JN057409

KIWAMERO!

極めろ!
TOEFL iBT® テスト
リーディング・リスニング解答力

第2版

TOEFL and TOEFL iBT are registered trademarks of ETS.
This publication is not endorsed or approved by ETS.

森田鉄也　日永田伸一郎　山内勇樹

スリーエーネットワーク

本書は小社既刊『極めろ！　TOEFL iBTテスト リーディング・リスニング解答力』に、2023年7月26日実施分「TOEFL iBTテスト」から導入された新形式問題の対策を加え、内容を加筆・修正した改訂版です。

Published by 3A Corporation.
Trusty Kojimachi Bldg., 2F, 4, Kojimachi 3-Chome, Chiyoda-ku, Tokyo 102-0083, Japan

ISBN978-4-88319-943-3 C0082

First published 2024
Printed in Japan

はじめに

2019年につづき2023年よりTOEFL iBTがまた新しくなりました。問題数が減少し、試験時間がさらに短くなりました。8～9ページで出題形式について詳しく解説します。

TOEIC L&Rの参考書は世にごまんとありますが、TOEFL iBTの対策書はいわゆる単語帳を除いて数えるほどしかありません。需要がないわけではありません。ではなぜなのか？作るのがとても大変だからです。内容は専門的で、使われる表現もTOEICに比べはるかに難しいのです。また、選択肢も非常に巧妙にできており、TOEFLのような問題を再現するのは難題です。

その難題に取り組んだのが本書です。到底1人で作成できるわけがないと思い、2人の専門家に助けを依頼しました。

1人はアメリカ留学専門サポートセンターUSA Clubの山内勇樹先生です。TOEFLを長年にわたって教えておられる、日本では数少ないTOEFLの専門家です。USA Clubのネイティブチームとともに問題を作成すれば本物に近い良問を作れると考え、お願いしました。

もう1人は日永田伸一郎先生です。TOEFLに関する知識もさることながら、予備校の講師として教える力にも長けていて、これまでの本とは違った切り口の解説を書いていただけるのではないかと思い、依頼しました。事実、今までにはない最も詳しい解説のTOEFL参考書になりました。

しかし、これだけの頭脳を集結させても問題の作成は難航しました。何度も会議を重ね、修正に修正を加えてここにようやく完成したのが本書です。汗と涙の結晶と言うにふさわしい本書をお使いになって、ぜひ目標点を達成してください。

著者代表　森田鉄也

目次

はじめに …… 3
目次 …… 4
TOEFL iBT テストについて …… 6
TOEFL iBT テストはこう変わる！ …… 8
本書のコンセプト・使い方 …… 11
音声について …… 13
USA Club Web 学習の使い方 …… 13

Chapter 1 **Reading Section** …… 15

Unit 1 リーディングセクションの解答戦略 …… 16

TOEFL iBT Reading Section の概要
設問のパターン
解き方 TIPS

Unit 2 本試験形式問題演習 …… 20

リーディング問題 1 …… 20
リーディング問題 2 …… 62
リーディング問題 3 …… 104
リーディング問題 4 …… 144
リーディング問題 5 …… 186
リーディング問題 6 …… 226

Chapter 2 Listening Section

Chapter 2 Listening Section …… 267

Unit 1 リスニングセクションの解答戦略 …… 268

TOEFL iBT Listening Section の概要
設問のパターン
何を意識して聞くべきか？
解き方 TIPS
メモの取り方について
メモと記憶

Unit 2 本試験形式問題演習 …… 272

リスニング問題 1 会話 …… 272
リスニング問題 2 講義 …… 290
リスニング問題 3 会話 …… 318
リスニング問題 4 講義 …… 336
リスニング問題 5 講義 …… 358
リスニング問題 6 会話 …… 382
リスニング問題 7 講義 …… 402
リスニング問題 8 会話 …… 426
リスニング問題 9 講義 …… 446
リスニング問題 10 講義 …… 470

TOEFL iBTテストについて

TOEFL iBTとは？

TOEFL iBTとは大学で学ぶための語学能力を証明する資格の1つです。主に北米圏に留学するために用いられることが多いです。試験そのものの詳細な情報は公式サイトをご覧ください。

TOEFL iBTは、一般的な日本人にとって極めて困難なテストです。よく「日本人はReadingとListeningは得意だが、SpeakingやWritingは苦手である」と言われます。ところが、早慶国公立などの難関大学に合格するレベルの学生でも、ReadingやListeningで高得点を取ることは容易ではありません。さらにSpeakingやWritingに関しては、ほとんどの日本人が苦手意識を持っているでしょう。

英語で自分の意見を主張する、データをまとめる、という経験を積んでいない人にとっては、TOEFLのSpeakingとWritingセクションはパフォーマンスが出しにくいセクションになりがちです。また、英会話自体は経験がある、英文メールは書いたことはある、という場合であっても、TOEFLは「アカデミックな英語」を中心としたテスト内容になっていますから、専門性の高い内容の英語であっても、一定のレベルで対応できるようにしておかなければいけません。英語ネイティブでも困ってしまう場合もあります。

このように非常に難しい試験ですが、裏を返せば100点以上取ることができれば、英語の基礎力が身につきつつあることを証明できるわけです。壁は高いですが、頑張りましょう！

試験を受ける上でのアドバイス

1. 体調を整える

TOEFLは2時間集中して受け続ける必要のあるテストです。十分な睡眠と、適度な朝食を必ず取りましょう（朝ごはんを食べすぎると眠くなるかもしれません）。コンディションを整えてから受けることにより、より良い結果が望めるでしょう。

2. 早く会場に向かう

ほとんどの会場では、到着した順に試験を開始します。言い換えれば、試験は一斉開始ではありません。そのため、遅く到着すると、他の人がスピーキングをしている中で、リスニングを聞くという可能性が生じます。これは、リスニングの点数を著しく下げる可能性があるため、なるべく早く会場に向かいましょう。

3. 試験会場に向かうまで

確実に理解できる音声を聞きながら向かうのが良いでしょう。本書の音声や公式問題集の音声などを聞くことにより、本番をイメージしつつ、知識を確認できます。わからない音声を聞き流すことは無意味なので、必ず理解できるものを聞きましょう。

4. 試験会場で

読んだことのある英文を復習することをお勧めします。できれば本書の英文や公式問題集の英文が良いでしょう。できれば、何度も復習したがためにスムーズに読むことができる英文を読み、頭を活性化しましょう。

5. 試験中

多くの受験者にとっては、英語で上手く話せるか？　という問題以前に、周りに人がいる状況で堂々と英語で話す、自信を持って英語を話す、ということ自体が気持ち的に難しい、という状況もよく見受けられます。周りも皆自分で精一杯で、誰も他の受験者のパフォーマンスに集中して、一喜一憂している人はいません。試験会場で英語の実力を上げることはできないので、それまでに練習してきたベストが出せるよう、自分のSpeaking に集中しましょう。Writing においては、慎重になりすぎていつもよりタイピング速度が落ちる、という傾向が多くの受験者に見られますので、時間と単語数を定期的にチェックしながらペースを保って書き進めていきましょう。

6. 試験終了後

その日の感想や試験内容を可能な限り記録しておきましょう。自分の感触と実際の試験結果がかみ合わないことがよくあります。記録を付けることにより、手ごたえを正確に把握することができます。

7. 試験結果

テスト日から4~8日後にWeb で確認することができます。どきどきしながら待ちましょう。納得のいかない結果の場合は、リスコア（rescore）＝ 再採点を依頼することができます。詳細は公式サイトをご覧ください。

TOEFL iBT テストはこう変わる！

2023年7月26日以降、TOEFL試験が変更となりました。大きな変更点は2つです。
①試験時間が約3時間→約2時間に変更
②Writingセクションにおける「Independent task」というエッセーが「Academic Discussion task」という名前のWritingに変更
また、小さな変更として「休憩時間がなくなった」というものがあります。

反対に、変わらない項目は以下の通りです。
・テストの難易度・種類・長さ・傾向
・Reading、Listening、Speaking、Writingというセクションの順番
・トータルの点数や採点基準
・受験料

つまり、諸条件に変更はありません。「試験時間が短くなった」「Writingセクションの問題が変わった」この2つが変わった項目になります。

変更内容について、具体的に見ていきましょう。テストはReading、Listening、Speaking、Writingの順番で進行していきます。Speakingセクションを除いて、それぞれのセクションで何かしらの変更がありました。

セクション	変更前	変更後（2023年7月26日～）
リーディング	長文の数：3～4（各10問） 時間：54～72分	長文の数：2（各10問） 時間：35分
リスニング	講義の数：3～4（各6問） 会話の数：2～3（各5問） 総設問数：28問～39問 時間：41～57分	講義の数：3（各6問） 会話の数：2（各5問） 総設問数：28問 時間：36分
（休憩）	あり（10分）	なし
スピーキング（変更なし）	全体の問題数：4問 Independent 1問 Integrated 3問 時間：17分	全体の問題数：4問 Independent 1問 Integrated 3問 時間：16分
ライティング	全体の問題数：2問 Integrated 1問（20分） Independent 1問（30分）	全体の問題数：2問 Integrated 1問（20分） Academic Discussion 1問（10分）
試験時間	約3時間	約2時間

Reading

以前は3～4つパッセージが提供されていました。3つが規定数であり、ダミー問題という採点されないパッセージが出された場合は4つになっていました。このパッセージ数が、必ず2つになりました。ダミー問題はもう出題されません。すなわち、採点されない問題はないということです。1パッセージあたり10問というのは変わりませんが、Readingのトータル時間は54～72分→35分に変更となりました。

Listening

講義形式では、3～4題あったものが3題に固定されました。対話形式では、2～3題あったものが2題に固定されました。採点されない問題はありません。

Speaking

おおむね変更はありません。ただ、以前よりも問題にバリエーションが見られるようになったため、注意が必要です。

Writing

Independent task（30分）というエッセーが廃止され、代わりにAcademic Discussion task（10分）が導入されました。

これらが大きな変更点となります。総じて、テスト時間が短縮され、今まで約3時間だったものが約2時間になります。

対策について

この形式変更を受けて、対策も少し変える必要があります。

●うっかりミスを減らす

まず、一問を落とすことに対するダメージが大きくなります。これまでは問題数が多かったため、うっかり一問を落としてしまってもダメージが比較的小さかったでしょう。しかし、問題数が減ったということは、一問を落とすことによるダメージが比較的大きくなるということです。つまり、より集中力を持って失点を防ぐことが大事になってきます。練習の時からケアレスミスを減らし、集中して問題を解くということが重要になるでしょう。

●集中力・持久力をつける

休憩がないため、2時間集中してテストに取り組む必要があります。これまでは休憩があったため、途中で一度リフレッシュできました。しかし、今回は休憩なくテストが進んでいきます。対策としては、模擬試験などを同じ条件で受け、2時間強集中し続けることができる持久力を備えていくことが大事になります。せっかく英語力があっても、その力を発揮できなければ点数に悪影響が出てしまいます。模擬試験を活用して、集中力・持久力をつけていきましょう。

●「Academic Discussion taskの対策」については、本シリーズの『スピーキング・ライティング編』をご覧ください。

本書のコンセプト・使い方

本書のコンセプト

本書の特徴は「著者の思考法を追体験する」というものです。リーディングに関しては、本文の読み方と設問へのアプローチについて、著者の頭の中にある思考法を可能な限り再現してみました。また、リスニングに関しては、どの部分をメモに取り記憶しているのかをまとめています。本番の試験と似た本書の問題で、ぜひ高得点を取る人の思考法を体感してください。ただし、どのようなテストであれ、高得点を支えるものは「土台となる英語力」にほかなりません。本書は、ある程度の基礎力を持ち、TOEFL100点以上を目指す人を対象に、問題を解く上でのコツや考え方を伝えることを目的としています。

本書の使い方

リーディング

まずは、1題につき17分で解いてみましょう。17分で終わらない場合は、超過した時間を記録して全て解きましょう。解答するときは根拠を探しながら解いてください。このとき、本文への書き込みは避けましょう。というのも、実際の試験では書き込みができないからです。その後、解説を丹念に読み、著者がどのように問題に取り組んでいるのかを体験してください。最後に和訳や語句説明を参考にして、全ての文を精読しましょう。ここで得た知識が、また新しい文を読むときに役立つはずです。

リスニング

まずは、メモ用紙と鉛筆を用意し、問題文を集中して聞きましょう。このとき、メモを取りながら、可能な限り内容を記憶してください。聞き終わったら、5分以内で設問を解きましょう。その後、リーディングと同じように解説を熟読してください。最後に、和訳と語句を参考にして精読し、音源を繰り返し聞いて、全て聞き取れるようにしましょう。

英語学習全般について

TOEFL iBTで90点前後を取るためには特別な対策は不要です。その前に基礎知識をしっかり身に付けてください。まずは、大学受験レベルの文法・語法・単語・熟語を理解して覚えることです。こうした知識を蓄えておけば、いずれ必ず役に立ちます。基礎力を身に付けるには、大量に読み、大量に聞き、大量に書き、大量に話すことが不可欠です。ですが、やみくもにインプットばかりしていては逆効果です。理解できない英文を何時間聞き流していても、理解できるようにはなりません。理解を伴ったインプットこそが力になります。文法や語法、語彙を頼りに、目の前の文章を正しく理解し、その中から1つでもライティングやスピーキングに活用できる表現を吸収していくことが理想です。その後TOEFLに頻出するテーマに関する基本単語を覚えましょう。生物学・地学・経済・歴史など、テーマは多岐にわたります。繰り返しになりますが、TOEFL iBTは高度な英語力を必要とします。おそらく多くの方は、高得点を取るのに苦労することでしょう。それでも、夢や目標のため高得点を目指す方にとり、本書が一筋の光明をもたらすものとなれば、著者にとってこれほどうれしいことはありません。一人の学習者としても、読者の皆さまの成功を祈っております。

音声について

リスニング問題で使用する音声は以下の方法で、すべて無料で聞くことができます。

パソコン・スマートフォンで聞く

インターネットにつながるパソコン・スマートフォンで、
「https://www.3anet.co.jp/np/books/5651」にアクセスしてください。

- ダウンロードする場合、音声ファイルはMP3形式です。圧縮（zip形式）されているので、パソコン上で解凍してください。
- MP3プレイヤーへの取り込み方法などは各メーカーにお問い合わせください。
- ファイルダウンロード、ストリーミング再生には通信費が発生する場合があります。

USA Club Web学習の使い方

アメリカ留学専門サポートセンター、USA Clubのサイトで、試験本番と同じようにWebで本書の問題を解くことができます。

1. アカウントを作成する

アカウント作成ページにアクセスします。
「**extester.com**」にアクセスして、メールアドレスとお名前をご入力ください。アカウント作成が終わりましたら、ご入力いただいたメールアドレスに、ログインページとログインID、パスワードをお送りいたします。

＊アカウントの作成には、通常2～3営業日頂戴いたしております。また大型連休や年末年始、お盆の期間など、通常よりも日数を要する期間もございますので、予めご了承くださいませ。

2. ログインする

ログインページにアクセスして、お送りしたログインIDとパスワードを入力し、「ログイン」をクリックします。

＊アクティベーションコードを聞かれた際は以下の通りです。
buffet-edu

3. 問題を選ぶ

トップページ左メニューの「ディレクトリ」から、「極めろ！TOEFL iBT®テスト リーディング・リスニング解答力」を選択します。取り組む問題を選択して、「受講」をクリックして、問題を解き始めることができます。

＊解いたことのある問題をクリックすると、「受講」と「結果」というボタンが表示されます。

4. 問題を解く

取り組む問題を選択して、「受講」をクリックすると、問題を解き始めることができます。解答を提出する場合は、緑色の「次のページへ進む」をクリックし、さらに次のページで「提出」をクリックしてください。解答を提出すると、これまでの解答と正答が確認できます。解答を中断する場合は、画面左下の赤い「中断」をクリックしてください（中断すると解答は保存されません）。

5. 採点する

トップメニューの下にある「成績」をクリックします。成績画面の「教材名」にある解いた問題の名前をクリックすると採点結果が詳細に表示されます。問題ごとに個別に確認したい場合には、「3. 問題を選ぶ」の「受講」ボタンの隣に表示される「結果」をクリックしてください。

「USA Club Web学習の使い方」についてのお問い合わせ先

usaclub@sapiens-sapiens.com

Chapter 1

Reading Section

Unit 1 **リーディングセクションの解答戦略**
TOEFL iBT Reading Section の概要
設問のパターン
解き方 TIPS

Unit 2 **本試験形式問題演習**

アイコン一覧

訳

語句

文法解説

正解

Unit 1 リーディングセクションの解答戦略

TOEFL iBT Reading Sectionの概要

問題量： 700語前後の英文が2題出題。

時　間： 35分。1つの英文につき17 ～ 18分が目安。

内　容： 理系は、生物学や地球科学が頻出。文系は、歴史や経済、芸術が頻出。

その他： パソコン上で受験するため、本文への書き込みは不可。普段の学習から、本文への書き込みをしないよう心がけるとよい。ただし、全セクションで、テスト監督者が配布する紙にメモを取ることは可能。

設問のパターン

1. 事実を問う問題

本文に「明確に」書かれていることを問う問題。このタイプには理由を問うものも含まれる。最もオーソドックスな出題形式。正解の選択肢は、本文から言い換えられていることが多い。また間違いの選択肢は、あえて本文の表現を使って引っかけてくることが多い。

2. 事実ではないものを問う問題

設問にNOTやEXCEPTが含まれる問題。残りの3つは正しい内容の選択肢となる。選択肢のうち、正しい内容は本文中の段落全体にまたがって述べられることもあり、時間と手間がかかる問題。正解となる「誤った内容」の選択肢は、本文と明らかに矛盾するか、本文に記述がない。

3. 推論問題

本文の内容から論理的に推論される選択肢を選ぶ問題。あくまで解答の根拠は文中にある。ただし、本文の内容を言い換えたものがそのまま正解となるとは限らない。設問にinferやimply、suggestなどが用いられる。

4. 筆者の意図を問う問題

筆者がある情報を提示した理由を問う問題。その文が、文中で果たす論理的役割を考える。

5. 語彙問題

単語の意味を問う問題。文脈判断ではなく純粋な知識で解く問題が多い。近年、難易度が上がっている。

6. 指示語問題

代名詞などが指示するものを問う問題。頻出ではないが、比較的簡単に解けるものが多い。

7. 文を簡潔に言い換える問題

文構造を正しく把握し、その文の中心的な意味を理解することがポイント。

8. 文挿入問題

文と文の論理関係に着目して解く問題。具体と抽象、原因と結果、代名詞や指示語などに注目すると解きやすい。

9. 表を完成させる問題

表を埋める形式の内容一致問題。頻出ではないが、事実を問う問題と同じように、本文に書かれていることが問われる。

10. 文要約問題

本文の主旨と一致する英文を３つ選ぶ問題。重要な内容をまとめている選択肢が正解となる。複数の段落にまたがった内容が１つの選択肢に入っていることも多い。なお、誤った内容の選択肢は、本文に反する内容であることが多い。具体例や枝葉末節の情報も誤りとなる。

解き方 TIPS

1. メモを取るべきか？

ほとんど全ての設問が段落ごとに解けるので、メモを取る必要は基本的にない。ただし、最後の要約問題に向けて、大意を簡単に書き取ることは有益だろう（なお、筆者は一切メモを取らない）。

2. 設問を読んでから解くべきか、英文を読んでから設問に入るべきか？

どちらでもよいが、筆者は設問を読んでから解くようにしている。先に設問を読むことにより、探すべき情報が明確になるからだ。

3. 段落ごとに解くべきか、全ての英文を読んでから解くべきか？

ほぼ全ての設問において、参照すべき段落が明示されている。よって、段落ごとに解くことが期待されている。

4. 問題を解く際、段落全体を読むべきか？

基本的に、問題の参照箇所がかぶることは少ない。つまり、ある段落の前半部分に関する設問が出題されていれば、後半部分を熟読する必要はないことが多いのだ。設問に関連する箇所を詳しく読むことで、時間を節約しよう。

5. スキャニング（飛ばし読み）をするべきか？

筆者は全て読むようにしている。内容一致問題は、細部まで読み込むことを要求することが多い。飛ばし読みはかえって時間の無駄になってしまう。丁寧に読んでも十分に終わるように読解力をつけよう。

6. 英文を読むときに意識するべきことは？

一文一文を丁寧に読みつつ、設問に対する解答を探すというスタンスで読むこと。同時に、英文の論理展開に注目するとよい。「具体と抽象」「原因と結果」「言い換え」「譲歩⇒逆接⇒主張」などの基本的な論理関係に着目することにより、文章全体を「論理的意味のカタマリ」として見ることができるようになる。

7. 最初に注目すべきポイントは？

タイトルと第1段落の内容から、本文全体の方向性がわかることが多い。ただ、最近は内容が大きく展開していく英文も多いため、第1段落からその後の内容を推測できないものもある。あくまで参考程度にしておこう。

8. 解き方の基本スタンスは？

まずは設問に含まれる特徴的な語句から参照箇所を特定する。そのとき、そのキーワードが含まれる英文やキーワードに関連する英文だけでなく、その前後の英文を読んで、文脈を理解することが重要。

9. 消去法は使うべきか？

語彙問題を除いて、基本的には消去法を使うこと。正解だと思っても、他の選択肢が誤りであることを確認しよう。

10. 求められる語彙レベルについて

非常に高いレベルの語彙力が求められている。大学受験よりもさらに上のレベルが必要。特に、一般的な語彙に加えて、生物学や地学などに関する専門的な語句はある程度覚えておいたほうがよい。

11. 語彙問題について

語彙問題では知識の有無が問われているので10秒で解くこと。ただ、最近はかなり難しい単語が問われることも多いので、1～2問わからないものがあっても気にしないこと。他の問題に時間をかけることも高得点の秘訣。

12. 誤った内容の選択肢について

誤りの選択肢にはいくつかのパターンがある。

(1) 本文と逆の内容

最も単純なパターン。否定したり、逆の意味の単語を用いたりすることが多い。

(2) 本文に無関係な内容

本文中の単語を用いて、無関係な内容になっていることが多い。

(3) 一部が誤りの内容

これは厄介な選択肢。書いてある内容の一部は正しいが、残りの部分が明らかに誤りといったケース。

(4) 言い過ぎの内容

これも厄介な選択肢。「全て」「～のみ」「必ず」など強い修飾語句が入る。

13. 長文の難易度について

英文の難易度にはばらつきがある。難しい英文と簡単な英文が混在していることが多い。もし仮に1つ目の長文に予想以上の時間を奪われたとしても、次の長文が比較的簡単である可能性がある。焦らずに、丁寧に解答していこう。

Unit 2 本試験形式問題演習

リーディング問題 1 | Archaeology

MESOLITHIC COMPLEXITY IN SCANDINAVIA

問題演習の流れ

- □ 解答時間は17分を目標にしましょう。
- □ 英文 ⇒ 問題 ⇒ 正解・解説レクチャー ⇒ 訳 という流れで学習します。
- □ 3回解けるように、3回分のマークシートを各問題に用意しています。解く日付を記入してからマークしてください。

Web解答方法

- □ 本試験では各選択肢の左に表示されるマークをクリックして解答します。本試験と同様の方法で取り組みたい場合は、Webで解答できます。
- □ インターネットのつながるパソコン・スマートフォンで、以下のサイトにアクセスしてWeb上で解答してください。

extester.com

- □ 操作方法は、p.13 ~ 14の「USA Club Web学習の使い方」をご参照ください。

学習の記録

学習開始日	年　　月　　日	学習終了日	年　　月　　日
学習開始日	年　　月　　日	学習終了日	年　　月　　日
学習開始日	年　　月　　日	学習終了日	年　　月　　日

リーディング問題1 英文

MESOLITHIC COMPLEXITY IN SCANDINAVIA

While Northern Scandinavia was still covered by an ice sheet around 10,000 BC, with little hope of sustaining lasting settlements, the Mesolithic[1] Southern Scandinavia was able to support continuous settlements all the way into the following Neolithic[2] epoch and onward. After the glaciers of the ice age retreated far enough north over Europe, forests soon began to spring up throughout this land, which was previously difficult to live on. Throughout what is now Denmark, as well as southern regions of Sweden and Finland, hunter-gatherers moved in and began to exploit the indigenous animal life of the land, sea, and rivers, as well as the local nutrient-rich plants. These post-glacial cultures are seen as a perfect example of the way the Mesolithic man lived. From collecting shells on the coast to making a journey to seasonal hunting grounds, they left behind one of the greatest sites of archaeological treasures. Many remains have been found in previously waterlogged locations like rivers and swamps, which preserved them in the thick mud. Through investigations, our understanding of Mesolithic Scandinavia has grown greatly over the last fifty years, making it clearer now that there was a gradual shift towards a more sedentary lifestyle, which merges with the introduction of farming into Europe in the following era.

The first Mesolithic culture to emerge in the Scandinavian southern lands was the Maglemosian culture, which lends its name to the first stage of the Maglemose-Kongemose-Ertebølle sequence. The Maglemosian culture is characterized by the use of wood, bone, and flint tools, and people in this era lived mostly in forested as well as wetland environments. Some societies at that time survived on hunting and fishing in fixed locations, although others were nomadic, meaning they migrated to better hunting grounds as the seasons allowed. The sea levels during the Maglemose period (9,000–6,000 BC) were much lower than they are today, not reaching their current heights until the very end of this period. There were a higher number of suitable coastal locations for fishing, where the Maglemosians would make good use of spears. With sufficient land and food supplies in many parts of their society, people did not have to relocate frequently, which facilitated the sedentary nature of their life.

Kongemosen, a big island in current day Denmark, is the name of the next Mesolithic culture and period in this region. Though fairly similar to their predecessors, the Kongemose culture was able to produce more sophisticated blade weapons and tools, expanding their flint and stone arsenal. An increasing artisan trend started to appear amongst the Kongemose as more of their tools and weapons were found to be etched with detailed geometric patterns. Due to the elevated sea levels by the start of this period, many previous coastal settlements were flooded under the Baltic Sea, which undermined their fishing habits. Thus, more dependence was placed on hunting than before. Hunters were now taking down wilder and larger game such as boar and deer, which may explain the increased size and significance of weaponry seen in this era. In fact, the Kongemose settlement was able to kill the most dangerous animals in the forests, including wolves, bears, aurochs, and elks. People chose to push themselves to develop better technology and stay in one place rather than move to other places. In fact, they could do so as long as they were able to find enough animals to hunt. Although this culture had a relatively short lifespan (6,000–5,200 BC) compared to the periods that come before and after, the short time period does not cancel out the importance of this fierce culture.

The Ertebølle culture (5,300–3,950 BC) took its time in development, but returning to the waves, the Ertebølle revived the Maglemosian traditions of fishing and even expanded it to taking on the larger inhabitants of the sea, whales. Their mastery of navigating inland rivers was impressive for the age and as such, their economy began to lean again towards marine treasures such as sharks, seals, and a variety of fish. Being able to travel for a long distance and hunt, people no longer had to relocate the entire community and change their place of residence, further accelerating the sedentary characteristics of their lifestyle. The discovery in the archaeological artifacts from this era points towards a great food surplus for this culture, and with concerns for procuring food gone, people could spend less time hunting and more time on something new, including farming and making pottery for storing food. Although the Ertebølle were not fully an agrarian society, we do see the rapid development of farming; they did use domestic grain to some extent to supplement their food supply.

The Ertebølle culture was the last culture marking the Mesolithic age. The survival of the Maglemosian, Kongemosen, and Ertebølle cultures was aided by the hospitable climate of this region. This ocean coast area attracted the Scandinavian ancestors throughout the Mesolithic periods. The move to the Neolithic age was triggered when they began to domesticate animals and exploit the land suitable for cultivation. Upon the transition from the Mesolithic to Neolithic era, people learned to become more accustomed to a permanently sedentary life in their society. It grew increasingly complex, and as a result, larger sized military or religious groups readily formed and strong leaders and hierarchies began to emerge. All these new cultural proliferations stand upon the long-lasted cultures during the Mesolithic ages.

1. Mesolithic: The middle part of the Stone Age
2. Neolithic: The last part of the Stone Age following the Mesolithic era

1. According to paragraph 1, why was early Northern Scandinavia before 10,000 BC difficult for human settlement?

(A) Ice covering the land throughout northern Europe made stable settlements virtually impossible.
(B) The lack of available resources made it difficult for continuous survival.
(C) Scandinavia and the remaining parts of Europe were only connected by glaciers, which people could not cross.
(D) There was little forest in which people could live because of destruction by earlier settlers around 10,000 BC.

2. Which of the sentences below best expresses the essential information in the highlighted sentence in the passage? Incorrect choices change the meaning in important ways or leave out essential information.

(A) The 50-year survey indicates that Scandinavians started living a more sedentary life because they had already practiced agriculture.
(B) From fifty years ago until now, there was a belief that farming in Europe, which had begun even before people's life became sedentary, faded away little by little.
(C) We now have a better research-based understanding of how the transition to sedentary living appeared and how it continued on to a more farming-intensive time seen in Europe.
(D) It is now clear, based on scholastic studies, that people in Scandinavia became increasingly sedentary over a long time due to the development of farming in Europe.

PARAGRAPH 1

While Northern Scandinavia was still covered by an ice sheet around 10,000 BC, with little hope of sustaining lasting settlements, the Mesolithic[1] Southern Scandinavia was able to support continuous settlements all the way into the following Neolithic[2] epoch and onward. After the glaciers of the ice age retreated far enough north over Europe, forests soon began to spring up throughout this land, which was previously difficult to live on. Throughout what is now Denmark, as well as southern regions of Sweden and Finland, hunter-gatherers moved in and began to exploit the indigenous animal life of the land, sea, and rivers, as well as the local nutrient-rich plants. These post-glacial cultures are seen as a perfect example of the way the Mesolithic man lived. From collecting shells on the coast to making a journey to seasonal hunting grounds, they left behind one of the greatest sites of archaeological treasures. Many remains have been found in previously waterlogged locations like rivers and swamps, which preserved them in the thick mud. Through investigations, our understanding of Mesolithic Scandinavia has grown greatly over the last fifty years, making it clearer now that there was a gradual shift towards a more sedentary lifestyle, which merges with the introduction of farming into Europe in the following era.

1. Mesolithic: The middle part of the Stone Age
2. Neolithic: The last part of the Stone Age following the Mesolithic era

3. According to paragraph 2, what can be inferred about the availability of food resources during the Maglemosian period?

(A) The food supply from the forest was rich whereas the marine food supply was not.
(B) While some places were rich in resources, there were also other places where the food was scanty.
(C) People spent most of their time in the forested areas because they could hunt as much as they needed.
(D) They relied on other nomadic people for their daily food supply.

PARAGRAPH 2

The first Mesolithic culture to emerge in the Scandinavian southern lands was the Maglemosian culture, which lends its name to the first stage of the Maglemose-Kongemose-Ertebølle sequence. The Maglemosian culture is characterized by the use of wood, bone, and flint tools, and people in this era lived mostly in forested as well as wetland environments. Some societies at that time survived on hunting and fishing in fixed locations, although others were nomadic, meaning they migrated to better hunting grounds as the seasons allowed. The sea levels during the Maglemose period (9,000–6,000 BC) were much lower than they are today, not reaching their current heights until the very end of this period. There were a higher number of suitable coastal locations for fishing, where the Maglemosians would make good use of spears. With sufficient land and food supplies in many parts of their society, people did not have to relocate frequently, which facilitated the sedentary nature of their life.

4. According to paragraph 3, all of the following are effects from elevated sea levels EXCEPT:

(A) People started to rely more on hunting.
(B) Parts of their habitats sank under the sea.
(C) The settlers' fishery was negatively affected.
(D) Changes in climate occurred.

5. According to paragraph 3, what can be inferred from the increased size in their weaponry?

(A) The increase of wildlife required them to use bigger weaponry for fishing.
(B) Prior weapons were unable to protect people from attacks by dangerous animals.
(C) The rise in hunting made necessary the weapons which were greater in size.
(D) It was not until they managed to develop large weapons that people started hunting bigger animals.

PARAGRAPH 3

Kongemosen, a big island in current day Denmark, is the name of the next Mesolithic culture and period in this region. Though fairly similar to their predecessors, the Kongemose culture was able to produce more sophisticated blade weapons and tools, expanding their flint and stone arsenal. An increasing artisan trend started to appear amongst the Kongemose as more of their tools and weapons were found to be etched with detailed geometric patterns. Due to the elevated sea levels by the start of this period, many previous coastal settlements were flooded under the Baltic Sea, which undermined their fishing habits. Thus, more dependence was placed on hunting than before. Hunters were now taking down wilder and larger game such as boar and deer, which may explain the increased size and significance of weaponry seen in this era. In fact, the Kongemose settlement was able to kill the most dangerous animals in the forests, including wolves, bears, aurochs, and elks. People chose to push themselves to develop better technology and stay in one place rather than move to other places. In fact, they could do so as long as they were able to find enough animals to hunt. Although this culture had a relatively short lifespan (6,000–5,200 BC) compared to the periods that come before and after, the short time period does not cancel out the importance of this fierce culture.

6. According to paragraph 4, what contributed the most to the Ertebølle culture's sedentary life?

(A) Pottery-making skills with which they were able to store more food supplies
(B) New farming techniques they learned during the time they could afford
(C) The discovery of new materials to produce larger hunting tools
(D) Superior skills in navigating through waterways and catching ocean resources

PARAGRAPH 4

The Ertebølle culture (5,300–3,950 BC) took its time in development, but returning to the waves, the Ertebølle revived the Maglemosian traditions of fishing and even expanded it to taking on the larger inhabitants of the sea, whales. Their mastery of navigating inland rivers was impressive for the age and as such, their economy began to lean again towards marine treasures such as sharks, seals, and a variety of fish. Being able to travel for a long distance and hunt, people no longer had to relocate the entire community and change their place of residence, further accelerating the sedentary characteristics of their lifestyle. The discovery in the archaeological artifacts from this era points towards a great food surplus for this culture, and with concerns for procuring food gone, people could spend less time hunting and more time on something new, including farming and making pottery for storing food. Although the Ertebølle were not fully an agrarian society, we do see the rapid development of farming; they did use domestic grain to some extent to supplement their food supply.

7. In paragraph 5, the word "exploit" in the passage is closest in meaning to

(A) expand
(B) utilize
(C) protect
(D) raise

8. According to paragraph 5, what can be inferred about the transition from the Mesolithic era to the Neolithic era?

(A) The availability of tillable land encouraged the entire community to reside in one place for long time.
(B) The transition was difficult for many to accept, which led to the formation of military associations.
(C) The sudden shift in cultural and religious ideas was undertaken by a new strong leader.
(D) Many were accustomed to former traditional ways of life, which made a sedentary life unappealing yet adaptable.

PARAGRAPH 5

The Ertebølle culture was the last culture marking the Mesolithic age. The survival of the Maglemosian, Kongemosen, and Ertebølle cultures was aided by the hospitable climate of this region. This ocean coast area attracted the Scandinavian ancestors throughout the Mesolithic periods. The move to the Neolithic age was triggered when they began to domesticate animals and exploit the land suitable for cultivation. Upon the transition from the Mesolithic to Neolithic era, people learned to become more accustomed to a permanently sedentary life in their society. It grew increasingly complex, and as a result, larger sized military or religious groups readily formed and strong leaders and hierarchies began to emerge. All these new cultural proliferations stand upon the long-lasted cultures during the Mesolithic ages.

9. Look at the four squares [■] that indicate where the following sentence could be added to the passage.

This shift strongly encouraged the structural and cultural development of Scandinavian society.

Where would the sentence best fit?

PARAGRAPH 5

The Ertebølle culture was the last culture marking the Mesolithic age. The survival of the Maglemosian, Kongemosen, and Ertebølle cultures was aided by the hospitable climate of this region. This ocean coast area attracted the Scandinavian ancestors throughout the Mesolithic periods. The move to the Neolithic age was triggered when they began to domesticate animals and exploit the land suitable for cultivation. **A** Upon the transition from the Mesolithic to Neolithic era, people learned to become more accustomed to a permanently sedentary life in their society. **B** It grew increasingly complex, and as a result, larger sized military or religious groups readily formed and strong leaders and hierarchies began to emerge. **C** All these new cultural proliferations stand upon the long-lasted cultures during the Mesolithic ages. **D**

10. Directions: An introductory sentence containing a brief summary of the passage is provided below. Complete the summary by selecting the best THREE answer choices that express the main ideas of the passage.

The history of Scandinavia had various cultures intertwined within it, which led it to its long survival and eventual migration and transition to more sedentary lifestyles.

Answer Choices

(A) Hunter-gatherers of Mesolithic Scandinavia actively traveled along coastlines in order to collect shells.

(B) Maglemosian culture, the first one to come in the Mesolithic era of Scandinavia, relied mostly on fishing with spears and hunting for survival.

(C) The Kongemose culture made advanced weaponry and focused on hunting large forest animals for their main source of food, while people in the Ertebølle culture engaged themselves actively in fishing.

(D) The favorable climate, abundant resources, and technological developments encouraged people during the later phase of the Mesolithic era to live a more and more sedentary life.

(E) The Mesolithic civilization influenced all three Scandinavian cultures to merge into sedentary ways of life after the introduction of militaristic and religious groups.

(F) The Mesolithic civilization consisted mostly of farmers from other parts of the land, including Europe.

リーディング問題 1

正解一覧……38
解説レクチャー……38~51
訳……52~61

1. **(A)** 2. **(C)** 3. **(B)** 4. **(D)** 5. **(C)**
6. **(D)** 7. **(B)** 8. **(A)** 9. **(B)** 10. **(B) (C) (D)**

第1段落｜問1～2 解説レクチャー

❶While Northern Scandinavia was still covered by an ice sheet around 10,000 BC, with little hope of sustaining lasting settlements, the Mesolithic Southern Scandinavia was able to support continuous settlements all the way into the following Neolithic epoch and onward. ❷After the glaciers of the ice age retreated far enough north over Europe, forests soon began to spring up throughout this land, which was previously difficult to live on. ❸Throughout what is now Denmark, as well as southern regions of Sweden and Finland, hunter-gatherers moved in and began to exploit the indigenous animal life of the land, sea, and rivers, as well as the local nutrient-rich plants. ❹These post-glacial cultures are seen as a perfect example of the way the Mesolithic man lived. ❺From collecting shells on the coast to making a journey to seasonal hunting grounds, they left behind one of the greatest sites of archaeological treasures. ❻Many remains have been found in previously waterlogged locations like rivers and swamps, which preserved them in the thick mud. ❼Through investigations, our understanding of Mesolithic Scandinavia has grown greatly over the last fifty years, making it clearer now that there was a gradual shift towards a more sedentary lifestyle, which merges with the introduction of farming into Europe in the following era.

1. According to paragraph 1, why was early Northern Scandinavia before 10,000 BC difficult for human settlement?

(A) Ice covering the land throughout northern Europe made stable settlements virtually impossible.
(B) The lack of available resources made it difficult for continuous survival.
(C) Scandinavia and the remaining parts of Europe were only connected by glaciers, which people could not cross.
(D) There was little forest in which people could live because of destruction by earlier settlers around 10,000 BC.

第1段落によると、紀元前1万年以前の北スカンジナビアは、なぜ人間にとって住むのが難しい場所でしたか。

(A) 北ヨーロッパ全体の土地を覆っていた氷によって、定住は実質的に不可能であったため。

(B) 手に入る資源がなく、継続的に生活していくことが困難だったため。
(C) スカンジナビアとその他のヨーロッパの地域は氷河でしかつながっておらず、その氷河も人々は渡ることができなかったため。
(D) 紀元前1万年頃、先に定住した人によって森が破壊され、人が定住できる森がほとんどなかったため。

早速、本文を読んでいきましょう。❶は「北スカンジナビアが氷床に覆われ、定住を続けることができる見込みがほぼなかったのに対して、中石器時代の南スカンジナビアは新石器時代までずっと定住することが可能であった」という内容です。「氷床に覆われていた」というのが定住を阻んでいた理由ですね。よって、問1の正解は(A)です。❷にまた、「氷河が後退して、以前は住みにくかった土地に…」とあるのもヒントになります。なお、(B)は常識的に考えれば正しいですが、本文に記述がないので誤りです。(C)や(D)も本文に記述がありません。

□ virtually：ほとんど、事実上（≒almost）　□ destruction：破壊

2. Which of the sentences below best expresses the essential information in the highlighted sentence in the passage? Incorrect choices change the meaning in important ways or leave out essential information.

(A) The 50-year survey indicates that Scandinavians started living a more sedentary life because they had already practiced agriculture.
(B) From fifty years ago until now, there was a belief that farming in Europe, which had begun even before people's life became sedentary, faded away little by little.
(C) We now have a better research-based understanding of how the transition to sedentary living appeared and how it continued on to a more farming-intensive time seen in Europe.
(D) It is now clear, based on scholastic studies, that people in Scandinavia became increasingly sedentary over a long time due to the development of farming in Europe.

次のうちどの文が、ハイライト表示した文の重要な情報を最もよく表していますか。不正解の選択肢は、意味を大きく変えたり重要な情報を抜かしたりしています。

(A) スカンジナビア人はすでに農耕を行っていたので、さらに定住的な生活を始めたということを、50年にわたる調査が示している。
(B) 人々の生活が定住的になる前に始まったヨーロッパの農耕は、徐々に衰退していったと、50年前から今日まで考えられていた。

(C) どのようにして定住生活への移行が始まったのか、そしてそれがどのように農耕の時代へと続いたのかについて、研究に基づいてよりよく理解できるようになった。
(D) スカンジナビアの人々はヨーロッパでの農耕の発展により、長い時間をかけてますます定住的になっていったことが、学術研究から現在明らかになっている。

❼を精読しましょう。ポイントは「スカンジナビアでは人々が定住するようになり、その後、農耕を行うようになったことが、これまでの研究でわかった」ということですね。では選択肢を詳しく見ていきましょう。(A)、(B)、(D)は全て「農耕の発達→定住」という流れなのですが、本文で見たのは「定住→農耕の発達」という順番です。よって前後関係が逆なので、どれも誤りです。(C)は「どのように定住生活への変化が生じたのか、そしてそれが農耕の時代へとどのように続いたのかがわかるようになった」という意味です。「定住→農耕の発達」という順番で書かれているので、(C)が正解です。選択肢の難しさに惑わされることなく、前後関係や論理関係の矛盾に気付けるかどうかがポイントでした。

□ fade away:徐々に衰退する　□ -intensive:～をとても必要とする

第2段落｜問3解説レクチャー

❶The first Mesolithic culture to emerge in the Scandinavian southern lands was the Maglemosian culture, which lends its name to the first stage of the Maglemose-Kongemose-Ertebølle sequence. ❷The Maglemosian culture is characterized by the use of wood, bone, and flint tools, and people in this era lived mostly in forested as well as wetland environments. ❸Some societies at that time survived on hunting and fishing in fixed locations, although others were nomadic, meaning they migrated to better hunting grounds as the seasons allowed. ❹The sea levels during the Maglemose period (9,000–6,000 BC) were much lower than they are today, not reaching their current heights until the very end of this period. ❺There were a higher number of suitable coastal locations for fishing, where the Maglemosians would make good use of spears. ❻With sufficient land and food supplies in many parts of their society, people did not have to relocate frequently, which facilitated the sedentary nature of their life.

3. According to paragraph 2, what can be inferred about the availability of food resources during the Maglemosian period?

(A) The food supply from the forest was rich whereas the marine food supply was not.
(B) While some places were rich in resources, there were also other places where the food was scanty.
(C) People spent most of their time in the forested areas because they could hunt as much as they needed.
(D) They relied on other nomadic people for their daily food supply.

第2段落によると、マグレモーゼ期の食料資源の入手の可能性について何が推測できますか。

(A) 森からの食料供給は十分であったが、海からの食料供給は不足していた。
(B) 資源が豊かな場所もあれば、食料が足りていない場所もあった。
(C) 人々は必要なだけ狩猟することができたため、大半の時間を森で過ごした。
(D) 日々の食料供給は、他の遊牧民に頼っていた。

問3は「マグレモーゼ時代における食料調達に関して推測されること」を問うています。the availability of food resourcesをキーワードとして読み進めましょう。❶は「中石器時代の最初の文化はマグレモーゼ文化と呼ばれ、これはマグレモーゼ文化、コンゲモーゼ文化、エルテベレ文化という一連の流れにおける最初の段階である」と述べています。❷には「マグレモーゼ文化の人々は木や骨や火打ち道具などを使い、森や湿地に住んでいた」とあります。さらに、❸は「ある特定の場所で狩猟や漁をして生活する社会もあれば、色々な場所に移住してそのような活動を行う社会もあった」と述べています。食料に関する内容はここまでなので、選択肢を詳しく見ていきましょう。(A)は本文に一致しません。森から得られる食料と、海から得られる食料を比べている記述はありません。(B)は「ある地域は食料が豊富で、他の地域は少なかった」という意味です。❸は、つまり「十分に食料が調達できる地域もあれば、そうではないので移住をしなければいけない地域もあった」ということを示唆します。選択肢の内容に一致するため、(B)が正解です。(C)は本文に一致しません。「人々が森で大半の時間を過ごした」という記述はありません。(D)も本文に一致しません。「他の遊牧民に頼った」という記述はありません。

□ whereas SV:～する一方で　□ scanty:不足した

第3段落｜問4〜5 解説レクチャー

❶Kongemosen, a big island in current day Denmark, is the name of the next Mesolithic culture and period in this region. ❷Though fairly similar to their predecessors, the Kongemose culture was able to produce more sophisticated blade weapons and tools, expanding their flint and stone arsenal. ❸An increasing artisan trend started to appear amongst the Kongemose as more of their tools and weapons were found to be etched with detailed geometric patterns. ❹Due to the elevated sea levels by the start of this period, many previous coastal settlements were flooded under the Baltic Sea, which undermined their fishing habits. ❺Thus, more dependence was placed on hunting than before. ❻Hunters were now taking down wilder and larger game such as boar and deer, which may explain the increased size and significance of weaponry seen in this era. ❼In fact, the Kongemose settlement was able to kill the most dangerous animals in the forests, including wolves, bears, aurochs, and elks. ❽People chose to push themselves to develop better technology and stay in one place rather than move to other places. ❾In fact, they could do so as long as they were able to find enough animals to hunt. ❿Although this culture had a relatively short lifespan (6,000–5,200 BC) compared to the periods that come before and after, the short time period does not cancel out the importance of this fierce culture.

4. According to paragraph 3, all of the following are effects from elevated sea levels EXCEPT:

(A) People started to rely more on hunting.
(B) Parts of their habitats sank under the sea.
(C) The settlers' fishery was negatively affected.
(D) Changes in climate occurred.

第3段落によると、海面が上昇することにより生じた影響について、正しくないものは次の中でどれですか。

(A) 人々はますます狩猟に依存するようになった。
(B) 彼らの居住地の一部は海の下に沈んだ。
(C) 定住者の漁労は、悪影響を受けた。
(D) 気候変動が起きた。

問4は「海面が上昇することにより生じた影響ではないもの」を問うています。まず❶〜❸は「コンゲモーゼ文化は、以前の文化よりも精巧な武器を使うようになった」と述べています。「海面上昇」の話題がまだ登場していないので、さくっと読み進めましょう。❹のDue to the elevated sea levelsが設問のポイントですね。ここから集中しましょう。まず、❹は「海面が上昇したため、沿岸の居住地が水没し、漁労が難しくなった」と説明しています。これは、選択肢の(B)と(C)に対応しますね。さらに、❺には「狩猟に依存するようになった」とあります。これは選択肢の(A)に対応します。(D)については言及がありません。よって(D)が正解です。

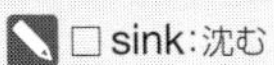
□ sink：沈む

5. According to paragraph 3, what can be inferred from the increased size in their weaponry?

(A) The increase of wildlife required them to use bigger weaponry for fishing.
(B) Prior weapons were unable to protect people from attacks by dangerous animals.
(C) The rise in hunting made necessary the weapons which were greater in size.
(D) It was not until they managed to develop large weapons that people started hunting bigger animals.

第3段落によると、武器が大きくなったことにより何が推測できますか。

(A) 野生生物が増えたことにより、漁労にさらに大きな武器を使わざるをえなくなった。
(B) 以前の武器は、危険な動物の攻撃から人を守れなかった。
(C) 狩猟が盛んになると、より大きな武器が必要になった。
(D) より大きな武器を作るようになってはじめて、より大型の動物を狩るようになった。

問5は、「武器が大きくなったことにより推測されること」を問うています。では続きを読み進めましょう。❻～❼は「狩猟者がより大型の獲物を狩るようになったため、武器が大きくなった」と述べています。❽～❾は「武器の技術が発展するにつれて、獲物がいる限り一カ所に留まって生活することができるようになった」と説明しています。❿は「コンゲモーゼ文化は短かったが、重要だった」と述べ、段落を締めています。では選択肢を検討しましょう。漁労から狩猟へと移行したと本文にはあったので(A)はfor fishingが誤りです。(B)は「以前の武器は危険な動物から人々を守れなかった」という意味ですが、本文にはこれを示唆する内容はありません。(C)のThe rise in huntingは「狩猟が盛んになる」という意味です。❺のmore dependence was placed on hunting than beforeから十分に推測できます。さらに、❻のwhich may explain the increased size ... of weaponryは「結果として、武器が大きくなった」という意味です。つまり、よりどう猛かつ大型の獲物を狩るようになった結果、武器が大きくなったので、(C)が正解となります。なお、(D)は「より大きな武器を作るようになってはじめて、より大型の動物を狩るようになった」ということですが、これは❺～❻の内容と因果関係が逆なので誤りです。

□ it is not until X that SV: Xしてはじめて～する

第４段落｜問６解説レクチャー

❶The Ertebølle culture (5,300–3,950 BC) took its time in development, but returning to the waves, the Ertebølle revived the Maglemosian traditions of fishing and even expanded it to taking on the larger inhabitants of the sea, whales. ❷Their mastery of navigating inland rivers was impressive for the age and as such, their economy began to lean again towards marine treasures such as sharks, seals, and a variety of fish. ❸Being able to travel for a long distance and hunt, people no longer had to relocate the entire community and change their place of residence, further accelerating the sedentary characteristics of their lifestyle. ❹The discovery in the archaeological artifacts from this era points towards a great food surplus for this culture, and with concerns for procuring food gone, people could spend less time hunting and more time on something new, including farming and making pottery for storing food. ❺Although the Ertebølle were not fully an agrarian society, we do see the rapid development of farming; they did use domestic grain to some extent to supplement their food supply.

6. According to paragraph 4, what contributed the most to the Ertebølle culture's sedentary life?

(A) Pottery-making skills with which they were able to store more food supplies
(B) New farming techniques they learned during the time they could afford
(C) The discovery of new materials to produce larger hunting tools
(D) Superior skills in navigating through waterways and catching ocean resources

第４段落によると、エルテベレ文化の定住生活の最大の原因となったものは何ですか。

(A) さらに多くの食料を保存できる壺を作る技術
(B) 余裕のあるときに学んだ新たな農耕技術
(C) より大きな狩猟道具を生産できる新たな材料の発見
(D) 水路を航行して、海の資源を捕る優れた技術問6は「エルテベレ文化の定住生活の最大の原因となったもの」を選ぶ問題です。❶は「エルテベレ人はマグレモーゼ文化の漁労を復活させ、クジラのような大型動物を狩るようになった」と述べています。さらなる具体説明として、❷には「内陸部の河川を迷わずに進めるようになったので、海の生き物のウエートが再び大きくなっていった」とあります。❸は「長距離を移動して狩りをすることができるようになったので、定住化がさらに進んだ」と説明しています。つまり、内陸部の河川を進む技術を身に付けることで、長距離の移動が可能になったということです。ここまで読むと(D)が正解だとわかりますね。他の選択肢はどれも本文の内容とは無関係です。段落後半の内容を確認してから第5段落に進みましょう。

第５段落｜問 7～8 解説レクチャー

❶The Ertebølle culture was the last culture marking the Mesolithic age. ❷The survival of the Maglemosian, Kongemosen, and Ertebølle cultures was aided by the hospitable climate of this region. ❸This ocean coast area attracted the Scandinavian ancestors throughout the Mesolithic periods. ❹The move to the Neolithic age was triggered when they began to domesticate animals and exploit the land suitable for cultivation. ❺Upon the transition from the Mesolithic to Neolithic era, people learned to become more accustomed to a permanently sedentary life in their society. ❻It grew increasingly complex, and as a result, larger sized military or religious groups readily formed and strong leaders and hierarchies began to emerge. ❼All these new cultural proliferations stand upon the long-lasted cultures during the Mesolithic ages.

7. In paragraph 5, the word "exploit" in the passage is closest in meaning to

(A) expand (B) utilize
(C) protect (D) raise

第5段落のexploitと最も近い意味のものはどれですか。

(A) 拡大する (B) 利用する
(C) 保護する (D) 上昇する

問7のexploitは「活用する、利用する」という意味なので、(B) utilizeが正解です。exploitの「搾取する」という意味も覚えておきましょう。

8. According to paragraph 5, what can be inferred about the transition from the Mesolithic era to the Neolithic era?

(A) The availability of tillable land encouraged the entire community to reside in one place for long time.
(B) The transition was difficult for many to accept, which led to the formation of military associations.
(C) The sudden shift in cultural and religious ideas was undertaken by a new strong leader.
(D) Many were accustomed to former traditional ways of life, which made a sedentary life unappealing yet adaptable.

第5段落によると、中石器時代から新石器時代への移行に関して推測できることは何ですか。

(A) 耕作可能な土地を利用できたので、地域社会全体が長期にわたって一カ所に留まることができた。
(B) 新石器時代への移行が多くの人にとって受け入れ難かったため、軍事同盟の結成に至った。
(C) 文化や宗教の思想における急激な変化は新たな力強い指導者によってもたらされた。
(D) 多くの人々は以前の生活に慣れていたので、定住生活は魅力的ではないが、融通が利くものになった。

問8は「中石器時代から新石器時代への移行に関して推測できること」を問うています。では、最後の段落も集中して読み進めましょう。❶〜❸は「エルテベレ文化は、中石器時代に特徴的な最後の文化であった。快適な気候のおかげで沿岸部に人々が住み始めた」と説明しています。❹は「新石器時代への移行は、動物を飼育し、耕作に適した土地を利用し始めたときに始まった」、❺は「人々は定住生活に慣れていった」、❻は「社会はますます複雑化し、その結果、より大きな軍事集団や宗教集団が容易に形成されるようになり、強い指導者や階級社会が現れた」という意味です。つまり、❹〜❻で新石器時代の特徴を説明しているわけですね。最後に❼でこれら全ての新しい文化が拡散したのは、中石器時代に続いた文化に立脚していると締めくくっています。では選択肢を詳しく見ていきましょう。(A)は「耕作可能な土地を利用できたので、地域社会全体が長期にわたって一カ所に留まることができた」という意味です。これは、❹と❺の内容から推察できます。(B)は「新石器時代への移行が受け入れ難かった」が誤りです。❺と矛盾します。(C)は「新たな力強い指導者によってもたらされた」が誤りです。社会が複雑になって様々な変化が現れ、その後リーダーが出てきたのであって、(C)は本文と順序が逆になっています。(D)は「多くの人々は以前の生活に慣れていたので、定住生活は魅力的ではなかった」が誤りです。❺にはこれとは逆のことが書いてあります。よって、正解は(A)です。

□tillable：耕作可能な　□reside：住む　□association：同盟　□undertake X：Xに着手する
□yet：だが（≒but）

問9解説レクチャー

9. Look at the four squares [■] that indicate where the following sentence could be added to the passage.

This shift strongly encouraged the structural and cultural development of Scandinavian society.

Where would the sentence best fit?

❶The Ertebølle culture was the last culture marking the Mesolithic age. ❷The survival of the Maglemosian, Kongemosen, and Ertebølle cultures was aided by the hospitable climate of this region. ❸This ocean coast area attracted the Scandinavian ancestors throughout the Mesolithic periods. ❹The move to the Neolithic age was triggered when they began to domesticate animals and exploit the land suitable for cultivation. **A** ❺Upon the transition from the Mesolithic to Neolithic era, people learned to become more accustomed to a permanently sedentary life in their society. **D** ❻It grew increasingly complex, and as a result, larger sized military or religious groups readily formed and strong leaders and hierarchies began to emerge. **C** ❼All these new cultural proliferations stand upon the long-lasted cultures during the Mesolithic ages. **D**

次の文が以下のパッセージで追加されうる箇所を示す4つの■を見てください。

この変化はスカンジナビアの社会における構造的かつ文化的な発展を強く促した。

この文は、どこに置くのが最もよいですか。

問9の文は「この変化はスカンジナビアの社会における構造的かつ文化的な発展を強く促した」という意味です。指示表現と論理展開に注目しましょう。This shiftが主語なので、前の文は変化や移行に関する内容のはずです。また、後半は「社会の発展」とあるので、続く文も同じような内容であることが予想されます。この2つの条件を頭に入れて読んでいくと、❺には「中石器時代から新石器時代への移行」が述べられており、続く❻では「宗教や社会における発展」が述べられています。よって正解は**B**です。❻のItは挿入文のScandinavian societyを指しています。

問 10 解説レクチャー

10. Directions: An introductory sentence containing a brief summary of the passage is provided below. Complete the summary by selecting the best THREE answer choices that express the main ideas of the passage.

The history of Scandinavia had various cultures intertwined within it, which led it to its long survival and eventual migration and transition to more sedentary lifestyles.

(A) Hunter-gatherers of Mesolithic Scandinavia actively traveled along coastlines in order to collect shells.

(B) Maglemosian culture, the first one to come in the Mesolithic era of Scandinavia, relied mostly on fishing with spears and hunting for survival.

(C) The Kongemose culture made advanced weaponry and focused on hunting large forest animals for their main source of food, while people in the Ertebølle culture engaged themselves actively in fishing.

(D) The favorable climate, abundant resources, and technological developments encouraged people during the later phase of the Mesolithic era to live a more and more sedentary life.

(E) The Mesolithic civilization influenced all three Scandinavian cultures to merge into sedentary ways of life after the introduction of militaristic and religious groups.

(F) The Mesolithic civilization consisted mostly of farmers from other parts of the land, including Europe.

指示：パッセージの簡単な要約を含む紹介文を以下に記載しています。パッセージの中の最も重要な考えを示している文を3つ選んで要約を完成させてください。

スカンジナビアの歴史は、その中で様々な文化が絡み合うことで長期にわたって続き、やがて移住と変遷を経て、さらに定住生活の傾向が進んだ。

(A) 中石器時代のスカンジナビアの狩猟採集民は貝殻を採取するために海岸沿いを活発に移動した。

(B) マグレモーゼ文化は、スカンジナビアの中石器時代の最初の文化だが、主にもりを使った漁労や狩猟に生き残りをかけていた。

(C) コンゲモーゼ文化は、最新の武器を作り、主な食料源として大型の森の動物を捕獲したのに対し、エルテベレ文化の人々は主に漁労に従事した。

(D) 望ましい気候と十分な資源、技術の発達により、中石器時代後期の人々はますます定住するようになった。

(E) 軍事集団や宗教集団が現れた後に、中石器時代の文明に影響を受けたスカンジナビアの3つの文化は、定住的生活様式に融合した。

(F) 中石器時代の文明は、ヨーロッパなど別の土地から来た農民が主体であった。

(A)は第1段落❺に書いてある内容ですが、これはあくまで具体例の一つにすぎません。このように枝葉末節をとらえた選択肢は、保留としておきましょう。(B)はマグレモーゼ文化の特徴をまとめています。これは第2段落全体の内容をとらえているものなので、正解である可能性が高いです。(C)は「コンゲモーゼ文化は発達した武器で大型の動物を捕らえていたのに対し、エルテベレ文化は主に漁労に従事した」という意味です。これは第3～4段落で説明されていたそれぞれの文化の特徴を端的にとらえているので、正解である可能性が高いです。(D)ですが中石器時代後期の人々が定住するようになった要因を述べています。これは、第5段落の内容と一致するため、正解の可能性が高いです。(E)は「軍事集団や宗教集団が現れた後に、定住生活を送るようになった」という部分が誤りです。第5段落の❺～❻によると、定住生活を送るようになった後に、軍事集団や宗教集団が現れたというのが正しい流れです。つまり、前後関係が逆なので誤りです。(F)は「中石器時代の文明は農民が主体であった」という意味です。ただ、農耕の発達について説明があるのは第4段落❺ですが、その時期は明確には述べられていません。よって(F)は誤りです。よって、(B)、(C)、(D)が正解です。

□ abundant：豊富な　□ phase：時期　□ merge into X：Xへと融合する

PARAGRAPH 1

❶While Northern Scandinavia was still covered by an ice sheet around 10,000 BC, with little hope of sustaining lasting settlements, the Mesolithic[1] Southern Scandinavia was able to support continuous settlements all the way into the following Neolithic[2] epoch and onward.

❷After the glaciers of the ice age retreated far enough north over Europe, forests soon began to spring up throughout this land, which was previously difficult to live on.

❸Throughout what is now Denmark, as well as southern regions of Sweden and Finland, hunter-gatherers moved in and began to exploit the indigenous animal life of the land, sea, and rivers, as well as the local nutrient-rich plants.

❹These post-glacial cultures are seen as a perfect example of the way the Mesolithic man lived.

❺From collecting shells on the coast to making a journey to seasonal hunting grounds, they left behind one of the greatest sites of archaeological treasures.

❻Many remains have been found in previously waterlogged locations like rivers and swamps, which preserved them in the thick mud.

❼Through investigations, our understanding of Mesolithic Scandinavia has grown greatly over the last fifty years, making it clearer now that there was a gradual shift towards a more sedentary lifestyle, which merges with the introduction of farming into Europe in the following era.

1. Mesolithic: The middle part of the Stone Age
2. Neolithic: The last part of the Stone Age following the Mesolithic era

❶紀元前1万年頃、まだ北スカンジナビアが氷床に覆われ、定住を続けられる望みがほぼなかったのに対して、中石器時代[1]の南スカンジナビアでは次の新石器時代[2]までずっと、またそれ以降も定住することが可能であった。

❷氷河時代の氷河がヨーロッパの北端まで後退した後しばらくして、以前は定住が難しかった土地全体に森が誕生した。

❸現在のスウェーデンやフィンランドの南部およびデンマークに当たる地域には、狩猟採集民が移住し、その地域の栄養分豊富な植物を採取するだけでなく、その土地、海域、河川に元から生息する動物を捕り始めた。

❹この後氷期の文化は、中石器時代の人類の生活様式の適例である。

❺彼らは海岸で貝殻を採取し、また季節に応じて狩猟場へと移動することによって、考古学的に貴重な品々が眠る土地の一つを後世に残した。

❻多くの貴重な遺物は、川や沼など、以前は水辺だった土地で見つかっている。そうした川や沼の厚い泥の中に保存されていたのだ。

❼調査を通じて、中石器時代のスカンジナビアに対する我々の理解は過去50年間で大いに進歩した。その結果、より定住的な生活スタイルへとゆるやかに移行していき、続く時代におけるヨーロッパへの農耕の導入と定住的な生活スタイルが融合したことが、明らかとなっている。

1. 中石器時代の：石器時代の中期
2. 新石器時代の：中石器時代に続く石器時代最後の時期

＊語句問題に出る可能性あり

❶ □ *lasting：持続可能な
□ settlement：定住
□ all the way：(時間的に) ずっと
□ onward：その後も、その先も

❷ □ spring up：生じる

❸ □ as well as X：Xに加えて
□ move in：移住する
□ *exploit X：Xを利用する
□ *indigenous：その地域に根付いている

❺ □ leave X behind：Xを後に残す

❻ □ remains：遺物
□ waterlogged：極度に水のしみ込んだ
□ swamp：沼
□ mud：泥

❼ □ *sedentary：定住的な、座りっぱなしの
□ *merge with X：Xと融合する
□ introduction of X into Y：XをYへと導入すること (introduce X into Yの名詞化)

❺ From <u>collecting shells on the coast</u> (X) to <u>making a journey to seasonal hunting grounds</u> (Y)

→from X to Y：XからYに至るまで（具体例を提示する表現）

❼ <u>making</u> (V′) <u>it</u> (O′) <u>clearer</u> (C′) now (that ...)

itはthat節を指す仮目的語。nowは単なる副詞で、now thatという熟語の一部ではない。

PARAGRAPH 2

❶The first Mesolithic culture to emerge in the Scandinavian southern lands was the Maglemosian culture, which lends its name to the first stage of the Maglemose-Kongemose-Ertebølle sequence.

❷The Maglemosian culture is characterized by the use of wood, bone, and flint tools, and people in this era lived mostly in forested as well as wetland environments.

❸Some societies at that time survived on hunting and fishing in fixed locations, although others were nomadic, meaning they migrated to better hunting grounds as the seasons allowed.

❹The sea levels during the Maglemose period (9,000–6,000 BC) were much lower than they are today, not reaching their current heights until the very end of this period.

❺There were a higher number of suitable coastal locations for fishing, where the Maglemosians would make good use of spears.

❻With sufficient land and food supplies in many parts of their society, people did not have to relocate frequently, which facilitated the sedentary nature of their life.

❶スカンジナビアの南部地域に現れた最初の中石器文化はマグレモーゼ文化と呼ばれ、マグレモーゼ文化、コンゲモーゼ文化、エルテベレ文化という一連の流れにおける最初の段階でその名が登場する。

❷マグレモーゼ文化は、木や骨、火打ち道具を使用したことに特徴があり、この時代の人々は、たいてい森や湿地帯に住んでいた。

❸当時、ある特定の場所で狩猟や漁労をして生活する社会もあれば、季節がよければよりよい猟場に移住する、いわゆる遊牧民としての生活をする社会もあった。

❹マグレモーゼ期（紀元前9000年～6000年）の海面の高さは今よりもずっと低く、この時代の末期になってようやく現在の高さまで上昇した。

❺マグレモーゼの人々がもりを利用して魚を捕るのに最適な沿岸地域も数多くあった。

❻社会には十分な土地と食料があったため、人々は頻繁に移住する必要がなくなり、生活は定住的な性格をますます帯びるようになっていった。

＊語句問題に出る可能性あり

❶ □ *emerge：生じる
□ sequence：一連の流れ、続きもの

❷ □ *be characterized by X：Xによって特徴づけられる

❸ □ *fixed：特定の
□ nomadic：遊牧民の
□ migrate：移住する

❺ □ *suitable：適切な
□ *make good use of X：Xを活用する

❻ □ *sufficient：十分な
□ relocate：移住する
□ *facilitate X：Xを促進する

❶ which lends its name to the first stage ...
(lends = V, its name = X, the first stage = Y)

lend X to Yは「XをYに貸す」が直訳。「それ（マグレモーゼ）はその名前を最初の段階に与えた」→「それが、最初の段階の名前となった」

PARAGRAPH 3

❶Kongemosen, a big island in current day Denmark, is the name of the next Mesolithic culture and period in this region.

❷Though fairly similar to their predecessors, the Kongemose culture was able to produce more sophisticated blade weapons and tools, expanding their flint and stone arsenal.

❸An increasing artisan trend started to appear amongst the Kongemose as more of their tools and weapons were found to be etched with detailed geometric patterns.

❹Due to the elevated sea levels by the start of this period, many previous coastal settlements were flooded under the Baltic Sea, which undermined their fishing habits.

❺Thus, more dependence was placed on hunting than before.

❻Hunters were now taking down wilder and larger game such as boar and deer, which may explain the increased size and significance of weaponry seen in this era.

❼In fact, the Kongemose settlement was able to kill the most dangerous animals in the forests, including wolves, bears, aurochs, and elks.

❽People chose to push themselves to develop better technology and stay in one place rather than move to other places.

❾In fact, they could do so as long as they were able to find enough animals to hunt.

❿Although this culture had a relatively short lifespan (6,000–5,200 BC) compared to the periods that come before and after, the short time period does not cancel out the importance of this fierce culture.

❶コンゲモーゼ（現在のデンマークにある大きな島）は、この地域における中石器時代の次の文化および時期の名称である。

❷それ以前の文化とかなり似た点も多いが、コンゲモーゼ文化はより精巧な刃物の武器や道具を作るようになり、火打ち石や石の武器が増えていった。

❸多くの道具や武器に細かい幾何学模様の描写が見つかるようになり、コンゲモーゼの人々が次第に意匠を凝らすようになっていった。

❹この時代が始まるまでに海面が上昇したため、以前の沿岸の居住地はバルト海に沈み、漁労の習慣が失われた。

❺これにより、以前にも増して狩猟に依存するようになった。

❻狩猟者はイノシシやシカといった、よりどう猛かつ大型の獲物を狩るようになったが、この時代の武器が大きくなり、その重要性も増したのはそのためかもしれない。

❼事実、コンゲモーゼの定住者らは、オオカミ、クマ、オーロックス、ヘラジカなど森で最も危険な動物を仕留めることができるようになった。

❽人々はどこかへ移動することよりも、一カ所に留まり、よりよい道具を作ることを選んだ。

❾実際、狩猟の対象となる獲物がそこにいる限り、定住することが可能であった。

❿この文化は、前後の時代と比較してかなり期間が短い（紀元前6000年～5200年）が、だからといってこの荒々しい文化の重要性を消し去ることはできない。

＊語句問題に出る可能性あり

❶ □ *current：現在の

❷ □ predecessor：先駆者、前に存在したものや人
□ sophisticated：洗練された
□ flint：火打ち石
□ arsenal：武器

❸ □ artisan：職人

❹ □ undermine X：Xを台無しにする
□ settlement：定住地

❻ □ *game：獲物
□ weaponry：武器
□ aurochs：オーロックス
□ elks：ヘラジカ

❾ □ as long as SV：～する限り（条件を表す接続詞句）

❿ □ cancel out X：Xを打ち消す
□ lifespan：寿命
□ compared to X：Xと比較すると
□ fierce：激しい、どう猛な

❺ more dependence was placed on hunting (X)

→place more dependence on X「Xに頼る」の受け身の形

PARAGRAPH 4

❶The Ertebølle culture (5,300–3,950 BC) took its time in development, but returning to the waves, the Ertebølle revived the Maglemosian traditions of fishing and even expanded it to taking on the larger inhabitants of the sea, whales.

❷Their mastery of navigating inland rivers was impressive for the age and as such, their economy began to lean again towards marine treasures such as sharks, seals, and a variety of fish.

❸Being able to travel for a long distance and hunt, people no longer had to relocate the entire community and change their place of residence, further accelerating the sedentary characteristics of their lifestyle.

❹The discovery in the archaeological artifacts from this era points towards a great food surplus for this culture, and with concerns for procuring food gone, people could spend less time hunting and more time on something new, including farming and making pottery for storing food.

❺Although the Ertebølle were not fully an agrarian society, we do see the rapid development of farming; they did use domestic grain to some extent to supplement their food supply.

❶エルテベレ文化（紀元前5300年～3950年）はその発展に時間を要したが、エルテベレ人は海に戻ると、マグレモーゼ文化の漁労の伝統を復活させ、クジラのような大型動物を捕獲するところまで発展させた。

❷内陸部の河川を迷わずに進めるようになったことは、その時代にしては驚異的であり、同様に経済に関しても、サメ、アザラシ、様々な魚類など海の生き物のウエートが再び大きくなっていった。

❸長距離を移動して狩りができるようになったので、社会全体を移動させ、集落を変える必要がなくなり、それにより彼らの生活スタイルは、さらに定住化の様相を帯びるようになった。

❹この時代の考古学的遺物の発見により、この文化には食料の余剰があったことがわかり、食料調達の心配がなくなったため、エルテベレ文化の人々は狩猟よりも農耕や食品を貯蔵する壺の作成など新しいことに時間を費やすことができた。

❺エルテベレ人は完全に農耕社会だったわけではないが、それでも農耕の急激な発達を見ることができる。彼らは食料の供給を補うために、自らが育てた穀物をある程度活用していた。

＊語句問題に出る可能性あり

❶□take on X：Xを捕獲する
□inhabitant：住民、ある場所に存在する生き物

❷□*impressive：素晴らしい
□for the age：その時代にしては
(例) He looks young for his age.
(彼は年齢の割に若く見える)
□lean towards X：Xに傾く、Xを好む
□treasure：資源
□seal：アザラシ
□a variety of X：様々なX

❸□*accelerate X：Xを促進する
□characteristic of X：Xの特徴

❹□archaeological：考古学的な
□artifact：遺物
□surplus：余剰の
□*procure X：Xを調達する
□pottery：壺
□store X：Xを蓄える

❺□not fully：完全に～というわけではない（部分否定）
□*domestic：居住区内の、国内の、家庭内の
□to some extent：ある程度
□supplement X：Xを補う

PARAGRAPH 5

❶The Ertebølle culture was the last culture marking the Mesolithic age.

❷The survival of the Maglemosian, Kongemosen, and Ertebølle cultures was aided by the hospitable climate of this region.

❸This ocean coast area attracted the Scandinavian ancestors throughout the Mesolithic periods.

❹The move to the Neolithic age was triggered when they began to domesticate animals and exploit the land suitable for cultivation.

❺Upon the transition from the Mesolithic to Neolithic era, people learned to become more accustomed to a permanently sedentary life in their society.

❻It grew increasingly complex, and as a result, larger sized military or religious groups readily formed and strong leaders and hierarchies began to emerge.

❼All these new cultural proliferations stand upon the long-lasted cultures during the Mesolithic ages.

❶エルテベレ文化は、中石器時代に特徴的な最後の文化であった。

❷マグレモーゼ文化、コンゲモーゼ文化、エルテベレ文化が続いたのは、この地域の快適な気候のおかげであった。

❸この沿岸部は、中石器時代を通して、スカンジナビア人の祖先を魅了した。

❹新石器時代への移行は、動物を飼育し、耕作に適した土地を利用し始めたときに始まった。

❺中石器時代から新石器時代への変遷期にあっては、人々の社会が長期にわたって一カ所に留まる生活習慣がますます定着していった。

❻社会はますます複雑化し、その結果、より大きな軍事集団や宗教集団が容易に形成されるようになり、強い指導者や階級社会が誕生するようになった。

❼これら全ての新しい文化が拡散したのは、中石器時代に長く続いた文化があったためである。

＊語句問題に出る可能性あり

❶ □ mark X：Xを特徴づける

❷ □ *aid X：Xを助ける
□ *hospitable：快適な

❹ □ *trigger X：Xを引き起こす
□ domesticate X：Xを家畜化する

❺ □ transition：変遷
□ become accustomed to X：Xに慣れる

❻ □ as a result：その結果
□ *readily：容易に
□ hierarchy：階級

❼ □ *proliferation：拡散

リーディング問題 2 | Earth Science

EARLY LIFE–FORMS AND EARTH'S ATMOSPHERE

問題演習の流れ

- □ 解答時間は17分を目標にしましょう。
- □ 英文 ⇒ 問題 ⇒ 正解・解説レクチャー ⇒ 訳 という流れで学習します。
- □ 3回解けるように、3回分のマークシートを各問題に用意しています。解く日付を記入してからマークしてください。

Web解答方法

- □ 本試験では各選択肢の左に表示されるマークをクリックして解答します。本試験と同様の方法で取り組みたい場合は、Webで解答できます。
- □ インターネットのつながるパソコン・スマートフォンで、以下のサイトにアクセスしてWeb上で解答してください。

extester.com

- □ 操作方法は、p.13 ～ 14の「USA Club Web学習の使い方」をご参照ください。

学習の記録

学習開始日	年　月　日	学習終了日	年　月　日
学習開始日	年　月　日	学習終了日	年　月　日
学習開始日	年　月　日	学習終了日	年　月　日

リーディング問題 2　英文

EARLY LIFE—FORMS AND EARTH'S ATMOSPHERE

The key drivers that have resulted in the livable atmosphere that the Earth has today are many and complicated, with interactions that spanned billions of years to shape the world as we know it. Of the eight planets orbiting the Sun, four—Mercury, Venus, Earth, and Mars—are called terrestrial planets, created by successive collisions of meteorites. The remaining four—Jupiter, Saturn, Uranus, and Neptune—are called Jovian planets, which are basically gigantic balls made of gas. Among all these planets, only our Earth has an atmosphere that is said to be habitable for organisms. The mechanisms of how a mass of meteorites or barren rocks initially generated an atmosphere and how the Earth became a thriving menagerie of life can be broken down into two key steps with a few supporting drivers.

To begin with, the Earth did not start out with the atmosphere that we have now. Indeed, the Earth had a so-called "primordial atmosphere" early in its history, but the atmosphere at one point became non-existent, owing to the Sun's rays, or solar winds, blasting away the hydrogen and helium based gases that had been around the Earth's surface. The hydrogen and helium gases being the two lightest among all, it was relatively easy for the solar winds to strip those gases from the early Earth. It can be said that for a certain length of time, the Earth was almost atmosphereless with only a tiny volume of remnants composed of relatively heavier elements. The atmosphere was not replenished until early volcanic activities released certain types of gases in addition to those light gases, which led to the creation of the "second atmosphere." The eruptions released the compounds of water, carbon dioxide, and methane, many of which were fundamentally important for the formation, growth, and proliferation of various living organisms.

There was, however, still a distinct lack of oxygen in this early outpouring of gas. The long-term changes that have gifted us with an oxygen-rich atmosphere in present times began with the evolution of the first photosynthetic life forms. These small cyanobacteria—found virtually anywhere including oceans, rocks, soil, etc.—would convert sunlight and carbon dioxide into oxygen. The early oxygen production was rather limited, however, and the vast majority of it was absorbed into meteorites and rocks due to the small amount produced. A saturation point for these rocks was eventually reached, and as such they could absorb no more oxygen, allowing it to remain free in the atmosphere. Only once a sufficient amount of oxygen was present in the atmosphere did it begin to protect life forms enough to enable them to move from the great oceans onto land, developing respiration in the meantime. The oxygen in the atmosphere mutated to provide even more protection for life forms. Ozone (three oxygen atoms bonded together) was a much better shield against the harmful effects of UV radiation.

During the initial part of the Proterozoic period (2,500–541 million years ago), with the atmosphere gradually changing but life barely becoming more complicated than the algae that had kicked off the whole process of oxygenation, the planet was kept warm. This is due in part to a high level of methane, a greenhouse gas. The oxygen level remained relatively low. At the end of the Proterozoic period, however, there was a sudden rise in the level of oxygen, resulting in an ice age as the oxygen effectively removed the methane from the atmosphere, reducing the greenhouse effect and allowing this significant cooling. The difference in the amount of methane in this ancient atmosphere compared to what we have now really cannot be understated. After the oxygen spike, there were only around 1.8 parts per million of methane in the atmosphere, while before this event, there were around 100 parts per million. Considering that methane is a much more effective greenhouse gas than CO_2, it should be no surprise that such a drastic reduction could have brought about global glaciation and what is referred to as a "snowball Earth."

With the surface of the Earth completely covered by ice and the ocean frozen, glacial activities of the mass of ice facilitated the mixing of elements and compounds that were once present only in the mountainous or oceanic regions, thereby exchanging and stirring up numerous nutrients on a global scale. In addition, the thick ice itself contained many different types of minerals and compounds, all of which poured into the mountains and oceans as the ice gradually melted away. Enriched with these ingredients, a richer variety of algae evolved and oxygen levels began to rise through their process of photosynthesis. This caused not only the composition of the atmosphere to change, but it also produced more complex life forms, like sponges and other animals. The atmosphere affects life on the planet. In the same way, activities of organisms affect the atmosphere. For example, the photosynthetic algae produce oxygen in abundance, without which there would not have been the evolution of animals. Although this process has taken billions of years, our Earth is now supporting life that is very different to its ancestors, with varying needs and prospects. As we move forward into the future, how will our atmosphere change in another billion years? There is the term "anthroposphere," which refers to the part of the natural environment that is made or modified by human activities. Rigorous research is being conducted about determining how the anthroposphere and atmosphere interact and shape our future Earth.

1. According to paragraph 1, what is true about the formation of the Earth?

(A) It was created through the process of a mass of meteorites colliding with one another, which, over time, helped generate the atmosphere we have today.
(B) It was created by a gigantic ball of gas which fused into the Earth's atmosphere.
(C) There were only a few factors that contributed to the formation of the Earth.
(D) With the formation of the Earth came an atmosphere that caused many complicated organisms to come into existence.

PARAGRAPH 1

The key drivers that have resulted in the livable atmosphere that the Earth has today are many and complicated, with interactions that spanned billions of years to shape the world as we know it. Of the eight planets orbiting the Sun, four—Mercury, Venus, Earth, and Mars—are called terrestrial planets, created by successive collisions of meteorites. The remaining four—Jupiter, Saturn, Uranus, and Neptune—are called Jovian planets, which are basically gigantic balls made of gas. Among all these planets, only our Earth has an atmosphere that is said to be habitable for organisms. The mechanisms of how a mass of meteorites or barren rocks initially generated an atmosphere and how the Earth became a thriving menagerie of life can be broken down into two key steps with a few supporting drivers.

2. In paragraph 2, the word "remnants" in the passage is closest in meaning to

(A) rare substances
(B) something that cannot be seen
(C) gases with unknown elements
(D) things that are left over

PARAGRAPH 2

To begin with, the Earth did not start out with the atmosphere that we have now. Indeed, the Earth had a so-called "primordial atmosphere" early in its history, but the atmosphere at one point became non-existent, owing to the Sun's rays, or solar winds, blasting away the hydrogen and helium based gases that had been around the Earth's surface. The hydrogen and helium gases being the two lightest among all, it was relatively easy for the solar winds to strip those gases from the early Earth. It can be said that for a certain length of time, the Earth was almost atmosphereless with only a tiny volume of remnants composed of relatively heavier elements. The atmosphere was not replenished until early volcanic activities released certain types of gases in addition to those light gases, which led to the creation of the "second atmosphere." The eruptions released the compounds of water, carbon dioxide, and methane, many of which were fundamentally important for the formation, growth, and proliferation of various living organisms.

3. According to paragraphs 2 and 3, how were the first primordial atmosphere and the second atmosphere different?

(A) The hydrogen and helium that were present in the primordial atmosphere were absent in the second one.
(B) The second atmosphere contained constituents vital for the development of life.
(C) Oxygen released by volcanic activities took up a large volume of the second atmosphere.
(D) The second atmosphere was filled with cyanobacteria capable of producing oxygen without light.

4. According to paragraph 3, all of the following is true about oxygen in the second atmosphere EXCEPT:

(A) Oxygen could stay in the air because there was a limit to the amount of oxygen that rocks could take in.
(B) Rocks and meteorites served as the primary source of oxygen generation.
(C) An oxygen-rich atmosphere made it possible for some animals to breathe on land.
(D) Ozone layers provided a more effective protection against UV rays.

PARAGRAPH 3

There was, however, still a distinct lack of oxygen in this early outpouring of gas. The long-term changes that have gifted us with an oxygen-rich atmosphere in present times began with the evolution of the first photosynthetic life forms. These small cyanobacteria—found virtually anywhere including oceans, rocks, soil, etc.—would convert sunlight and carbon dioxide into oxygen. The early oxygen production was rather limited, however, and the vast majority of it was absorbed into meteorites and rocks due to the small amount produced. A saturation point for these rocks was eventually reached, and as such they could absorb no more oxygen, allowing it to remain free in the atmosphere. Only once a sufficient amount of oxygen was present in the atmosphere did it begin to protect life forms enough to enable them to move from the great oceans onto land, developing respiration in the meantime. The oxygen in the atmosphere mutated to provide even more protection for life forms. Ozone (three oxygen atoms bonded together) was a much better shield against the harmful effects of UV radiation.

5. According to paragraph 4, all of the following were true about the Proterozoic period EXCEPT:

(A) Oxygen-producing algae could be found.
(B) The temperature of the atmosphere dramatically decreased.
(C) The dramatic evolution of complex life forms was observed.
(D) The amounts of methane in the atmosphere greatly changed.

6. According to paragraph 4, the reduced level of methane toward the end of the Proterozoic period resulted in

(A) a spike in the concentration of carbon dioxide
(B) a marked rise in the sea level
(C) a reduction of living organisms on the Earth
(D) enhanced formation of glacier

PARAGRAPH 4

During the initial part of the Proterozoic period (2,500–541 million years ago), with the atmosphere gradually changing but life barely becoming more complicated than the algae that had kicked off the whole process of oxygenation, the planet was kept warm. This is due in part to a high level of methane, a greenhouse gas. The oxygen level remained relatively low. At the end of the Proterozoic period, however, there was a sudden rise in the level of oxygen, resulting in an ice age as the oxygen effectively removed the methane from the atmosphere, reducing the greenhouse effect and allowing this significant cooling. The difference in the amount of methane in this ancient atmosphere compared to what we have now really cannot be understated. After the oxygen spike, there were only around 1.8 parts per million of methane in the atmosphere, while before this event, there were around 100 parts per million. Considering that methane is a much more effective greenhouse gas than CO_2, it should be no surprise that such a drastic reduction could have brought about global glaciation and what is referred to as a "snowball Earth."

7. Which of the sentences below best expresses the essential information in the highlighted sentence in the passage? Incorrect choices change the meaning in important ways or leave out essential information.

(A) Because the Earth was covered with a tremendous amount of ice, the exchange of nutrients between oceanic and mountainous regions was accelerated on a global scale.
(B) Ice started to cover the Earth's surface on a global scale, which caused the movement of parts of the massive ice to stir up substances on the Earth.
(C) During early Earth times, an abundant ice build-up created mountain and ocean movements which caused the facilitation of glacier activities.
(D) Thanks to the movements of glaciers, substances essential for life forms were brought to every corner of the world.

8. According to paragraph 5, what can be inferred about "anthroposphere"?

(A) Human activities may have future implications for the Earth in the long run.
(B) It has been proven that human activity has negative impacts on the Earth.
(C) Activities of all living organisms including humans shape the anthroposphere.
(D) Changes in the anthroposphere exert the greatest impact on the atmosphere.

PARAGRAPH 5

With the surface of the Earth completely covered by ice and the ocean frozen, glacial activities of the mass of ice facilitated the mixing of elements and compounds that were once present only in the mountainous or oceanic regions, thereby exchanging and stirring up numerous nutrients on a global scale. In addition, the thick ice itself contained many different types of minerals and compounds, all of which poured into the mountains and oceans as the ice gradually melted away. Enriched with these ingredients, a richer variety of algae evolved and oxygen levels began to rise through their process of photosynthesis. This caused not only the composition of the atmosphere to change, but it also produced more complex life forms, like sponges and other animals. The atmosphere affects life on the planet. In the same way, activities of organisms affect the atmosphere. For example, the photosynthetic algae produce oxygen in abundance, without which there would not have been the evolution of animals. Although this process has taken billions of years, our Earth is now supporting life that is very different to its ancestors, with varying needs and prospects. As we move forward into the future, how will our atmosphere change in another billion years? There is the term "anthroposphere," which refers to the part of the natural environment that is made or modified by human activities. Rigorous research is being conducted about determining how the anthroposphere and atmosphere interact and shape our future Earth.

9. Look at the four squares [■] that indicate where the following sentence could be added to the passage.

The evolution of our atmosphere has gone hand in hand with the evolution of life on our planet.

Where would the sentence best fit?

PARAGRAPH 5

With the surface of the Earth completely covered by ice and the ocean frozen, glacial activities of the mass of ice facilitated the mixing of elements and compounds that were once present only in the mountainous or oceanic regions, thereby exchanging and stirring up numerous nutrients on a global scale. In addition, the thick ice itself contained many different types of minerals and compounds, all of which poured into the mountains and oceans as the ice gradually melted away. **A** Enriched with these ingredients, a richer variety of algae evolved and oxygen levels began to rise through their process of photosynthesis. **B** This caused not only the composition of the atmosphere to change, but it also produced more complex life forms, like sponges and other animals. **C** The atmosphere affects life on the planet. **D** In the same way, activities of organisms affect the atmosphere. For example, the photosynthetic algae produce oxygen in abundance, without which there would not have been the evolution of animals. Although this process has taken billions of years, our Earth is now supporting life that is very different to its ancestors, with varying needs and prospects. As we move forward into the future, how will our atmosphere change in another billion years? There is the term "anthroposphere," which refers to the part of the natural environment that is made or modified by human activities. Rigorous research is being conducted about determining how the anthroposphere and atmosphere interact and shape our future Earth.

10. Directions: An introductory sentence containing a brief summary of the passage is provided below. Complete the summary by selecting the best THREE answer choices that express the main ideas of the passage.

The gradual changes over time of the Earth's atmosphere have made it a sustainable planet for many living organisms today.

Answer Choices

(A) Living creatures have made an important contribution to the formation of the atmosphere we have today.
(B) By the end of the Proterozoic period, most of the Earth had frozen over due to a sudden rise in oxygen, but this was a necessary step toward the formation of a livable atmosphere.
(C) The beginning of the Proterozoic period was characterized by a great and sharp decrease in methane gas, leading to an extremely cold climate.
(D) The conditions of the primordial atmosphere on early Earth were able to sustain bacterial life forms and their proliferation.
(E) UV light can be effectively filtered out by a sufficient amount of oxygen forming the so-called ozone layer.
(F) The Earth once lacked an atmosphere, but some volcanic activities and the first photosynthetic life forms provided essential substances that created the current atmosphere.

リーディング問題 2

正解一覧 80
解説レクチャー .... 80~93
訳 .... 94~103

1. **(A)** 2. **(D)** 3. **(B)** 4. **(B)** 5. **(C)**
6. **(D)** 7. **(D)** 8. **(A)** 9. **(C)** 10. **(A) (B) (F)**

第1段落｜問1 解説レクチャー

❶The key drivers that have resulted in the livable atmosphere that the Earth has today are many and complicated, with interactions that spanned billions of years to shape the world as we know it. ❷Of the eight planets orbiting the Sun, four—Mercury, Venus, Earth, and Mars—are called terrestrial planets, created by successive collisions of meteorites. ❸The remaining four—Jupiter, Saturn, Uranus, and Neptune—are called Jovian planets, which are basically gigantic balls made of gas. ❹Among all these planets, only our Earth has an atmosphere that is said to be habitable for organisms. ❺The mechanisms of how a mass of meteorites or barren rocks initially generated an atmosphere and how the Earth became a thriving menagerie of life can be broken down into two key steps with a few supporting drivers.

1. According to paragraph 1, what is true about the formation of the Earth?

(A) It was created through the process of a mass of meteorites colliding with one another, which, over time, helped generate the atmosphere we have today.
(B) It was created by a gigantic ball of gas which fused into the Earth's atmosphere.
(C) There were only a few factors that contributed to the formation of the Earth.
(D) With the formation of the Earth came an atmosphere that caused many complicated organisms to come into existence.

第1段落によると、地球の形成について正しいものはどれですか。

(A) 地球は隕石の塊が衝突し合いながら形成され、やがてそれは、我々が今日有する大気をつくり出すことに一役買った。
(B) 地球の大気に融合した巨大な球体のガスにより形成された。
(C) 地球の形成の一因となった要因はほとんどなかった。
(D) 地球の形成とともに、数多くの複雑な生物が生まれる原因となる大気ができた。

問1は「地球の形成に関して正しいもの」を問うています。❶は「生命が生存可能な大気を作り出した要因（driver）は数多くあり、複雑である」と述べています。❷で「地球を含むいくつかの惑星は、隕石の衝突によってつくり出された」とあります。ここは「地球の形成」に関わる箇所なのでヒントになりそうです。❸は「ガスからなる惑星」について述べています。その後、❹が「太陽系の惑星の中で、生物が生存できる大気を持つのは地球だけである」と説明しています。❺は「隕石や岩が大気をつくり、地球が生物が繁栄する場所となったメカニズムは、2つの重要な段階に分けられる」とあります。では、選択肢を詳しく見ていきましょう。(A)は「地球は隕石が衝突することにより形成され、それが大気をつくり出すことに一役買った」とあります。まさに、❷の「地球を含むいくつかの惑星は、隕石の衝突によってつくり出された」と、❺の「隕石や岩が大気をつくり…」という内容に一致しますね。(B)は❷と矛盾します。地球はガスでできているのではありません。(C)はonly a few「ほとんどない」という記述が❶のThe key drivers ... are many and complicatedと矛盾します。問題は(D)です。(D)は「地球の形成と同時に大気が生じた」という意味です。❶のwith interactions that spanned billions of years to shape the world as we know itにより、実際には何十億年もかかったということがわかります。つまり、地球の形成と生命が生存可能な大気の形成は、同時ではなかったことを示唆しています。一方、(A)の選択肢はover timeとあり、「長い時間をかけて大気が生じた」ことを示しています。よって(A)が正解です。

□ collide with X：Xと衝突する　□ come into existence：存在するようになる

第2段落｜問2解説レクチャー

❶To begin with, the Earth did not start out with the atmosphere that we have now. ❷Indeed, the Earth had a so-called "primordial atmosphere" early in its history, but the atmosphere at one point became non-existent, owing to the Sun's rays, or solar winds, blasting away the hydrogen and helium based gases that had been around the Earth's surface. ❸The hydrogen and helium gases being the two lightest among all, it was relatively easy for the solar winds to strip those gases from the early Earth. ❹It can be said that for a certain length of time, the Earth was almost atmosphereless with only a tiny volume of remnants composed of relatively heavier elements. ❺The atmosphere was not replenished until early volcanic activities released certain types of gases in addition to those light gases, which led to the creation of the "second atmosphere." ❻The eruptions released the compounds of water, carbon dioxide, and methane, many of which were fundamentally important for the formation, growth, and proliferation of various living organisms.

2. In paragraph 2, the word "remnants" in the passage is closest in meaning to

(A) rare substances
(B) something that cannot be seen
(C) gases with unknown elements
(D) things that are left over

第2段落のremnantsと最も近い意味のものはどれですか。

(A) 珍しい物質
(B) 見ることができない何か
(C) 成分のわからない気体
(D) 残されたもの

問2のremnantsは「残りもの、遺物」という意味なので、(D)が正解です。remnantはremain「残る」と同語源の単語だとわかれば覚えやすいです。段落全体の内容を確認してから第3段落に進みましょう。

第3段落｜問3~4 解説レクチャー

❶There was, however, still a distinct lack of oxygen in this early outpouring of gas. ❷The long-term changes that have gifted us with an oxygen-rich atmosphere in present times began with the evolution of the first photosynthetic life forms. ❸These small cyanobacteria—found virtually anywhere including oceans, rocks, soil, etc.—would convert sunlight and carbon dioxide into oxygen. ❹The early oxygen production was rather limited, however, and the vast majority of it was absorbed into meteorites and rocks due to the small amount produced. ❺A saturation point for these rocks was eventually reached, and as such they could absorb no more oxygen, allowing it to remain free in the atmosphere. ❻Only once a sufficient amount of oxygen was present in the atmosphere did it begin to protect life forms enough to enable them to move from the great oceans onto land, developing respiration in the meantime. ❼The oxygen in the atmosphere mutated to provide even more protection for life forms. ❽Ozone (three oxygen atoms bonded together) was a much better shield against the harmful effects of UV radiation.

3. According to paragraphs 2 and 3, how were the first primordial atmosphere and the second atmosphere different?

(A) The hydrogen and helium that were present in the primordial atmosphere were absent in the second one.
(B) The second atmosphere contained constituents vital for the development of life.
(C) Oxygen released by volcanic activities took up a large volume of the second atmosphere.
(D) The second atmosphere was filled with cyanobacteria capable of producing oxygen without light.

第2、第3段落によると、最初の原始大気と第二の大気の違いは何ですか。

(A) 原始大気に存在していた水素とヘリウムは、第二の大気には存在しなかった。
(B) 第二の大気は、生物の進化に必要不可欠な物質を含んでいた。
(C) 火山活動で放出された酸素が、第二の大気の大部分を占めていた。
(D) 第二の大気は、光がなくても酸素を生成できるシアノバクテリアで満たされていた。

問3は「最初の原始大気と第二の大気の違いは何か」を問うています。まず最初の原始大気は、第2段落❷に出てきます。先ほど読んだ通り、この原始大気は太陽風によって消滅してしまいました。その結果、❹にある通り地球にはほぼ大気のない期間が存在したのです。ところが、❺によると「火山活動によって放出された気体が、再び大気をつくり出した」とあります。これが第二の大気ですね。❻には「その大気は生物の発展に必要不可欠である多くの物質を含んでいた」とあります。(A)は「水素とヘリウムは、第二の大気には存在しなかった」が本文と矛盾しています。第2段落❺にin addition to those light gasesとあるため、第二の大気にも水素やヘリウムが含まれていたとわかります。(B)は「第二の大気は、生物の発展に必要不可欠である物質が含まれていた」という意味ですが、これは❻に一致します。第2段落を参照すれば、問3は(B)が正解だとわかりますが、(C)と(D)を誤りだと確定するには、第3段落まで読む必要があります。第3段落の❶には「初期の段階で大量に流出した気体には酸素が含まれていなかった」とあります。言い換えれば、第二の大気には酸素がはじめ存在していなかったということです。❷には「光合成を行う最初の生命体が進化したことで、酸素が豊富に含まれる大気が生まれた」とあります。さらに❸では「シアノバクテリアが太陽光と二酸化炭素を酸素に変換していた」と述べています。さて、(C)は明らかに❶の内容と矛盾します。また、(D)のwithout lightは❸と矛盾しています。以上から正解は(B)です。

□ constituent: 構成要素　□ take up X: Xを占める

4. According to paragraph 3, all of the following is true about oxygen in the second atmosphere EXCEPT:

(A) Oxygen could stay in the air because there was a limit to the amount of oxygen that rocks could take in.
(B) Rocks and meteorites served as the primary source of oxygen generation.
(C) An oxygen-rich atmosphere made it possible for some animals to breathe on land.
(D) Ozone layers provided a more effective protection against UV rays.

第3段落によると、第二の大気に存在した酸素に関して正しくないものは、次の中でどれですか。

(A) 岩が吸収できる酸素の量には限界があったので、酸素が大気中に残ることができた。
(B) 岩や隕石が主要な酸素生成の源として機能した。
(C) 酸素が豊富に含まれる大気によって、陸地で呼吸できるようになった動物もいた。
(D) オゾン層がさらに効果的に紫外線からの保護の役割を果たした。

問4は「第二の大気に存在した酸素に関して正しくないもの」を選ぶ問題です。段落の最後まで読んでから、1つ1つの選択肢を検討します。❹〜❽をまとめると以下のようになります。「初期の酸素は、その大半が隕石や岩の中に吸収された。その後、岩が吸収できる酸素の量が限界に達したので、吸収できない酸素が大気中に残ることになった。大気中に十分な量の酸素が存在するようになってはじめて、生物が地上で生息できるようになった。また、酸素が結合してオゾン層が形成され、紫外線から生物を守るようになった」とここでは、酸素がどのように生物の発展に役立ったのかが説明されています。では選択肢を見ていきましょう。(A)は大気中に酸素が残った経緯を述べています。a saturation pointは「飽和点」、つまり「これ以上酸素を吸収できない点」を意味するので、「岩が吸収できる酸素の量には限界がある」という❺の記述に一致します。(B)は「岩や隕石が、酸素生成の源として機能した」とありますが、❷〜❸にあるように光合成を行う生物が酸素をつくったわけです。本文と矛盾しているため、(B)が正解です。(C)は❻の内容に一致します。(D)は❽に一致しますね。

□ take in X: Xを吸収する　□ layer: 層

第4段落｜問5〜6 解説レクチャー

❶During the initial part of the Proterozoic period (2,500–541 million years ago), with the atmosphere gradually changing but life barely becoming more complicated than the algae that had kicked off the whole process of oxygenation, the planet was kept warm. ❷This is due in part to a high level of methane, a greenhouse gas. ❸The oxygen level remained relatively low. ❹At the end of the Proterozoic period, however, there was a sudden rise in the level of oxygen, resulting in an ice age as the oxygen effectively removed the methane from the atmosphere, reducing the greenhouse effect and allowing this significant cooling. ❺The difference in the amount of methane in this ancient atmosphere compared to what we have now really cannot be understated. ❻After the oxygen spike, there were only around 1.8 parts per million of methane in the atmosphere, while before this event, there were around 100 parts per million. ❼Considering that methane is a much more effective greenhouse gas than CO_2, it should be no surprise that such a drastic reduction could have brought about global glaciation and what is referred to as a "snowball Earth."

5. According to paragraph 4, all of the following were true about the Proterozoic period EXCEPT:

(A) Oxygen-producing algae could be found.
(B) The temperature of the atmosphere dramatically decreased.
(C) The dramatic evolution of complex life forms was observed.
(D) The amounts of methane in the atmosphere greatly changed.

第4段落によると、原生代について正しくないものは次のうちどれですか。

(A) 酸素を生成する藻類が存在した。
(B) 大気の温度が劇的に下がった。
(C) 複雑な生命体の劇的な進化が見られた。
(D) 大気中のメタンの量が大きく変わった。

問5は「原生代に関して正しくないもの」を選ぶ問題です。では、読んでみましょう。❶には「原生代の初期は、酸素を作るきっかけとなった藻類程度の生物しかおらず、地球は暖かいままだった」とあります。この段階でまず、選択肢の(A)が正しいとわかります。be found（＋場所）で「（～に）存在している」という意味です。❷によると、地球が暖かかった理由はメタンガスによるものだとわかります。❸には「酸素濃度が低かった」ともあります。❹は原生代末期について述べています。「突然、酸素の量が増え、地球を暖めていたメタンガスが減り、その結果、地球が氷河期へと入った」ことがわかります。ここで、(B)の「気温が劇的に下がった」という記述が正しいとわかります。なぜなら、初期は暖かかった（❶）が、末期では寒くなった（❹）とあるからです。また、❹から(D)の「大気中のメタンガスの量が大きく変化した」という記述も正しいとわかります。よって、本文に該当する記述のない(C)が正解となります。

6. According to paragraph 4, the reduced level of methane toward the end of the Proterozoic period resulted in

(A) a spike in the concentration of carbon dioxide
(B) a marked rise in the sea level
(C) a reduction of living organisms on the Earth
(D) enhanced formation of glacier

第4段落によると、原生代末期ごろメタンの濃度が減少した結果、何が起こりましたか。

(A) 二酸化炭素の濃度が上昇した
(B) 海面が著しく上昇した
(C) 地球上の生物が減少した
(D) 氷河の形成が促進された

問6は「原生代末期にかけて生じたメタンガスの濃度の減少が何をもたらしたか」を問うています。❻は「酸素が爆発的に増えたため、メタンガスの濃度が100 ppmから1.8 ppmに減少した」と説明しています。さらに❼では「そのような現象により、地球規模での氷河期が訪れた」とあります。よって、氷河について述べている(D)が正解ですね。

□ marked:著しい

第5段落｜問7~8 解説レクチャー

❶With the surface of the Earth completely covered by ice and the ocean frozen, glacial activities of the mass of ice facilitated the mixing of elements and compounds that were once present only in the mountainous or oceanic regions, thereby exchanging and stirring up numerous nutrients on a global scale. ❷In addition, the thick ice itself contained many different types of minerals and compounds, all of which poured into the mountains and oceans as the ice gradually melted away. ❸Enriched with these ingredients, a richer variety of algae evolved and oxygen levels began to rise through their process of photosynthesis. ❹This caused not only the composition of the atmosphere to change, but it also produced more complex life forms, like sponges and other animals. ❺The atmosphere affects life on the planet. ❻In the same way, activities of organisms affect the atmosphere. ❼For example, the photosynthetic algae produce oxygen in abundance, without which there would not have been the evolution of animals. ❽Although this process has taken billions of years, our Earth is now supporting life that is very different to its ancestors, with varying needs and prospects. ❾As we move forward into the future, how will our atmosphere change in another billion years? ❿There is the term “anthroposphere,” which refers to the part of the natural environment that is made or modified by human activities. ⓫Rigorous research is being conducted about determining how the anthroposphere and atmosphere interact and shape our future Earth.

7. Which of the sentences below best expresses the essential information in the highlighted sentence in the passage? Incorrect choices change the meaning in important ways or leave out essential information.

(A) Because the Earth was covered with a tremendous amount of ice, the exchange of nutrients between oceanic and mountainous regions was accelerated on a global scale.
(B) Ice started to cover the Earth's surface on a global scale, which caused the movement of parts of the massive ice to stir up substances on the Earth.
(C) During early Earth times, an abundant ice build-up created mountain and ocean movements which caused the facilitation of glacier activities.
(D) Thanks to the movements of glaciers, substances essential for life forms were brought to every corner of the world.

次のうちどの文が、ハイライト表示した文の重要な情報を最もよく表していますか。不正解の選択肢は、意味を大きく変えたり、重要な情報を抜かしたりしています。

(A) 地球は膨大な量の氷に覆われていたので、海と山の栄養素の交換が地球規模で加速化した。
(B) 氷が地球規模で表面を覆い始め、それによって巨大な氷の一部の動きが地球上の物質を混ぜ合わせた。
(C) 地球誕生初期の頃、氷が大量に積み重なったことで山や海の動きを形成し、それが氷河の活動を促進した。
(D) 氷河の活動により、生命体に不可欠な物質が世界中に行き渡った。

問7は文を簡潔に言い換える問題です。まず❶を精読しましょう。With the surface ... completely covered ... は「地球の表面が完全に氷で覆われている状態で」という意味です。いわゆる「付帯状況のwith」と呼ばれる形です。glacial activities ... facilitated the mixing of elements and compounds ... は「氷河の活動が、山や海にしか存在しなかった物質が混ざり合うのに一役買った」と直訳できます。最後にthereby exchanging以降の部分は「それにより、地球規模で非常に多くの栄養素が行き渡った」という意味です。つまり、氷河の活動により、地球規模で栄養素が行き渡ったということです。(A)はthe exchange of nutrients between oceanic and mountainous regionsの部分が誤りです。「海と山にある栄養素が交換された」という意味ですが、本文が述べていることは「海や山にしかなかった栄養素が世界規模で混ぜ合わされた」ということです。(B)は、本文のthereby exchanging以降の内容がすっぽりと抜けているため誤りです。(C)は、氷河の話しかしていないので論外です。(D)は「氷河の活動により、生命に必要な物質が世界中へと運ばれた」という意味です。本文のポイントに合致するので、(D)が正解ですね。

□ **build-up**:徐々に増えること

8. According to paragraph 5, what can be inferred about “anthroposphere”?

(A) Human activities may have future implications for the Earth in the long run.
(B) It has been proven that human activity has negative impacts on the Earth.
(C) Activities of all living organisms including humans shape the anthroposphere.
(D) Changes in the anthroposphere exert the greatest impact on the atmosphere.

第5段落によると、「人類圏」について何が推測できますか。

(A) 長い目で見れば、人間の活動は今後の地球に影響を与えるかもしれない。
(B) 人間の活動は地球に悪影響を与えていることが証明された。
(C) 人間を含むあらゆる生物の活動が人類圏を形作る。
(D) 人類圏の変化が大気圏に最大の影響を及ぼしている。

問8は「人類圏に関して推察されること」を問うています。can be inferredとあるので直接的な記述がなくても正解になり得ます。では、anthroposphereというキーワードを探しながら読み進めましょう。⓾でanthroposphereが定義されています。「人間が手を加えた自然環境の部分」という意味です。その後、⓫に「人類圏と大気圏がどのように地球の未来を決定づけるのかは、研究中である」という記述があります。では、選択肢を検討しましょう。(A)ですが、⓫で「人類圏が地球に影響を与える可能性があること」が示唆されていました。また⓾により人類圏は人間活動に端を発することがわかります。よって「人間活動が地球の将来に影響を与える可能性がある」と言えるので(A)が正解です。(B)ですが、本文では人間が悪影響をもたらすかどうかまで踏み込んではいませんし、証明されてもいないので誤りです。(C)はall living organismsが言い過ぎです。人類圏はあくまで「人間活動によってもたらされる変化」のことです。(D)は「人類圏における変化が大気圏に最も大きな影響をもたらす」という意味ですが、本文にはそういった記述がありません。

□ exert X: X（影響など）を及ぼす

問 9 解説レクチャー

9. Look at the four squares [■] that indicate where the following sentence could be added to the passage.

The evolution of our atmosphere has gone hand in hand with the evolution of life on our planet.

Where would the sentence best fit?

❶With the surface of the Earth completely covered by ice and the ocean frozen, glacial activities of the mass of ice facilitated the mixing of elements and compounds that were once present only in the mountainous or oceanic regions, thereby exchanging and stirring up numerous nutrients on a global scale. ❷In addition, the thick ice itself contained many different types of minerals and compounds, all of which poured into the mountains and oceans as the ice gradually melted away. **A** ❸Enriched with these ingredients, a richer variety of algae evolved and oxygen levels began to rise through their process of photosynthesis. **B** ❹This caused not only the composition of the atmosphere to change, but it also produced more complex life forms, like sponges and other animals. **C** ❺The atmosphere affects life on the planet. **D** ❻In the same way, activities of organisms affect the atmosphere.

次の文が以下のパッセージで追加されうる箇所を示す4つの■を見てください。

大気の進化は、私たちの惑星の生命の進化と密接に関係してきた。

この文はどこに置くのが最もよいですか。

問9は文挿入問題ですが、この一文に論理展開を示す語句であるディスコースマーカーや指示表現がありません。このような場合は、本文中の論理展開や指示表現に注目しましょう。挿入文は「大気の進化は、生命の進化と密接に関連してきた」という意味ですね。では本文を読みましょう。❷は「氷そのものが多くのミネラルや化合物を含んでいた」と述べています。続く❸のthese ingredientsという指示表現は、❷のminerals and compoundsを指します。よって、Aに挿入文は入りません。さて、❸には「藻類が進化を遂げ、光合成により酸素濃度が上昇した」とあります。続く❹は「このことは、大気の構成要素を変えただけでなく、より複雑な生命体を生み出した」と述べています。❹における「このこと（This)」は、❸の内容を指すと考えるのが自然でしょう。よってBにも挿入文は入りません。❺は「大気は地球上の生物に影響を与える」とあり、続く❻には「生物が大気に影響をもたらす」と、❺とは逆のことが述べられています。つまり、大気と地球上の生物が相互に作用し合っており、❻のIn the same wayによって❺と❻の関連性が示されているということです。よってDにも挿入文は入りません。そこで、❹を見てみると、caused not only the composition of the atmosphere to changeの部分が挿入文のThe evolution of our atmosphereに、❹のproduced more complex life formsが挿入文のthe evolution of lifeに対応しているとわかります。前文の言い換えになっているのでCが正解です。

問10解説レクチャー

10. Directions: An introductory sentence containing a brief summary of the passage is provided below. Complete the summary by selecting the best THREE answer choices that express the main ideas of the passage.

The gradual changes over time of the Earth's atmosphere have made it a sustainable planet for many living organisms today.

(A) Living creatures have made an important contribution to the formation of the atmosphere we have today.
(B) By the end of the Proterozoic period, most of the Earth had frozen over due to a sudden rise in oxygen, but this was a necessary step toward the formation of a livable atmosphere.
(C) The beginning of the Proterozoic period was characterized by a great and sharp decrease in methane gas, leading to an extremely cold climate.
(D) The conditions of the primordial atmosphere on early Earth were able to sustain bacterial life forms and their proliferation.
(E) UV light can be effectively filtered out by a sufficient amount of oxygen forming the so-called ozone layer.
(F) The Earth once lacked an atmosphere, but some volcanic activities and the first photosynthetic life forms provided essential substances that created the current atmosphere.

指示：パッセージの簡単な要約を含む紹介文を以下に記載しています。パッセージの中の最も重要な考えを示している文を3つ選んで要約を完成させてください。

地球の大気が徐々に変化することにより、地球は今日の多くの生物にとって持続可能な惑星となった。

(A) 今ある大気の形成に、生物が大きく貢献してきた。
(B) 原生代の終わりまでには、酸素濃度が急激に上がったため、地球の大部分が凍ってしまった。だが、それは生命が生存可能な大気を作るために必要な段階だった。
(C) 原生代の初期は、メタンガスの大量かつ急激な減少に特徴づけられ、極端に寒い気候へとつながった。
(D) 初期の地球における原始の大気の状態は、バクテリアの生命体とその増殖を維持することができるようなものだった。
(E) 紫外線は、いわゆるオゾン層を形成する十分な酸素によって効果的に遮断できる。
(F) かつて地球に大気がない時期もあったが、火山活動や初期の光合成を行う生物により、現在の大気を作り出す上で不可欠な物質が生成された。

あと一息です、頑張りましょう。(A)は「今ある大気をつくることに、生物が大きく貢献した」という意味です。第5段落の❻にactivities of organisms affect the atmosphereとあります。さらに、本文の主旨は「現在の大気が形成される過程」なので、「生物がその一因であった」という内容は重要だと考えられます。よって(A)は正解の可能性が高いですね。(B)は「原生代の終わりまでには、酸素濃度が急激に上がったため、地球の大部分が凍ってしまった。だが、それは生命が生存可能な大気をつくるために必要な段階だった」という意味です。第4段落には「酸素が増えメタンガスが減ったため、地球が凍った」という説明がありました。また第5段落では「氷河の活動によって地球規模で様々な栄養素がもたらされた」という説明もありました。よって(B)も正解の可能性が高いです。(C)はThe beginningの部分が、第4段落の内容と矛盾します。メタンガスが減ったのは原生代の初期ではなく終盤だからです。(D)ですが、原始大気についての説明がある第2段落を読む限り、原始大気と生命を直接結びつけている記述は見られません。(E)は本文の内容に一致しますが、オゾン層の話はあくまで酸素がどのように役立ったのかの一例にすぎないので、本文の内容をまとめるものとは言えません。(F)は「地球に大気がない時期もあったが、火山活動や初期の光合成を行う生物により、現在の大気をつくり出す上で不可欠な物質が生成された」という意味です。これは第2段落の内容に一致しますね。よって、(A)、(B)、(F)が正解です。

□ filter out X: Xを取り除く

PARAGRAPH 1

❶The key drivers that have resulted in the livable atmosphere that the Earth has today are many and complicated, with interactions that spanned billions of years to shape the world as we know it.

❷Of the eight planets orbiting the Sun, four—Mercury, Venus, Earth, and Mars—are called terrestrial planets, created by successive collisions of meteorites.

❸The remaining four—Jupiter, Saturn, Uranus, and Neptune—are called Jovian planets, which are basically gigantic balls made of gas.

❹Among all these planets, only our Earth has an atmosphere that is said to be habitable for organisms.

❺The mechanisms of how a mass of meteorites or barren rocks initially generated an atmosphere and how the Earth became a thriving menagerie of life can be broken down into two key steps with a few supporting drivers.

❶今日の地球が有する、生命が生存可能な大気がつくられた要因は数多くあり、複雑である。それらの要因が何十億年もの間影響しあって、我々が知っているこの世界が形成された。

❷太陽を周回する8つの惑星のうちの4つ（水星、金星、地球、火星）は地球型惑星と呼ばれ、隕石の衝突が幾度も起きたことによって作り出された。

❸残りの4惑星（木星、土星、天王星、海王星）は木星型惑星と呼ばれ、基本的にはガスからなる巨大な球体である。

❹これら太陽系の惑星のうち、生物が生存できると言われる大気を持つのは、我々の住む地球だけである。

❺どのようにして隕石の塊、不毛な岩が大気をつくるに至ったのか、またどのようにして地球が様々な生物の繁栄する場所となったのかというメカニズムは、いくつかの補足的な要素とともに、2つの重要な段階に分けられる。

❶ □ driver：要因
□ span：ある期間にわたって存在する【動詞】

❷ □ Of the eight planets：8つの惑星のうち
□ terrestrial：地球型の、地球上の

❸ □ remaining：残りの【形容詞】
□ gigantic：巨大な

❹ □ habitable：居住可能な
□ organism：生物

❺ □ mass：塊
□ meteorite：隕石
□ barren：不毛な
□ menagerie：動物の集団
□ break X down into Y：XをYに分割する

❶ the world (as we know it)「我々が知っているような世界」

as we know itはthe worldを修飾する形容詞節。

PARAGRAPH 2

❶To begin with, the Earth did not start out with the atmosphere that we have now.

❷Indeed, the Earth had a so-called "primordial atmosphere" early in its history, but the atmosphere at one point became non-existent, owing to the Sun's rays, or solar winds, blasting away the hydrogen and helium based gases that had been around the Earth's surface.

❸The hydrogen and helium gases being the two lightest among all, it was relatively easy for the solar winds to strip those gases from the early Earth.

❹It can be said that for a certain length of time, the Earth was almost atmosphereless with only a tiny volume of remnants composed of relatively heavier elements.

❺The atmosphere was not replenished until early volcanic activities released certain types of gases in addition to those light gases, which led to the creation of the "second atmosphere."

❻The eruptions released the compounds of water, carbon dioxide, and methane, many of which were fundamentally important for the formation, growth, and proliferation of various living organisms.

❶まず、今ある大気は、最初から地球に存在したわけではない。

❷確かに、地球の初期の頃には「原始大気」と呼ばれるものがあったが、太陽光や太陽風が、地球の表面を覆う水素やヘリウムで構成されたガスを吹き飛ばしたために一時、大気が存在しなくなった。

❸水素とヘリウムは最も軽い2つの気体なので、太陽風がこれらの気体を初期の地球から吹き飛ばすのは容易なことであった。

❹地球はある一定の期間、ほぼ大気が存在せず、比較的重い元素で構成されたものがわずかに残っていたと言うことができる。

❺ようやく、初期の火山活動が水素などの軽い気体に加えてある種の気体を放出し、これが「第二の大気」の生成へとつながったのである。

❻火山の爆発は、水、二酸化炭素、メタンなどの化合物を放出した。これらの多くは、様々な生物の生成、成長、増殖において、極めて重要であった。

＊語句問題に出る可能性あり

❶□start out with X：Xで始まる

❷□so-called X：いわゆるX、Xと呼ばれるもの
□primordial：原始の
□owing to X：Xが原因で
□blast X away (away X)：Xを吹き飛ばす

❸□strip X from Y：XをYから引きはがす

❹□remnant：残存物
□composed of X：Xで構成された

❺□*replenish X：Xを再び満たす
□a certain X：あるX、何らかのX（前置修飾のcertainは「何らかの」という意味）
□lead to X：Xという結果をもたらす

❻□eruption：噴火
□*compound：化合物
□*proliferation：増殖、拡散

❷ the hydrogen and helium based gases「水素やヘリウムで構成されたガス」

hydrogen and helium basedがgasesを修飾している。

❸ The hydrogen and helium gases (S′) being (V′) the two lightest (C′) among all

beingはいわゆる分詞構文。The hydrogen and helium gasesはbeingに対する意味上の主語。

❻ many of which (S′) were (V′) ...「それらの中の多くは」

ofは「範囲」を表す。（例）some of the people

PARAGRAPH 3

❶There was, however, still a distinct lack of oxygen in this early outpouring of gas.

❷The long-term changes that have gifted us with an oxygen-rich atmosphere in present times began with the evolution of the first photosynthetic life forms.

❸These small cyanobacteria—found virtually anywhere including oceans, rocks, soil, etc.—would convert sunlight and carbon dioxide into oxygen.

❹The early oxygen production was rather limited, however, and the vast majority of it was absorbed into meteorites and rocks due to the small amount produced.

❺A saturation point for these rocks was eventually reached, and as such they could absorb no more oxygen, allowing it to remain free in the atmosphere.

❻Only once a sufficient amount of oxygen was present in the atmosphere did it begin to protect life forms enough to enable them to move from the great oceans onto land, developing respiration in the meantime.

❼The oxygen in the atmosphere mutated to provide even more protection for life forms.

❽Ozone (three oxygen atoms bonded together) was a much better shield against the harmful effects of UV radiation.

❶だが、初期の段階で大量に放出した気体には、まだ酸素が全く存在しなかった。

❷現在見られるような酸素を豊富に持つ大気をもたらした長期的変化は、光合成を行う最初の生命体が進化したことで始まった。

❸これらの小さなシアノバクテリア（海、岩、土など実際どこにでもいる）は、太陽光や二酸化炭素を酸素に変換していた。

❹しかし、初期の酸素の生成は比較的限られていて、その量の少なさのためにその大半が隕石や岩の中に吸収された。

❺やがてこれらの岩が飽和点に達したために、これ以上酸素を吸収できなくなり、酸素が大気中に残ることになった。

❻十分な量の酸素が大気中に存在するようになってはじめて、海洋から陸地へと移動できるように酸素が生命体を保護するようになり、呼吸器官が進化し始めたのである。

❼大気中の酸素が変化して、生命体をさらに保護するようになった。

❽オゾン（3つの酸素原子が結合したもの）が有害な紫外線から生物を守るためのはるかに優れた層を形成した。

＊語句問題に出る可能性あり

❶ □ distinct：明らかな
□ outpouring：流出すること

❷ □ gift X with Y：XにYを与える
□ photosynthetic：光合成を行う

❸ □ including X：Xを含めて【前置詞】
□ *convert X into Y：XをYに変換する

❹ □ rather：ある程度（≒ fairly）

❺ □ saturation point：飽和点
□ as such：それゆえ、したがって

❻ □ respiration：呼吸
□ in the meantime：その間に、一方で

❼ □ *mutate：変化する
□ even：より一層

❺ allowing it to remain ...
いわゆる分詞構文。意味上の主語は直前の内容全体。... they could absorb no more oxygen, which allowed it to remain ...と同じ意味。whichは前述の内容を指す。

❻ Only [M] (once a sufficient amount of oxygen [S] was [V] present [C] in the atmosphere) did it begin [S V] to ...
onceは副詞節をつくる接続詞。onlyのような（準）否定語が、副詞句や副詞節、前置詞句を修飾し文頭に置かれると、主節が疑問倒置と同じ語順になる。

PARAGRAPH 4

❶During the initial part of the Proterozoic period (2,500–541 million years ago), with the atmosphere gradually changing but life barely becoming more complicated than the algae that had kicked off the whole process of oxygenation, the planet was kept warm.

❷This is due in part to a high level of methane, a greenhouse gas.

❸The oxygen level remained relatively low.

❹At the end of the Proterozoic period, however, there was a sudden rise in the level of oxygen, resulting in an ice age as the oxygen effectively removed the methane from the atmosphere, reducing the greenhouse effect and allowing this significant cooling.

❺The difference in the amount of methane in this ancient atmosphere compared to what we have now really cannot be understated.

❻After the oxygen spike, there were only around 1.8 parts per million of methane in the atmosphere, while before this event, there were around 100 parts per million.

❼Considering that methane is a much more effective greenhouse gas than CO_2, it should be no surprise that such a drastic reduction could have brought about global glaciation and what is referred to as a "snowball Earth."

❶原生代初期の頃（25億～5億4100万年前）、大気は徐々に変化していたが、酸素供給の一連の過程のきっかけとなった藻類程度の生物しかおらず、地球は暖かいままだった。

❷これは、1つには温室効果ガスであるメタンの濃度が高かったからである。

❸酸素濃度は比較的低いままだった。

❹しかし原生代末期には、突然酸素の量が増え、酸素が効果的に大気からメタンを除去し、温室効果を減少させて地球を寒冷化したため、氷河期に入った。

❺この古代の大気中におけるメタンの量と現在の量を比較したときの差を実際よりも小さく言ってはならない。

❻酸素が爆発的に増えたため、大気中のメタンガス濃度は、増加前の約100 ppmから約1.8 ppmに減少した。

❼メタンは二酸化炭素よりもはるかに影響力の強い温室効果ガスであることを考えると、メタンの大幅な減少が地球の氷河作用や、いわゆる「スノーボールアース（全球凍結）」と呼ばれる現象をもたらしたことは何ら驚くべきことではない。

❶ □ barely：ほとんど～しない（≒ hardly / scarcely）
□ alga：藻、複数形はalgae
□ kick off X：Xを始める

❷ □ greenhouse gas：温室効果ガス

❺ □ understate X：Xを実際より少なく言う

❻ □ spike：爆発的に増えること

❼ □ drastic：大幅な
□ glaciation：氷河作用
□ refer to X as Y：XをYと呼ぶ

❷ due (in part) to
due to（～が原因で）という表現のあいだに、in part（部分的には）が挿入されている。

❹ there was a sudden rise ... oxygen, resulting in an ...
→there was a sudden rise ... oxygen, which resulted in an ...と解釈する。whichは前述の内容を指す。

❹ the oxygen effectively removed ... atmosphere, reducing the greenhouse effect and allowing this ...
→the oxygen effectively removed ... atmosphere, which reduced the greenhouse effect and allowed this ...と解釈する。whichは前述の内容を指す。

PARAGRAPH 5

❶With the surface of the Earth completely covered by ice and the ocean frozen, glacial activities of the mass of ice facilitated the mixing of elements and compounds that were once present only in the mountainous or oceanic regions, thereby exchanging and stirring up numerous nutrients on a global scale.

❷In addition, the thick ice itself contained many different types of minerals and compounds, all of which poured into the mountains and oceans as the ice gradually melted away.

❸Enriched with these ingredients, a richer variety of algae evolved and oxygen levels began to rise through their process of photosynthesis.

❹This caused not only the composition of the atmosphere to change, but it also produced more complex life forms, like sponges and other animals.

❺The atmosphere affects life on the planet.

❻In the same way, activities of organisms affect the atmosphere.

❼For example, the photosynthetic algae produce oxygen in abundance, without which there would not have been the evolution of animals.

❽Although this process has taken billions of years, our Earth is now supporting life that is very different to its ancestors, with varying needs and prospects.

❾As we move forward into the future, how will our atmosphere change in another billion years?

❿There is the term "anthroposphere," which refers to the part of the natural environment that is made or modified by human activities.

⓫Rigorous research is being conducted about determining how the anthroposphere and atmosphere interact and shape our future Earth.

❶地球表面が完全に氷で覆われ、海洋も凍結したため、氷の塊による氷河の活動が、山や海にしか存在しなかった元素や化合物が混ざり合うのに一役買った。ゆえに、地球規模で非常に多くの栄養素がかき回されることとなった。

❷さらに、厚い氷自体に様々な鉱物や化合物が多く含まれており、氷が徐々に解けるにつれ、そうした鉱物が山脈や海洋に注がれることとなった。

❸こうした成分を豊富に含んだ様々な藻類は進化を遂げ、光合成の過程で酸素濃度が上昇し始めた。

❹これにより、大気中の成分が変化しただけでなく、海綿動物などのさらに複雑な生命体が生まれた。

❺大気は地球上の生命に影響を与える。

❻同様に、生物の活動も大気に影響を与える。

❼例えば、光合成をする藻類は大量の酸素を生成するが、これがなかったら、動物の進化はなかったであろう。

❽この過程を経るのに数十億年かかったが、私たちの地球は、様々な（生物学上の）必要性や将来への可能性を併せ持った、その原種からはかなり変化した生命体を支えているのだ。

❾未来へと進む中で、私たちの大気は次の10億年でどう変化していくのだろうか。

❿自然環境の中で、人間の活動によって作られたか、手を加えられた部分を表す言葉に「人類圏」というものがある。

⓫人類圏と大気圏がいかに関係し合い、どのように地球の未来を決定づけるのかについては、綿密な研究が行われている。

＊語句問題に出る可能性あり

❶ □ *facilitate X: Xを促進する
□ compound: 物質
□ thereby: それによって【副詞】
□ stir up X: Xをかき回す

❸ □ photosynthesis: 光合成

❹ □ sponge: 海綿動物

❻ □ in abundance: 豊富に

❼ □ varying: 様々な【形容詞】(vary「変化する」という動詞の現在分詞から派生)

❽ □ another billion years: さらなる10億年(anotherは「追加の」という意味)

❾ □ *modify X: Xを変える

❿ □ rigorous: 綿密な

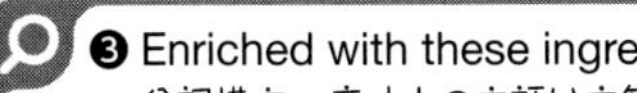

❸ Enriched with these ingredients

分詞構文。意味上の主語は主節の主語のa richer variety of algaeである。過去分詞なので、a richer variety of algae was enriched with these ingredientsと解釈する。

リーディング問題 3 | Ecology

HOW SOIL IS FORMED

問題演習の流れ

- □ 解答時間は17分を目標にしましょう。
- □ 英文 ⇒ 問題 ⇒ 正解・解説レクチャー ⇒ 訳 という流れで学習します。
- □ 3回解けるように、3回分のマークシートを各問題に用意しています。解く日付を記入してからマークしてください。

Web解答方法

- □ 本試験では各選択肢の左に表示されるマークをクリックして解答します。本試験と同様の方法で取り組みたい場合は、Webで解答できます。
- □ インターネットのつながるパソコン・スマートフォンで、以下のサイトにアクセスしてWeb上で解答してください。

extester.com

- □ 操作方法は、p.13 ～ 14の「USA Club Web学習の使い方」をご参照ください。

学習の記録

学習開始日	年　月　日	学習終了日	年　月　日
学習開始日	年　月　日	学習終了日	年　月　日
学習開始日	年　月　日	学習終了日	年　月　日

リーディング問題3　英文

HOW SOIL IS FORMED

Soil is composed of three major components: minerals that came from eroded rocks, organic matter that originated from plants and animals, and a variety of organisms that are living in the soil. These elements that soil consists of are collectively known as the parent material, which is often found directly below the soil. However, it could be located a great distance away due to wind, water, or glaciers having transported it over the centuries or millennia. Alongside air and water, soil is considered one of the three major natural resources that are indispensable for sustaining the life of organisms living in soil. The organisms in soil and organic matter that they deposit become parts of the parent material. Soil exhibits different features depending on what its parent material was and how the soil was created. The formation of soil is called "pedogenesis," a Greek word that means "soil origin."

The very origin of soil is rocks, and pedogenesis all starts from the erosion of rocks. The eroding processes can be categorized into two major types: physical disintegration and chemical disintegration. Physical processes are often triggered by the physical contact of rocks with something else. Strong wind or water streams carry rocks from one place to another, and during its course, parts of the rock become chipped away, splitting the initially larger mass into several smaller pieces. Earthquakes, floods, typhoons, and other meteorological or geological events cause physical disintegration. Importantly, physical disintegration can happen without physical collisions. Thunder hitting and breaking rocks, differences of temperature causing cracks and eventually the breakdown of rocks, and frozen water expanding in volume and splitting rocks are all examples of this kind of physical disintegration. Chemical disintegration, on the other hand, is caused by chemical reactions, not by physical erosion. For example, oxygen ions, when combined with the minerals in rocks, make the rocks brittle. This process, called oxidation, exemplifies the chemical reaction that decomposes rocks. Rusting is another example of oxidation you can readily see: oxygen ions react with substances in steel and alter the chemical property of the material.

Besides oxidation, hydration—water molecules reacting with minerals—and carbonation—carbon dioxide turning into carbonic acid and reacting with rocks—are known to accelerate the disintegration of rocks.

Decomposed rocks eventually become the major constituent of soil, but those grains and particles derived from rocks do not necessarily stay where they were initially formed. As the rain starts to collect, at some point a gully—a small narrow valley—will form, and it allows the water to flow quite fast and increase the rate of erosion. Taken to the extreme, in tropical climates where the rain can be torrential, the gullies that are formed become deep and soil in one location can be easily displaced. In general, the vast amount of water found on the Earth has played its role in moving soil from source to destination. Using the example of rivers, we can see how topsoil is transported along its throughways. As it is washed into the river, the smaller particles will be carried the furthest as their weight makes them much easier for the stream to keep carrying them. Some particles can even reach the end point of the river, the ocean. Larger pieces of earth such as sand will fall to the bottom of the river much faster. Similarly, the distribution of soil and its components is largely affected by the movement of water on the Earth.

Though seemingly the least physical in presence, wind also plays a significant role in pedogenesis. In fact, wind is able to convey vast quantities of soil. One example is a strong wind blowing eastward around China. This continuous wind flings up yellow sand in arid regions such as the Takla Makan Desert and Ocher Plateau, both of which are located west of China. With sufficient force, the distances that soil can travel due to wind has no limit; particles can even cross oceans and reach a far-off land. It is worth pointing out that the prevailing winds[1] often shape the composition of soils in this way, moving the eroded material to a place where it can combine with other soil and create something completely different. For example, fine soil that has actually been generated in North African deserts can be seen in many parts of southern England.

One last crucial component of pedogenesis is biological factors. Soil serves as a bedrock for many plants to grow on. These plants take nutrients and water from the soil for their growth and in return, thcy donate chemicals that were originally absent in the soil, for example, through processes like carbon fixation or photosynthesis. Slowly but steadily, plants leave a great volume of organic materials, adding tremendous value to the chemical portfolio of the soil. The same mechanism and cycle apply to living organisms. Worms, ants, mites, and all other organisms are important parts of soil and pedogenesis. Due to the vast diversity of rock particles, minerals, and organisms existing in a particular soil, it is entirely possible to analyze the composition of soil and distinguish soil from place to place. The diversity of soil composition, referred to as pedodiversity, is the result of highly complex mechanisms and routes that soil in each place took through the process of pedogenesis.

1. Prevailing winds: A wind that blows over a particular area most of the time

1. According to paragraph 1, parent material is referred to as

(A) elements that make up the main part of soil
(B) minerals and organic matter that animals and plants produce
(C) rocks that are made up of various minerals
(D) organic matter that parent animals leave in the soil

PARAGRAPH 1

Soil is composed of three major components: minerals that came from eroded rocks, organic matter that originated from plants and animals, and a variety of organisms that are living in the soil. These elements that soil consists of are collectively known as the parent material, which is often found directly below the soil. However, it could be located a great distance away due to wind, water, or glaciers having transported it over the centuries or millennia. Alongside air and water, soil is considered one of the three major natural resources that are indispensable for sustaining the life of organisms living in soil. The organisms in soil and organic matter that they deposit become parts of the parent material. Soil exhibits different features depending on what its parent material was and how the soil was created. The formation of soil is called "pedogenesis," a Greek word that means "soil origin."

2. According to paragraph 2, all of the following are true about physical disintegration EXCEPT:

(A) It requires the physical contact of rocks with something.
(B) It can happen in many different ways.
(C) It serves as one of the steps of pedogenesis.
(D) It is not the only way rocks can be disintegrated.

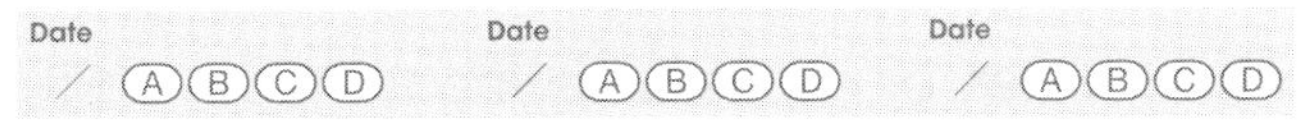

3. In paragraph 2, why was rusting mentioned?

(A) To explain the process of oxidation
(B) To show that iron reacts with oxygen
(C) To give a common example of oxidation
(D) To prove that iron is harder than rocks

PARAGRAPH 2

The very origin of soil is rocks, and pedogenesis all starts from the erosion of rocks. The eroding processes can be categorized into two major types: physical disintegration and chemical disintegration. Physical processes are often triggered by the physical contact of rocks with something else. Strong wind or water streams carry rocks from one place to another, and during its course, parts of the rock become chipped away, splitting the initially larger mass into several smaller pieces. Earthquakes, floods, typhoons, and other meteorological or geological events cause physical disintegration. Importantly, physical disintegration can happen without physical collisions. Thunder hitting and breaking rocks, differences of temperature causing cracks and eventually the breakdown of rocks, and frozen water expanding in volume and splitting rocks are all examples of this kind of physical disintegration. Chemical disintegration, on the other hand, is caused by chemical reactions, not by physical erosion. For example, oxygen ions, when combined with the minerals in rocks, make the rocks brittle. This process, called oxidation, exemplifies the chemical reaction that decomposes rocks. Rusting is another example of oxidation you can readily see: oxygen ions react with substances in steel and alter the chemical property of the material. Besides oxidation, hydration—water molecules reacting with minerals—and carbonation—carbon dioxide turning into carbonic acid and reacting with rocks—are known to accelerate the disintegration of rocks.

4. According to paragraph 3, how does rain contribute to pedogenesis?

(A) Rocks hit by rain split into multiple smaller pieces.
(B) It reacts with rocks in the gully and causes disintegration.
(C) Water from rain results in rapid streams, which escalates erosion.
(D) It brings eroded particles from one place to another.

5. From information in paragraph 3, which of the following can be inferred about topsoil made up only of very small particles when it is washed away in the river?

(A) All particles of the topsoil will be brought all the way to the ocean.
(B) The soil is washed away if the river is deep enough.
(C) All of the particles sink to the bottom of the river quickly.
(D) Heavier parts of it are unlikely to travel to the sea.

PARAGRAPH 3

Decomposed rocks eventually become the major constituent of soil, but those grains and particles derived from rocks do not necessarily stay where they were initially formed. As the rain starts to collect, at some point a gully—a small narrow valley—will form, and it allows the water to flow quite fast and increase the rate of erosion. Taken to the extreme, in tropical climates where the rain can be torrential, the gullies that are formed become deep and soil in one location can be easily displaced. In general, the vast amount of water found on the Earth has played its role in moving soil from source to destination. Using the example of rivers, we can see how topsoil is transported along its throughways. As it is washed into the river, the smaller particles will be carried the furthest as their weight makes them much easier for the stream to keep carrying them. Some particles can even reach the end point of the river, the ocean. Larger pieces of earth such as sand will fall to the bottom of the river much faster. Similarly, the distribution of soil and its components is largely affected by the movement of water on the Earth.

6. In paragraph 4, the word "arid" in the passage is closest in meaning to

(A) dry
(B) remote
(C) interesting
(D) mysterious

7. In paragraph 4, why did the author touch upon the Takla Makan Desert and Ocher Plateau?

(A) To specify regions around China that are extremely hot
(B) To give an example of how wind affects the process of photosynthesis
(C) To show how a large quantity of yellow sand is present
(D) To indicate some places where wind affects the transportation of soil

PARAGRAPH 4

Though seemingly the least physical in presence, wind also plays a significant role in pedogenesis. In fact, wind is able to convey vast quantities of soil. One example is a strong wind blowing eastward around China. This continuous wind flings up yellow sand in arid regions such as the Takla Makan Desert and Ocher Plateau, both of which are located west of China. With sufficient force, the distances that soil can travel due to wind has no limit; particles can even cross oceans and reach a far-off land. It is worth pointing out that the prevailing winds[1] often shape the composition of soils in this way, moving the eroded material to a place where it can combine with other soil and create something completely different. For example, fine soil that has actually been generated in North African deserts can be seen in many parts of southern England.

1. Prevailing winds: A wind that blows over a particular area most of the time

8. Which of the following statements does paragraph 5 support?

(A) Plants and animals have the greatest influence on the characteristics of soil.
(B) Pedogenesis plays an important role in the variation of soil properties.
(C) One can identify the origin of soil just by looking at the organisms living in the soil.
(D) Pedogenesis can occur without the existence of plants and animals.

PARAGRAPH 5

One last crucial component of pedogenesis is biological factors. Soil serves as a bedrock for many plants to grow on. These plants take nutrients and water from the soil for their growth and in return, they donate chemicals that were originally absent in the soil, for example, through processes like carbon fixation or photosynthesis. Slowly but steadily, plants leave a great volume of organic materials, adding tremendous value to the chemical portfolio of the soil. The same mechanism and cycle apply to living organisms. Worms, ants, mites, and all other organisms are important parts of soil and pedogenesis. Due to the vast diversity of rock particles, minerals, and organisms existing in a particular soil, it is entirely possible to analyze the composition of soil and distinguish soil from place to place. The diversity of soil composition, referred to as pedodiversity, is the result of highly complex mechanisms and routes that soil in each place took through the process of pedogenesis.

9. Look at the four squares [■] that indicate where the following sentence could be added to the passage.

Indeed, the characteristics of soil greatly influence creatures located in the soil and vice versa.

Where would the sentence best fit?

PARAGRAPH 1

Soil is composed of three major components: minerals that came from eroded rocks, organic matter that originated from plants and animals, and a variety of organisms that are living in the soil. These elements that soil consists of are collectively known as the parent material, which is often found directly below the soil. **A** However, it could be located a great distance away due to wind, water, or glaciers having transported it over the centuries or millennia. **B** Alongside air and water, soil is considered one of the three major natural resources that are indispensable for sustaining the life of organisms living in soil. **C** The organisms in soil and organic matter that they deposit become parts of the parent material. **D** Soil exhibits different features depending on what its parent material was and how the soil was created. The formation of soil is called "pedogenesis," a Greek word that means "soil origin."

10. Directions: An introductory sentence containing a brief summary of the passage is provided below. Complete the summary by selecting the best THREE answer choices that express the main ideas of the passage.

The composition of soil relies on several outside factors for their role in pedogenesis.

Answer Choices

(A) In many ways, soil has a great impact on living organisms and vice versa.

(B) Soil composition consists of the breakdown of eroded materials from living organisms and plant life.

(C) The formation of soil through rock erosion is a fundamental part of pedogenesis.

(D) The flow of water on the Earth plays a more significant role in the movement of sand than wind does.

(E) Although sometimes unnoticeable, natural phenomena such as water streams and wind do contribute to the diversifying soil contents.

(F) The first step of pedogenesis is the so-called physical disintegration, followed by the chemical disintegration.

リーディング問題 3

正解一覧……………………………122
解説レクチャー…………122~133
訳…………………………………134~143

1. **(A)** 2. **(A)** 3. **(C)** 4. **(C)** 5. **(D)**
6. **(A)** 7. **(D)** 8. **(B)** 9. **(C)** 10. **(A) (C) (E)**

第1段落｜問1 解説レクチャー

❶Soil is composed of three major components: minerals that came from eroded rocks, organic matter that originated from plants and animals, and a variety of organisms that are living in the soil. ❷These elements that soil consists of are collectively known as the parent material, which is often found directly below the soil. ❸However, it could be located a great distance away due to wind, water, or glaciers having transported it over the centuries or millennia. ❹Alongside air and water, soil is considered one of the three major natural resources that are indispensable for sustaining the life of organisms living in soil. ❺The organisms in soil and organic matter that they deposit become parts of the parent material. ❻Soil exhibits different features depending on what its parent material was and how the soil was created. ❼The formation of soil is called "pedogenesis," a Greek word that means "soil origin."

1. According to paragraph 1, parent material is referred to as

(A) elements that make up the main part of soil
(B) minerals and organic matter that animals and plants produce
(C) rocks that are made up of various minerals
(D) organic matter that parent animals leave in the soil

第1段落によると、母材とは何を表しますか。

(A) 土を主に構成している要素
(B) 動物や植物が生成する鉱物や有機物
(C) 様々な鉱物から成る岩
(D) 親動物が土壌に残す有機物

問1は母材が何かを問うものです。parent materialというキーワードを探しながら読みましょう。❶は「土の主な3つの構成要素」を述べています。❷は「土を構成するこれらの要素はまとめて母材と呼ばれ、土の真下にある」と述べています。「これらの要素（These elements）」は❶の「主な構成要素」を指すので、(A)が正解です。

第２段落｜問2～3 解説レクチャー

❶The very origin of soil is rocks, and pedogenesis all starts from the erosion of rocks. ❷The eroding processes can be categorized into two major types: physical disintegration and chemical disintegration. ❸Physical processes are often triggered by the physical contact of rocks with something else. ❹Strong wind or water streams carry rocks from one place to another, and during its course, parts of the rock become chipped away, splitting the initially larger mass into several smaller pieces. ❺Earthquakes, floods, typhoons, and other meteorological or geological events cause physical disintegration. ❻Importantly, physical disintegration can happen without physical collisions. ❼Thunder hitting and breaking rocks, differences of temperature causing cracks and eventually the breakdown of rocks, and frozen water expanding in volume and splitting rocks are all examples of this kind of physical disintegration. ❽Chemical disintegration, on the other hand, is caused by chemical reactions, not by physical erosion. ❾For example, oxygen ions, when combined with the minerals in rocks, make the rocks brittle. ❿This process, called oxidation, exemplifies the chemical reaction that decomposes rocks. ⓫Rusting is another example of oxidation you can readily see: oxygen ions react with substances in steel and alter the chemical property of the material. ⓬Besides oxidation, hydration—water molecules reacting with minerals—and carbonation—carbon dioxide turning into carbonic acid and reacting with rocks—are known to accelerate the disintegration of rocks.

2. According to paragraph 2, all of the following are true about physical disintegration EXCEPT:

(A) It requires the physical contact of rocks with something.
(B) It can happen in many different ways.
(C) It serves as one of the steps of pedogenesis.
(D) It is not the only way rocks can be disintegrated.

第2段落によると、物理的風化について正しくないものは次のうちのどれですか。

(A) 物理的風化は、岩が何かと物理的に接触することを必要とする。
(B) 物理的風化は、様々な方法で発生しうる。
(C) 物理的風化は、土壌生成の段階の１つとして機能する。
(D) 物理的風化以外にも岩が風化する方法はある。

問2は物理的風化に関して正しくないものを選ぶ問題です。physical disintegrationに関する記述が登場する箇所で、選択肢を突き合わせて確認してみましょう。❶は「土壌生成は岩の浸食により始まる」と述べています。さらに❷で「岩の浸食には2種類あり、その1つが物理的風化である」とあります。つまり、土壌生成は物理的風化により始まると言えるため、(C)は本文に一致します。❷に戻ると、「岩の浸食には物理的風化と化学的風化の2種類が存在する」と述べられています。これは(D)「物理的風化は岩が風化する唯一の方法というわけではない」に一致します。続く❸では「物理的な浸食は、岩が何か別のものとぶつかることにより生じる」とあり、❹～❺はその具体例です。強風や水の流れ、地震や洪水など様々な要因により物理的な浸食が生じます。これは(B)「物理的風化はさまざまな方法で生じうる」に一致します。さらに読み進めていくと、❻は「物理的風化は物理的な衝突がなくても生じうる」と説明しています。これは(A)「物理的風化は岩が何かとぶつかることを必要とする」に矛盾しています。よって(A)が正解です。

□ disintegrate：崩壊させる、分解する

3. In paragraph 2, why was rusting mentioned?

(A) To explain the process of oxidation
(B) To show that iron reacts with oxygen
(C) To give a common example of oxidation
(D) To prove that iron is harder than rocks

第2段落で、なぜ腐食について述べられているのですか。

(A) 酸化の過程を説明するため
(B) 鉄が酸素と反応することを示すため
(C) 酸化の身近な例を示すため
(D) 鉄は岩より硬いことを証明するため

問3は「腐食」に言及している理由を問うています。❼は物理的な接触のない物理的風化の具体例です。本問とは無関係です。さて、❽から化学的風化、つまり化学変化による浸食についての説明がなされます。❾には「酸素イオンが岩の鉱物と結びつくと、岩が砕ける」とあります。そして、これが酸化の例だと❿で述べられています。⓫に「腐食」が登場します。ここでは酸化の別の例として腐食を挙げています。Rusting is another example ... you can readily seeとあるので、簡単に見られることをcommon exampleと表した(C)が正解です。

第3段落｜問4~5解説レクチャー

❶Decomposed rocks eventually become the major constituent of soil, but those grains and particles derived from rocks do not necessarily stay where they were initially formed. ❷As the rain starts to collect, at some point a gully—a small narrow valley—will form, and it allows the water to flow quite fast and increase the rate of erosion. ❸Taken to the extreme, in tropical climates where the rain can be torrential, the gullies that are formed become deep and soil in one location can be easily displaced. ❹In general, the vast amount of water found on the Earth has played its role in moving soil from source to destination. ❺Using the example of rivers, we can see how topsoil is transported along its throughways. ❻As it is washed into the river, the smaller particles will be carried the furthest as their weight makes them much easier for the stream to keep carrying them. ❼Some particles can even reach the end point of the river, the ocean. ❽Larger pieces of earth such as sand will fall to the bottom of the river much faster. ❾Similarly, the distribution of soil and its components is largely affected by the movement of water on the Earth.

4. According to paragraph 3, how does rain contribute to pedogenesis?

(A) Rocks hit by rain split into multiple smaller pieces.
(B) It reacts with rocks in the gully and causes disintegration.
(C) Water from rain results in rapid streams, which escalates erosion.
(D) It brings eroded particles from one place to another.

第3段落によると、雨は土壌生成においてどのような役割を持っていますか。

(A) 雨に打たれた岩は、砕けて複数の小さな石になる。
(B) 雨裂で岩と反応して、風化を引き起こす。
(C) 雨水で流れが急になり、浸食を加速させる。
(D) 雨はある場所から別の場所へ、浸食した砂利を運ぶ。

問4は「雨がどのように土壌生成を引き起こしているか」を問うています。「雨」というキーワードを探しながら読みましょう。❶には「ぼろぼろになった岩が最終的に土の構成要素になるが、岩からできた粒は別の所へ運ばれる」とあります。❷で雨と浸食に関する説明があり、❸ではその極端な例が述べられています。まとめると、雨が降ることにより小さな谷が作られ、そこに水が流れて浸食が生じるということです。これは(C)「雨水で流れが急になり、浸食を加速させる」に一致します。(A)は「雨が岩を砕く」ということですが、本文に記述がありません。(B)は「雨が岩と反応する」という意味ですが、これも本文に記述がありません。(D)は「雨が、浸食された岩の粒子をある場所から別の場所へと移動させる」という意味ですが、移動させるのは「雨」ではなく「雨によってつくられた水の流れ」ですので誤りです。よって、(C)が正解です。

5. From information in paragraph 3, which of the following can be inferred about topsoil made up only of very small particles when it is washed away in the river?

(A) All particles of the topsoil will be brought all the way to the ocean.
(B) The soil is washed away if the river is deep enough.
(C) All of the particles sink to the bottom of the river quickly.
(D) Heavier parts of it are unlikely to travel to the sea.

第3段落の情報から、非常に小さな粒によって構成されている表土が川で流されるとき、それに関して推測されることは次のうちどれですか。

(A) 表土の全ての粒が最終的に海まで運ばれる。
(B) 川が十分に深ければ、土が流される。
(C) 全ての粒は川底にすぐに沈む。
(D) 重い粒は海まで流されにくい。

問5は「非常に小さな粒からなる表土が川で流されるとき、推測されること」を問うています。topsoilというキーワードを探しながら❹以降を読みましょう。❹は「水は土を水源地から移動させる」と述べています。❺からtopsoilについての話が登場します。表土がどのように運ばれるのかを見てみましょう。❻～❼で「表土が川へ流されると、より小さな粒は軽いので最も遠くまで運ばれ、中には河口まで流れ着くものもある」と述べられています。一方、❽には「砂利などの大きい粒は川底にいち早く沈む」とあります。では選択肢を見ていきましょう。(A)は「全ての粒が海まで流される」という意味ですが、❽と矛盾します。(B)は「川が十分に深ければ」とありますが、本文には川の深さに関する記述はありません。(C)ですが、川底にすぐに沈むのは粒の大きなものです。よって(C)は誤りです。(D)については❼に「小さな粒は軽いので海まで流れる」が、❽では「大きい粒は川底に沈む」とあります。これは大きい粒は海まで移動することなく、途中で川底に落ちるということなので(D)が正解です。

第4段落｜問6～7 解説レクチャー

❶Though seemingly the least physical in presence, wind also plays a significant role in pedogenesis. ❷In fact, wind is able to convey vast quantities of soil. ❸One example is a strong wind blowing eastward around China. ❹This continuous wind flings up yellow sand in arid regions such as the Takla Makan Desert and Ocher Plateau, both of which are located west of China. ❺With sufficient force, the distances that soil can travel due to wind has no limit; particles can even cross oceans and reach a far-off land. ❻It is worth pointing out that the prevailing winds often shape the composition of soils in this way, moving the eroded material to a place where it can combine with other soil and create something completely different. ❼For example, fine soil that has actually been generated in North African deserts can be seen in many parts of southern England.

6. In paragraph 4, the word "arid" in the passage is closest in meaning to

(A) dry　(B) remote
(C) interesting　(D) mysterious

第4段落のaridと最も近い意味のものはどれですか。

(A) 乾燥した　(B) 遠い
(C) 興味深い　(D) 神秘的な

問6のaridは「乾燥した」という意味なので(A) dryが正解です。aridはやや難しい単語ですが、TOEFLでは頻出です。

7. In paragraph 4, why did the author touch upon the Takla Makan Desert and Ocher Plateau?

(A) To specify regions around China that are extremely hot
(B) To give an example of how wind affects the process of photosynthesis
(C) To show how a large quantity of yellow sand is present
(D) To indicate some places where wind affects the transportation of soil

第4段落で、筆者はなぜタクラマカン砂漠や黄土高原について言及したのですか。

(A) 非常に暑い中国近隣の地域を特定するため
(B) 光合成の過程に風がどう影響を与えるかについての例を示すため
(C) どれほど大量の黄砂が存在するのかを示すため
(D) 風が土の移動に影響する場所をいくつか示すため

問7は「筆者がタクラマカン砂漠や黄土高原に言及した理由」を問うています。このキーワードを探しながら読みましょう。❶には「風も土壌生成に関して重要な役割を担う」とあります。❷は「風は多くの土を運ぶことができる」と述べています。❸は例として「中国付近で東に吹く風」を提示し、❹はその具体的な説明としてタクラマカン砂漠や黄土高原などの地名を挙げています。つまり、黄砂が風の影響を受ける場所の具体例を示しているため、(D)が正解です。段落後半は設問と関係ありませんが目を通しておきましょう。❺は「風によって飛ばされた土は、海を越えることもある」と述べています。❻は「卓越風は浸食した物質をある場所へ運び、そこで他の土と組み合わさって全く異なった土を作る」とあり、その具体例として、❼は「北アフリカの砂漠で生まれた細かな土が、イングランド南部の多くの地域で見られる」と述べています。このことから、北アフリカの土が風によってイングランドまで運ばれていると推測できます。

□ specify X: Xを特定する

第５段落｜問８解説レクチャー

❶One last crucial component of pedogenesis is biological factors. ❷Soil serves as a bedrock for many plants to grow on. ❸These plants take nutrients and water from the soil for their growth and in return, they donate chemicals that were originally absent in the soil, for example, through processes like carbon fixation or photosynthesis. ❹Slowly but steadily, plants leave a great volume of organic materials, adding tremendous value to the chemical portfolio of the soil. ❺The same mechanism and cycle apply to living organisms. ❻Worms, ants, mites, and all other organisms are important parts of soil and pedogenesis. ❼Due to the vast diversity of rock particles, minerals, and organisms existing in a particular soil, it is entirely possible to analyze the composition of soil and distinguish soil from place to place. ❽The diversity of soil composition, referred to as pedodiversity, is the result of highly complex mechanisms and routes that soil in each place took through the process of pedogenesis.

8. Which of the following statements does paragraph 5 support?

(A) Plants and animals have the greatest influence on the characteristics of soil.
(B) Pedogenesis plays an important role in the variation of soil properties.
(C) One can identify the origin of soil just by looking at the organisms living in the soil.
(D) Pedogenesis can occur without the existence of plants and animals.

第5段落の内容が支持する主張は、次のうちどれですか。

(A) 動植物は、土の組成に一番影響を与えている。
(B) 土壌生成は、土の組成における違いを生み出す点で重要な役割を持つ。
(C) 土に生息する生物を見るだけで、どこの土かを特定することができる。
(D) 土壌生成は動植物の存在なしに発生しうる。

問8は「第5段落の内容が支持する主張」、つまり第5段落の内容から言えることを問うています。❶で土壌生成の重要な要素として生物を挙げています。❸は「これらの植物は自らの成長のために土から栄養素や水を取り込み、その代わりに炭素固定や光合成などの過程を通して、土壌にもともと存在しなかった化学物質を提供する」という意味ですが、ポイントは「植物と土が共存関係にある」ということです。❹は「植物は大量の有機物を残していくことにより、土の組成をより豊かにする」と述べています。続く❺には「同じメカニズムが生物にも当てはまる」とあり、話が植物から生物へと発展します。❻は生物の具体例です。❼は「組成の多様性により、土を特定することが可能である」と述べています。❽で「土の組成における多様性は、複雑なメカニズムの結果である」と述べて締めくくっています。では選択肢を検討しましょう。(A)はthe greatest influenceが誤りです。「影響力が最も大きい」ことを示唆する内容はありません。(B)は「土壌生成は、土の組成の多様性を生み出す上で、重要な役割を持つ」という意味で、❽に一致します。「複雑なメカニズム」とは土壌生成のことであり、それが多様性（diversity）を生み出すと述べられています。正解は(B)です。(C)はjust by looking at the organismsが誤りです。土の組成に影響を与えるのは生物だけではありません。justは「～だけ」という意味なので、本文に矛盾します。(D)は論外です。動植物は土の生成に必要不可欠です。

問9解説レクチャー

9. Look at the four squares [■] that indicate where the following sentence could be added to the passage.

Indeed, the characteristics of soil greatly influence creatures located in the soil and vice versa.

Where would the sentence best fit?

❶Soil is composed of three major components: minerals that came from eroded rocks, organic matter that originated from plants and animals, and a variety of organisms that are living in the soil. ❷These elements that soil consists of are collectively known as the parent material, which is often found directly below the soil. **A** ❸However, it could be located a great distance away due to wind, water, or glaciers having transported it over the centuries or millennia. **B** ❹Alongside air and water, soil is considered one of the three major natural resources that are indispensable for sustaining the life of organisms living in soil. **C** ❺The organisms in soil and organic matter that they deposit become parts of the parent material. **D** ❻Soil exhibits different features depending on what its parent material was and how the soil was created. ❼The formation of soil is called "pedogenesis," a Greek word that means "soil origin."

次の文が以下のパッセージで追加されうる箇所を示す4つの■を見てください。

土の特徴がその土中に生息する生物に大きな影響を与えることは確かであり、その逆もまた、しかりである。

この文はどこに置くのが最もよいですか。

問9は文挿入問題です。「土の特徴がその中に生息する生物に大きな影響を与えることは確かであり、その逆もまたしかりである」という意味です。Indeedは、直前の内容を強調したり、追加で説明したりする場合によく用いられます。よって、直前に「土と生物の関係性」が述べられていると予想できますね。本文中のディスコースマーカーや指示表現にも注目しながら、読み進めましょう。❷～❸は「土を構成するこれらの要素はまとめて母材と呼ばれ、土の真下にあることが多い。だが、風、水、氷河が長い時間をかけて母材を遠くまで運ぶこともある」という意味です。❷と❸は逆接という論理的関連性があるので、Aに挿入文は入りません。❹は「土は生命を維持するために必要不可欠な資源の1つ」と述べています。ここで「土と生物の関係」が登場しますので❹の前のBにも挿入文は入りません。❺は「土にいる有機体は有機物を堆積し、それが母材の一部となる」と述べています。これは「土の中に住む有機体（生物）が、土の特徴に影響を与えている」ということです。挿入文の「逆もまたしかり」の部分を具体的に説明しているため、Cが正解です。

問10解説レクチャー

10. Directions: An introductory sentence containing a brief summary of the passage is provided below. Complete the summary by selecting the best THREE answer choices that express the main ideas of the passage.

The composition of soil relies on several outside factors for their role in pedogenesis.

(A) In many ways, soil has a great impact on living organisms and vice versa.
(B) Soil composition consists of the breakdown of eroded materials from living organisms and plant life.
(C) The formation of soil through rock erosion is a fundamental part of pedogenesis.
(D) The flow of water on the Earth plays a more significant role in the movement of sand than wind does.
(E) Although sometimes unnoticeable, natural phenomena such as water streams and wind do contribute to the diversifying soil contents.
(F) The first step of pedogenesis is the so-called physical disintegration, followed by the chemical disintegration.

指示：パッセージの簡単な要約を含む紹介文を以下に記載しています。パッセージの中の最も重要な考えを示している文を3つ選んで要約を完成させてください。

土壌の組成は、土壌生成におけるいくつかの外部要因の役割に依存する。

(A) 多くの点において、土は生物に大きな影響を与え、その逆もまたしかりである。
(B) 土壌の組成は、生物や植物由来の物質が腐食した分解物からなる。
(C) 岩の衝突による土の形成は、土壌生成における重要な要素だ。
(D) 風よりも地球上の水の流れの方が土砂の運搬において重要である。
(E) 気付かないこともあるが、川や風のような自然現象は土の組成を多様化させることにつながる。
(F) 土壌生成の第一歩は、いわゆる物理的統合であり、その後、化学的風化が続く。

最後の問題です。(A)は「多くの点において、土は生物に大きな影響を与え、その逆もまたしかりである」という意味です。これは第5段落の❸~❺に一致します。❸~❹には「植物と土が相互に作用している」とありました。そして❺で「同じことが生物にも当てはまる」とあります。さらに第5段落全体の重要なテーマなので、正解となる可能性が高いです。(B)はeroded materials from living organisms and plant lifeが誤りです。「生物や植物から生まれた腐食物質」という記述は本文中にありません。(C)は「岩の衝突によって土が生成されることは、土壌生成における重要な要素だ」という意味です。まさに、第2段落全体の内容に対応しますね。これも正解となる可能性が高いです。(D)については、第3段落で「水の流れ」の重要性、第4段落では風の重要性について述べられています。しかし、どちらの方が重要ということは本文では述べられていません。(E)は「気付かないこともあるが、川や風のような自然現象は土の組成を多様化させることにつながる」という意味です。第3段落では川が、第4段落では風が土を運ぶことにより、場所によって土の組成が変わるという説明がありました。よって、(E)は正解となる可能性が高いです。(F)は「物理的風化の後に、化学的風化が生じる」と述べていますが、この前後関係は本文に記述がありません。よって、(A)、(C)、(E)が正解です。

□ vice versa:逆もまたしかり　□ unnoticeable:気付かれることのない

PARAGRAPH 1

❶Soil is composed of three major components: minerals that came from eroded rocks, organic matter that originated from plants and animals, and a variety of organisms that are living in the soil.

❷These elements that soil consists of are collectively known as the parent material, which is often found directly below the soil.

❸However, it could be located a great distance away due to wind, water, or glaciers having transported it over the centuries or millennia.

❹Alongside air and water, soil is considered one of the three major natural resources that are indispensable for sustaining the life of organisms living in soil.

❺The organisms in soil and organic matter that they deposit become parts of the parent material.

❻Soil exhibits different features depending on what its parent material was and how the soil was created.

❼The formation of soil is called "pedogenesis," a Greek word that means "soil origin."

❶土は、主に3つの構成要素 ―浸食した岩からできた鉱物、動物や植物から生じる有機物、および土の中に生息する様々な物質―から成っている。

❷土を構成するこれらの要素は母材と総称され、土の真下にあることが多い。

❸しかし母材は、何百年、何千年もかけて、風や水、氷河に運ばれて、遠くまで移動することもある。

❹空気や水とともに、土は土壌に生息する生物の命を支えるうえで必要不可欠な3つの主要な天然資源の1つと考えられる。

❺土の中の生物やこうした生物が残していく有機物が母材の一部となるのである。

❻土壌は、母材の構成成分と生成過程によって様々な特徴を呈する。

❼土の生成は、「土壌の始まり」という意味のギリシャ語であるpedogenesis（土壌生成）と呼ばれる。

＊語句問題に出る可能性あり

❶□ *be composed of X: Xで構成されている
□ eroded: 浸食した
□ originate from X: Xを起源とする

❷□ consist of X: Xで構成されている
□ collectively: まとめて

❸□ be located ＋ 場所: ～にある
□ millennium: 千年

❹□ alongside X: Xと合わせて、Xとともに【前置詞】
□ indispensable: 必要不可欠な

❺□ deposit X: Xを堆積する

❻□ exhibit X: Xを呈する、示す
□ depending on X: Xによって【前置詞句】

❸ due to (wind, water, or glaciers having transported it ...)
(wind, water, or glaciers = S′, having transported = V′, it = O′)

wind, water, or glaciersは意味上の主語、having transportedは動名詞でdue toの目的語。

PARAGRAPH 2

❶The very origin of soil is rocks, and pedogenesis all starts from the erosion of rocks.

❷The eroding processes can be categorized into two major types: physical disintegration and chemical disintegration.

❸Physical processes are often triggered by the physical contact of rocks with something else.

❹Strong wind or water streams carry rocks from one place to another, and during its course, parts of the rock become chipped away, splitting the initially larger mass into several smaller pieces.

❺Earthquakes, floods, typhoons, and other meteorological or geological events cause physical disintegration.

❻Importantly, physical disintegration can happen without physical collisions.

❼Thunder hitting and breaking rocks, differences of temperature causing cracks and eventually the breakdown of rocks, and frozen water expanding in volume and splitting rocks are all examples of this kind of physical disintegration.

❽Chemical disintegration, on the other hand, is caused by chemical reactions, not by physical erosion.

❾For example, oxygen ions, when combined with the minerals in rocks, make the rocks brittle.

❿This process, called oxidation, exemplifies the chemical reaction that decomposes rocks.

⓫Rusting is another example of oxidation you can readily see: oxygen ions react with substances in steel and alter the chemical property of the material.

⓬Besides oxidation, hydration—water molecules reacting with minerals—and carbonation—carbon dioxide turning into carbonic acid and reacting with rocks—are known to accelerate the disintegration of rocks.

❶土の起源はそもそも岩石であり、土壌生成は岩の浸食に端を発する。

❷浸食の過程は、主に次の2つのタイプに分けられる。1つは物理的風化、もう1つは化学的風化である。

❸物理的過程は、岩が直接別の何かに物理的に接触することによって引き起こされることが多い。

❹強い風や水の流れが岩を動かし、やがて岩の一部分が削られ、最初は大きな岩の塊だったものが砕けて、いくつかの石になっていく。

❺地震、洪水、台風およびその他の気象や地質的な事象が物理的風化を引き起こす。

❻重要なことだが、物理的風化は物理的衝突がなくても起きることがある。

❼落雷で岩が砕けたり、気候の変化によって岩にひびが入りやがて岩が割れたり、水が凍る際に体積が増えて岩が割れたりすることなども全て、物理的風化の例である。

❽一方、化学的風化は、物理的浸食ではなく化学反応によって引き起こされる。

❾例えば、酸素イオンが岩の中の鉱物と結合すると、岩は砕けやすくなる。

❿この酸化と呼ばれる過程が岩を分解する化学反応の例である。

⓫腐食も容易にみられる酸化のもう1つの例である。つまり、酸素イオンが鋼鉄内の物質と化学反応を起こし、金属の化学的性質を変化させるのだ。

⓬酸化の他に、水和（水分子が鉱物に反応する）や炭酸化（二酸化炭素が炭酸に変化し岩に反応する）なども岩の風化を加速させることで知られている。

＊語句問題に出る可能性あり

❶ □ the very origin of soil：土の起源そのもの
（形容詞のveryは名詞を強調している）
□ erosion：浸食

❷ □ categorize X into Y：XをYに分ける
□ disintegration：風化、分離、解体

❸ □ trigger X：Xを引き起こす

❹ □ stream：流れ
□ chip away X：Xを削る
□ split X into Y：XをYに分割する

❺ □ meteorological：気象の

❻ □ *collision：衝突

❾ □ *brittle：もろい【形容詞】

❿ □ exemplify X：Xの例となる
□ decompose X：Xを分解する

⓫ □ rust：腐食する
□ *alter X：Xを変える

⓬ □ *accelerate X：Xを促進する、Xを加速させる

❼ differences of temperature causing <u>cracks</u> [and] eventually <u>the breakdown</u> of rocks
andはcracksとthe breakdownを並べている。

PARAGRAPH 3

❶Decomposed rocks eventually become the major constituent of soil, but those grains and particles derived from rocks do not necessarily stay where they were initially formed.

❷As the rain starts to collect, at some point a gully—a small narrow valley—will form, and it allows the water to flow quite fast and increase the rate of erosion.

❸Taken to the extreme, in tropical climates where the rain can be torrential, the gullies that are formed become deep and soil in one location can be easily displaced.

❹In general, the vast amount of water found on the Earth has played its role in moving soil from source to destination.

❺Using the example of rivers, we can see how topsoil is transported along its throughways.

❻As it is washed into the river, the smaller particles will be carried the furthest as their weight makes them much easier for the stream to keep carrying them.

❼Some particles can even reach the end point of the river, the ocean.

❽Larger pieces of earth such as sand will fall to the bottom of the river much faster.

❾Similarly, the distribution of soil and its components is largely affected by the movement of water on the Earth.

❶ぼろぼろになった岩が最終的に土の主要な構成要素になるが、そのような岩からできた粒は必ずしもそれができた場所に留まるとは限らない。

❷雨が降り続くと、ある時点で、雨裂（小さな狭い谷）が形成され、それにより水の流れが速くなり、浸食のスピードも速まる。

❸極端に言うと、豪雨が頻繁にみられる熱帯気候では、形成された雨裂が深さを増し、ある部分の土がたちまち流されてしまう。

❹一般に、地球上にある膨大な量の水は水源地から目的地まで土を運ぶ役割を果たしてきた。

❺川の例で言えば、流れに沿って表土が運ばれていく様子を見ることができる。

❻表土が川へと押し流されると、砂などは軽いため、川の流れに乗って簡単に遠くまで運ばれていく。

❼河口、つまり海までたどり着く砂さえある。

❽砂利のように土中で粒の大きなものは川底にいち早く沈む。

❾同様に、土やその構成要素の運搬は、地球上の水の動きによって大きく影響を受けるのである。

＊語句問題に出る可能性あり

❶ □ *constituent：構成物
□ particle：粒子
□ *be derived from X：Xから生じる

❷ □ collect：集まる
□ gully：雨裂
□ valley：谷

❸ □ taken to the extreme：極端に言うと
□ torrential：土砂降りの
□ displace X：Xの場所を(無理やり)移す

❺ □ topsoil：表土
□ throughway：流れ

❶ where they were initially formed
whereは「～する場所に、～する場所で」という意味の副詞節を作る。

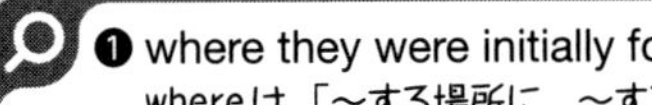

❾ the distribution of soil and its components
andはsoilとits componentsを並べている。

PARAGRAPH 4

❶Though seemingly the least physical in presence, wind also plays a significant role in pedogenesis.

❷In fact, wind is able to convey vast quantities of soil.

❸One example is a strong wind blowing eastward around China.

❹This continuous wind flings up yellow sand in arid regions such as the Takla Makan Desert and Ocher Plateau, both of which are located west of China.

❺With sufficient force, the distances that soil can travel due to wind has no limit; particles can even cross oceans and reach a far-off land.

❻It is worth pointing out that the prevailing winds[1] often shape the composition of soils in this way, moving the eroded material to a place where it can combine with other soil and create something completely different.

❼For example, fine soil that has actually been generated in North African deserts can be seen in many parts of southern England.

1. Prevailing winds: A wind that blows over a particular area most of the time

❶実際には存在がわかりにくいが、風も土壌生成に重要な役割を果たしている。

❷実は、風は大量の土を運ぶことができる。

❸一例として、中国付近で東向きに吹く風が挙げられる。

❹この不断に吹く風が、中国西部のタクラマカン砂漠や黄土高原などの乾燥地帯の黄砂を巻き上げる。

❺風が強ければ土が運ばれる距離は限りがなく、その砂塵は海を越え、はるか遠くの陸地にまで届くことさえある。

❻卓越風[1]はしばしばこのようにして土を構成し、浸食した物質を他の土と混ざり合うような場所へ運び、完全に異なったものを形成している、ということは特筆に値するだろう。

❼例えば、北アフリカの砂漠で実はできたきめの細かい土は、イングランド南部の様々な地域でみられる。

1. 卓越風：ある地域で頻繁に吹く風

＊語句問題に出る可能性あり

❶□ *significant：重要な

❹□ fling up X：Xを持ち上げる
□ arid：乾燥した
□ west of China：中国西部に

❺□ far-off：遠く離れた

❼□ *fine soil：細かい、非常に小さい

❶ **Though seemingly the least physical in presence**
「存在という点では最も物理的ではない」→「物理的な存在感が最も少ない」Though (it is) seemingly the least physical ...のようにSVを補って読む。

PARAGRAPH 5

❶One last crucial component of pedogenesis is biological factors.

❷Soil serves as a bedrock for many plants to grow on.

❸These plants take nutrients and water from the soil for their growth and in return, they donate chemicals that were originally absent in the soil, for example, through processes like carbon fixation or photosynthesis.

❹Slowly but steadily, plants leave a great volume of organic materials, adding tremendous value to the chemical portfolio of the soil.

❺The same mechanism and cycle apply to living organisms.

❻Worms, ants, mites, and all other organisms are important parts of soil and pedogenesis.

❼Due to the vast diversity of rock particles, minerals, and organisms existing in a particular soil, it is entirely possible to analyze the composition of soil and distinguish soil from place to place.

❽The diversity of soil composition, referred to as pedodiversity, is the result of highly complex mechanisms and routes that soil in each place took through the process of pedogenesis.

❶最後に、もう一つ土壌生成において重要な要素は、生物学的要因である。

❷土は、多くの植物の成長の土台となる。

❸これらの植物は自らの成長のために土から栄養素や水を取り込み、その代わりに炭素固定や光合成などの過程を通して、土壌にもともと存在しなかった化学物質を提供する。

❹植物は、ゆっくりだが確実に、大量の有機物を残し、土の中の化学的成分に多大な貢献をしている。

❺同様のメカニズムやサイクルが生物にも当てはまる。

❻ミミズ、アリ、ダニ、その他あらゆる生物は土や土壌生成の重要な一部を成す。

❼岩からできた石や砂、鉱物そして特定の土に生息する生物には豊かな多様性が見られるので、土の構成要素を分析し、その土地ごとに土を区別することは十分可能である。

❽土壌多様性と呼ばれる土の構成要素の多様性は、各場所の土が土壌生成で経験した非常に複雑なメカニズムや経路の産物なのだ。

＊語句問題に出る可能性あり

❶□ *crucial：とても重要な

❷□ serve as X：Xとして機能する
□ bedrock：地盤

❸□ in return：お返しに
□ donate X：Xを提供する
□ fixation：固定化

❹□ steadily：確実に
□ tremendous：とてつもない
□ portfolio：構成要素

❺□ apply to X：Xに当てはまる

❼□ *diversity：多様性
□ distinguish X：Xを見分ける

リーディング問題 4 | Marine Biology

THE ORIGIN OF CORAL REEFS

問題演習の流れ

- □ 解答時間は17分を目標にしましょう。
- □ 英文 ⇒ 問題 ⇒ 正解・解説レクチャー ⇒ 訳 という流れで学習します。
- □ 3回解けるように、3回分のマークシートを各問題に用意しています。解く日付を記入してからマークしてください。

Web解答方法

- □ 本試験では各選択肢の左に表示されるマークをクリックして解答します。本試験と同様の方法で取り組みたい場合は、Webで解答できます。
- □ インターネットのつながるパソコン・スマートフォンで、以下のサイトにアクセスしてWeb上で解答してください。

extester.com

- □ 操作方法は、p.13 ~ 14の「USA Club Web学習の使い方」をご参照ください。

学習の記録

学習開始日	年　月　日	学習終了日	年　月　日
学習開始日	年　月　日	学習終了日	年　月　日
学習開始日	年　月　日	学習終了日	年　月　日

リーディング問題 4　英文

THE ORIGIN OF CORAL REEFS

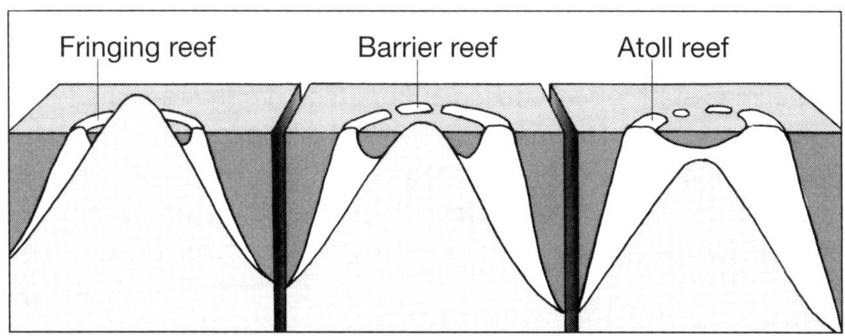

Coral reefs originate from microscopic organisms but grow into humongous structures teeming with the greatest diversity of life on planet Earth. Existing only under the ocean, coral reefs are often called "rainforests of the ocean." Importantly, "corals" and "reefs" are not exactly the same. "Corals" are living organisms and "reefs" are basically rocky masses. Therefore, coral reefs are masses that are composed of a bunch of corals. Baby corals called coral larvae swim through the oceans, and they seek out suitable rocks to which they attach themselves. The larvae turn into coral polyps. A special skeleton made of calcium carbonate starts forming from the bottom of the polyps' skin. This skeleton protects the corals from many predators that might come across them, but it also forms the base to which other coral larvae can attach themselves, and there they begin to grow skeletons of their own. This process repeats itself, growing into an enormous number of coral polyps all attached to each other, some dying off but more growing on top of the ancestors to raise the coral reefs upwards. The energy required for this kind of growth is huge, and only with desirable environmental conditions can corals of various types and shapes continue to grow.

The three main types of coral reefs found on Earth are "fringing," "barrier," and "atoll" reefs. Fringing reefs grow quite close to the coast of islands, leaving just short patches of lagoons[1] between themselves and the shoreline; they are also the most common. Second are the barrier reefs, which form further away from the coast, leaving a larger lagoon. They can actually reach the surface of the water, making them a barrier to marine navigation. The most well known of this type is the Great Barrier Reef off the coast of Australia. Finally there are the atoll reefs, which are unique in that they form a ring around a collapsed or collapsing volcanic island. Once the island has sunk a sufficient amount, the reefs retain the lagoon and sometimes start to form beaches from their eroded remains. Atolls are also some of the most life filled coral reefs of all types. Allowed to grow for sufficient time and with favorable ocean currents, some atolls will become habitable islands, with leftover materials from the collapsed volcano and the sand of the atoll mixing to become a fertile home for different flora and even fauna.

For each type of coral reefs, there are many different species of corals, all with their own natural rates of growth. The two most important growth factors are salinity (i.e., how salty the ocean water is) and water temperature, with the latter being dominant. First, without sufficient levels of salt, the corals cannot keep growing, or they may even die out. Any area that receives large quantities of fresh water from their adjacent island is much less livable for the corals because salinity must remain high enough and constant. While salinity definitely plays a crucial role in corals' health, temperature is known to exert the greatest impact. Only in the water with a livable temperature range can corals keep growing. The ideal temperature range is between 21 and 29 degrees Celsius. On the other hand, if the temperature is too high or too low, the growth of corals is seriously inhibited, even if there is a sufficient amount of salt in the water. Most coral reefs fail to form if the water stays below 18 or above 35 degrees Celsius. They are extremely sensitive to warm temperature in particular. Why is that? The answer lies in the symbiotic algae called zooxanthellae, which are also known to contribute to the growth of both corals and coral reefs.

The activities of zooxanthellae play a critical role in the life cycle of corals. Sunlight reaches the corals, and permits the symbiotic algae partners to perform photosynthesis. The process of photosynthesis provides corals with enough oxygen, which is essential for their healthy growth. Photosynthesis also produces materials important for producing calcium carbonate skeletons. In return, corals provide a shelter for the algae. Warm water disturbs their relationship. As the water temperature increases, the rate of photosynthesis becomes faster, which produces more oxygen, eventually to an abnormal and toxic level. The corals must expel these too-excited algae. This is how warm temperature agitates the symbiotic relationship and hinders the development of coral reefs. Now we realize that this is one example of how environmental changes such as global warming can devastate the environment.

Corals of all species and coral reefs of all types are sensitive to changes in the surrounding environment. Their growth rates change drastically or they sometimes become extinct if the local water conditions change even slightly. Not only does the temperature change caused by global warming have a direct effect on the coral, but also the melting of glaciers exerts an additional impact. The melting of glaciers releases non-salty fresh water, which guarantees a significant decrease in salinity of the ocean. Besides, as glaciers melt away, the sea level rises. This means that less light can reach the algae; as a result, algae cannot perform photosynthesis as much, and less food is available for the corals. Intuitively or counter-intuitively, phenomena occurring above the sea level, such as global warming and the ensuing glacier melting, are intimately related to the phenomena observed under the water.

1. Lagoon: A stretch of shallow water surrounded by a low sandbank or coral reef

1. In paragraph 1, which of the following best describes the relationship of corals and coral reefs?

(A) Larvae represent corals and polyps represent coral reefs.
(B) Corals make up the hard skeleton of coral reefs.
(C) They both indicate the same thing, which is a group of polyps.
(D) Coral reefs are made up of corals and calcium carbonate-based skeletons.

2. According to paragraph 1, which of the following best describes how corals grow?

(A) Upward currents of the ocean provide energy for the corals to expand in size.
(B) New larvae continuously add to a structure made of older corals.
(C) Some old parts of corals die off, which protect the new polyps that are growing taller.
(D) Each coral polyp increases in size and eventually splits into two identical units.

PARAGRAPH 1

Coral reefs originate from microscopic organisms but grow into humongous structures teeming with the greatest diversity of life on planet Earth. Existing only under the ocean, coral reefs are often called "rainforests of the ocean." Importantly, "corals" and "reefs" are not exactly the same. "Corals" are living organisms and "reefs" are basically rocky masses. Therefore, coral reefs are masses that are composed of a bunch of corals. Baby corals called coral larvae swim through the oceans, and they seek out suitable rocks to which they attach themselves. The larvae turn into coral polyps. A special skeleton made of calcium carbonate starts forming from the bottom of the polyps' skin. This skeleton protects the corals from many predators that might come across them, but it also forms the base to which other coral larvae can attach themselves, and there they begin to grow skeletons of their own. This process repeats itself, growing into an enormous number of coral polyps all attached to each other, some dying off but more growing on top of the ancestors to raise the coral reefs upwards. The energy required for this kind of growth is huge, and only with desirable environmental conditions can corals of various types and shapes continue to grow.

3. In paragraph 2, the Great Barrier Reef was mentioned for what main purpose?

(A) To compare the characteristics of barrier reefs with other kinds of reefs
(B) To show that it is the largest reef of all types
(C) To give an existing example of a barrier reef
(D) To exemplify how barrier reefs may discourage marine navigation

4. Which of the sentences below best expresses the essential information in the highlighted sentence in the passage? Incorrect choices change the meaning in important ways or leave out essential information.

(A) Suitable conditions created from volcanic material and sand over time result in a living habitat that supports the life of various organisms.
(B) It takes a long time for atolls to become a fertile dwelling for many species if materials produced by volcanic activities do not reach the atolls.
(C) Without appropriate ocean currents, creatures cannot proliferate for a long time around the atolls that contain substances from volcanoes.
(D) When materials produced from collapsing volcanoes react with atolls, they become a comfortable home for animals and plants living in the ocean.

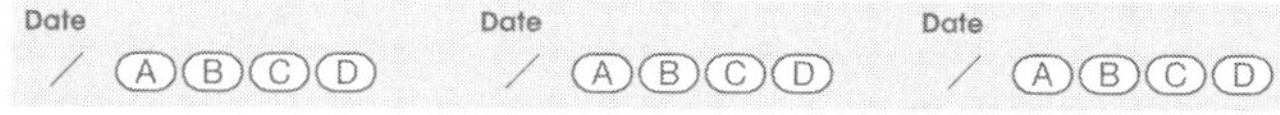

PARAGRAPH 2

The three main types of coral reefs found on Earth are "fringing," "barrier," and "atoll" reefs. Fringing reefs grow quite close to the coast of islands, leaving just short patches of lagoons[1] between themselves and the shoreline; they are also the most common. Second are the barrier reefs, which form further away from the coast, leaving a larger lagoon. They can actually reach the surface of the water, making them a barrier to marine navigation. The most well known of this type is the Great Barrier Reef off the coast of Australia. Finally there are the atoll reefs, which are unique in that they form a ring around a collapsed or collapsing volcanic island. Once the island has sunk a sufficient amount, the reefs retain the lagoon and sometimes start to form beaches from their eroded remains. Atolls are also some of the most life filled coral reefs of all types. Allowed to grow for sufficient time and with favorable ocean currents, some atolls will become habitable islands, with leftover materials from the collapsed volcano and the sand of the atoll mixing to become a fertile home for different flora and even fauna.

1. Lagoon: A stretch of shallow water surrounded by a low sandbank or coral reef

5. In paragraph 3, the word "adjacent" in the passage is closest in meaning to

(A) isolated
(B) neighboring
(C) similar
(D) grouped

PARAGRAPH 3

For each type of coral reefs, there are many different species of corals, all with their own natural rates of growth. The two most important growth factors are salinity (i.e., how salty the ocean water is) and water temperature, with the latter being dominant. First, without sufficient levels of salt, the corals cannot keep growing, or they may even die out. Any area that receives large quantities of fresh water from their adjacent island is much less livable for the corals because salinity must remain high enough and constant. While salinity definitely plays a crucial role in corals' health, temperature is known to exert the greatest impact. Only in the water with a livable temperature range can corals keep growing. The ideal temperature range is between 21 and 29 degrees Celsius. On the other hand, if the temperature is too high or too low, the growth of corals is seriously inhibited, even if there is a sufficient amount of salt in the water. Most coral reefs fail to form if the water stays below 18 or above 35 degrees Celsius. They are extremely sensitive to warm temperature in particular. Why is that? The answer lies in the symbiotic algae called zooxanthellae, which are also known to contribute to the growth of both corals and coral reefs.

6. Which of the following best describes the relationship between paragraphs 3 and 4?

(A) Paragraph 3 brings up two important factors for the survival of corals and paragraph 4 explains why one is more important than the other.
(B) Paragraph 3 illustrates why corals cannot grow in a certain environment and paragraph 4 proves the validity of the explanation.
(C) Paragraph 3 explains two key factors for the growth of corals and paragraph 4 provides the specific mechanism of one of them.
(D) Paragraph 3 discusses theories about how corals grow in optimum environments and paragraph 4 gives specific examples of the optimum environments.

7. According to paragraph 4, which of the following illustrates the mechanism of how the symbiotic relationship is disturbed?

(A) Warm water causes algae to release poison, which destroys corals.
(B) Algae, when extremely excited, slow down the process of photosynthesis.
(C) Accelerated photosynthesis results in the production of excessive gas.
(D) An abnormal amount of calcium carbonate disturbs the corals.

PARAGRAPH 4

The activities of zooxanthellae play a critical role in the life cycle of corals. Sunlight reaches the corals, and permits the symbiotic algae partners to perform photosynthesis. The process of photosynthesis provides corals with enough oxygen, which is essential for their healthy growth. Photosynthesis also produces materials important for producing calcium carbonate skeletons. In return, corals provide a shelter for the algae. Warm water disturbs their relationship. As the water temperature increases, the rate of photosynthesis becomes faster, which produces more oxygen, eventually to an abnormal and toxic level. The corals must expel these too-excited algae. This is how warm temperature agitates the symbiotic relationship and hinders the development of coral reefs. Now we realize that this is one example of how environmental changes such as global warming can devastate the environment.

8. According to paragraph 5, melting glaciers affect coral reefs in all of the following ways EXCEPT:

(A) Ice melting lowers the ocean temperature, which is unfavorable to corals.
(B) What happens above the sea level has profound implications for corals.
(C) It limits the rate of photosynthesis performed by algae.
(D) Melted ice, which is non-salty, dramatically changes the salinity of ocean.

PARAGRAPH 5

Corals of all species and coral reefs of all types are sensitive to changes in the surrounding environment. Their growth rates change drastically or they sometimes become extinct if the local water conditions change even slightly. Not only does the temperature change caused by global warming have a direct effect on the coral, but also the melting of glaciers exerts an additional impact. The melting of glaciers releases non-salty fresh water, which guarantees a significant decrease in salinity of the ocean. Besides, as glaciers melt away, the sea level rises. This means that less light can reach the algae; as a result, algae cannot perform photosynthesis as much, and less food is available for the corals. Intuitively or counter-intuitively, phenomena occurring above the sea level, such as global warming and the ensuing glacier melting, are intimately related to the phenomena observed under the water.

9. Look at the four squares [■] that indicate where the following sentence could be added to the passage.

Temperatures of this range can be often observed in the tropics.

Where would the sentence best fit?

PARAGRAPH 3

For each type of coral reefs, there are many different species of corals, all with their own natural rates of growth. The two most important growth factors are salinity (i.e., how salty the ocean water is) and water temperature, with the latter being dominant. First, without sufficient levels of salt, the corals cannot keep growing, or they may even die out. Any area that receives large quantities of fresh water from their adjacent island is much less livable for the corals because salinity must remain high enough and constant. **A** While salinity definitely plays a crucial role in corals' health, temperature is known to exert the greatest impact. **B** Only in the water with a livable temperature range can corals keep growing. **C** The ideal temperature range is between 21 and 29 degrees Celsius. **D** On the other hand, if the temperature is too high or too low, the growth of corals is seriously inhibited, even if there is a sufficient amount of salt in the water. Most coral reefs fail to form if the water stays below 18 or above 35 degrees Celsius. They are extremely sensitive to warm temperature in particular. Why is that? The answer lies in the symbiotic algae called zooxanthellae, which are also known to contribute to the growth of both corals and coral reefs.

10. Directions: An introductory sentence containing a brief summary of the passage is provided below. Complete the summary by selecting the best THREE answer choices that express the main ideas of the passage.

Corals are considered one of the most diverse living organisms on Earth, varying in species type and growth rate.

Answer Choices

(A) In order for coral reefs to grow, the temperature of the water must be within a certain range and a certain level of salt concentration is essential.

(B) Three main reef types are formed in the same manner in the same location, yet their appearances are quite different.

(C) Changes in the environment including global warming and glaciers melting may lead to the extinction of corals.

(D) Even if the water temperature is stable, high salinity levels prevent corals from continuous growth.

(E) There exist different types of corals possessing distinctive characteristics, and they grow at different rates.

(F) Global warming has a greater and more direct influence on a particular type of coral reefs than the melting of glaciers does.

リーディング問題 4

正解一覧 …… 162
解説レクチャー …… 162~175
訳 …… 176~185

1. **(D)** 2. **(B)** 3. **(C)** 4. **(A)** 5. **(B)**
6. **(C)** 7. **(C)** 8. **(A)** 9. **(D)** 10. **(A) (C) (E)**

第1段落｜問1～2 解説レクチャー

❶Coral reefs originate from microscopic organisms but grow into humongous structures teeming with the greatest diversity of life on planet Earth. ❷Existing only under the ocean, coral reefs are often called "rainforests of the ocean." ❸Importantly, "corals" and "reefs" are not exactly the same. ❹"Corals" are living organisms and "reefs" are basically rocky masses. ❺Therefore, coral reefs are masses that are composed of a bunch of corals. ❻Baby corals called coral larvae swim through the oceans, and they seek out suitable rocks to which they attach themselves. ❼The larvae turn into coral polyps. ❽A special skeleton made of calcium carbonate starts forming from the bottom of the polyps' skin. ❾This skeleton protects the corals from many predators that might come across them, but it also forms the base to which other coral larvae can attach themselves, and there they begin to grow skeletons of their own. ❿This process repeats itself, growing into an enormous number of coral polyps all attached to each other, some dying off but more growing on top of the ancestors to raise the coral reefs upwards. ⓫The energy required for this kind of growth is huge, and only with desirable environmental conditions can corals of various types and shapes continue to grow.

1. In paragraph 1, which of the following best describes the relationship of corals and coral reefs?

(A) Larvae represent corals and polyps represent coral reefs.
(B) Corals make up the hard skeleton of coral reefs.
(C) They both indicate the same thing, which is a group of polyps.
(D) Coral reefs are made up of corals and calcium carbonate-based skeletons.

第1段落によると、サンゴとサンゴ礁の関係を最も適切に説明しているものは次のうちどれですか。

(A) 幼生はサンゴのことであり、ポリプはサンゴ礁のことである。
(B) サンゴがサンゴ礁の堅い骨格を構成する。
(C) 両方ともポリプの群体であり、同じものを指す。
(D) サンゴ礁はサンゴと炭酸カルシウムを主成分とした骨格で構成されている。

問1は、「サンゴとサンゴ礁の関係性」について最も適切なものを選ぶ問題です。では本文を読んでいきましょう。❶~❷には「サンゴ礁は微小な有機体から生じるが、地球上で最も多様な生物が群がる、巨大な構造体へと成長する。海中のみに生存するサンゴ礁は、しばしば海の熱帯雨林と呼ばれている」とあります。ここはあくまで導入部です。❸はImportantlyにより、ここから重要な内容が始まることがわかりますね。「サンゴと礁は全く同じではない」と説明しています。❹~❺によると「サンゴは生命体のことで、礁は岩のようなカタマリのことであり、サンゴ礁とは多くのサンゴによって構成されたカタマリ」であるとわかります。❻以降はサンゴ礁がどのようにしてできるかを説明しています。まず、幼生のサンゴが適当な岩にくっつきます。それがサンゴポリプになり、そこから炭酸カルシウムから成る骨格が形成されます。この骨格は外敵から身を守るだけではなく、他のサンゴの幼生がくっつくための足場となります。この過程を繰り返しながら、サンゴ礁は巨大化していくということです。最後に⓫で「このような成長に必要なエネルギーは膨大であり、環境条件が望ましい場合のみ、様々な種類や形のサンゴが成長し続けることができる」と述べています。では選択肢を検討しましょう。(A)は「幼生=サンゴ、ポリプ=サンゴ礁」という意味です。❼によると幼生はポリプへと成長するので、幼生とポリプが同一物だとわかります。また、❸にはサンゴとサンゴ礁は別物であると書いてあります。❸と❼に矛盾するため(A)は誤りです。(B)は「サンゴはサンゴ礁の堅い骨格を構成する」と述べていますが、❽と矛盾します。骨格は炭酸カルシウムから成るものです。(C)は「両方とも同じものを指す」と述べていますが、❸と矛盾します。(D)は「サンゴ礁はサンゴと炭酸カルシウムの骨格によって作られる」と述べています。❺と❽の内容に一致します。よって(D)が正解です。

2. According to paragraph 1, which of the following best describes how corals grow?

(A) Upward currents of the ocean provide energy for the corals to expand in size.
(B) New larvae continuously add to a structure made of older corals.
(C) Some old parts of corals die off, which protect the new polyps that are growing taller.
(D) Each coral polyp increases in size and eventually splits into two identical units.

第1段落によると、サンゴがどのように成長するかを最も適切に説明しているものは次のうちどれですか。

(A) 上昇海流がサンゴが大きくなるためのエネルギーを提供する。
(B) 新たな幼生が、古いサンゴによって構成される構造体を絶えず大きくする。
(C) サンゴの古い部分が死に、それが高く育っている新しいポリプを守る。
(D) それぞれのサンゴポリプはサイズが大きくなり、最終的に2つの全く同じ物体に分裂する。

問2は「サンゴが成長する過程」に関して正しいものを選ぶ問題です。基本的には❻以降を参照すれば十分でしょう。では選択肢を検討していきましょう。(A)は「上昇海流がサンゴにエネルギーを与える」と述べていますが、本文に記述がありません。(B)は「新たな幼生が、古いサンゴによって構成される構造体を絶えず大きくする」と述べています。❽~❿の記述に一致するので、(B)が正解です。(C)は「サンゴの古い部分が死ぬと、それが新しいポリプを守る」と述べていますが、本文に記述がありません。サンゴを守るのは、炭酸カルシウムから成る骨のようなものです。(D)は「サンゴポリプはサイズが大きくなると、最終的に2つの全く同じ物体に分裂する」と述べていますが、本文には全く記述がありません。

□upward: 上昇の □add to X: Xを大きくする □identical: 全く同じの

第2段落｜問3~4 解説レクチャー

❶The three main types of coral reefs found on Earth are "fringing," "barrier," and "atoll" reefs. ❷Fringing reefs grow quite close to the coast of islands, leaving just short patches of lagoons between themselves and the shoreline; they are also the most common. ❸Second are the barrier reefs, which form further away from the coast, leaving a larger lagoon. ❹They can actually reach the surface of the water, making them a barrier to marine navigation. ❺The most well known of this type is the Great Barrier Reef off the coast of Australia. ❻Finally there are the atoll reefs, which are unique in that they form a ring around a collapsed or collapsing volcanic island. ❼Once the island has sunk a sufficient amount, the reefs retain the lagoon and sometimes start to form beaches from their eroded remains. ❽Atolls are also some of the most life filled coral reefs of all types. ❾Allowed to grow for sufficient time and with favorable ocean currents, some atolls will become habitable islands, with leftover materials from the collapsed volcano and the sand of the atoll mixing to become a fertile home for different flora and even fauna.

3. In paragraph 2, the Great Barrier Reef was mentioned for what main purpose?

(A) To compare the characteristics of barrier reefs with other kinds of reefs
(B) To show that it is the largest reef of all types
(C) To give an existing example of a barrier reef
(D) To exemplify how barrier reefs may discourage marine navigation

第2段落において、グレートバリアリーフが言及された主な目的は何ですか。

(A) 堡礁の特徴を他の種類の礁と比較するため
(B) 全ての種類の礁で堡礁が最も大きいことを示すため
(C) 実際に存在する堡礁の例を挙げるため
(D) 堡礁がどのように海洋航行を妨げるかという実例を示すため

問3は「グレートバリアリーフ」について触れている理由を聞く問題です。では、読んでいきましょう。❶で「礁には主に3種類ある」と述べており、❷で裾礁の説明をしています。❸～❺が堡礁（バリアリーフ）についての説明です。まず、「海岸から遠いところで成長し、大きなラグーンを形成する」とあります。さらに「堡礁は水面に達することもあり、海洋航行の妨げとなることがある」と説明されています。その後、最も有名な堡礁は、オーストラリア沖にあるグレートバリアリーフであると述べられています。グレートバリアリーフは堡礁の具体例なので正解は(C)です。

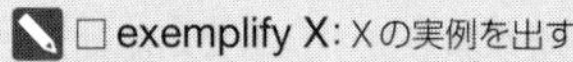
□ exemplify X: Xの実例を出す

4. Which of the sentences below best expresses the essential information in the highlighted sentence in the passage? Incorrect choices change the meaning in important ways or leave out essential information.

(A) Suitable conditions created from volcanic material and sand over time result in a living habitat that supports the life of various organisms.
(B) It takes a long time for atolls to become a fertile dwelling for many species if materials produced by volcanic activities do not reach the atolls.
(C) Without appropriate ocean currents, creatures cannot proliferate for a long time around the atolls that contain substances from volcanoes.
(D) When materials produced from collapsing volcanoes react with atolls, they become a comfortable home for animals and plants living in the ocean.

次のうちどの文が、ハイライト表示した文の重要な情報を最もよく表していますか。不正解の選択肢は、意味を大きく変えたり、重要な情報を抜かしたりしています。

(A) 火山物質や砂から時間をかけて作られた適切な環境は、様々な生物の命を支えるすみかを作り出してくれる。
(B) 火山活動により生み出された物質が環礁に到達しなければ、環礁が豊かな住みかになるのには時間がかかる。
(C) 適度の海流なくしては、生物は火山の物質を含む環礁の周りで長期間にわたり繁殖できない。
(D) 沈下が進んでいる火山の物質が環礁と反応すると、環礁は海で生息する動物や植物の快適なすみかとなる。

問4は❾を読むだけで解けますが、❻～❽にも目を通しておきましょう。3つ目の環礁は、火山の周りに輪を作る独特なサンゴ礁で、最も生物種が豊富とあります。❾は「十分な時間をかけて、好都合の海流下で成長できれば、居住可能な島となる。海中に沈んだ火山から残った物質や環礁の砂が混ざり合い、様々な植物相や動物相にとってさえも豊かな生息地になる」という意味です。では選択肢を見ていきましょう。(A)は「火山物質や砂から時間をかけて作られた適切な環境は、様々な生物の命を支えるすみかを作り出してくれる」という意味ですが、これは今見た❾の内容を十分に反映していると言えそうです。念のために他の選択肢も確認しましょう。(B)は「火山活動により生み出された物質が環礁に到達しなければ、豊かなすみかになるのに時間がかかる」という意味ですが、こういった関係は本文からは読み取れません。(C)は「適切な潮流がなければ、環礁の周りでは生物は繁殖できない」という意味です。ただこれは、海流の要因にしか焦点があてられておらず、❾の言い換えとしては不適切です。(D)は「火山から生じた物質が環礁と反応すると」という箇所が誤りです。本文に記述がありません。よって(A)が正解です。

□ result in X：Xという結果になる　□ dwelling：すみか　□ proliferate：増殖する

第3段落｜問5解説レクチャー

❶For each type of coral reefs, there are many different species of corals, all with their own natural rates of growth. ❷The two most important growth factors are salinity (i.e., how salty the ocean water is) and water temperature, with the latter being dominant. ❸First, without sufficient levels of salt, the corals cannot keep growing, or they may even die out. ❹Any area that receives large quantities of fresh water from their adjacent island is much less livable for the corals because salinity must remain high enough and constant. ❺While salinity definitely plays a crucial role in corals' health, temperature is known to exert the greatest impact. ❻Only in the water with a livable temperature range can corals keep growing. ❼The ideal temperature range is between 21 and 29 degrees Celsius. ❽On the other hand, if the temperature is too high or too low, the growth of corals is seriously inhibited, even if there is a sufficient amount of salt in the water. ❾Most coral reefs fail to form if the water stays below 18 or above 35 degrees Celsius. ❿They are extremely sensitive to warm temperature in particular. ⓫Why is that? ⓬The answer lies in the symbiotic algae called zooxanthellae, which are also known to contribute to the growth of both corals and coral reefs.

5. In paragraph 3, the word "adjacent" in the passage is closest in meaning to

(A) isolated
(B) neighboring
(C) similar
(D) grouped

第3段落のadjacentと最も近い意味のものはどれですか。

(A) 孤立した
(B) 近隣の
(C) 類似の
(D) 群を成した

問5のadjacentは「隣接した」という意味の形容詞なので、**(B) neighboring**が正解です。**adjacent to X**「Xに近い」という形でよく使われます。**close to**の代わりにスピーキングやライティングでぜひ使ってみてください。

第4段落｜問6〜7 解説レクチャー

❶The activities of zooxanthellae play a critical role in the life cycle of corals. ❷Sunlight reaches the corals, and permits the symbiotic algae partners to perform photosynthesis. ❸The process of photosynthesis provides corals with enough oxygen, which is essential for their healthy growth. ❹Photosynthesis also produces materials important for producing calcium carbonate skeletons. ❺In return, corals provide a shelter for the algae. ❻Warm water disturbs their relationship. ❼As the water temperature increases, the rate of photosynthesis becomes faster, which produces more oxygen, eventually to an abnormal and toxic level. ❽The corals must expel these too-excited algae. ❾This is how warm temperature agitates the symbiotic relationship and hinders the development of coral reefs. ❿Now we realize that this is one example of how environmental changes such as global warming can devastate the environment.

6. Which of the following best describes the relationship between paragraphs 3 and 4?

(A) Paragraph 3 brings up two important factors for the survival of corals and paragraph 4 explains why one is more important than the other.
(B) Paragraph 3 illustrates why corals cannot grow in a certain environment and paragraph 4 proves the validity of the explanation.
(C) Paragraph 3 explains two key factors for the growth of corals and paragraph 4 provides the specific mechanism of one of them.
(D) Paragraph 3 discusses theories about how corals grow in optimum environments and paragraph 4 gives specific examples of the optimum environments.

第3段落と第4段落の関係を最も適切に説明しているものは次の中でどれですか。

(A) 第3段落は、サンゴの生存にとって重要な2つの要因を提示し、第4段落はなぜ一方が他方よりも重要なのかを説明している。
(B) 第3段落は、なぜサンゴが特定の環境下では成長できないかを説明し、第4段落はその説明の妥当性を証明している。
(C) 第3段落は、サンゴの成長にとって重要な2つの要因を説明し、第4段落はそのうちの1つの特定の仕組みを提供している。
(D) 第3段落は、サンゴが最適な環境下においてどのように成長するのかについての理論を議論し、第4段落は最適な環境の具体例を挙げている。

問6は「第3段落と第4段落の関係性」を問うています。まず、第3段落では「塩分濃度」と「水温」が成長に重要であると述べられています。とくに、第3段落の❷から「水温の方が塩分濃度より重要である」とわかります。また、第4段落の要旨は「水温が高すぎると光合成が活発になり過ぎるため、サンゴに悪影響がある」というものです。つまり、第3段落に出てくる水温について、第4段落でさらに詳しく説明しています。では選択肢を見ていきましょう。(A)にはparagraph 4 explains why one is more important than the otherとありますが、理由を説明しているわけではありません。(B)はwhy corals cannot grow in a certain environmentが誤りです。逆に「成長に必要な要素」を説明するのが第3段落の役割でした。(C)はtwo key factors for the growthが「塩分濃度」と「水温」に対応します。また、the specific mechanism of one of themは第4段落で述べられている「水温が光合成にもたらす影響」を指すと考えられるので、(C)が正解です。(D)はspecific examples of the optimum environmentsが誤りです。「最適な環境」ではなくサンゴ礁の成長が阻害される例について述べています。

□ validity：妥当性　□ optimum：最適な

7. According to paragraph 4, which of the following illustrates the mechanism of how the symbiotic relationship is disturbed?

(A) Warm water causes algae to release poison, which destroys corals.
(B) Algae, when extremely excited, slow down the process of photosynthesis.
(C) Accelerated photosynthesis results in the production of excessive gas.
(D) An abnormal amount of calcium carbonate disturbs the corals.

第4段落によると、どのようにして共生関係が乱されるのかについて、その仕組みを説明しているものは次の中でどれですか。

(A) 温かい水は藻に毒を排出させ、この毒がサンゴを破壊する。
(B) 極めて活発になった藻は、光合成のスピードを遅らせる。
(C) 加速した光合成は、過剰な気体の生成をもたらす。
(D) 異常な量の炭酸カルシウムがサンゴの邪魔をする。

問7は「共生関係が乱されるメカニズム」について説明しているものを選ぶ問題です。では続きを読んでいきましょう。❶でまず、褐虫藻が重要だと述べています。❷は「太陽の光がサンゴに到達すると、パートナーである褐虫藻は光合成を行うことができる」と述べています。❸～❹には「光合成は酸素を提供するとともに、炭酸カルシウムの骨格の形成に重要である物質を生成する」とあります。❺は「そのお返しとして、サンゴは藻にすみかを提供する」と述べています。つまり、サンゴと褐虫藻は切っても切れない関係にあるわけですね。❻は「温水は関係に支障をきたす」と述べています。第3段落❻にもサンゴの成長における水温の重要性に触れていましたね。❼には「水温が上がるにつれて光合成が活発になり、最終的には異常で有害なレベルの多くの酸素を生み出す」とあります。❽では「サンゴは、このように活発になり過ぎた藻を追い出さなければならない」と説明されています。つまり、共生関係が解消されてしまうがゆえに、サンゴが滅びてしまうわけです。最後に❿で、問題の一例として地球温暖化を挙げています。では選択肢を見ていきましょう。(A)は「毒を出す」という記述が誤りです。あくまで酸素を出すだけです。(B)は「活発になった藻類が光合成の速度を下げる」という記述が誤りです。むしろ速度は上がります。(C)は「活発になった光合成は過度に気体を供給することになる」という意味です。❼に一致するため、(C)が正解です。(D)に書いてあるような炭酸カルシウムの働きに関する記述は本文にないため、誤りです。

第5段落｜問8 解説レクチャー

❶Corals of all species and coral reefs of all types are sensitive to changes in the surrounding environment. ❷Their growth rates change drastically or they sometimes become extinct if the local water conditions change even slightly. ❸Not only does the temperature change caused by global warming have a direct effect on the coral, but also the melting of glaciers exerts an additional impact. ❹The melting of glaciers releases non-salty fresh water, which guarantees a significant decrease in salinity of the ocean. ❺Besides, as glaciers melt away, the sea level rises. ❻This means that less light can reach the algae; as a result, algae cannot perform photosynthesis as much, and less food is available for the corals. ❼Intuitively or counter-intuitively, phenomena occurring above the sea level, such as global warming and the ensuing glacier melting, are intimately related to the phenomena observed under the water.

8. According to paragraph 5, melting glaciers affect coral reefs in all of the following ways EXCEPT:

(A) Ice melting lowers the ocean temperature, which is unfavorable to corals.
(B) What happens above the sea level has profound implications for corals.
(C) It limits the rate of photosynthesis performed by algae.
(D) Melted ice, which is non-salty, dramatically changes the salinity of ocean.

第5段落によると、融解しつつある氷河がサンゴ礁に与える影響として正しくないものはどれですか。

(A) 氷河の融解は海水温度を下げるが、これはサンゴにとって好ましくない。
(B) 海面上で起こることが、サンゴに大きな影響を与える。
(C) 藻類が行う光合成の速度を制限する。
(D) 塩分を含まない溶けた氷は、海水の塩分濃度を大幅に変える。

問8は「溶けつつある氷河がサンゴ礁に与える影響」ではないものを問うています。❶～❸は「サンゴ礁の成長は周りの環境によって左右されるが、地球温暖化によってもたらされた温度変化が、サンゴに直接的な影響を与えるだけでなく、氷河の融解もサンゴにさらなる影響を及ぼす」と述べています。❹以下がポイントとなりそうです。❹は「氷河の融解は、塩分を含まない真水を放出し、確実に海水の塩分濃度の大幅な低下を引き起こす」と説明しています。この内容は(D)「溶けた氷は海水の塩分濃度を大幅に変える」に一致します。さらに❻を見ると「これは藻に届く光が少なくなることを意味し、結果として、光合成を以前ほど行うことができなくなり、サンゴが得られる食料が少なくなる」と説明されています。この内容は(C)「藻類が行う光合成の速度を制限する」に一致します。❼は「地球温暖化やその後生じる氷河の融解などの海面上で起こっている現象は、海面下で見られる現象と密接に関係している」と述べています。この内容は(B)「海面上で生じることがサンゴに大きな影響を与える」に一致します。よって、本文に記述がない(A)「氷河の融解は海水温度を下げる」が正解です。

□ unfavorable：望ましくない　□ profound：深い、大きな　□ implication：影響（通常複数形）

問9解説レクチャー

9. Look at the four squares [■] that indicate where the following sentence could be added to the passage.

Temperatures of this range can be often observed in the tropics.

Where would the sentence best fit?

❶For each type of coral reefs, there are many different species of corals, all with their own natural rates of growth. ❷The two most important growth factors are salinity (i.e., how salty the ocean water is) and water temperature, with the latter being dominant. ❸First, without sufficient levels of salt, the corals cannot keep growing, or they may even die out. ❹Any area that receives large quantities of fresh water from their adjacent island is much less livable for the corals because salinity must remain high enough and constant. **A** ❺While salinity definitely plays a crucial role in corals' health, temperature is known to exert the greatest impact. **B** ❻Only in the water with a livable temperature range can corals keep growing. **C** ❼The ideal temperature range is between 21 and 29 degrees Celsius. **D** ❽On the other hand, if the temperature is too high or too low, the growth of corals is seriously inhibited, even if there is a sufficient amount of salt in the water. ❾Most coral reefs fail to form if the water stays below 18 or above 35 degrees Celsius. ❿They are extremely sensitive to warm temperature in particular. ⓫Why is that? ⓬The answer lies in the symbiotic algae called zooxanthellae, which are also known to contribute to the growth of both corals and coral reefs.

次の文が以下のパッセージで追加されうる箇所を示す4つの■を見てください。

この温度域は熱帯地方でしばしば見られる。

この文は、どこに置くのが最もよいですか。

問9の挿入文は「この温度域は熱帯地方でしばしば見られる」という意味です。指示表現とディスコースマーカーに注目しましょう。this rangeとあるので「範囲」を示すような表現がある英文を探します。❶~❸の部分はさくっと読みましょう。❶は「それぞれのサンゴ礁の種類に対し、独自の自然成長速度を有した多くの異なる種のサンゴが存在する」、❷は「最も重要な2つの成長要因は塩分濃度（海水がどのくらい塩分を含んでいるのか）と水温であり、後者が支配的な要因である」、❸は「塩分濃度が十分でなければ、サンゴは成長を維持できない」という意味です。さて、❹から設問に関わるので、じっくりと読みましょう。❹は「大量の真水が入ると塩分濃度が下がるので、サンゴの生息に適さない」と述べています。「範囲」についての言及がないためⒶは誤りです。❺は「温度が最も大きな影響を及ぼす」とあります。まだ「範囲」の記述はありません。Ⓑも誤りです。❼は「理想的な温度は21~29度だ」とあります。「範囲」なので、答えはⒹです。今回は比較的簡単でしたね。1分程度で解きたい問題です。

問10解説レクチャー

10. Directions: An introductory sentence containing a brief summary of the passage is provided below. Complete the summary by selecting the best THREE answer choices that express the main ideas of the passage.

Corals are considered one of the most diverse living organisms on Earth, varying in species type and growth rate.

(A) In order for coral reefs to grow, the temperature of the water must be within a certain range and a certain level of salt concentration is essential.
(B) Three main reef types are formed in the same manner in the same location, yet their appearances are quite different.
(C) Changes in the environment including global warming and glaciers melting may lead to the extinction of corals.
(D) Even if the water temperature is stable, high salinity levels prevent corals from continuous growth.
(E) There exist different types of corals possessing distinctive characteristics, and they grow at different rates.
(F) Global warming has a greater and more direct influence on a particular type of coral reefs than the melting of glaciers does.

指示：パッセージの簡単な要約を含む紹介文を以下に記載しています。パッセージの中の最も重要な考えを示している文を3つ選んで要約を完成させてください。

様々な種があり、成長速度も異なるため、サンゴは地球上で最も多様な生物と考えられている。

(A) サンゴ礁が成長するためには、水温がある一定の範囲内にあるべきで、一定の塩分濃度が必要不可欠だ。
(B) 主要な3種類の礁は、同じ方法で同じ場所に形成されるが、見た目はかなり異なる。
(C) 温暖化や氷河の融解を含む環境の変化は、サンゴの絶滅につながるかもしれない。
(D) たとえ水温が安定していても、塩分濃度が高ければ、サンゴが継続的に成長し続けることは難しい。
(E) それぞれに特徴を有する様々な種類のサンゴが存在し、成長速度も異なる。
(F) 地球温暖化の方が、氷河の融解よりも、さらに大きく直接的な影響を特定の種類のサンゴ礁に与える。

最後の問題です。(A)は「サンゴ礁が成長するためには、水温が決まった範囲内であり、ある程度の塩分濃度が必要不可欠だ」という意味です。これは第3段落の要旨に一致するため、正解の可能性が高いです。(B)は「主な3種類のサンゴ礁は同じ場所に同じ方法でつくられる」と述べていますが、これは第2段落の内容に反します。(C)は「温暖化や氷河の融解を含む環境の変化は、多くのサンゴが絶滅することにつながるかもしれない」という意味です。第4段落❿から第5段落の内容に一致するため、正解の可能性が高いです。(D)は「塩分濃度が高ければサンゴの継続的な成長を阻害する」という部分が誤りです。塩分濃度に関して触れているのは第3段落❷～❹ですが、サンゴの成長には高い塩分濃度が必要だとあります。これは(D)の記述と明らかに矛盾します。(E)は第3段落の内容に一致しています。正解の可能性が高いです。(F)の「地球温暖化の方が、氷河の融解よりも大きな影響を与える」という比較は本文にはありません。「地球温暖化によって、氷河が溶ける」という因果関係が述べられていますが、どちらが大きな影響かとは書かれていません。よって、(A)、(C)、(E)が正解です。

□ manner:方法　□ extinction:絶滅

PARAGRAPH 1

❶Coral reefs originate from microscopic organisms but grow into humongous structures teeming with the greatest diversity of life on planet Earth.

❷Existing only under the ocean, coral reefs are often called "rainforests of the ocean."

❸Importantly, "corals" and "reefs" are not exactly the same.

❹"Corals" are living organisms and "reefs" are basically rocky masses.

❺Therefore, coral reefs are masses that are composed of a bunch of corals.

❻Baby corals called coral larvae swim through the oceans, and they seek out suitable rocks to which they attach themselves.

❼The larvae turn into coral polyps.

❽A special skeleton made of calcium carbonate starts forming from the bottom of the polyps' skin.

❾This skeleton protects the corals from many predators that might come across them, but it also forms the base to which other coral larvae can attach themselves, and there they begin to grow skeletons of their own.

❿This process repeats itself, growing into an enormous number of coral polyps all attached to each other, some dying off but more growing on top of the ancestors to raise the coral reefs upwards.

⓫The energy required for this kind of growth is huge, and only with desirable environmental conditions can corals of various types and shapes continue to grow.

❶サンゴ礁は微小な有機体から生じるが、地球上で最も多様な生物が群がる、巨大な構造体へと成長する。

❷海中にのみ生息するサンゴ礁は、しばしば海の熱帯雨林と呼ばれている。

❸重要な点だが、サンゴと礁は全く同じというわけではない。

❹サンゴは生命体であり、礁は基本的に岩のような塊である。

❺したがって、サンゴ礁は多くのサンゴによって構成された塊なのだ。

❻サンゴ幼生と呼ばれる生まれて間もないサンゴは、海を漂い、付着するのに適した岩を探す。

❼サンゴ幼生はサンゴポリプに変化する。

❽炭酸カルシウムで構成される特殊な骨格が、ポリプの皮膚の最下部から形成され始める。

❾この骨格は、遭遇し得る捕食動物からサンゴを守るだけではなく、他のサンゴ幼生が付着することができる足場となり、サンゴ幼生はそこで自身の骨格を育むのだ。

❿この過程を繰り返し、互いにくっついた膨大な数のサンゴポリプに成長する。死ぬものもいるが、より多くのサンゴ幼生が原種の上で育ち、サンゴ礁を上の方へと成長させていくのだ。

⓫このような成長に必要なエネルギーは膨大であり、環境条件が望ましい場合のみ、様々な種類や形のサンゴが成長し続けることができる。

＊語句問題に出る可能性あり

❶ □ coral reef：サンゴ礁
□ originate from X：Xから生じる
□ humongous：巨大な
□ *teeming with X：Xでいっぱいの
□ diversity：多様性

❹ □ mass：塊

❺ □ a bunch of X：多くのX

❻ □ larvae→larva「幼虫」の複数形

❼ □ polyp：ポリプ

❽ □ skeleton：骨格

❾ □ predator：捕食動物

❿ □ *enormous：巨大な
□ die off：死ぬ
□ ancestor：原種

PARAGRAPH 2

❶The three main types of coral reefs found on Earth are “fringing,” “barrier,” and “atoll” reefs.

❷Fringing reefs grow quite close to the coast of islands, leaving just short patches of lagoons[1] between themselves and the shoreline; they are also the most common.

❸Second are the barrier reefs, which form further away from the coast, leaving a larger lagoon.

❹They can actually reach the surface of the water, making them a barrier to marine navigation.

❺The most well known of this type is the Great Barrier Reef off the coast of Australia.

❻Finally there are the atoll reefs, which are unique in that they form a ring around a collapsed or collapsing volcanic island.

❼Once the island has sunk a sufficient amount, the reefs retain the lagoon and sometimes start to form beaches from their eroded remains.

❽Atolls are also some of the most life filled coral reefs of all types.

❾Allowed to grow for sufficient time and with favorable ocean currents, some atolls will become habitable islands, with leftover materials from the collapsed volcano and the sand of the atoll mixing to become a fertile home for different flora and even fauna.

1. Lagoon: A stretch of shallow water surrounded by a low sandbank or coral reef

❶地球上では、裾礁(きょしょう)、堡礁(ほしょう)、そして環礁(かんしょう)の3つの種類の礁が見られる。

❷裾礁は島の海岸にかなり近いところで成長し、海岸線との間に小さなラグーンを形成する。また、裾礁は最も一般的な礁である。

❸2つ目は、海岸からかなり離れた場所で形成され、大きなラグーンを持つ堡礁だ。

❹堡礁は水面に達することもあり、海洋航行の妨げとなることがある。

❺このタイプのサンゴ礁で最も広く認知されているのが、オーストラリア沖にあるグレートバリアリーフだ。

❻最後に環礁がある。環礁は、沈下もしくは沈下中の火山島の周りに環を形成するという点で独特である。

❼島が十分に沈むと、礁にはラグーンが残り、浸食された残余物から時には浜が形成され始める。

❽また、環礁は全てのサンゴ礁の中で、最も生命に満ちたサンゴ礁でもある。

❾十分な時間をかけて、好都合の海流下で成長できれば、居住可能な島となる。海中に沈んだ火山から残った物質や環礁の砂が混ざり合い、様々な植物相や動物相にとってさえも豊かな生息地になる。

1. ラグーン：砂洲やサンゴ礁に囲まれてできた浅い水面

※語句問題に出る可能性あり

❷ □ patch：他の部分とは異なる小さな部分

❸ □ further away → far away (furtherはfarの比較級)

❹ □ marine navigation：海洋航行

❻ □ *unique：独特な
□ in that SV：～という点で【慣用表現】

❼ □ *sufficient：十分な
□ *retain X：Xを維持する

❾ □ leftover：残った、残りの【形容詞】
□ fertile：肥沃な
□ flora：植物相
□ fauna：動物相

❾ with leftover materials ... and the sand ... mixing ...

いわゆる「付帯状況」のwithである。materialsとthe sandが意味上の主語で、mixingが意味上の述語。
(例) He was sitting with his eyes closed.

PARAGRAPH 3

❶For each type of coral reefs, there are many different species of corals, all with their own natural rates of growth.

❷The two most important growth factors are salinity (i.e., how salty the ocean water is) and water temperature, with the latter being dominant.

❸First, without sufficient levels of salt, the corals cannot keep growing, or they may even die out.

❹Any area that receives large quantities of fresh water from their adjacent island is much less livable for the corals because salinity must remain high enough and constant.

❺While salinity definitely plays a crucial role in corals' health, temperature is known to exert the greatest impact.

❻Only in the water with a livable temperature range can corals keep growing.

❼The ideal temperature range is between 21 and 29 degrees Celsius.

❽On the other hand, if the temperature is too high or too low, the growth of corals is seriously inhibited, even if there is a sufficient amount of salt in the water.

❾Most coral reefs fail to form if the water stays below 18 or above 35 degrees Celsius.

❿They are extremely sensitive to warm temperature in particular.

⓫Why is that?

⓬The answer lies in the symbiotic algae called zooxanthellae, which are also known to contribute to the growth of both corals and coral reefs.

❶それぞれのサンゴ礁の種類に対し、独自の自然に成長する速度を有した多くの異なる種のサンゴが生息する。

❷最も重要な2つの成長要因は塩分濃度（海水がどのくらい塩分を含んでいるのか）と水温であり、後者が支配的な要因である。

❸第一に、塩分濃度が十分でなければ、サンゴは成長し続けられない。つまり、場合によっては、サンゴは死んでしまうかもしれない。

❹塩分濃度は、十分に高くかつ一定でなければならないので、サンゴにとって、隣り合った島から大量の真水が流れ込んでくる地域は生息にほとんど適さない。

❺塩分濃度は、サンゴの健康状態に極めて大きな影響を与えることは確実であるが、温度が最も大きな影響を及ぼすことが知られている。

❻サンゴは、生息できる温度の範囲内の水の中でしか成長を続けられないのである。

❼理想的な温度域は摂氏21度から29度である。

❽一方、温度が高すぎたり低すぎたりすると、たとえ塩分を十分に含んだ水の中であっても、サンゴの成長は著しく抑えられる。

❾水温が摂氏18度未満、あるいは摂氏35度を上回っている場合、サンゴ礁はほとんど形成されない。

❿サンゴ礁は特に暖かい温度に極めて敏感なのである。

⓫それはなぜなのだろうか。

⓬その答えは、サンゴとサンゴ礁両方の成長に貢献することでも知られている、褐虫藻と呼ばれる共生藻に見ることができる。

＊語句問題に出る可能性あり

❷□salinity：塩分濃度

❹□adjacent：隣り合った
□*constant：一定の

❺□crucial：極めて重大な
□exert X：X（力や影響力）を行使する

❼□*ideal：理想的な

❽□*inhibit X：Xを阻害する

❾□fail to V：～し損ねる

❿□be sensitive to X：Xに対して敏感な
□in particular：特に

⓬□symbiotic：共生関係の
□contribute to X：Xに貢献する

❶ all with their own natural rates ... → all (being) with their own natural rates ...
(all = S′, being = V′, with their own natural rates = M′)

分詞構文のbeingが省略されていると解釈する。all（＝全ての種）が意味上の主語で、being以下が述語となる。

PARAGRAPH 4

❶The activities of zooxanthellae play a critical role in the life cycle of corals.

❷Sunlight reaches the corals, and permits the symbiotic algae partners to perform photosynthesis.

❸The process of photosynthesis provides corals with enough oxygen, which is essential for their healthy growth.

❹Photosynthesis also produces materials important for producing calcium carbonate skeletons.

❺In return, corals provide a shelter for the algae.

❻Warm water disturbs their relationship.

❼As the water temperature increases, the rate of photosynthesis becomes faster, which produces more oxygen, eventually to an abnormal and toxic level.

❽The corals must expel these too-excited algae.

❾This is how warm temperature agitates the symbiotic relationship and hinders the development of coral reefs.

❿Now we realize that this is one example of how environmental changes such as global warming can devastate the environment.

❶褐虫藻の活動は、サンゴのライフサイクルに極めて重要な役割を果たす。

❷太陽の光がサンゴに到達すると、パートナーである共生藻は光合成を行うことができる。

❸光合成の過程はサンゴに十分な酸素を提供するが、これが健全な成長に不可欠なのだ。

❹また、光合成は炭酸カルシウムの骨格の形成に重要な物質を生成する。

❺そのお返しとして、サンゴは藻にすみかを提供するのである。

❻温水は彼らの関係に支障をきたす。

❼水温が上がるにつれて、光合成の速度が速くなり、最終的には異常で有害なレベルになるまで多くの酸素を生み出すのだ。

❽サンゴは、このように活発になり過ぎた藻を追い出さなければならない。

❾暖かい温度は、このように共生関係をかき乱し、そしてサンゴ礁の成長を邪魔するのである。

❿これは、地球温暖化などの環境変化が、どのようにして環境を破壊するのかという一例であることがわかる。

*語句問題に出る可能性あり

❶□play a role：役割を果たす
□critical：重要な

❷□permit X to V：Xに〜することを可能にする、許可する
□symbiotic：共生の

❸□provide X with Y：XにYを提供する

❺□shelter：すみか

❻□*disturb X：Xを乱す

❼□abnormal：異常な
□*toxic：毒性の

❽□*expel X：Xを追い出す
□excited：活発になった

❾□*agitate X：Xをかき乱す
□*hinder X：Xを阻害する

❿□*devastate X：Xを破壊する

PARAGRAPH 5

❶Corals of all species and coral reefs of all types are sensitive to changes in the surrounding environment.

❷Their growth rates change drastically or they sometimes become extinct if the local water conditions change even slightly.

❸Not only does the temperature change caused by global warming have a direct effect on the coral, but also the melting of glaciers exerts an additional impact.

❹The melting of glaciers releases non-salty fresh water, which guarantees a significant decrease in salinity of the ocean.

❺Besides, as glaciers melt away, the sea level rises.

❻This means that less light can reach the algae; as a result, algae cannot perform photosynthesis as much, and less food is available for the corals.

❼Intuitively or counter-intuitively, phenomena occurring above the sea level, such as global warming and the ensuing glacier melting, are intimately related to the phenomena observed under the water.

❶あらゆる種のサンゴやサンゴ礁も周辺環境の変化に敏感である。

❷周りの水の状態がほんの少し変わっただけでも、成長速度が大幅に変化し、時には絶滅することもある。

❸地球温暖化によってもたらされた温度変化が、サンゴに直接的な影響を与えるだけでなく、氷河の融解もさらなる影響を及ぼす。

❹氷河の融解は、塩分を含まない真水を放出し、確実に海水の塩分濃度を大幅に低下させる。

❺加えて、氷河が溶けるにつれて海水面が上昇する。

❻これは藻に届く光が少なくなることを意味し、結果として、光合成を以前ほど行うことができなくなり、サンゴが得られる食料が少なくなる。

❼私たちの直感通り、あるいは直感に反して、地球温暖化やその後生じる氷河の融解などの海面上で起こっている現象は、海面下で見られる現象と密接に関係しているのである。

＊語句問題に出る可能性あり

❶ □ surrounding：周りの【形容詞】

❷ □ drastically：劇的に
□ become extinct：絶滅する

❹ □ *guarantee X：X を確約する、保証する

❺ □ besides：さらに【副詞】

❼ □ intuitively：直感的に、直感通りに
□ *ensue：続いて生じる
□ intimately：密接に
□ phenomenon：現象

❻ algae cannot perform photosynthesis as much
as muchは比較表現。「太陽光が十分に届く場合と比べると、それほど光合成を行えるわけではない」という意味。

リーディング問題 5 | History

THE COLLAPSE OF THE MAYANS

問題演習の流れ

- ☐ 解答時間は17分を目標にしましょう。
- ☐ 英文 ⇒ 問題 ⇒ 正解・解説レクチャー ⇒ 訳 という流れで学習します。
- ☐ 3回解けるように、3回分のマークシートを各問題に用意しています。解く日付を記入してからマークしてください。

Web解答方法

- ☐ 本試験では各選択肢の左に表示されるマークをクリックして解答します。本試験と同様の方法で取り組みたい場合は、Webで解答できます。
- ☐ インターネットのつながるパソコン・スマートフォンで、以下のサイトにアクセスしてWeb上で解答してください。

extester.com

- ☐ 操作方法は、p.13 ~ 14の「USA Club Web学習の使い方」をご参照ください。

学習の記録

学習開始日	年　月　日	学習終了日	年　月　日
学習開始日	年　月　日	学習終了日	年　月　日
学習開始日	年　月　日	学習終了日	年　月　日

リーディング問題 5 英文

THE COLLAPSE OF THE MAYANS

It only took one hundred years for the collapse of the Mayan civilization, which is just a small fraction of its three-thousand-year history. The Mayans abandoned their cities, their great monuments, and pyramids, all for reasons unknown. Investigations as to what could have caused the Mayan civilization to collapse are still continuing. The Mayan empire in 800 AD spanned from the Northern reaches of modern Honduras, to the central lands of what is now Mexico. In reality, however, this empire consisted of city-states, each with its own autonomy and each competing for power against the others. These cities were homes to a large number of people, and the demand on local resources to supply their food was massive. Although the culture did reach its peak from 600 to 800 AD, it could not prevent the unknown cause of people abandoning all that had been constructed. The cities went quiet and the stonemasons ceased to build their great monuments. There are at least five different competing theories on how the Mayan civilization collapsed, each one picking at either a social or environmental factor as the key cause.

One of the oldest theories developed and later modified by earlier scholars points to the theory of a disastrous event. This holds that a particular geological event wiped out the Mayan people. The theory is still quite common with some researchers. British archaeologist Euan Mackie proposed an earthquake theory in his article published in 1961, which was relatively a long time ago. However, some findings such as the hundred-year time frame of destruction, along with the different city abandonment periods, call for many anthropologists to conduct more research concerning this possible theory. Surely, if a massive earthquake, volcanic eruption or large tidal wave had been the cause, the city-states would all have been abandoned simultaneously. The following theory deals with warfare. It was first believed that the Maya was a peaceful culture; however, stone carvings depicting war between city-states over resources, land, and prestige found otherwise. It is possible that the destruction of "Dos Pilas," now located in Petén, Guatemala, around 750 AD could have started a domino effect, mainly because trade and other important operations between the city-states collapsed due to fear of aggression.

These are just two of the possible theories that could have occurred, which leads us to the theory of over-population. Proponents of this theory include Professor Richard B. Gill. He argues that as civilizations advanced and cities grew, so did their population. The cities started to suffer from severe food supply shortages. This extreme and continuous scarcity of food led to the fall of the civilization. Professor Arthur A. Demarest proposed yet another theory, which involves civil discontent. His findings through stone art have shown that the Maya were one of the most volatile, unstable state-level societies in the New World, especially after 600 AD. The working class of the Mayan society faced issues such as being overworked, underfed, and competing in an ever-growing social caste. Many people also suffered from great pressure and intensive labor to build increasingly elaborate monuments for authorities. All of these resulted in extreme fatigue building up in the working class and this could no doubt provide a cause for rebellion in the lower echelons.

Last but not least is the longest-standing theory that is based on environmental change. The article proposed by Professor Douglas Kennett expounded on this through the possibility of an extended drought between 1020 and 1100 AD due to sudden climate change, resulting in the final collapse. As the Mayans only cultivated a limited range of crops, with some hunting and fishing to make up for their food supply, a sudden climate change could have easily caused the destruction of their food supply. Some scenarios include drought, with record high temperatures being seen towards the end of their civilization, thus further reducing the tight margins of food available for these barely subsisting cities. The poor replenishment of the soil may have also caused these environmental factors to manifest more significantly, as runoff and nutrient levels were just not enough to provide the yields that were needed to keep the population fed.

Truly, there is little consensus on which theory could have been the decisive factor to the Mayan collapse. Perhaps the combination of these proposed theories or even the discovery of the unknown truth may reveal this mystery. It can be seen that many of the challenges the Mayan civilization faced ages ago are quite similar to those found in our society today. With the advancement of technology, it is conceivable that we may solve the mystery in time, leading us to the guidance of our very own civilization and steering us away from our very own extinction.

1. According to paragraph 1, how was the Mayan empire divided?

(A) It was divided into small independent cities which were highly competitive.

(B) Cities were independent but dependent on each other for many resources.

(C) There were several city-sized nations that cooperated to fight against outside enemies.

(D) It was one large independent city separated into many smaller dependent units.

PARAGRAPH 1

It only took one hundred years for the collapse of the Mayan civilization, which is just a small fraction of its three-thousand-year history. The Mayans abandoned their cities, their great monuments, and pyramids, all for reasons unknown. Investigations as to what could have caused the Mayan civilization to collapse are still continuing. The Mayan empire in 800 AD spanned from the Northern reaches of modern Honduras, to the central lands of what is now Mexico. In reality, however, this empire consisted of city-states, each with its own autonomy and each competing for power against the others. These cities were homes to a large number of people, and the demand on local resources to supply their food was massive. Although the culture did reach its peak from 600 to 800 AD, it could not prevent the unknown cause of people abandoning all that had been constructed. The cities went quiet and the stonemasons ceased to build their great monuments. There are at least five different competing theories on how the Mayan civilization collapsed, each one picking at either a social or environmental factor as the key cause.

2. In paragraph 2, the author questions the theory described in the article published in 1961 for which of the following reasons?

(A) There is no evidence that destructive earthquakes or waves happened.
(B) Some rulers did not end up abandoning their territories.
(C) The publication of the book is too old for it to be trusted.
(D) It took a very long time for the entire society to abandon the cities.

3. According to paragraph 2, the warfare theory states that

(A) Mayans, originally of a peaceful nature, were attacked by invaders and lost the war
(B) the destruction of "Dos Pilas" was caused by the lack of trade and trust between the cities
(C) people in Maya, who were initially thought to be peaceful, fought within the city
(D) city-states lost most of their resources due to war and people had to leave cities for trading

PARAGRAPH 2

One of the oldest theories developed and later modified by earlier scholars points to the theory of a disastrous event. This holds that a particular geological event wiped out the Mayan people. The theory is still quite common with some researchers. British archaeologist Euan Mackie proposed an earthquake theory in his article published in 1961, which was relatively a long time ago. However, some findings such as the hundred-year time frame of destruction, along with the different city abandonment periods, call for many anthropologists to conduct more research concerning this possible theory. Surely, if a massive earthquake, volcanic eruption or large tidal wave had been the cause, the city-states would all have been abandoned simultaneously. The following theory deals with warfare. It was first believed that the Maya was a peaceful culture; however, stone carvings depicting war between city-states over resources, land, and prestige found otherwise. It is possible that the destruction of "Dos Pilas," now located in Petén, Guatemala, around 750 AD could have started a domino effect, mainly because trade and other important operations between the city-states collapsed due to fear of aggression.

4. In paragraph 3, the word "elaborate" in the passage is closest in meaning to

(A) huge
(B) complex
(C) widespread
(D) gorgeous

5. According to paragraph 3, which of the following best describes Professor Arthur A. Demarest's theory?

(A) Severe stress caused by social hierarchy was the ultimate cause of the destruction.
(B) Creation of monuments put tremendous pressure on the ruling class.
(C) Rebellions would not have occurred if people's mental health had been cared for.
(D) Food shortages could not support the life of working people, which led to the collapse.

PARAGRAPH 3

These are just two of the possible theories that could have occurred, which leads us to the theory of over-population. Proponents of this theory include Professor Richard B. Gill. He argues that as civilizations advanced and cities grew, so did their population. The cities started to suffer from severe food supply shortages. This extreme and continuous scarcity of food led to the fall of the civilization. Professor Arthur A. Demarest proposed yet another theory, which involves civil discontent. His findings through stone art have shown that the Maya were one of the most volatile, unstable state-level societies in the New World, especially after 600 AD. The working class of the Mayan society faced issues such as being overworked, underfed, and competing in an ever-growing social caste. Many people also suffered from great pressure and intensive labor to build increasingly elaborate monuments for authorities. All of these resulted in extreme fatigue building up in the working class and this could no doubt provide a cause for rebellion in the lower echelons.

6. In paragraph 4, what can be inferred about Professor Douglas Kennett's theory?

(A) It is the least reliable theory among others.
(B) The theory combined several existing theories.
(C) It has been continuously receiving support from scholars.
(D) This theory was the last one that was proposed.

7. In paragraph 4, the environment-based theory explains all of the following EXCEPT

(A) the possible scenario of how the entire civilization became weakened
(B) what might have caused the final collapse of civilization
(C) roughly when the destructive events happened
(D) how the Mayans could have coped with the drastic change

PARAGRAPH 4

Last but not least is the longest-standing theory that is based on environmental change. The article proposed by Professor Douglas Kennett expounded on this through the possibility of an extended drought between 1020 and 1100 AD due to sudden climate change, resulting in the final collapse. As the Mayans only cultivated a limited range of crops, with some hunting and fishing to make up for their food supply, a sudden climate change could have easily caused the destruction of their food supply. Some scenarios include drought, with record high temperatures being seen towards the end of their civilization, thus further reducing the tight margins of food available for these barely subsisting cities. The poor replenishment of the soil may have also caused these environmental factors to manifest more significantly, as runoff and nutrient levels were just not enough to provide the yields that were needed to keep the population fed.

8. According to paragraph 5, why does the author state that "there is little consensus of which theory could have been the decisive factor"?

(A) To argue that all of the theories provide insufficient evidence to the collapse
(B) To support the idea that the collapse might not have been due to one sole reason
(C) To show that the collapse was dependent upon all of the theories
(D) To challenge the idea that the theories do not provide a reliable source

PARAGRAPH 5

Truly, there is little consensus on which theory could have been the decisive factor to the Mayan collapse. Perhaps the combination of these proposed theories or even the discovery of the unknown truth may reveal this mystery. It can be seen that many of the challenges the Mayan civilization faced ages ago are quite similar to those found in our society today. With the advancement of technology, it is conceivable that we may solve the mystery in time, leading us to the guidance of our very own civilization and steering us away from our very own extinction.

9. Look at the four squares [■] that indicate where the following sentence could be added to the passage.

Despite the improved agricultural techniques acquired, they could not maintain local production.

Where would the sentence best fit?

PARAGRAPH 3

These are just two of the possible theories that could have occurred, which leads us to the theory of over-population. Proponents of this theory include Professor Richard B. Gill. **A** He argues that as civilizations advanced and cities grew, so did their population. **B** The cities started to suffer from severe food supply shortages. **C** This extreme and continuous scarcity of food led to the fall of the civilization. **D** Professor Arthur A. Demarest proposed yet another theory, which involves civil discontent. His findings through stone art have shown that the Maya were one of the most volatile, unstable state-level societies in the New World, especially after 600 AD. The working class of the Mayan society faced issues such as being overworked, underfed, and competing in an ever-growing social caste. Many people also suffered from great pressure and intensive labor to build increasingly elaborate monuments for authorities. All of these resulted in extreme fatigue building up in the working class and this could no doubt provide a cause for rebellion in the lower echelons.

10. Directions: An introductory sentence containing a brief summary of the passage is provided below. Complete the summary by selecting the best THREE answer choices that express the main ideas of the passage.

There are a number of theories pertaining to the collapse of the Mayan civilization.

Answer Choices

(A) Five theories provide evidence that the Mayans were thinking and living in different ways than we do today.
(B) Some findings such as stone art have allowed us to change our old views toward Mayan life and characteristics.
(C) Many theories about the collapse of the Mayan civilization can be divided into environment-based theories and society-based ones.
(D) Mayans relied on hunting and fishing for their food resources, which were disrupted by wars and environmental changes.
(E) Despite vigorous academic endeavors, there is still much to be discovered about the collapse of the Mayan civilization.
(F) Over-population was the main cause for their food shortage and the eventual starvation of their entire civilization.

リーディング問題 5

正解一覧……………………………… 204
解説レクチャー…………204~215
訳………………………………216~225

1. **(A)** 2. **(D)** 3. **(B)** 4. **(B)** 5. **(A)**
6. **(C)** 7. **(D)** 8. **(B)** 9. **(B)** 10. **(B) (C) (E)**

第1段落｜問1解説レクチャー

❶It only took one hundred years for the collapse of the Mayan civilization, which is just a small fraction of its three-thousand-year history. ❷The Mayans abandoned their cities, their great monuments, and pyramids, all for reasons unknown. ❸Investigations as to what could have caused the Mayan civilization to collapse are still continuing. ❹The Mayan empire in 800 AD spanned from the Northern reaches of modern Honduras, to the central lands of what is now Mexico. ❺In reality, however, this empire consisted of city-states, each with its own autonomy and each competing for power against the others. ❻These cities were homes to a large number of people, and the demand on local resources to supply their food was massive. ❼Although the culture did reach its peak from 600 to 800 AD, it could not prevent the unknown cause of people abandoning all that had been constructed. ❽The cities went quiet and the stonemasons ceased to build their great monuments. ❾There are at least five different competing theories on how the Mayan civilization collapsed, each one picking at either a social or environmental factor as the key cause.

1. According to paragraph 1, how was the Mayan empire divided?

(A) It was divided into small independent cities which were highly competitive.
(B) Cities were independent but dependent on each other for many resources.
(C) There were several city-sized nations that cooperated to fight against outside enemies.
(D) It was one large independent city separated into many smaller dependent units.

第1段落によると、マヤ帝国はどのように分割されていましたか。

(A) 非常に競争心の強い、小さな独立した都市に分けられていた。
(B) 都市は独立していたが、多くの資源を互いに依存していた。
(C) いくつかの都市ぐらいの大きさの国家が存在し、外敵と戦うため協力していた。
(D) 多数の小さな従属したユニットに分けられた、1つの大きな独立した都市国家であった。

問1は「マヤ帝国がどのように分割されていたのか」を問うています。では読んでいきましょう。❶で「マヤ文明の崩壊」がテーマであること、❷～❸で「マヤ文明の崩壊の原因を解明する調査は、現在も行われている」ことがわかります。❺には「マヤ帝国は都市国家で構成されており、それぞれが自治権を持ち、お互いに争っていた」とあります。では、選択肢を見ていきましょう。(A)は「非常に競争心の強い、小さな独立した都市に分けられていた」という意味です。これが正解です。❺のwith … autonomyをindependent、competingの部分をcompetitiveと言い換えています。(B)のdependent on each otherと(C)のcooperatedは❺のcompeting for powerと矛盾します。(D)は、one large independent cityが誤りです。❺のconsisted of city-statesと矛盾します。マヤは「独立した1つの都市」ではなく、「複数の都市国家」で構成されていたのです。残りの部分は設問と関係ありませんが、目を通しておきましょう。❹～❻ではマヤ帝国の大まかな説明が行われていましたが、❼～❽で「マヤ崩壊の話」へと戻ります。❾は、マヤ崩壊の原因に関して少なくとも5つの説があることに触れており、続く段落でその説を検証していくと想定できますね。では、次の段落に進みましょう。

第2段落｜問2～3 解説レクチャー

❶One of the oldest theories developed and later modified by earlier scholars points to the theory of a disastrous event. ❷This holds that a particular geological event wiped out the Mayan people. ❸The theory is still quite common with some researchers. ❹British archaeologist Euan Mackie proposed an earthquake theory in his article published in 1961, which was relatively a long time ago. ❺However, some findings such as the hundred-year time frame of destruction, along with the different city abandonment periods, call for many anthropologists to conduct more research concerning this possible theory. ❻Surely, if a massive earthquake, volcanic eruption or large tidal wave had been the cause, the city-states would all have been abandoned simultaneously. ❼The following theory deals with warfare. ❽It was first believed that the Maya was a peaceful culture; however, stone carvings depicting war between city-states over resources, land, and prestige found otherwise. ❾It is possible that the destruction of “Dos Pilas,” now located in Petén, Guatemala, around 750 AD could have started a domino effect, mainly because trade and other important operations between the city-states collapsed due to fear of aggression.

2. In paragraph 2, the author questions the theory described in the article published in 1961 for which of the following reasons?

(A) There is no evidence that destructive earthquakes or waves happened.
(B) Some rulers did not end up abandoning their territories.
(C) The publication of the book is too old for it to be trusted.
(D) It took a very long time for the entire society to abandon the cities.

第2段落において、1961年に発表の論文で説明されている説に筆者が異議を唱えている理由は何ですか。

(A) 壊滅的な地震や津波が起こった証拠は存在しない。
(B) 領土を放棄しなかった支配者もいた。
(C) あまりにも昔に出版された本なので、信用できない。
(D) マヤ社会全体が都市国家を放棄するのに、とても長い時間がかかった。

問2は「1961年の論文で説明されている説に筆者が異議を唱えている理由」を問うています。キーワードは1961年ですね。では読み進めましょう。❶～❸は1つ目の説について述べています。「災害によってマヤ文明が滅びた」という説ですね。❹には「イギリス人考古学者Euan Mackieは、比較的古い、1961年に発表した論文で、地震によってマヤ文明が滅びたと提唱した」とあります。次の❺がポイントです。「しかしながら、都市を放棄した時期がバラバラであり、文明の崩壊が100年にわたって生じたことが調査で判明したため、この説に関しては人類学者によるさらなる研究が必要である」と述べられています。さらに、❻には「もし巨大地震や火山噴火、津波が生じていれば、人々は同時に都市国家を捨てていただろう」という説明もあります。ここが問2の根拠になります。では、選択肢を詳しく見ていきましょう。(A)はno evidenceという内容の記述が本文にないので誤りです。実際に地震や津波が「あった」という明確な記述はありませんが、同時に「なかった」という記述もありません。(B)は本文に記述がありません。(C)は難しいです。確かにこの説が提唱されたのは比較的昔であると述べられていますが、それ自体が批判の直接的な理由ではありません。よって(C)も誤りです。(D)は「マヤ社会全体が都市国家を放棄するのに、とても長い時間がかかった」という意味です。これは❺の「だが、マヤが100年かかって崩壊した」と、❻の「災害が原因であれば滅亡は同時に起こったはずだ」という記述に一致します。よって、(D)が正解です。

□ end up Ving：結局～することになる

3. According to paragraph 2, the warfare theory states that

(A) Mayans, originally of a peaceful nature, were attacked by invaders and lost the war
(B) the destruction of "Dos Pilas" was caused by the lack of trade and trust between the cities
(C) people in Maya, who were initially thought to be peaceful, fought within the city
(D) city-states lost most of their resources due to war and people had to leave cities for trading

第2段落において、武力衝突説が主張していることはどれですか。

(A) もともとは平和的であったマヤ人は、侵略者に攻撃され、戦争に敗れた
(B) Dos Pilasの崩壊は、都市間の通商と信頼関係が失われたことによって引き起こされた
(C) 平和的であると思われていたマヤの人々は、都市国家内で戦った
(D) 都市国家は戦争により資源のほとんどを失い、人々は貿易のため都市を離れなければならなかった

問3は「武力衝突説」の内容を問うています。では続きを読んでいきましょう。❽は「マヤは平和的な文化だと考えられていたが、資源、土地、そして名声をめぐる都市国家間の争いを描いた石の彫刻によって、そうではないことがわかった」と述べています。❾には「Dos Pilasの崩壊が波及効果をもたらした可能性が考えられる。侵略の恐怖により、主に都市国家間の通商その他の重要な活動が破たんしたのだ」とあります。Dos Pilasが崩壊した後、他の都市国家にもその影響があったかもしれない、ということですね。では選択肢を詳しく見ていきましょう。(A)は本文と一致しません。選択肢では「マヤ人はもともと平和的であった」と言い切っていますが、これは先に見た❽と矛盾します。また、「侵略者に攻撃され、戦争に敗れた」という記述もありません。(B)は「Dos Pilasの崩壊は、都市間の通商と信頼関係がなくなったことによって引き起こされた」という意味です。これは❾に一致します。本文の「侵略を恐れていた」という記述は、「都市間の信頼関係が失われた」ということを示します。よって、(B)が正解です。(C)の前半の内容は確かに本文に一致しますが、後半のwithin the cityというのは❽ between city-states「都市国家間」と矛盾します。よって、(C)は誤りです。(D)は本文に記述がありません。

第 3 段落｜問 4〜5 解説レクチャー

❶These are just two of the possible theories that could have occurred, which leads us to the theory of over-population. ❷Proponents of this theory include Professor Richard B. Gill. ❸He argues that as civilizations advanced and cities grew, so did their population. ❹The cities started to suffer from severe food supply shortages. ❺This extreme and continuous scarcity of food led to the fall of the civilization. ❻Professor Arthur A. Demarest proposed yet another theory, which involves civil discontent. ❼His findings through stone art have shown that the Maya were one of the most volatile, unstable state-level societies in the New World, especially after 600 AD. ❽The working class of the Mayan society faced issues such as being overworked, underfed, and competing in an ever-growing social caste. ❾Many people also suffered from great pressure and intensive labor to build increasingly elaborate monuments for authorities. ❿All of these resulted in extreme fatigue building up in the working class and this could no doubt provide a cause for rebellion in the lower echelons.

4. In paragraph 3, the word "elaborate" in the passage is closest in meaning to

(A) huge　　(B) complex
(C) widespread　　(D) gorgeous

第 3 段落の elaborate と最も近い意味のものはどれですか。

(A) 大きい　　(B) 複雑な
(C) 蔓延した　　(D) 豪華な

問 4 の elaborate は「手の込んだ、精巧な」という意味です。よって「複雑な」という意味の (B) complex が正解です。(D) の gorgeous で迷うかもしれませんが、これは見た目が「美しい、きらびやかな」という意味合いです。一方、elaborate は「手の込んだ、念入りに作られた」というニュアンスがあります。

5. According to paragraph 3, which of the following best describes Professor Arthur A. Demarest's theory?

(A) Severe stress caused by social hierarchy was the ultimate cause of the destruction.
(B) Creation of monuments put tremendous pressure on the ruling class.
(C) Rebellions would not have occurred if people's mental health had been cared for.
(D) Food shortages could not support the life of working people, which led to the collapse.

第3段落によると、Arthur A. Demarest教授の説を最も適切に説明しているものはどれですか。

(A) 階級社会によって生み出された極度のストレスが、崩壊の究極の原因となった。
(B) 記念建造物の建設は、支配者階級の人々に大きな圧力をかけた。
(C) 人々の精神の健康がケアされていたら、反乱は起こらなかったであろう。
(D) 食料不足により労働者の生活を支えることができず、それが文明の崩壊につながった。

問5は「Arthur A. Demarestの説を最も適切に説明するもの」を問うています。では、読み進めましょう。まず、❶～❺は本問と関係ない説の話なのでさらっと読み進めます（後ほど問9の解説で詳しく説明します）。❻からArthur A. Demarestが提唱した説ですね。この説は、「市民の不満と関係している」と述べています。❼は「マヤは非常に不安定な国家社会であった」と説明しています。❽～❾から「マヤの人々が、過酷な労働環境と階級制、重圧によって苦しんでいた」ということがわかります。❿は「その結果、労働者階級の人々は極度に疲弊し、下層部が反乱を起こした可能性もある」と結論付けています。(A)は「階級社会によって生み出された極度のストレスが、崩壊の究極の原因となった」という意味です。❾のMany people also suffered from great pressureにより「極度のストレスを感じていた」ことは間違いないでしょう。また❽のin an ever-growing social casteや「労働者階級」という表現により、階級社会であったこともわかります。よって、(A)が正解です。(B)は「支配者階級にも圧力がかかっていた」と述べていますが、本文には該当する記述がありません。(C)の英文はいわゆる「仮定法」です。「人々の精神の健康がケアされていたら、反乱は生じなかったであろう」という意味ですが、裏を返せば「人々の精神の健康がケアされていなかったので、反乱が起こった」ということです。ですが、本文にはこの因果関係が明示されていません。よって(C)も誤りです。(D)は「食料不足により労働者の生活を支えることができず、それが文明の崩壊につながった」という意味です。こちらも本文にこの因果関係は明示されていません。❿は「疲弊した結果、反乱につながった」と述べています。「食料不足で滅びた」というわけではないのです。

□ ultimate：最終的な　□ tremendous：多大な

第4段落｜問6～7 解説レクチャー

❶Last but not least is the longest-standing theory that is based on environmental change. ❷The article proposed by Professor Douglas Kennett expounded on this through the possibility of an extended drought between 1020 and 1100 AD due to sudden climate change, resulting in the final collapse. ❸As the Mayans only cultivated a limited range of crops, with some hunting and fishing to make up for their food supply, a sudden climate change could have easily caused the destruction of their food supply. ❹Some scenarios include drought, with record high temperatures being seen towards the end of their civilization, thus further reducing the tight margins of food available for these barely subsisting cities. ❺The poor replenishment of the soil may have also caused these environmental factors to manifest more significantly, as runoff and nutrient levels were just not enough to provide the yields that were needed to keep the population fed.

6. In paragraph 4, what can be inferred about Professor Douglas Kennett's theory?

(A) It is the least reliable theory among others.
(B) The theory combined several existing theories.
(C) It has been continuously receiving support from scholars.
(D) This theory was the last one that was proposed.

第4段落のDouglas Kennett教授の説について何が推測できますか。

(A) この説は数ある説の中で最も信頼性がない。
(B) この説は既存の説を組み合わせたものだった。
(C) この説は継続的に学者の支持を受けて来た。
(D) この説は最後に提唱された。

問6は「Douglas Kennettの説に関して推測されること」を問うています。❶～❷により､「環境変化を根拠とした最も長く支持されてきた説があり、Douglas Kennettがそれを説明した」ことがわかります。❶のlongest-standingは「最も長い間支持されてきた」という意味なので、(C)が正解です。これと同じ理由で(A)のthe least reliableは誤りだとわかります。(B)は「既存の説を組み合わせた」とありますが、本文に記述はありません。(D)は「最後に提唱された」という部分が誤りです。確かに❶でLast but not leastとありますが、これは「主要な5つの説の中で最後に紹介するもの」という意味であり、「提唱された順番が最後」という意味ではありません。

□ existing：既存の

7. In paragraph 4, the environment-based theory explains all of the following EXCEPT

(A) the possible scenario of how the entire civilization became weakened
(B) what might have caused the final collapse of civilization
(C) roughly when the destructive events happened
(D) how the Mayans could have coped with the drastic change

第4段落によると、環境説が説明していないものは次の中でどれですか。

(A) 文明全体の弱体化があり得るシナリオ
(B) 何が文明の最終的な崩壊をもたらしたのか
(C) いつごろ壊滅的な出来事が起こったのか
(D) マヤ人がどうすれば急激な変化に対処できたか

問7は「環境説が説明していないもの」を選ぶ問題です。では続きを読みましょう。❷は「気候変動により長期にわたる干ばつがあり、それが最終的な文明の崩壊につながった可能性」に触れています。これは選択肢の(A)と(B)に一致しますね。❷にはさらに、「1020年から1100年の間に干ばつが発生した」ともあるので、(C)も本文に一致します。(D)は「マヤ人がどうすれば急激な変化に対処できたのか」という意味ですが、それについては述べられていません。よって、(D)が正解です。段落後半の部分は設問と関係ありませんが、目を通しておきましょう。❸~❺では環境説によるマヤ文明崩壊のシナリオを詳しく説明しています。

第5段落｜問8解説レクチャー

❶Truly, there is little consensus on which theory could have been the decisive factor to the Mayan collapse. ❷Perhaps the combination of these proposed theories or even the discovery of the unknown truth may reveal this mystery. ❸It can be seen that many of the challenges the Mayan civilization faced ages ago are quite similar to those found in our society today. ❹With the advancement of technology, it is conceivable that we may solve the mystery in time, leading us to the guidance of our very own civilization and steering us away from our very own extinction.

8. According to paragraph 5, why does the author state that “there is little consensus of which theory could have been the decisive factor”?

(A) To argue that all of the theories provide insufficient evidence to the collapse
(B) To support the idea that the collapse might not have been due to one sole reason
(C) To show that the collapse was dependent upon all of the theories
(D) To challenge the idea that the theories do not provide a reliable source

第5段落によると、「どの説がマヤ文明崩壊の決定的な要因だったのかについて、意見の一致がほとんど見られない」と筆者が述べた理由は何ですか。

(A) どの説も、文明の崩壊に関する十分な証拠を提供できていないことを主張するため
(B) 文明の崩壊は単独の原因によるものではないという考えを支持するため
(C) 文明の崩壊は全ての説に依拠していたということを示すため
(D) 説が信頼できる情報源に基づいていないという考えに異議を唱えるため

問8は「どの説がマヤ文明崩壊の決定的な要因だったのかについて、意見の一致がほとんど見られない」と筆者が述べた理由は何かを問うています。では、読んでいきましょう。❶は問題文が含まれる文ですね。❷には「これまで提示された説の組み合わせ、または未知なる真実の発見が、この謎を明らかにするかもしれない」とあります。❶の「意見の一致が見られない」という記述と「説の組み合わせ」という記述により、筆者は「マヤ文明崩壊を単独で説明できる説は今のところない」と主張しているのです。では選択肢を詳しく見ていきましょう。(A)は「どの説も証拠が不十分だと主張するため」という意味です。ですが、筆者が主張したいことは「それぞれの説を支える証拠が不十分だ」ということではなく、「1つの説だけでは足りない」ということです。よって(A)は誤りです。(B)は「文明の崩壊は単独の原因によるものではないという考えを支持するため」という意味です。これは❶～❷の内容から、

十分に推察可能です。よって(B)が正解です。(C)は「全ての説に依拠していた」というのが誤りです。「全て」とは限りません。(D)は二重否定なので、つまりは「説が信頼できる情報源に基づいていることを主張するため」と解釈できます。ところが、❷で筆者は「新事実が謎を解き明かすかもしれない」とぼやかしているので、それぞれの説に十分な信ぴょう性があることはうかがえません。よって、(D)は誤りです。段落後半の内容も確認しておきましょう。❸ではマヤ文明が直面した課題と今日我々が直面している課題は似通っていると述べています。❹はまとめると、「マヤ文明の崩壊の謎がわかれば、現代に生きる我々の教訓になる」という意味です。

問 9 解説レクチャー

9. Look at the four squares [■] that indicate where the following sentence could be added to the passage.

Despite the improved agricultural techniques acquired, they could not maintain local production.

Where would the sentence best fit?

❶These are just two of the possible theories that could have occurred, which leads us to the theory of over-population. ❷Proponents of this theory include Professor Richard B. Gill. **A** ❸He argues that as civilizations advanced and cities grew, so did their population. **B** ❹The cities started to suffer from severe food supply shortages. **C** ❺This extreme and continuous scarcity of food led to the fall of the civilization. **D** ❻Professor Arthur A. Demarest proposed yet another theory, which involves civil discontent. ❼His findings through stone art have shown that the Maya were one of the most volatile, unstable state-level societies in the New World, especially after 600 AD. ❽The working class of the Mayan society faced issues such as being overworked, underfed, and competing in an ever-growing social caste. ❾Many people also suffered from great pressure and intensive labor to build increasingly elaborate monuments for authorities. ❿All of these resulted in extreme fatigue building up in the working class and this could no doubt provide a cause for rebellion in the lower echelons.

次の文章が以下のパッセージで追加されうる箇所を示す4つの■を見てください。

より進歩した農業技術を手に入れたにもかかわらず、彼らはその土地で耕作を続けることができなかった。

この文章は、どこに置くのが最もよいですか。

挿入文は「より進歩した農業技術を手に入れたにもかかわらず、彼らはその土地で耕作を続けることができなかった」という意味です。選択肢には、指示表現やディスコースマーカーがありません。この場合は、本文の指示表現に注意しつつ、内容のつながりも意識しましょう。では、本文を読みます。❶で「人口増加による崩壊説」を紹介するとわかります。❷はその説の支持者であるRichard B. Gillの名前を出しており、続く❸のHeはこの人物を指しています。よって、🅰に挿入文は入りません。❸は「文明が進歩し都市が成長するとともに、人口も増加した」という意味です。❹は「都市は深刻な食料不足に悩まされ始めた」と述べています。「人口が増えたので、食料不足が生じた」という因果関係が見えますが、ここに挿入文を入れると、さらに論理関係が明確になります。「人口が増えた → 耕作を続けることができなかった → 食料不足が生じた」とうまくつながります。よって、🅱が正解です。❹のsevere food supply shortagesを受けて、❺ではThis extreme and continuous scarcity of foodと続けているので、🅲に挿入文は入りません。また、❺は「文明が崩壊した」と述べているため、ここで説明は終わりです。よって🅳にも挿入文は入りません。消去法でも🅱が正解だとわかります。

問10 解説レクチャー

10. Directions: An introductory sentence containing a brief summary of the passage is provided below. Complete the summary by selecting the best THREE answer choices that express the main ideas of the passage.

There are a number of theories pertaining to the collapse of the Mayan civilization.

(A) Five theories provide evidence that the Mayans were thinking and living in different ways than we do today.
(B) Some findings such as stone art have allowed us to change our old views toward Mayan life and characteristics.
(C) Many theories about the collapse of the Mayan civilization can be divided into environment-based theories and society-based ones.
(D) Mayans relied on hunting and fishing for their food resources, which were disrupted by wars and environmental changes.

(E) Despite vigorous academic endeavors, there is still much to be discovered about the collapse of the Mayan civilization.
(F) Over-population was the main cause for their food shortage and the eventual starvation of their entire civilization.

指示：パッセージの簡単な要約を含む紹介文を以下に掲載しています。パッセージ中の最も重要な考えを表している文を3つ選んで、要約を完成させてください。

マヤ文明の崩壊に関する説は多数存在する。

(A) 5つの説は、マヤの人々が今日の我々とは異なる考え方を持ち、異なる生活を送っていたことの証拠を提供する。
(B) 石細工などの研究の成果によって、我々が持っていたマヤの人々の生活や特徴に関する古い考えを改めることができた。
(C) マヤ文明の崩壊に関する多くの説は、環境を基盤とするものと社会を基盤とするものに分類できる。
(D) マヤの人々は食料を狩猟や漁業に依存したが、それは戦争と環境変化によって妨げられた。
(E) 活発な学術的取り組みにもかかわらず、マヤ文明の崩壊に関してわからないことが多くある。
(F) 人口過剰が食料不足とその後の文明全体の飢えの主たる原因であった。

最後の問題です。落ち着いて取り組みましょう。(A)の内容は本文に登場していますが、マヤ文明崩壊の説とは無関係なため不正解です。(B)は第2段落❺や❽、第3段落❼などに一致します。様々な発見により、説が進歩してきたわけです。複数箇所の内容に一致する選択肢は正解の可能性が高いです。(C)は「多くの説が環境か社会的要因を基盤とするものに分類できる」という意味です。環境に関する要因については第2段落で災害、第3段落で食料不足、第4段落で干ばつや気候変動が述べられています。また、第2段落では戦争、第3段落では社会制度といった社会的要因について述べられているので、これは正解の可能性が高いです。(D)は第4段落❸に、with some hunting and fishing to make up for their food supplyとありますが、これは「足りない食料を補うために狩猟や漁業を営んだ」という意味です。よって(D)のrelied onという記述は言いすぎです。また、第4段落で述べられているのは「気候変動が文明の崩壊につながったという説」なので選択肢のwarsも誤りです。(E)は「マヤ文明の崩壊に関してわからないことが多くある」という意味です。これは第1段落の内容に一致します。また第5段落の❶で、「滅亡の原因については意見の一致が得られていない」ともあるので、この選択肢は正解の可能性が高いです。(F)は第3段落で述べられている内容だと考えられますが、これは本文全体で紹介のある5つの説の内の1つの説明にすぎません。また、同段落では人口過剰がマヤ文明の滅亡の原因だったと述べていますが、(F)では「文明全体の飢えの主たる原因」とあり、本文の内容とずれます。よって、(B)、(C)、(E)が正解です。

□ disrupt X: Xを妨害する　□ starvation: 飢饉

PARAGRAPH 1

❶It only took one hundred years for the collapse of the Mayan civilization, which is just a small fraction of its three-thousand-year history.

❷The Mayans abandoned their cities, their great monuments, and pyramids, all for reasons unknown.

❸Investigations as to what could have caused the Mayan civilization to collapse are still continuing.

❹The Mayan empire in 800 AD spanned from the Northern reaches of modern Honduras, to the central lands of what is now Mexico.

❺In reality, however, this empire consisted of city-states, each with its own autonomy and each competing for power against the others.

❻These cities were homes to a large number of people, and the demand on local resources to supply their food was massive.

❼Although the culture did reach its peak from 600 to 800 AD, it could not prevent the unknown cause of people abandoning all that had been constructed.

❽The cities went quiet and the stonemasons ceased to build their great monuments.

❾There are at least five different competing theories on how the Mayan civilization collapsed, each one picking at either a social or environmental factor as the key cause.

❶マヤ文明は、その3000年の歴史のほんの一部であるわずか100年の間に崩壊した。

❷理由はわかっていないが、マヤの人々は、都市、巨大な記念碑、そしてピラミッドを放棄したのだ。

❸マヤ文明の崩壊の原因を解明する調査は、現在も行われている。

❹西暦800年当時、マヤ帝国は現在のホンジュラス北部地域からメキシコ中部にまで及んだ。

❺しかし実際には、マヤ帝国は都市国家で構成されており、それぞれが自治権を持ち、お互いに争っていた。

❻これらの都市国家は多くの人口を有しており、食料を供給するためのその土地の資源の需要は莫大なものであった。

❼マヤの文化は、600年から800年の間に最盛期を迎えたが、その後、それまでに建設されたもの全てを放棄するに至った理由である未知の出来事を回避することができなかった。

❽都市は静けさに包まれ、石工たちは壮大な記念碑の建設をやめたのだ。

❾マヤ文明の崩壊の原因については、少なくとも5つの競合する説があり、それぞれが社会的あるいは環境的要因のどちらか一方を主な原因として挙げている。

＊語句問題に出る可能性あり

❶ □ *collapse：崩壊【名詞】、崩壊する【動詞】
□ civilization：文明
□ fraction：断片、一部

❷ □ *abandon X：Xを放棄する

❸ □ *as to X：Xに関して（≒about）

❹ □ empire：帝国
□ span：ある期間にわたって存在する

❻ □ resource：資源
□ massive：莫大な

❼ □ reach one's peak：～の最盛期を迎える

❽ □ stonemason：石工
□ monument：記念碑

❾ □ competing：競合する

❺ each with its own autonomy and each competing for power

eachを意味上の主語とする分詞構文。each (S′) (being) (V′) with its own autonomy (M′)と解釈する。

❼ people (S′) abandoning (V′) all

peopleは意味上の主語で、abandoningは動名詞。

❾ each one (S′) picking (V′) ...

each oneを意味上の主語とする分詞構文。

PARAGRAPH 2

❶One of the oldest theories developed and later modified by earlier scholars points to the theory of a disastrous event.

❷This holds that a particular geological event wiped out the Mayan people.

❸The theory is still quite common with some researchers.

❹British archaeologist Euan Mackie proposed an earthquake theory in his article published in 1961, which was relatively a long time ago.

❺However, some findings such as the hundred-year time frame of destruction, along with the different city abandonment periods, call for many anthropologists to conduct more research concerning this possible theory.

❻Surely, if a massive earthquake, volcanic eruption or large tidal wave had been the cause, the city-states would all have been abandoned simultaneously.

❼The following theory deals with warfare.

❽It was first believed that the Maya was a peaceful culture; however, stone carvings depicting war between city-states over resources, land, and prestige found otherwise.

❾It is possible that the destruction of "Dos Pilas," now located in Petén, Guatemala, around 750 AD could have started a domino effect, mainly because trade and other important operations between the city-states collapsed due to fear of aggression.

❶先代の学者によって提唱され、後に修正された最も初期の説の一つは、壊滅的な出来事に目を向けている。

❷この説によると、ある地質学的な出来事が、マヤ人を全滅させたというのだ。

❸この説は、現在でも一部の研究者に支持されている。

❹イギリス人考古学者Euan Mackieは、比較的古い1961年に発表の論文で、地震によってマヤ文明が滅びたのだと提唱した。

❺しかしながら、都市を放棄した時期がバラバラであり、文明の崩壊が100年にわたって生じたことが調査で判明したため、この説に関しては人類学者によるさらなる研究が必要である。

❻もし巨大地震や火山噴火、津波が生じていれば、人々は同時に都市国家を捨てていただろう。

❼次の説は武力衝突に言及している。

❽マヤの人々は平和的な文化を有していたと考えられていたが、資源、土地、そして名声をめぐる都市国家間の争いを描いた石の彫刻が出てきたことによって、そうではないことがわかった。

❾750年頃のDos Pilas（現在のグアテマラ、ペテン県にある）の崩壊が波及効果をもたらした可能性が考えられ、その主な理由は、侵略の恐怖により、主に都市国家間の通商その他の重要な活動が破たんしたというものだ。

＊語句問題に出る可能性あり

❶□*modify X：Xを修正する
□point to X：Xを指摘する
□disastrous：壊滅的な

❷□hold that SV：～と述べる
□geological：地質学的な
□wipe out X：Xを全滅させる

❹□tidal：潮の

❺□time frame：時間の枠
□along with X：Xがあるので、Xとともに
□abandonment：放棄
□call for X to V：Xに～することを要求する
□concerning X：Xに関して

❻□*simultaneously：同時に

❼□deal with X：Xを扱う
□warfare：武力衝突

❽□carving：彫刻
□depict X：Xを描く
□prestige：名声
□[find/think/believe] otherwise：そうではないと思う
(例) Most people believe he is right, but I think otherwise.
(ほとんどの人は彼が正しいと思っているが、私はそうは思わない)

❾□domino effect：波及効果

PARAGRAPH 3

❶These are just two of the possible theories that could have occurred, which leads us to the theory of over-population.

❷Proponents of this theory include Professor Richard B. Gill.

❸He argues that as civilizations advanced and cities grew, so did their population.

❹The cities started to suffer from severe food supply shortages.

❺This extreme and continuous scarcity of food led to the fall of the civilization.

❻Professor Arthur A. Demarest proposed yet another theory, which involves civil discontent.

❼His findings through stone art have shown that the Maya were one of the most volatile, unstable state-level societies in the New World, especially after 600 AD.

❽The working class of the Mayan society faced issues such as being overworked, underfed, and competing in an ever-growing social caste.

❾Many people also suffered from great pressure and intensive labor to build increasingly elaborate monuments for authorities.

❿All of these resulted in extreme fatigue building up in the working class and this could no doubt provide a cause for rebellion in the lower echelons.

❶これらの説は、何が起こり得たかを説明する説のほんの2つにすぎない。次に人口過剰説を紹介しよう。

❷この説を支持する研究者の一人がRichard B. Gill教授である。

❸教授によると、文明が進歩し都市が成長するにつれて人口も増加した。

❹都市は深刻な食料不足に悩まされ始めた。

❺この極度の食料不足が続いたことにより、文明の衰退につながった。

❻一方、Arthur A. Demarest教授は、市民の不満に関わる別の説を提唱した。

❼教授の石細工の研究によると、特に600年以降、マヤ文明は新世界で最も突発的な変化が生じやすい、不安定な国家社会の1つであったというのだ。

❽マヤの労働者階級の人々は、過重労働、栄養不足、そしてますます激しさを増す社会階級内の競争などの問題に直面していた。

❾また、多くの人々はますます精巧さを増す、支配者のための記念建造物建設の強制や、激しい労働に苦しんでいた。

❿その結果、労働者階級の人々は極度に疲弊し、下層部が反乱を起こした可能性もある。

＊語句問題に出る可能性あり

❷ □ *proponent：支持者

❹ □ food (supply) shortages：食料不足

❺ □ *scarcity：不足

❻ □ yet another：さらに別の（yetは「さらに」の意味）
□ *discontent：不満

❼ □ *volatile：不安定な、突発的な変化が生じやすい

❽ □ face X：Xに直面する【動詞】
□ underfed：十分に食料を与えられていない【形容詞】
□ caste：階級

❾ □ *intensive：激しい
□ elaborate：精巧な
□ authority：支配者

❿ □ *fatigue：疲労
□ *rebellion：反乱
□ echelon：階層

❸ as civilizations advanced and cities grew, so did their population → … , their population grew too
「…が成長するにつれて、人口も増えた」 as SV … , so SV ～で「…するにつれて、～する」という意味。so SV ～のSVは疑問文の語順になることがある。
（例）I like coffee, and so does she.「私はコーヒーが好きですが、彼女もそうです。」

PARAGRAPH 4

❶Last but not least is the longest-standing theory that is based on environmental change.

❷The article proposed by Professor Douglas Kennett expounded on this through the possibility of an extended drought between 1020 and 1100 AD due to sudden climate change, resulting in the final collapse.

❸As the Mayans only cultivated a limited range of crops, with some hunting and fishing to make up for their food supply, a sudden climate change could have easily caused the destruction of their food supply.

❹Some scenarios include drought, with record high temperatures being seen towards the end of their civilization, thus further reducing the tight margins of food available for these barely subsisting cities.

❺The poor replenishment of the soil may have also caused these environmental factors to manifest more significantly, as runoff and nutrient levels were just not enough to provide the yields that were needed to keep the population fed.

❶最後に述べるが決して軽んじるべきでないのが、最も長く支持されてきた、環境変化を根拠とした説だ。

❷Douglas Kennett教授により発表された論文は、1020年から1100年まで続いた急激な気候変動を起因とする、文明の最終的な崩壊につながる長期的干ばつをもって、これ（環境変化を根拠とした説）を詳説している。

❸マヤの人々は限られた種類の農作物しか栽培せず、足りない食料を補うために狩猟や漁業を営んでいた。したがって、急激な気候変動が、食料供給を容易に崩壊させた可能性があるのだ。

❹いくつかのシナリオでは、彼らの文明の末期にかけて見られた記録的な高温を伴う干ばつが、かろうじて持ちこたえていた都市に残されたわずかな食料備蓄を、さらに減少させたとしている。

❺また、地表を流れる雨水や栄養分の水準が、人口を養うために必要であった収穫高を確保するのに全く十分ではなかったため、土壌の補充の不足が、環境要因をより顕著に表面化させたのかもしれない。

＊語句問題に出る可能性あり

❶ □ last but not least：最後だが重要である
□ long-standing：長い間存在する

❷ □ article：論文
□ *expound on X：Xを細かく説明する
□ *drought：干ばつ

❸ □ crop：農作物
□ make up for X：Xを補う

❹ □ drought：干ばつ
□ the tight margins of food：非常にわずかな食料
□ margin：ギリギリの状態
□ barely：かろうじて
□ *subsist：なんとか生き延びる

❺ □ replenishment：新たに供給すること（the poor replenishment of the soil は「新しい土壌がもたらされることがほとんどなかった」という意味）
□ *manifest：表面化する、顕在化する
□ runoff：地表を流れる雨水
□ *yield：収穫高
□ keep the population fed → feed X：Xに食料を与える

❹ thus further reducing
→thus＋現在分詞「このようにして～する（した）」

PARAGRAPH 5

❶Truly, there is little consensus on which theory could have been the decisive factor to the Mayan collapse.

❷Perhaps the combination of these proposed theories or even the discovery of the unknown truth may reveal this mystery.

❸It can be seen that many of the challenges the Mayan civilization faced ages ago are quite similar to those found in our society today.

❹With the advancement of technology, it is conceivable that we may solve the mystery in time, leading us to the guidance of our very own civilization and steering us away from our very own extinction.

❶実のところ、どの説がマヤ文明崩壊の決定的な要因だったのかについて、意見の一致はほとんど見られない。

❷もしかすると、これまで提示された説の組み合わせ、または未知なる真実の発見が、この謎を明らかにするかもしれない。

❸マヤ文明がはるか昔に直面した課題の多くは、今日の我々の社会に見られる問題とかなり似ていることがわかる。

❹技術の進歩により、ゆくゆくは、マヤ文明崩壊の謎を解明する可能性が考えられる。謎の解明は、我々を自らの文明の指針に導き、そして人類を滅亡から救うであろう。

＊語句問題に出る可能性あり

❶ □ *consensus on X：Xに関する意見の一致
□ decisive：決定的な

❷ □ reveal X：Xを明らかにする

❸ □ *challenge：困難

❹ □ *conceivable：考えうる
□ in time：ゆくゆくは
□ steer X away from Y：XをYからそらす
□ *extinction：絶滅

❸ those found in ... → those (challenges) found in ...
「those＋修飾語」は「the 複数名詞＋修飾語」の代用形。

Unit 2 本試験形式問題演習

リーディング問題6 | Zoology

BIRD COLONIES

問題演習の流れ

- □ 解答時間は17分を目標にしましょう。
- □ 英文 ⇒ 問題 ⇒ 正解・解説レクチャー ⇒ 訳 という流れで学習します。
- □ 3回解けるように、3回分のマークシートを各問題に用意しています。解く日付を記入してからマークしてください。

Web解答方法

- □ 本試験では各選択肢の左に表示されるマークをクリックして解答します。本試験と同様の方法で取り組みたい場合は、Webで解答できます。
- □ インターネットのつながるパソコン・スマートフォンで、以下のサイトにアクセスしてWeb上で解答してください。

extester.com

- □ 操作方法は、p.13 ～ 14の「USA Club Web学習の使い方」をご参照ください。

学習の記録

学習開始日	年　　月　　日	学習終了日	年　　月　　日
学習開始日	年　　月　　日	学習終了日	年　　月　　日
学習開始日	年　　月　　日	学習終了日	年　　月　　日

リーディング問題 6　英文

BIRD COLONIES

The definition of "colonies" when referring to birds differs greatly from when referring to humans. When used for birds, it indicates species of birds that build their nests in a communal, shared environment and display common traits that have been adapted to aid survivability. The size of these colonies can vary by orders of magnitude, with some limited to just a few breeding pairs, while others contain hundreds of thousands of birds. The variability in size may be specific to the species although climate factors and environmental conditions such as available space and feeding grounds also restrict the size of colonies. It is important for birds to consider where to form their colonies in consideration of various factors, which could be to their advantage.

Due to the avian abilities of most birds, their colonies are most often found in high, rocky, and inaccessible locations that would be extremely difficult for land-based predators to attack. This is why islands with steep cliffs or secluded mountainsides are the most popular colony locations for some bird species. These birds may return to the same, intact nesting locations over many years and even reuse the same nest and/or nesting materials. The colonies in such locations, however, can be easily spotted by the returning birds as there is a constant hustle and bustle of birds coming and going. A variety of mating rituals can be seen and the passionate cries of the hungry young can also be heard. In order to make sure birds do not lose their own nests, which all look quite similar, they leave themselves subtle visual clues to light the way home, though how exactly they identify their own nests is yet to be discovered.

Although it is often the case that birds create their nests in isolated locations, some birds are known to eschew isolation for safety in numbers. Depending on the availability of land and nesting techniques, some birds such as those belonging to the family of Laridae, or more commonly known as terns, may nest out on open ground within only a few feet or inches of each other. Under situations where natural enemies are not around, these birds could have more convenient access to their food resources that come in greater abundance and variety. Interestingly, these colonies are not made up of just one species. In certain instances, it is mutually beneficial for different species of birds to nest in close proximity to one another, making the best possible use of the local resources. Triangle Island in Canada, for instance, is known to be co-habited by gulls, tufted puffins, auks, auklets, and some other species. As long as competition for the resources does not become too fierce, these multi-species colonies can remain quite stable.

Some of the greatest merits of birds forming themselves into colonies are quite obvious. They are able to better protect their vulnerable offspring, as there are more birds of a mature age which could keep a lookout and raise the alarm if anything happens, as well as then taking the offensive against predators with their greater numbers. Mockingbirds found in North America are a good example. When their offspring are exposed to danger by predators, the adults cooperatively attack the predators or try to distract their attention from the young. This behavior is often referred to as "mobbing," which can be seen in many bird species. Besides mobbing, other benefits of forming an assemblage are not ones that would normally come to mind. Firstly, in the event of a mating partner's death there are still many more readily available partners in close vicinity to ensure continued breeding. The inborn nature of "promiscuity" observed in some species does contribute to the survival of a colony. Secondly, and sadly, by having large numbers of eggs and young chicks around, even if a predator were to come looking for food, they might get their fill before reaching for other birds' offspring. Essentially, the predators might become full on devouring a certain proportion of offspring, but there will always be more to continue the colony.

While there are clear advantages, no situation is without its disadvantages. As a colony grows, overconsumption of food sources may outstrip the available resources, putting great pressure on the food supply and thus leading to a potential colony collapse. This has been seen to be the case in larger colonies, but outside influences, such as climate shifts, human destruction of habitats, and natural disasters can cause similar problems with the food supply regardless of the size of the colony. By being together in a large group, such huge events could potentially wipe out the entire colony. Add to this the increased danger of disease caused by the unsanitary conditions of bird colonies and the ease with which that disease could spread at close quarters. This means that a single sick bird could transmit its illness colony-wide very easily, wiping it out within a short time. These and some other disadvantages of living in a colony make scholars doubt the overall benefits of bird colonies; however, recurring evolutionary behavior found in various different bird species provides them with an indication that the advantages of the colonies outweigh the disadvantages.

1. According to paragraph 1, all of the following determine the size of a bird colony EXCEPT

(A) the size of the birds
(B) climate conditions
(C) available land
(D) the species of the birds

PARAGRAPH 1

The definition of “colonies” when referring to birds differs greatly from when referring to humans. When used for birds, it indicates species of birds that build their nests in a communal, shared environment and display common traits that have been adapted to aid survivability. The size of these colonies can vary by orders of magnitude, with some limited to just a few breeding pairs, while others contain hundreds of thousands of birds. The variability in size may be specific to the species although climate factors and environmental conditions such as available space and feeding grounds also restrict the size of colonies. It is important for birds to consider where to form their colonies in consideration of various factors, which could be to their advantage.

2. In paragraph 2, the word "rituals" is closest in meaning to

(A) styles
(B) patterns
(C) strategies
(D) rules

3. According to paragraph 2, which of the following best describes how birds identify their nests?

(A) They look for similar nests that they have built.
(B) Distinct cries from offspring provide audible guidance.
(C) They leave a sign that helps them distinguish their nest.
(D) Sunlight serves as a navigation tool that shows the right position.

PARAGRAPH 2

Due to the avian abilities of most birds, their colonies are most often found in high, rocky, and inaccessible locations that would be extremely difficult for land-based predators to attack. This is why islands with steep cliffs or secluded mountainsides are the most popular colony locations for some bird species. These birds may return to the same, intact nesting locations over many years and even reuse the same nest and/or nesting materials. The colonies in such locations, however, can be easily spotted by the returning birds as there is a constant hustle and bustle of birds coming and going. A variety of mating rituals can be seen and the passionate cries of the hungry young can also be heard. In order to make sure birds do not lose their own nests, which all look quite similar, they leave themselves subtle visual clues to light the way home, though how exactly they identify their own nests is yet to be discovered.

4. What is one of the characteristics of the Laridae mentioned in paragraph 3?

(A) It has more advanced nest-making techniques than other birds.
(B) It creates tightly packed nests that shelter birds from a single species.
(C) It does not necessarily seek isolated areas to make a nest.
(D) Its nests are more widely found than those of other species.

5. In paragraph 3, Triangle Island in Canada was mentioned in order to

(A) show the importance of mutual help among different species for better survival
(B) identify what animals are living together on the island
(C) explain how several different animals are utilizing available food in the same area
(D) bring up an example of a multi-species colony that is effectively consuming resources

PARAGRAPH 3

Although it is often the case that birds create their nests in isolated locations, some birds are known to eschew isolation for safety in numbers. Depending on the availability of land and nesting techniques, some birds such as those belonging to the family of Laridae, or more commonly known as terns, may nest out on open ground within only a few feet or inches of each other. Under situations where natural enemies are not around, these birds could have more convenient access to their food resources that come in greater abundance and variety. Interestingly, these colonies are not made up of just one species. In certain instances, it is mutually beneficial for different species of birds to nest in close proximity to one another, making the best possible use of the local resources. Triangle Island in Canada, for instance, is known to be co-habited by gulls, tufted puffins, auks, auklets, and some other species. As long as competition for the resources does not become too fierce, these multi-species colonies can remain quite stable.

6. According to paragraph 4, the following are protection techniques for mockingbirds EXCEPT

(A) emitting an alarm signal when a potential threat has been detected
(B) physically attacking predators as a group
(C) trying to turn the predators' attention away from offspring
(D) distracting predators and guiding them into secluded areas

7. Which of the sentences below best expresses the essential information in the highlighted sentence in the passage? Incorrect choices change the meaning in important ways or leave out essential information.

(A) Even if some young birds are eaten by predators, those that survive will contribute to the existence of the colony.
(B) It is essential that the colony keep giving birth to the young so that enough of them survive and grow.
(C) Predators always become satisfied after eating a certain number of young birds, which ensures the colony's safety.
(D) There are always some predators that are aiming to hunt young birds only, threatening the continuity of the colony.

PARAGRAPH 4

Some of the greatest merits of birds forming themselves into colonies are quite obvious. They are able to better protect their vulnerable offspring, as there are more birds of a mature age which could keep a lookout and raise the alarm if anything happens, as well as then taking the offensive against predators with their greater numbers. Mockingbirds found in North America are a good example. When their offspring are exposed to danger by predators, the adults cooperatively attack the predators or try to distract their attention from the young. This behavior is often referred to as "mobbing," which can be seen in many bird species. Besides mobbing, other benefits of forming an assemblage are not ones that would normally come to mind. Firstly, in the event of a mating partner's death there are still many more readily available partners in close vicinity to ensure continued breeding. The inborn nature of "promiscuity" observed in some species does contribute to the survival of a colony. Secondly, and sadly, by having large numbers of eggs and young chicks around, even if a predator were to come looking for food, they might get their fill before reaching for other birds' offspring. Essentially, the predators might become full on devouring a certain proportion of offspring, but there will always be more to continue the colony.

8. According to paragraph 5, which of the following is true about a disease that spreads in a bird colony?

(A) A severe disease can kill as many as one fourth of the birds in a colony.
(B) A single infection has the potential to wipe out the entire colony.
(C) It can be spread even when the colony is clean.
(D) Such a disease is generally not as dangerous as climate shifts or natural disasters.

PARAGRAPH 5

While there are clear advantages, no situation is without its disadvantages. As a colony grows, overconsumption of food sources may outstrip the available resources, putting great pressure on the food supply and thus leading to a potential colony collapse. This has been seen to be the case in larger colonies, but outside influences, such as climate shifts, human destruction of habitats, and natural disasters can cause similar problems with the food supply regardless of the size of the colony. By being together in a large group, such huge events could potentially wipe out the entire colony. Add to this the increased danger of disease caused by the unsanitary conditions of bird colonies and the ease with which that disease could spread at close quarters. This means that a single sick bird could transmit its illness colony-wide very easily, wiping it out within a short time. These and some other disadvantages of living in a colony make scholars doubt the overall benefits of bird colonies; however, recurring evolutionary behavior found in various different bird species provides them with an indication that the advantages of the colonies outweigh the disadvantages.

9. Look at the four squares [■] that indicate where the following sentence could be added to the passage.

In fact, some of these locations are highly secure and no predators can successfully spot the nests for years.

Where would the sentence best fit?

PARAGRAPH 2

Due to the avian abilities of most birds, their colonies are most often found in high, rocky, and inaccessible locations that would be extremely difficult for land-based predators to attack. This is why islands with steep cliffs or secluded mountainsides are the most popular colony locations for some bird species. **A** These birds may return to the same, intact nesting locations over many years and even reuse the same nest and/or nesting materials. **B** The colonies in such locations, however, can be easily spotted by the returning birds as there is a constant hustle and bustle of birds coming and going. **C** A variety of mating rituals can be seen and the passionate cries of the hungry young can also be heard. **D** In order to make sure birds do not lose their own nests, which all look quite similar, they leave themselves subtle visual clues to light the way home, though how exactly they identify their own nests is yet to be discovered.

10. Directions: An introductory sentence containing a brief summary of the passage is provided below. Complete the summary by selecting the best THREE answer choices that express the main ideas of the passage.

The variation in size, species, and composition of large bird colonies has its advantages and disadvantages respectively.

Answer Choices

(A) Many birds form colonies in isolated places and thus can return to the same old nest, whereas some species prefer open fields for making nests.

(B) Bird colonies increase the likelihood of birds' survival by allowing them to cooperatively counterattack their enemies and by making it easy to find a mate.

(C) The advantages of large-scale colonies definitely outweigh the disadvantages of them and therefore they are more sustainable than secluded small groups.

(D) Colonies made up of multiple species are more widely found because those species can better utilize environmental resources.

(E) Although forming a colony may cause a great number of problems which could be disastrous, its benefits do seem to surpass the demerits.

(F) Evolutionary behaviors amongst bird species have proven to be the key to the colony's sustainability and survivability.

リーディング問題 6

正解一覧 ································ 244
解説レクチャー ············ 244~255
訳 ································ 256~265

1. **(A)** 2. **(B)** 3. **(C)** 4. **(C)** 5. **(D)**
6. **(D)** 7. **(A)** 8. **(B)** 9. **(B)** 10. **(A) (B) (E)**

第1段落｜問1解説レクチャー

❶The definition of "colonies" when referring to birds differs greatly from when referring to humans. ❷When used for birds, it indicates species of birds that build their nests in a communal, shared environment and display common traits that have been adapted to aid survivability. ❸The size of these colonies can vary by orders of magnitude, with some limited to just a few breeding pairs, while others contain hundreds of thousands of birds. ❹The variability in size may be specific to the species although climate factors and environmental conditions such as available space and feeding grounds also restrict the size of colonies. ❺It is important for birds to consider where to form their colonies in consideration of various factors, which could be to their advantage.

1. According to paragraph 1, all of the following determine the size of a bird colony EXCEPT

(A) the size of the birds
(B) climate conditions
(C) available land
(D) the species of the birds

第1段落によると、鳥のコロニーの大きさを決定しないものは次の中でどれですか。

(A) 鳥の大きさ
(B) 気候条件
(C) 利用可能な土地
(D) 鳥の種

問1は「鳥のコロニーの大きさを決定づける要因」ではないものを問うています。まず❶～❷は「コロニーの定義」についてなので「大きさ」とは無関係です。❸で大きさに関する記述が登場しますが、それを決める要因について触れているのは❹です。❹は「大きさのばらつきは、種に固有のものであるかもしれないが、気候要因や鳥が活用できる空間や餌場などといった環境条件もまた、コロニーの大きさを制限する」と述べています。(A)は本文に記述がないのでおそらく正解ですが、念のために(B)～(D)が一致するかどうかを確かめましょう。❹の中で、(B)はclimate factors、(C)はavailable space and feeding grounds、(D)はThe variability in size may be specific to the speciesという箇所にそれぞれ一致します。よって(A)が正解です。❺の内容は問1に影響しませんが、意味を確認してから次の段落に進みましょう。

第２段落｜問 2~3 解説レクチャー

❶Due to the avian abilities of most birds, their colonies are most often found in high, rocky, and inaccessible locations that would be extremely difficult for land-based predators to attack. ❷This is why islands with steep cliffs or secluded mountainsides are the most popular colony locations for some bird species. ❸These birds may return to the same, intact nesting locations over many years and even reuse the same nest and/or nesting materials. ❹The colonies in such locations, however, can be easily spotted by the returning birds as there is a constant hustle and bustle of birds coming and going. ❺A variety of mating rituals can be seen and the passionate cries of the hungry young can also be heard. ❻In order to make sure birds do not lose their own nests, which all look quite similar, they leave themselves subtle visual clues to light the way home, though how exactly they identify their own nests is yet to be discovered.

2. In paragraph 2, the word "rituals" is closest in meaning to

(A) styles
(B) patterns
(C) strategies
(D) rules

第２段落のritualsと最も近い意味のものはどれですか。

(A) 様式
(B) パターン
(C) 戦略
(D) 規則

問２のこの文脈におけるritualsは「習慣的行為」という意味なので、(B) patternsが正解です。なお、ritualには「儀式」という意味もありますので覚えておきましょう。

3. According to paragraph 2, which of the following best describes how birds identify their nests?

(A) They look for similar nests that they have built.
(B) Distinct cries from offspring provide audible guidance.
(C) They leave a sign that helps them distinguish their nest.
(D) Sunlight serves as a navigation tool that shows the right position.

第2段落によると、鳥が自分の巣を特定する方法を最もよく表しているのはどれですか。

(A) 彼らは自分たちが作った巣と似ている巣を探す。
(B) 子どもの泣き声を聞き分けて探す。
(C) 彼らは巣を見分ける手助けとなるしるしを残す。
(D) 日光が、正確な位置を示すナビの役割を果たす。

問3は「鳥がどのように自分の巣を特定するか」を問うています。参照箇所を探しましょう。❶～❷には「捕食者に襲われない場所に鳥が巣を作る」とあります。続く❸には「以前の巣や巣の材料を再利用することさえある」とあります。❹には「そのような場所のコロニーは常に鳥が行き交っているため、戻ってくる鳥はコロニーの場所を簡単に突き止めることができる」とあります。問3は「コロニー」ではなく「自分の巣」をどのように特定するのかを問うています。つまりここは解答の参照箇所ではありません。❺は具体的にコロニーの様子を描写しています。よって、❻が解答の参照箇所になります。they leave themselves subtle visual clues to light the way home「鳥は巣への道を示すかすかな視覚的手がかりを残す」とあるので、(C)が正解です。文中のclueをsignと言い換えています。

□ audible:はっきりと聞こえる

第3段落｜問4～5 解説レクチャー

❶Although it is often the case that birds create their nests in isolated locations, some birds are known to eschew isolation for safety in numbers. ❷Depending on the availability of land and nesting techniques, some birds such as those belonging to the family of Laridae, or more commonly known as terns, may nest out on open ground within only a few feet or inches of each other. ❸Under situations where natural enemies are not around, these birds could have more convenient access to their food resources that come in greater abundance and variety. ❹Interestingly, these colonies are not made up of just one species. ❺In certain instances, it is mutually beneficial for different species of birds to nest in close proximity to one another, making the best possible use of the local resources. ❻Triangle Island in Canada, for instance, is known to be co-habited by gulls, tufted puffins, auks, auklets, and some other species. ❼As long as competition for the resources does not become too fierce, these multi-species colonies can remain quite stable.

4. What is one of the characteristics of the Laridae mentioned in paragraph 3?

(A) It has more advanced nest-making techniques than other birds.
(B) It creates tightly packed nests that shelter birds from a single species.
(C) It does not necessarily seek isolated areas to make a nest.
(D) Its nests are more widely found than those of other species.

第3段落で述べられているカモメ科の特徴の1つは何ですか。

(A) 他の鳥よりも、巣を作るための手法が進んでいる。
(B) ただ1つの種から鳥を守るよう、ひしめき合って巣を作る。
(C) 巣作りに必ずしも孤立した場所を探すわけではない。
(D) その巣は、他の種の鳥の巣よりも広い範囲で見られる。

問4は「カモメ科の特徴の1つ」を問うています。Laridaeというキーワードを探しながら、本文を読みましょう。❶には「数が多いことによる安全性を求め、一部の鳥は孤立を避けることで知られている」とあります。❷でLaridaeが登場します。「お互い数フィートあるいは数インチしか離れていない開けた土地に巣を作る」と書いてあります。参照箇所が見つかったので、選択肢を確認してみましょう。(A)は本文に記述がありません。(B)はthat shelter birds from a single speciesが本文に一致しません。(C)は「巣作りに必ずしも孤立した場所を探すわけではない」とあり、本文の❷「開けた土地で巣を作る」に一致します。よって(C)が正解です。(D)のような比較は本文に記述がありません。

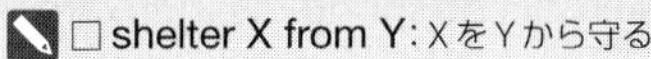

□ shelter X from Y: XをYから守る

5. In paragraph 3, Triangle Island in Canada was mentioned in order to

(A) show the importance of mutual help among different species for better survival
(B) identify what animals are living together on the island
(C) explain how several different animals are utilizing available food in the same area
(D) bring up an example of a multi-species colony that is effectively consuming resources

第3段落において、なぜカナダのTriangle Islandに言及したのですか。

(A) よりよく生き残るために、異種同士で互いに助け合うことの重要性を示すため
(B) その島でどの動物がともに暮らしているのかを特定するため
(C) 数種類の異なる動物が、同一地域で手に入る食料をどのように利用しているのかを説明するため
(D) 資源を効果的に消費している、多種から成るコロニーの例を挙げるため

問5は「Triangle Islandに言及している理由」を問うています。まずはTriangle Islandというキーワードを探しながら、読み進めましょう。❸には「これらの鳥は量、種類ともに豊富な食料資源をより簡単に手に入れることができる」とあります。❹〜❺には「異なる種の鳥が、近くで巣を作ることがある」とあります。そして❻でTriangle Islandが登場します。for instanceにより、❻が具体例であることがわかるので、(D)が正解です。他の選択肢には「例」という記述がありません。

□utilize X: Xを活用する　□bring up X: X(例など)を持ち出す

第4段落｜問6〜7 解説レクチャー

❶Some of the greatest merits of birds forming themselves into colonies are quite obvious. ❷They are able to better protect their vulnerable offspring, as there are more birds of a mature age which could keep a lookout and raise the alarm if anything happens, as well as then taking the offensive against predators with their greater numbers. ❸Mockingbirds found in North America are a good example. ❹When their offspring are exposed to danger by predators, the adults cooperatively attack the predators or try to distract their attention from the young. ❺This behavior is often referred to as "mobbing," which can be seen in many bird species. ❻Besides mobbing, other benefits of forming an assemblage are not ones that would normally come to mind. ❼Firstly, in the event of a mating partner's death there are still many more readily available partners in close vicinity to ensure continued breeding. ❽The inborn nature of "promiscuity" observed in some species does contribute to the survival of a colony. ❾Secondly, and sadly, by having large numbers of eggs and young chicks around, even if a predator were to come looking for food, they might get their fill before reaching for other birds' offspring. ❿Essentially, the predators might become full on devouring a certain proportion of offspring, but there will always be more to continue the colony.

6. According to paragraph 4, the following are protection techniques for mockingbirds EXCEPT

(A) emitting an alarm signal when a potential threat has been detected
(B) physically attacking predators as a group
(C) trying to turn the predators' attention away from offspring
(D) distracting predators and guiding them into secluded areas

第4段落によると、次の中でマネシツグミの防御策でないものはどれですか。

(A) 脅威になりそうなものが感知されたとき警告する
(B) 捕食動物を集団で物理的に攻撃する
(C) 捕食動物の注意を子どもからそらそうとする
(D) 捕食動物の気を散らし、遠く離れた場所へと誘導する

問6は「マネシツグミの防御策ではないもの」を問うています。mockingbirdsというキーワードを探しながら読みましょう。まず、❶でコロニーには明らかなメリットがあることが示されます。❷には、その具体例として「見張りをし、何か起こったら注意を呼びかけることができる十分に成長した鳥の数が多いので、彼らはひ弱な子どもを一層守ることができる。また、数的優位を利用して捕食動物に対して攻勢に出ることができる」とあります。❷の具体例として❸ではmockingbirdsが登場します。❹には「子どもが危険にさらされたとき、集団で外敵を攻撃し、子どもから気をそらすよう仕向ける」とあります。(A)は❷に一致します。❷のif anything happensが(A)のwhen a potential threat has been detectedに言い換えられています。(B)は❹のcooperatively attack the predatorsに一致します。cooperativelyがas a groupに言い換えられています。(C)は❹に一致します。distractがturn ... away、the youngがoffspringに言い換えられています。(D)「遠く離れた場所へと誘導する」という記述はありません。よって(D)が正解です。

□ emit X: Xを放出する　□ threat: 脅威　□ detect X: Xを感知する

7. Which of the sentences below best expresses the essential information in the highlighted sentence in the passage? Incorrect choices change the meaning in important ways or leave out essential information.

(A) Even if some young birds are eaten by predators, those that survive will contribute to the existence of the colony.
(B) It is essential that the colony keep giving birth to the young so that enough of them survive and grow.

(C) Predators always become satisfied after eating a certain number of young birds, which ensures the colony's safety.
(D) There are always some predators that are aiming to hunt young birds only, threatening the continuity of the colony.

次のうちどの文が、ハイライト表示した文の重要な情報を最もよく表していますか。不正解の選択肢は、意味を大きく変えたり、重要な情報を抜かしたりしています。

(A) たとえ幼い鳥が捕食動物に食べられたとしても、生き残ったものがコロニーの存続に貢献する。
(B) 十分な数の子どもが生き残って成長できるように、コロニーの鳥が子どもを生み続けることが不可欠である。
(C) 捕食動物は特定の数の幼い鳥を食べたら必ず満足するが、これがコロニーの安全を保証している。
(D) 子どものみを捕らえることを目的とする捕食動物が常に存在し、コロニーの継続を脅かしている。

⑩は「本質的には、捕食動物は一定数の子どもをむさぼり食い満腹になるかもしれないが、コロニーを存続させられるだけのさらに多くの子どもが常にいる」という意味です。ポイントは、食べられても、十分な数の子どもが残るということです。この内容に最も近いものは(A)です。devouringをeatenで、moreをthose that surviveで、continue the colonyをcontribute to the existence of the colonyで言い換えています。(B)は「子どもが食べられても」という条件がありません。(C)と(D)は「食べられなかった子どもがコロニーを存続させる」という記述がありません。特に(D)の「子どものみ」という記述は明らかに不適当です。よって(A)が正解です。

□so that SV:〜するようにするために(目的)　□threat X: Xを脅かす

第5段落｜問8解説レクチャー

❶While there are clear advantages, no situation is without its disadvantages. ❷As a colony grows, overconsumption of food sources may outstrip the available resources, putting great pressure on the food supply and thus leading to a potential colony collapse. ❸This has been seen to be the case in larger colonies, but outside influences, such as climate shifts, human destruction of habitats, and natural disasters can cause similar problems with the food supply regardless of the size of the colony. ❹By being together in a large group, such huge events could potentially wipe out the entire colony. ❺Add to this the increased danger of disease caused by the unsanitary conditions of bird colonies and the ease with which that disease could spread at close quarters. ❻This means that a single sick bird could transmit its illness colony-wide very easily, wiping it out within a short time. ❼These and some other disadvantages of living in a colony make scholars doubt the overall benefits of bird colonies; however, recurring evolutionary behavior found in various different bird species provides them with an indication that the advantages of the colonies outweigh the disadvantages.

8. According to paragraph 5, which of the following is true about a disease that spreads in a bird colony?

(A) A severe disease can kill as many as one fourth of the birds in a colony.
(B) A single infection has the potential to wipe out the entire colony.
(C) It can be spread even when the colony is clean.
(D) Such a disease is generally not as dangerous as climate shifts or natural disasters.

第5段落によると、次の中で鳥のコロニーで広がる病気に関して正しいものはどれですか。

(A) 重い病気は、コロニーの4分の1もの鳥を殺すことがある。
(B) たった1つの感染が、コロニー全体を絶滅させる可能性がある。
(C) 病気はコロニーが衛生的であっても広がることがある。
(D) そのような病気は一般的に、気候変動や自然災害ほど危険ではない。

問8は「コロニー内に広がる病気に関しての正しい記述」を問うています。❶～❹には「病気」に関する記述がないので、❺と❻の内容が参照箇所となります。❺には「コロニーでは病気が広がりやすい」とあります。また、❻には「一羽の鳥がコロニー全体に病気を広げ、結果として短期間でコロニーを簡単に絶滅させてしまうかもしれない」と書いてあります。では選択肢を見てみましょう。(A)のone fourthという具体的な数字は本文にないので誤りです。(B)は、❻に一致します。a single sick birdをa single infectionで、couldをhas the potentialで、colony-wideをentire colonyで言い換えていますね。(C)は「コロニーが衛生的であっても」という状況が本文にないので誤りです。(D)のように病気と他のものを比較している箇所は見当たらないので、誤りです。よって、正解は(B)です。❼の内容は問8に影響しませんが、内容を確認してから次に進みましょう。

問9解説レクチャー

9. Look at the four squares [■] that indicate where the following sentence could be added to the passage.

In fact, some of these locations are highly secure and no predators can successfully spot the nests for years.

Where would the sentence best fit?

❶Due to the avian abilities of most birds, their colonies are most often found in high, rocky, and inaccessible locations that would be extremely difficult for land-based predators to attack. ❷This is why islands with steep cliffs or secluded mountainsides are the most popular colony locations for some bird species. **A** ❸These birds may return to the same, intact nesting locations over many years and even reuse the same nest and/or nesting materials. **B** ❹The colonies in such locations, however, can be easily spotted by the returning birds as there is a constant hustle and bustle of birds coming and going. **C** ❺A variety of mating rituals can be seen and the passionate cries of the hungry young can also be heard. **D** ❻In order to make sure birds do not lose their own nests, which all look quite similar, they leave themselves subtle visual clues to light the way home, though how exactly they identify their own nests is yet to be discovered.

次の文章が以下のパッセージで追加されうる箇所を示す4つの■を見てください。

事実、これらの場所のいくつかは非常に安全で、捕食動物は何年もの間、巣を見つけることができない。

この文章は、どこに置くのが最もよいですか。

問9は文挿入問題です。選択肢のthese locationsという指示語に注目できれば、直前の文に「場所」に関する記述が来るとわかります。❷には「険しい崖や人里離れた山腹を持つ島」という「場所」に関する記述があります。ところが、❷のsome bird speciesを受けて、❸ではThese birdsと書いています。ですのでAに挿入文を入れると、❸のThese birdsの指示対象がわからなくなるため誤りです。さて、❸には「手付かずのまま残っている同じ営巣地」や「同じ巣」という「場所」に関する記述もあります。よって❸と挿入文は論理的につながります。さらに、❹の「ところが、戻ってくる鳥はコロニーの場所を簡単に突き止めることができる」という内容は、挿入文の「捕食動物は巣を見つけることができない」という内容と対比されています。よってBが正解です。

問10解説レクチャー

10. Directions: An introductory sentence containing a brief summary of the passage is provided below. Complete the summary by selecting the best THREE answer choices that express the main ideas of the passage.

The variation in size, species, and composition of large bird colonies has its advantages and disadvantages respectively.

(A) Many birds form colonies in isolated places and thus can return to the same old nest, whereas some species prefer open fields for making nests.
(B) Bird colonies increase the likelihood of birds' survival by allowing them to cooperatively counterattack their enemies and by making it easy to find a mate.
(C) The advantages of large-scale colonies definitely outweigh the disadvantages of them and therefore they are more sustainable than secluded small groups.
(D) Colonies made up of multiple species are more widely found because those species can better utilize environmental resources.
(E) Although forming a colony may cause a great number of problems which could be disastrous, its benefits do seem to surpass the demerits.
(F) Evolutionary behaviors amongst bird species have proven to be the key to the colony's sustainability and survivability.

指示：パッセージの簡単な要約を含む紹介文を以下に記載しています。パッセージの中の最も重要な考えを示している文を3つ選んで要約を完成させてください。

大規模な鳥のコロニーにおける大きさ、種、構成の変化には、利点と欠点の両方がある。

(A) 多くの鳥は孤立した場所にコロニーを作るので、同じ古い巣に戻ることができるが、巣を作る場所として開けた田畑を好む種もいる。
(B) 鳥のコロニーは、協力して敵に反撃することを可能にし、そして交尾相手を見つけやすくすることにより、鳥の生存率を向上させる。
(C) 大規模なコロニーの利点は欠点を確実に上回るので、大規模なコロニーは隔離された小さな群れよりも持続可能である。
(D) 種の数が多いと環境資源をより一層活用することができるので、多くの種によって構成されたコロニーはより広い範囲で見られる。
(E) コロニーを形成することは、破滅的になり得る非常に多くの問題を引き起こすものの、利点が欠点を上回っているようだ。
(F) 鳥類の進化的行動は、コロニーの持続可能性と生存可能性の鍵であることが証明された。

(A)は、孤立した場所に巣を作る鳥もいれば開けたところで巣を作る種もいる」という意味ですが、これは第2段落❶～❸や第3段落❶～❷に一致します。よって(A)は正解の可能性が高いです。(B)は、第4段落❹や❼に一致します。第4段落❼のreadily available「簡単に手に入る」が、(B)ではit easy to find a mate「簡単に相手を見つけることができる」で言い換えられていますね。よって(B)も正解の可能性が高いです。(C)ではdefinitely「確実に」が誤りです。第5段落❼を見れば言い過ぎだとわかります。また、選択肢の後半では「大規模なコロニーは隔離された小さな群れよりも持続可能」とありますが、これは第5段落❷以降と矛盾します。❷では「コロニーが大きくなるにつれて、食料が不足する」という問題点を指摘しています。よって(C)は誤りです。(D)には「環境資源をより一層活用することができる」とありますが、これは第3段落❺に一致しています。ところが、「こういったコロニーがより広範囲で見られる」という記述は本文にはありません。よって(D)は誤りです。第5段落❶～❻では食料不足や病気の蔓延などコロニーを崩壊させる要因についての説明があり、これは(E)に一致します。また、(E)の後半、「利点が欠点を上回っているようだ」も第5段落❼に言及されています。よって(E)は正解の可能性が高いです。(F)はproven「証明された」が誤りです。第5段落❼には、indication「示唆」とありますが、これはproven「証明された」とは違います。よって、解答は(A)、(B)、(E)となります。

□ whereas SV:～する一方で　□ likelihood:可能性　□ disastrous:悲惨な　□ surpass X:Xを上回る　□ amongst X:Xの中で　□ prove to be X:Xだとわかる　□ sustainability:持続可能性

PARAGRAPH 1

❶The definition of "colonies" when referring to birds differs greatly from when referring to humans.

❷When used for birds, it indicates species of birds that build their nests in a communal, shared environment and display common traits that have been adapted to aid survivability.

❸The size of these colonies can vary by orders of magnitude, with some limited to just a few breeding pairs, while others contain hundreds of thousands of birds.

❹The variability in size may be specific to the species although climate factors and environmental conditions such as available space and feeding grounds also restrict the size of colonies.

❺It is important for birds to consider where to form their colonies in consideration of various factors, which could be to their advantage.

❶コロニーの定義は、鳥に言及する場合と人間に言及する場合とでは大きく異なる。

❷鳥に使われた場合、共同の環境に巣を作り、生存の助けとなるような共通の特徴を持つ鳥の種を意味する。

❸コロニーの大きさにはかなりばらつきがあり、ほんの少数のつがいに限定されたコロニーもあれば、数十万羽の鳥を有するコロニーもある。

❹大きさのばらつきは、種に固有のものであるかもしれないが、気候要因や、鳥が活用できる空間や餌場などといった環境条件もまた、コロニーの大きさを制限する。

❺自分たちに有利に働き得る様々な要因を考慮し、どこにコロニーを形成するのかを考えることが、鳥たちにとって大切である。

＊語句問題に出る可能性あり

❶ □ colony：コロニー

❷ □ *indicate X：Xを意味する、Xを指示する
□ *communal：共有の
□ *adapt X：Xを徐々に身に着ける、徐々に変える
□ *aid X：Xを助ける

❸ □ vary：変わる
□ by orders of magnitude：かなりの程度
□ breeding pair：つがい

❹ □ variability：ばらつき
□ be specific to X：Xに固有である
□ feeding grounds：餌場
□ restrict X：Xを制限する

❺ □ in consideration of X：Xを考慮して
□ be to one's advantage：～の利益になる

❶ when referring to birds → when you refer to birds
「鳥について言及するとき」

❸ with some (colonies) limited ... 「コロニーの中には限定されているものもある」

付帯状況のwithに注目。

PARAGRAPH 2

❶Due to the avian abilities of most birds, their colonies are most often found in high, rocky, and inaccessible locations that would be extremely difficult for land-based predators to attack.

❷This is why islands with steep cliffs or secluded mountainsides are the most popular colony locations for some bird species.

❸These birds may return to the same, intact nesting locations over many years and even reuse the same nest and/or nesting materials.

❹The colonies in such locations, however, can be easily spotted by the returning birds as there is a constant hustle and bustle of birds coming and going.

❺A variety of mating rituals can be seen and the passionate cries of the hungry young can also be heard.

❻In order to make sure birds do not lose their own nests, which all look quite similar, they leave themselves subtle visual clues to light the way home, though how exactly they identify their own nests is yet to be discovered.

❶たいていの鳥が有している飛翔能力のため、鳥のコロニーはほとんどの場合、陸上の捕食動物が襲うことが極めて難しい、高くて岩が多く近づき難い場所に見られる。

❷険しい崖や人里離れた山腹を持つ島が、コロニーの場所として一部の鳥類に最も人気があるのはそのためである。

❸これらの鳥は、手付かずのまま残っている同じ営巣地に長年にわたって戻って行って、同じ巣や巣の材料を再利用することさえある。

❹ところが、そのような場所にできたコロニーは常に鳥が忙しく行き交っているため、戻ってくる鳥はコロニーの場所を簡単に突き止めることができるのだ。

❺様々な種類の交尾行動を見ることができ、また腹をすかせた若い鳥の激しい鳴き声も聞くことができる。

❻彼らが具体的にどのように自身の巣を特定しているのかは明らかになっていないが、外見が酷似した巣を見失わないように、鳥は巣へ戻る道を示すかすかな視覚的手がかりを残す。

＊語句問題に出る可能性あり

❶□avian：飛ぶことに関する
□most often：かなりの頻度で
□inaccessible：辿り着くことができない【形容詞】
□predator：捕食動物

❷□*steep：急な
□*secluded：隔離された

❸□*intact：手付かずの

❹□spot X：Xを突き止める
□*constant：一定の、常に生じる
□hustle and bustle：忙しく行き交う

❺□ritual：儀式

❻□*subtle：微妙な、かすかな
□*clue：手がかり
□be yet to V：まだ～していない、これから～する

PARAGRAPH 3

❶Although it is often the case that birds create their nests in isolated locations, some birds are known to eschew isolation for safety in numbers.

❷Depending on the availability of land and nesting techniques, some birds such as those belonging to the family of Laridae, or more commonly known as terns, may nest out on open ground within only a few feet or inches of each other.

❸Under situations where natural enemies are not around, these birds could have more convenient access to their food resources that come in greater abundance and variety.

❹Interestingly, these colonies are not made up of just one species.

❺In certain instances, it is mutually beneficial for different species of birds to nest in close proximity to one another, making the best possible use of the local resources.

❻Triangle Island in Canada, for instance, is known to be co-habited by gulls, tufted puffins, auks, auklets, and some other species.

❼As long as competition for the resources does not become too fierce, these multi-species colonies can remain quite stable.

❶鳥は巣を孤立した場所に作る場合が多いものの、数が多いことによる安全性を求め、一部の鳥は孤立を避けることで知られている。

❷土地や巣作りの方法がどのくらい使えるか次第だが、カモメ科に属する鳥、というよりアジサシの名のほうで知られている鳥などは、開けた土地でお互いに数フィートあるいは数インチしか離さずに巣を作る。

❸天敵が周りにいない状況下において、これらの鳥は量、種類ともに豊富な食料資源をより簡単に手に入れることができる。

❹興味深いことに、これらのコロニーはただ1つの種で構成されているわけではない。

❺場合によっては、異なる種の鳥が互いの近くに巣を作ることが双方に利益をもたらし、周辺の資源を最大限に生かすことになるのだ。

❻カナダにあるTriangle Islandは、カモメ、エトピリカ、ウミスズメ、小型のウミスズメやその他の種が共生していることで知られている。

❼資源をめぐる競争が激化しない限り、これらの複数種の生物が住むコロニーは、極めて安定した状態を保つことができるのである。

＊語句問題に出る可能性あり

❶ □ be the case：事実である（≒ be true）
□ isolated：孤立した
□ *eschew X：Xを避ける
□ safety in numbers：数が多いことによる安全性

❷ □ tern：アジサシ

❸ □ *convenient：便利な
□ have access to X：Xを手に入れることができる
□ in abundance：豊富に

❺ □ *mutually：お互いに、双方に
□ *in proximity to X：Xの近くに
□ the best possible X：考えうる限り最高のX

❼ □ as long as SV：～する限り【接続詞】
□ *fierce：激しい

❷ some birds such as those belonging ... → some birds (such as the birds belonging ...)

thoseはthe birdsの反復を避けるための代名詞。such asは前置詞で具体例を示す。

PARAGRAPH 4

❶Some of the greatest merits of birds forming themselves into colonies are quite obvious.

❷They are able to better protect their vulnerable offspring, as there are more birds of a mature age which could keep a lookout and raise the alarm if anything happens, as well as then taking the offensive against predators with their greater numbers.

❸Mockingbirds found in North America are a good example.

❹When their offspring are exposed to danger by predators, the adults cooperatively attack the predators or try to distract their attention from the young.

❺This behavior is often referred to as "mobbing," which can be seen in many bird species.

❻Besides mobbing, other benefits of forming an assemblage are not ones that would normally come to mind.

❼Firstly, in the event of a mating partner's death there are still many more readily available partners in close vicinity to ensure continued breeding.

❽The inborn nature of "promiscuity" observed in some species does contribute to the survival of a colony.

❾Secondly, and sadly, by having large numbers of eggs and young chicks around, even if a predator were to come looking for food, they might get their fill before reaching for other birds' offspring.

❿Essentially, the predators might become full on devouring a certain proportion of offspring, but there will always be more to continue the colony.

❶鳥がコロニーを形成することの最大のメリットのいくつかは、一目瞭然である。

❷見張りをし、何か起こったら注意を呼びかけることができる十分に成長した鳥の数が多いので、彼らはひ弱な子どもを一層守ることができる。また、数的優位を利用して、捕食動物に対して攻勢に出ることができる。

❸北アメリカで見られるマネシツグミが好例だ。

❹子どもが捕食動物によって危険にさらされたとき、マネシツグミの大人たちは、協力して捕食動物を襲ったり、捕食動物の関心を子どもからそらそうと試みるのだ。

❺この行動はしばしばモビングと呼ばれており、多くの鳥類で見ることができる。

❻モビングを除けば、群れをなすことの利点は簡単に思いつくものではない。

❼まず第一に、交尾の相手が死んだ場合でも、継続的な繁殖を保障するために、容易に交尾ができる相手がすぐ近くにたくさんいる。

❽一部の種で見られる先天的な性質である様々な相手との交尾が、コロニーの生存に貢献しているのである。

❾次に、悲しいことだが、たくさんの卵と幼いひなをそばに置いておくことにより、たとえ捕食動物が餌を求めてやってきたとしても、他の鳥の子どもに向かう前に満腹になる可能性がある。

❿要するに、捕食動物は一定数の子どもをむさぼり食い満腹になるかもしれないが、コロニーを存続させられるだけのさらに多くの子どもが常にいるであろうということだ。

＊語句問題に出る可能性あり

❶ □ *merits：利益

❷ □ vulnerable：脆弱な
□ *offspring：子ども
□ raise the alarm：警告する
□ X as well as Y：Xに加えて、Xでもある（「Yに加えてX」という意味もある）
□ then：そのとき、その場合
□ take the offensive：攻撃する

❹ □ be exposed to X：Xに晒される
□ *distract X：Xの注意をそらす

❺ □ refer to X as Y：XをYとみなす、XをYと呼ぶ
□ mob：群れをなして襲う

❻ □ besides：加えて
□ assemblage：群れ

❼ □ readily：簡単に
□ *available：手に入る
□ in vicinity：近くに
□ ensure X：Xを保障する

❽ □ inborn nature：生まれ持った性質
□ *contribute to X：Xに貢献する

❾ □ get one's fill：満腹になる

❿ □ *devour X：Xをむさぼる

❼ many more partners
manyはmoreを修飾し「差の程度が大きい」ということを示す。a lot more partnersやfar more partnersと書くことも可能。

❿ there will always be more
moreはmore offspringという意味。

PARAGRAPH 5

❶While there are clear advantages, no situation is without its disadvantages.

❷As a colony grows, overconsumption of food sources may outstrip the available resources, putting great pressure on the food supply and thus leading to a potential colony collapse.

❸This has been seen to be the case in larger colonies, but outside influences, such as climate shifts, human destruction of habitats, and natural disasters can cause similar problems with the food supply regardless of the size of the colony.

❹By being together in a large group, such huge events could potentially wipe out the entire colony.

❺Add to this the increased danger of disease caused by the unsanitary conditions of bird colonies and the ease with which that disease could spread at close quarters.

❻This means that a single sick bird could transmit its illness colony-wide very easily, wiping it out within a short time.

❼These and some other disadvantages of living in a colony make scholars doubt the overall benefits of bird colonies; however, recurring evolutionary behavior found in various different bird species provides them with an indication that the advantages of the colonies outweigh the disadvantages.

❶明らかな利点があるとはいえ、欠点がない状況は存在しない。

❷コロニーが大きくなるにつれて、食料の過剰消費が、利用可能な資源の量を超え、食料供給への大きな圧力となり、それがコロニー崩壊の可能性へとつながるのだ。

❸これは大きいコロニーで見られてきたことだが、コロニーの大きさにかかわらず、気候変動や人間による生息地の破壊、自然災害などの外的影響は、食料供給において似たような問題を引き起こす可能性がある。

❹大きな群れでいたがために、そのような大きな出来事が、コロニー全体を絶滅させてしまうかもしれないのだ。

❺さらに、コロニーの不衛生な状態により病気の危険が高まることや、病気が間近でたやすく広がる可能性があり得る。

❻これは、一羽の鳥がコロニー全体に病気を広げ、結果として短期間でコロニーを簡単に絶滅させてしまうかもしれないことを意味する。

❼コロニーを作って生きることのこうした欠点などから、学者はコロニーの全体的利点について疑念を抱いている。しかしながら、様々な鳥類で見られる繰り返される進化的行動は、コロニーの利点が欠点を上回っていることを学者に示している。

*語句問題に出る可能性あり

❷□ overconsumption：過剰消費
□ outstrip X：Xを超える
□ *potential：潜在的な

❸□ outside influence：外的影響（outsideは形容詞としてinfluencesを修飾している）
□ *regardless of X：Xに関係なく

❹□ wipe out X：Xを絶滅させる

❺□ unsanitary：不衛生な
□ at close quarters：非常に近い場所で、接近して

❻□ transmit X：Xを伝染させる

❼□ *recur：何度も生じる、繰り返される
□ outweigh X：Xより重要である

Chapter 2

Listening Section

Unit 1　リスニングセクションの解答戦略

TOEFL iBT Listening Section の概要
設問のパターン
何を意識して聞くべきか？
解き方 TIPS
メモの取り方について
メモと記憶

Unit 2　本試験形式問題演習

アイコン一覧

訳

語句

文法解説

正解

トラック番号

Unit 1 リスニングセクションの解答戦略

TOEFL iBT Listening Sectionの概要

問題量： 講義3題と会話文2題という構成。1回の試験につき28問出題される。

時　間： 36分。

内　容： 会話文は論文の資料集めの方法や、大学の施設を借りる方法など、大学生活で起こり得る状況を想定したものが多い。最近では、アカデミックな内容を含む会話文も出題されている。講義は学術的な内容が話題になる。生物学、地学、天文学、物理学、美術、音楽、心理学、ビジネスなど、内容は実に多岐にわたる。

その他： テスト監督者が配る紙にメモを取ることが可能。

設問のパターン

1. 文章全体のテーマや目的

必ず1つは出題される。英文の冒頭部を集中して聞くことが重要。

2. 内容一致

1カ所だけではなく複数箇所を参照して解く問題も出題される。会話文問題では非常に細かい内容が問われることもある。

3. 発言の目的や意図

ほぼ確実に出題される形式の1つ。文章の一部を聞きなおしてから解くパターンになることが多い。

4. 話者の見方

ある理論や手法などに対して、教授や生徒がどのように考えているのかを答える問題。聞き逃すことが多いので気を付けよう。

5. 推測

直接言及があるわけではないが、話の内容から推測できることを答える問題。What can be inferred ... ? のような英文で問われることが多い。難しい形式だが、内容を正しく理解していれば比較的容易に答えることができる。

6. 講義の構成

講義の内容ではなく構成を問う問題。比較的出題は少ない形式。"How does the professor organize his lecture?" や "How does the professor introduce the topic?" のような英文で問われる。

何を意識して聞くべきか？

文章の全てを記憶できるなら理想的だが、実際は極めて困難である。そこで、設問になる可能性がある箇所を意識しながら、メモを取って内容を記憶しよう。ここでは、特に注意するべきポイントをいくつか紹介する。

1. ディスコースマーカー

読解でディスコースマーカー（論理展開を示す語句）を意識することは基本だが、リスニングでも同様である。特に、「逆接」の後に続く内容は重要であることが多いので、必ずメモを取るようにしよう。

2. 話題の転換

会話文も講義も、いきなり本題に入る場合とそうでない場合がある。最初に世間話や前回の講義の内容を述べたうえで、本題に入ることも多い。その場合、本題に入る切り替えの部分を意識して聞くことが重要である。

3. 固有名詞

芸術作品の名前や建物の名前などの「固有名詞」や「特殊な語句」は必ず聞き取ること。その語句に言及した目的などが問われることが多い。

4. 講義における生徒の発言

講義では生徒が発言する機会がある。そのときの教授とのやり取りが狙われる傾向にある。主に発言の理由が問われる。講義内容と比べて、生徒の発言は聞き逃してしまうことが多い。誰がどのような目的で発言しているのかに注目しよう。

5. ある方法や理論に関する教授の見方

何らかの手法や理論についての講義が行われる場合、それらに対する見方を教授が述べることが多い。例えば、説得力のある理論か否か、役立つ手法か否か、将来性があるか否か、などである。文章の中盤から終盤にかけて述べられることが多い。

6. 順番や分類

ある現象が生じる順番や、ある物質（例えば石など）を分類する方法などは、狙われる傾向が強い。細かい内容を覚える必要はないが、大まかな順番や分類は必ずメモを取ること。

解き方 TIPS

1. 雑音をなるべく遮断する

他人の声が聞こえると、集中力が途切れてしまう。なるべく音声は最大にして、音源以外の音が入らないようにしよう。

2. 一瞬たりとも集中力を緩めない

少しでも集中を欠くと、残りの内容がわからなくなることがある。集中力を保つには日々の訓練が欠かせないが、試験直前においても強く意識しよう。

3. 冷静さを保つ

何を言っているのか全くわからない英文が出題されることもある。そんな場合でも、1カ所でも多く聞き取るつもりで、集中すること。決してあきらめてはいけない。

4. 難しい講義が出た場合

講義の内容が難しい場合、設問は比較的簡単であることが多い。そのような講義では、一から十まで聞き取るのではなく、主題を中心に理解すれば高得点を取れる可能性が高くなる。

5. メモの言語について

メモは英語でも日本語でもよい。もっと言えば、つづりなども問題にはならない。自分が後で見たときにわかるようにメモを取ればよいのだ。

メモの取り方について

リスニングではメモを取ることが許可されている。メモを取る場合は、できる限り簡潔に書くことが望ましい。キーワードや固有名詞などを中心にメモを取るとよいだろう。聞きながらメモを取るのは難しい作業だが、リスニング問題では同じ内容を繰り返し述べることがある。パラフレーズされているタイミングでメモを取れれば、重要なことを聞き漏らさないだろう。リスニング問題において最も避けるべきことは、メモに気を取られて音声を聞き逃してしまうことである。

メモと記憶

メモを見てから解答を選ぶことはほとんどないのかもしれない。むしろ、メモは記憶の補助だと考えるべきである。メモを取ることで、講義の内容を頭の中で整理しやすくなる。また、全体の流れを把握しながら聞くことも、講義の内容を覚える上で重要だ。

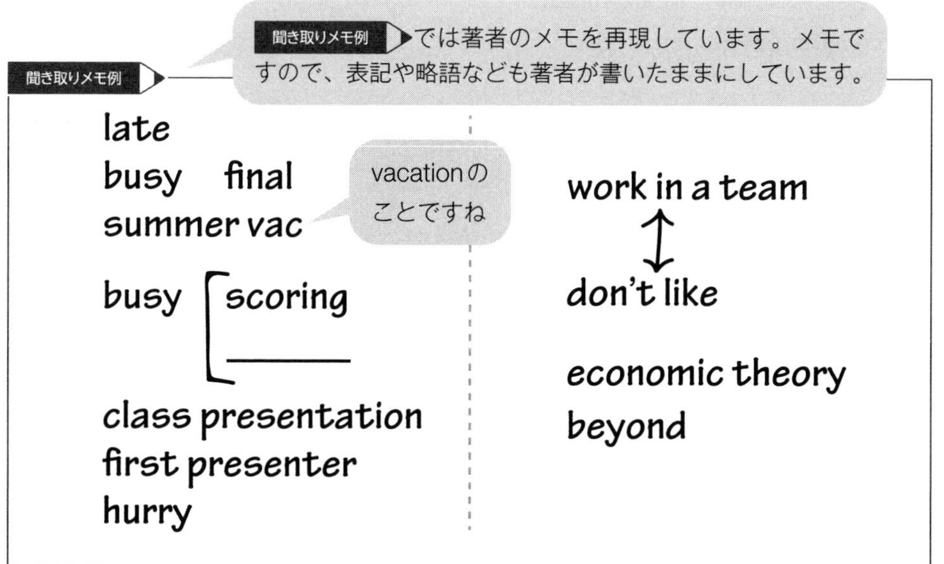

リスニング問題１ 会話

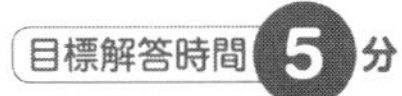

CAMPUS CONVERSATION

問題演習の流れ

- ☐ 音声が流れている間は、問題は読めません。会話が終わり、最初の問題音声が流れ始めたらページをめくって、5分以内に解答しましょう。
- ☐ 1問の解答時間は20秒を目安にしています。問題を読み上げた後に解答時間として20秒のポーズ（音声なし）が入っていますので、その間に解答をマークしてください。
- ☐ メモは自由に取ってください。
- ☐ 3回解けるように、3回分のマークシートを問題ページに用意しています。解く日付を記入してからマークしてください。

Web解答方法

- ☐ 本試験では各選択肢の左に表示されるマークをクリックして解答します。本試験と同様の方法で取り組みたい場合は、Webで解答できます。
- ☐ インターネットのつながるパソコン・スマートフォンで、以下のサイトにアクセスしてWeb上で解答してください。

extester.com

- ☐ 操作方法は、p.13 ～ 14の「USA Club Web学習の使い方」をご参照ください。

学習の記録

学習開始日	年　　月　　日	学習終了日	年　　月　　日
学習開始日	年　　月　　日	学習終了日	年　　月　　日
学習開始日	年　　月　　日	学習終了日	年　　月　　日

リスニング問題 1 会話 音声

 L01

聞き取りメモ

L01_Q1

1. What are the woman and the manager mainly discussing?

(A) How to improve communication skills
(B) Important regulations for living in the dorm
(C) Difficulties the woman experienced while living in a dorm
(D) How to be academically successful at university

L01_Q2

2. According to the manager, what challenges are often encountered by those new to the dorm? *Choose two answers.*

(A) Becoming accustomed to living away from their families
(B) Bringing in necessary furniture to their rooms
(C) Performing household chores
(D) Making friends with neighbors

L01_Q3

3. What can be inferred about the dorm residents?

(A) Most of them prefer to cook in their room.
(B) They are asking the school to renovate the dorm.
(C) They are prohibited from entering the kitchen after midnight.
(D) Not many students use land-line telephones.

L01_Q4

4. What does the manager say about the student gym?

(A) Students need to register before they can take a tour of it.
(B) Some new machines have been introduced.
(C) There is an additional membership fee to use the gym.
(D) It is open 24 hours a day on weekdays.

L01_Q5

5. Listen again to part of the conversation and then answer the question. Why does the manager say this?

(A) To argue that some students lack communication skills
(B) To encourage the woman to take a course on communication
(C) To remind the woman that acquiring communication skills takes courage
(D) To suggest there is something to learn outside of university class such as interpersonal skills

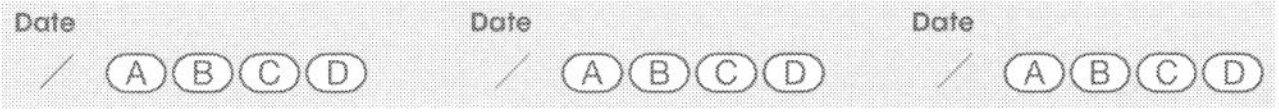

 1. **(B)**　2. **(A) (C)**　3. **(D)**　4. **(B)**　5. **(D)**

1～6 | 問 1～2 解説レクチャー

L01_Script01-06　M: Manager　S: Student

1
M: ❶Hello, I don't think I've seen you before. ❷Are you a freshman?
S: ❶Yes, I just moved in. ❷This is my first week here.

2
M: ❶Glad to have you here. ❷My name is Simon Binmore. ❸I'm the manager of the university dormitory. ❹Things can be a bit tough in the first couple of weeks, but I'm sure you'll come to like it here.
S: ❶Thank you, sir. ❷In fact, I'm still feeling quite nervous.

3
M: ❶I can imagine. ❷I get the feeling that the first hurdle for new students is being able to feel comfortable about being alone, separate from your family . . . you know. ❸And the next challenge is more physical in nature, like preparing meals or doing the laundry yourself.
S: ❶I think I'm still struggling to overcome the first one then. ❷I thought I would enjoy more privacy here, but I'm actually finding it difficult. ❸You know, this is my first time living alone, and . . .

4
M: Your life changed suddenly and you're a bit confused . . .
S: ❶Right. ❷Seems so. ❸Do you happen to have a minute now? ❹There's something I want to ask you about.

5
M: Sure, go ahead.
S: Are there any rules I should keep in mind?

6
M: ❶Well, obviously, I can't go over each of them now. ❷It would take me ages to do that! ❸However, there are some crucial ones I want you to know from the very beginning.
S: I'm all ears.

解説レクチャー

※1M：1の管理人の発言　1S：1の学生の発言

1M～1S：学生は引っ越してきたばかりの新入生です。
2M：この人物が寮の管理人であることがわかります。
2S～3M：学生が不安を覚えていることに対して、管理人もその気持ちを理解しています。とくに、家族から離れて一人で暮らすことや、自炊や洗濯などが大変だと述べています。
3S～4M：学生は、一人暮らしをすることにまだ不安を抱えていると明かしています。
4S～5S：学生は、寮に住むうえでのルールを確認したがっているとわかります。
6M：重要なルールだけを説明しようとしています。ちなみに、It would take me ages ... は「膨大な時間がかかる」という意味です。
6S：I'm all earsは「しっかりと耳を傾けます」という意味の慣用表現です。全身「耳」と考えると、覚えやすくなりますね。

聞き取りメモ例

freshman

1st wk

manager of dorm

nervous

away from family

meal
laundry

live alone

rules

L01_Q1

1. What are the woman and the manager mainly discussing?

(A) How to improve communication skills
(B) Important regulations for living in the dorm
(C) Difficulties the woman experienced while living in a dorm
(D) How to be academically successful at university

女性と管理人は主に何を話し合っていますか。

(A) コミュニケーション能力を向上させる方法
(B) 寮での生活にとって大切な規則
(C) 寮で生活するに当たって女性が経験した困難
(D) 大学で学業を成就する方法

5Sから、学生は寮に住むうえでのルールを確認したがっているとわかります。そして続く**6M**から管理人によるルールの説明があるため(B)が正解です。**5S**のrulesをregulationsで言い換えています。(A)は**11M**に関連する話がありますが、コミュニケーションスキルの改善方法について主に話しているわけではありません。局所的な情報ですので主旨とは言えません。(C)も学生が苦労していることは、局所的な情報ですので主旨ではありません。(D)は学業についての話は特に出てこないので誤りです。

L01_Q2

2. According to the manager, what challenges are often encountered by those new to the dorm? *Choose two answers.*

(A) Becoming accustomed to living away from their families
(B) Bringing in necessary furniture to their rooms
(C) Performing household chores
(D) Making friends with neighbors

管理人によれば、寮に新しく入ってきた人がよく直面する課題は何ですか。2つ選んでください。

(A) 家族と離れて暮らすことに慣れること
(B) 部屋に必要な家具を持ち込むこと
(C) 家事をすること
(D) 近くの人と友達になること

管理人は3M❷で「最初のハードルは一人でいることに慣れることだ」と述べています。よって、(A)は正解です。続く❸で「炊事や洗濯など」も大変だと述べています。よって「家事をする」という意味の(C)も正解です。正解は(A)と(C)です。(B)と(D)のような話は会話に出てきません。

□ be accustomed to Ving:〜することに慣れている　□ household chore:家事

7〜14｜問3〜4 解説レクチャー

L01_Script07-14

7 M: ❶The first rule is that you should be back in the dorm by 11:00 pm. ❷This is very important as all the doors are automatically locked at 11:00 pm sharp.

S: That's indeed an important rule to know then!

8 M: ❶Also, you should bear in mind that the use of fire isn't allowed in your room. ❷This includes using some cooking gear like a portable stove. ❸Besides, after midnight, you are not allowed to talk loudly on your cell phone.

S: Is there a space where I can talk on a phone around that time?

9 M: ❶Yes, there's a designated land-line telephone area in the dorm, but we might get rid of it in the near future. ❷Whenever I go there, it's almost always empty. ❸You know, people just communicate using their cell phones mostly. ❹And the space can be used more effectively for something else, like a shared kitchen space or something.

S: ❶Got it. ❷Anything else?

10 M: ❶Oh, another thing. ❷I also want you to be aware that you should refrain from making loud noises.

S: ❶Of course. ❷But, what should I do if my neighbor is too loud? ❸Am I supposed to make a complaint to you or just try to solve it on my own?

11 M: ❶Well, it really depends. ❷However, generally speaking, the first thing you should do is to try to sort it out yourself peacefully . . . by talking to your neighbor. ❸I know it takes a bit of courage to directly complain to your fellow students, but it's something you should get used to and become able to handle. ❹Besides, you don't get to learn these sorts of skills in your class, do you?

S: ❶I see your point. ❷What if my neighbor refuses to listen?

12 M: ❶If there's no sign of improving, let me know by all means. ❷I'll be happy to help.
S: ❶Thank you, sir. ❷Also, is there a place where I can work out in the dorm?

13 M: ❶Yes, there's a gym available for students to use free of charge on the first floor open from 7:00 am to 9:00 pm, Monday to Friday. ❷We've just installed some new equipment. ❸You're welcome to take a look. ❹Please note that you need to sign up and pay a $30 deposit prior to using the gym though.
S: ❶Sounds great. ❷I think I'll check it out now. ❸Thank you for your time.

14 M: No problem.

解説レクチャー

7M~**7S**:1つ目のルールは午後11時までに寮に戻らないといけないということです。11時ぴったりに寮の玄関が自動でロックされるそうです。

8M:さらに部屋で火を使うことは禁止されていると述べています。カセットコンロ(a portable stove)も禁止です。さらに、午前0時を過ぎてから携帯電話で話すことも禁止だと説明しています。

8S~**9M**:寮には固定電話を使える場所があるが、近い将来に撤去するかもしれないとのことです。it's almost always emptyは「ほぼいつも電話のブースが空である」という意味なので「使っている人がほとんどいない」ということですね。携帯電話を使う人が大半だと言っています。また、空いたスペースをキッチンなどに使うことも検討しているようです。

9S~**10M**:大きな音を立てることも避けるべきだと述べています。

10S~**11M**:近所の人がうるさい場合、まずは当事者同士で解決することを勧めています。対人スキルを学ぶ機会にもなると言っています。

12M:言っても聞かない場合は、管理人の出番です。

12S~**13M**:無料で使えるジムがあり、新しく機器も導入したと述べています。ジムを使う前に登録して30ドルの保証金を払う必要があるとのことです。

13S:これからジムを見に行くようです。

聞き取りメモ例

rules
- back by 11 ← lock
- ~~fire~~
- ~~talk~~ cell night

landline

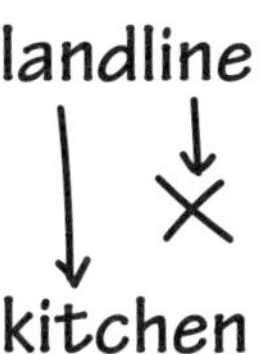

kitchen

noise
neighbor [complain / solve yourself]
let him know ←

work out
↓
gym 1st fl 7am~9pm
new equipment
sign up deposit

L01_Q3

3. What can be inferred about the dorm residents?

(A) Most of them prefer to cook in their room.
(B) They are asking the school to renovate the dorm.
(C) They are prohibited from entering the kitchen after midnight.
(D) Not many students use land-line telephones.

寮生について何が推測できますか。

(A) ほとんどの人が自分の部屋で料理をするのが好きだ。
(B) 寮を改装するよう大学に頼んでいる。
(C) 午前0時を過ぎるとキッチンへ入ることが禁じられている。
(D) 固定電話を使う学生はそれほど多くない。

管理人は9M❸で「ほとんどの人は携帯電話を使う」と述べています。9M❹でまた、固定電話を撤去するという発言もありました。ここからわかることは「固定電話を使う学生が少ない」ということなので、(D)が正解です。(A)は8M❶に「部屋で火を使ってはいけない」とあります。(B)は会話中に言及がありません。(C)についてですが、8M❸に「午前0時以降に禁止されていることは、携帯電話での通話」とあります。キッチンに入ることではありません。

□ prohibit X from Ving: Xが～することを禁止する

L01_Q4

4. What does the manager say about the student gym?

(A) Students need to register before they can take a tour of it.
(B) Some new machines have been introduced.
(C) There is an additional membership fee to use the gym.
(D) It is open 24 hours a day on weekdays.

学生のジムについて管理人は何を述べていますか。

(A) 学生は見学をする前に登録をする必要がある。
(B) いくつかの新しい器具が導入された。
(C) そのジムを使うための追加の会費がある。
(D) 平日は1日24時間開いている。

管理人は13M❷で、「新しい機器を導入した」と述べています。よって(B)が正解です。13M❷のequipmentをmachinesと、installをintroduceとそれぞれ言い換えていますね。ダミーの選択肢に惑わされずに(B)を選びましょう。(A)は13M❸に「いつでもジムを見学してよい」とありますが、13M❹に「ジムを使う前に登録する必要がある」とあります。(B)のtourとはジムを見学することなので、この段階では登録は不要です。(C)のような話は会話に出てきません。(D)は13M❶に「午前7時から午後9時まで」とあるため、誤りです。

問5 解説レクチャー

L01_Q5

5. Listen again to part of the conversation and then answer the question.

Manager:
I know it takes a bit of courage to directly complain to your fellow students, but it's something you should get used to and become able to handle. Besides, you don't get to learn these sorts of skills in your class, do you?

Why does the manager say this?

Besides, you don't get to learn these sort of skills in your class, do you?

(A) To argue that some students lack communication skills
(B) To encourage the woman to take a course on communication
(C) To remind the woman that acquiring communication skills takes courage
(D) To suggest there is something to learn outside of university class such as interpersonal skills

会話の一部をもう一度聞いて、設問に答えてください。

管理人：
あなたの同級生に直接苦情を言うことは少し勇気が要りますが、それに慣れて対処できるようになっておくべきです。それに、授業でこのようなスキルは学ぶ機会がないでしょう。

なぜ管理人は「それに、授業でこのようなスキルは学ぶ機会がないでしょうから」と言っていますか。

(A) 生徒の中にはコミュニケーション能力が不足している人もいると主張するため
(B) コミュニケーションについての授業を取るよう女性に勧めるため
(C) コミュニケーション能力を手に入れることは勇気が要ることだと女性に再確認するため
(D) 対人関係スキルのような、大学の授業以外で学べることがあると示唆するため

「隣の人との間で問題が生じた場合、直接その人と話をするには勇気が必要だが、このようなスキルは、大学の授業では学べない」と管理人は述べています。よって、(D)が正解です。(A)と(C)は発言内容から読み取ることはできません。(B)ですが、管理人は授業を取るのではなく、授業以外で学ぶべきことについて話しているため、この選択肢は誤りです。

□ acquire X: Xを習得する　□ interpersonal skill: 対人スキル

1–5 M: Manager S: Student

Listen to a conversation between a student and a university dormitory manager.

1
M: ❶Hello, I don't think I've seen you before.
❷Are you a freshman?
S: ❶Yes, I just moved in.
❷This is my first week here.

2
M: ❶Glad to have you here.
❷My name is Simon Binmore.
❸I'm the manager of the university dormitory.
❹Things can be a bit tough in the first couple of weeks, but I'm sure you'll come to like it here.
S: ❶Thank you, sir.
❷In fact, I'm still feeling quite nervous.

3
M: ❶I can imagine.
❷I get the feeling that the first hurdle for new students is being able to feel comfortable about being alone, separate from your family . . . you know.
❸And the next challenge is more physical in nature, like preparing meals or doing the laundry yourself.
S: ❶I think I'm still struggling to overcome the first one then.
❷I thought I would enjoy more privacy here, but I'm actually finding it difficult.
❸You know, this is my first time living alone, and . . .

4
M: Your life changed suddenly and you're a bit confused . . .
S: ❶Right.
❷Seems so.
❸Do you happen to have a minute now?
❹There's something I want to ask you about.

5
M: Sure, go ahead.
S: Are there any rules I should keep in mind?

生徒と大学寮の管理人との会話を聞きなさい。

1 M:❶こんにちは、今まであなたを見たことがありませんね。
❷１年生ですか。
S: ❶はい、ちょうど引っ越してきたところです。
❷今週がここでの１週目です。

2 M:❶来てくれてとてもうれしいです。
❷私の名前は Simon Binmore です。
❸この大学寮の管理人です。
❹最初の数週間は大変ですが、ここが気に入ると思いますよ。
S: ❶ありがとうございます。
❷実をいうと、まだかなり緊張しています。

3 M:❶よくわかります。
❷新入生にとっての最初の困難は、家族から離れ、一人でいることに慣れることだという感じがします。
❸そして次の課題は、ご飯を作ったり自分で洗濯をしたりと、もっと身体的な性質のものです。
S: ❶では私はまだ最初の課題を克服するのに苦労しているのだと思います。
❷ここではもっとプライバシーを享受できると思っていたのですが、それは実際難しいのだということがわかってきました。
❸これが初めての一人暮らしですし、それに…。

4 M:突然生活が変わって少し混乱している…。
S: ❶はい。
❷そのようです。
❸今少しお時間がありますか。
❹お聞きしたいことがあります。

5 M:いいですよ。どうぞ。
S: 覚えておくべきルールはありますか。

- □ dormitory：寮

1
- □ freshman：大学1年生
- □ move in：引っ越してくる

3
- □ in nature：性質上
- □ do the laundry：洗濯をする
- □ struggle to V：苦労して～する

4
- □ happen to V：偶然～する

5
- □ go ahead：どうぞ
- □ keep X in mind：Xを覚えておく

6–10

6 M: ❶Well, obviously, I can't go over each of them now.
❷It would take me ages to do that!
❸However, there are some crucial ones I want you to know from the very beginning.
S: I'm all ears.

7 M: ❶The first rule is that you should be back in the dorm by 11:00 pm.
❷This is very important as all the doors are automatically locked at 11:00 pm sharp.
S: That's indeed an important rule to know then!

8 M: ❶Also, you should bear in mind that the use of fire isn't allowed in your room.
❷This includes using some cooking gear like a portable stove.
❸Besides, after midnight, you are not allowed to talk loudly on your cell phone.
S: Is there a space where I can talk on a phone around that time?

9 M: ❶Yes, there's a designated land-line telephone area in the dorm, but we might get rid of it in the near future.
❷Whenever I go there, it's almost always empty.
❸You know, people just communicate using their cell phones mostly.
❹And the space can be used more effectively for something else, like a shared kitchen space or something.
S: ❶Got it.
❷Anything else?

10 M: ❶Oh, another thing.
❷I also want you to be aware that you should refrain from making loud noises.
S: ❶Of course.
❷But, what should I do if my neighbor is too loud?
❸Am I supposed to make a complaint to you or just try to solve it on my own?

6

M:❶ええ、もちろん、今一つ一つそれらを説明はできません。
❷それをすると、とんでもなく時間がかかってしまうでしょう！
❸しかし、一番始めに知っておいていただきたい重要なものがいくつかあります。
S: それを聞かせてください。

7

M:❶まず最初のルールは、午後11時までに寮に戻らなければいけないということです。
❷これは、午後11時ちょうどに自動的に全てのドアがロックされてしまうので、とても重要です。
S: それは知っておくべき本当に大切なルールですね！

8

M:❶また、部屋で火を使うことは許可されていないことも覚えておくべきです。
❷これは、カセットコンロのような調理器具を使うことも含みます。
❸また、午前0時を過ぎてから、携帯で通話することも許可されていません。
S: その時間に電話できる場所はありますか。

9

M:❶ええ。寮には固定電話を使える指定場所がありますが、将来撤去するかもしれません。
❷そこは、いつ行っても、ほとんどいつも空いています。
❸ご存じの通り、皆さんは携帯を使ってやり取りしますからね。
❹そしてそのスペースは他のもの、共有のキッチンスペースか何かとして有効に使えます。
S: ❶わかりました。
❷他には。

10

M:❶ああ、もう1つ。
❷大きな音を立てることは控えなければならないということにも注意していただきたいです。
S: ❶もちろん。
❷ところで、近くの人がうるさすぎたらどうすればいいでしょうか。
❸管理人さんに苦情を入れるべきですか、それとも自力でそれを解決しようとするべきですか。

6
- □ obviously：言うまでもなく
- □ go over X：Xを説明する
- □ ages：非常に長い時間
- □ crucial：重要な
- □ be all ears：耳を傾ける

7
- □ sharp：ちょうど

8
- □ bear in mind that SV：～ということを心に留めておく、覚えておく
- □ gear：器具
- □ stove：コンロ

9
- □ designated：指定された
- □ get rid of X：Xを取り除く
- □ (I) got it：わかりました

10
- □ refrain from Ving：～することを控える
- □ make a complaint：苦情を入れる
- □ on one's own：自力で

---

7 as all the doors are ... locked

asは接続詞で「理由」を表す。

11-14

11 M: ❶Well, it really depends.
❷However, generally speaking, the first thing you should do is to try to sort it out yourself peacefully . . . by talking to your neighbor.
❸I know it takes a bit of courage to directly complain to your fellow students, but it's something you should get used to and become able to handle.
❹Besides, you don't get to learn these sorts of skills in your class, do you?
S: ❶I see your point.
❷What if my neighbor refuses to listen?

12 M: ❶If there's no sign of improving, let me know by all means.
❷I'll be happy to help.
S: ❶Thank you, sir.
❷Also, is there a place where I can work out in the dorm?

13 M: ❶Yes, there's a gym available for students to use free of charge on the first floor open from 7:00 am to 9:00 pm, Monday to Friday.
❷We've just installed some new equipment.
❸You're welcome to take a look.
❹Please note that you need to sign up and pay a $30 deposit prior to using the gym though.
S: ❶Sounds great.
❷I think I'll check it out now.
❸Thank you for your time.

14 M: No problem.

11 M:❶それは本当に時と場合によります。
❷ですが、一般的に、まずは近くの人と話して、自力で円満に解決しようと試してみてください。
❸あなたの同級生に直接苦情を言うことは少し勇気が要りますが、それに慣れて対処できるようになっておくべきです。
❹それに、授業でこのようなスキルは学ぶ機会がないでしょうから。
S: ❶確かにそうですね。
❷もし近くの人が聞き入れることを拒んだら。

12 M:❶もし改善の兆候がない場合は、ぜひ私に知らせてください。
❷喜んでお力になります。
S: ❶ありがとうございます。
❷それと、寮内に運動できる場所はありますか。

13 M:❶ええ、月曜日から金曜日の午前7時から午後9時まで開いている、学生が無料で使えるジムが1階にあります。
❷ちょうど新しい器具をいくつか設置したところですよ。
❸ぜひ見てみてください。
❹しかし、ジムを使う前に、登録をして30ドルのデポジットを払う必要がありますので、注意してくださいね。
S: ❶いいですね。
❷今から見に行きます。
❸お時間をいただき、ありがとうございました。

14 M:いいえ、どういたしまして。

11
- □ it depends：時と場合による
- □ generally speaking：一般的に言って
- □ sort X out：Xを解決する

12
- □ by all means：ぜひとも
- □ work out：運動する

13
- □ free of charge：無料で
- □ deposit：保証金
- □ prior to X：Xの前に

リスニング問題 2 講義

目標解答時間 5 分

BUSINESS

問題演習の流れ

- □ 音声が流れている間は、問題は読めません。講義が終わり、最初の問題音声が流れ始めたらページをめくって、5分以内に解答しましょう。
- □ 1問の解答時間は20秒を目安にしています。問題を読み上げた後に解答時間として20秒のポーズ（音声なし）が入っていますので、その間に解答をマークしてください。
- □ メモは自由に取ってください。
- □ 3回解けるように、3回分のマークシートを問題ページに用意しています。解く日付を記入してからマークしてください。

Web解答方法

- □ 本試験では各選択肢の左に表示されるマークをクリックして解答します。本試験と同様の方法で取り組みたい場合は、Webで解答できます。
- □ インターネットのつながるパソコン・スマートフォンで、以下のサイトにアクセスしてWeb上で解答してください。

extester.com

- □ 操作方法は、p.13 ～ 14の「USA Club Web学習の使い方」をご参照ください。

学習の記録

学習開始日	年　　月　　日	学習終了日	年　　月　　日
学習開始日	年　　月　　日	学習終了日	年　　月　　日
学習開始日	年　　月　　日	学習終了日	年　　月　　日

リスニング問題2 講義 音声

 L02

Business

聞き取りメモ

L02_Q1

1. What is the professor mainly discussing?

(A) How giving discounts can be a powerful marketing tactic
(B) How effective a surprise gift is
(C) How human emotions can be classified
(D) How unexpected events can be used to catch customers' attention

L02_Q2

2. What can be inferred about the marketing industry today?

(A) Devising a campaign that can draw consumers' attention is becoming difficult.
(B) The marketing industry looks to neuroscientific journals for new ideas.
(C) Surprise marketing is the tactic most widely used in the industry today.
(D) Marketing companies have entirely changed the goal of marketing.

L02_Q3

3. Why can a free drink from a fast-food restaurant be effective?

(A) Because customers are often thirsty
(B) Because menu items are usually not free
(C) Because a free drink offer is very rare
(D) Because people do not have to choose their drinks

L02_Q4

4. Why does the professor talk about the example of British Rail?

(A) To show how powerful monetary incentives can be in marketing
(B) To demonstrate rewards are not always necessary to attract customers
(C) To remind students of the importance of being on time for meetings
(D) To examine how surprise marketing helped British Rail win a contract

L02_Q5

5. What can be inferred about a poorly laid out surprise marketing campaign?

(A) It can nonetheless be a powerful marketing campaign.
(B) It can lead to amplifying negative emotions of customers.
(C) It still remains to be seen whether bad campaign could lead to a disaster.
(D) It should be studied thoroughly for future reference.

L02_Q6

6. Listen again to part of the lecture and then answer the question.
What does the professor mean when he says this?

(A) Winning a contract is like a game that involves some risk.
(B) The tactics of the advertising company could have failed completely.
(C) The risky nature of the contract will cost the advertising company a lot of money.
(D) The advertising company could have won a contract using conventional tactics.

 1. **(D)**　2. **(A)**　3. **(B)**　4. **(B)**　5. **(B)**　6. **(B)**

問1 解説レクチャー

L02_Q1

1. What is the professor mainly discussing?

(A) How giving discounts can be a powerful marketing tactic
(B) How effective a surprise gift is
(C) How human emotions can be classified
(D) How unexpected events can be used to catch customers' attention

教授は主に何を議論していますか。

(A) 割引がいかに強力なマーケティング戦略となりうるか
(B) サプライズギフトがどれ程効果的か
(C) どのように人間の感情を分類できるか
(D) 顧客の注意を引くために予期しない出来事をどのように使えるか

講義はサプライズマーケティングがメインのテーマでした。これは「予想外の報酬などを与えることで、顧客の注意を引く」手法です。よって、(D)が正解です。(A)はサプライズマーケティングの一例です。主旨とは言えないので誤りです。(B)のサプライズギフトもサプライズマーケティングの一例にすぎません。(C)は講義で言及がありません。

□classify X: Xを分類する　□catch one's attention: ~の注意を引く

1~4 | 問2 解説レクチャー

L02_Script01-04　P: Professor　S: Student

1 P: ❶Marketing tactics have evolved significantly over the years as customers desire a more personalized experience. ❷However, the ultimate aim of marketing remains the same . . . sell your products. ❸Sell your services. ❹Basically, you wanna make your products or services memorable and unforgettable so that people keep buying what you offer. ❺One strategy for accomplishing this is "surprise marketing." ❻I'm sure you've received birthday presents on your birthday from your friends or parents. ❼It's nice to know there's somebody who celebrates your special day, isn't it? ❽But, you know what? ❾You're likely to feel happier if you get a present on a non-special day. ❿There's some neuroscientific research data indicating that the part of the human brain associated with pleasure showed increased activity when the event was unexpected. ⓫So, how people perceive a certain event differs depending on whether it's expected or unexpected.

2 P: ❶Today's consumers are exposed to a vast array of advertisements and digitalized experiences. ❷Therefore, it's extremely hard to come up with a campaign that stands out among many others out there. ❸Consequently, with increasing awareness of the power of surprise in the context of marketing, more and more marketing companies today are trying to incorporate elements of surprise into their marketing schemes. ❹So, what is this much-talked-about surprise marketing? ❺Any guesses? ❻Well, you guys should have a pretty good idea of it given what I have talked about so far.

3 S: Is it like giving out coupons or offering discounts?

4 P: ❶Yes, exactly, so that's one form of surprise marketing. ❷Coupons and discounts are good examples. ❸Surprise marketing tries to draw customers' attention by offering them something unexpected. ❹It starts by targeting groups of people who will receive an unexpected reward or experience. ❺Surprise campaigns include offering special privileges to loyal customers . . . or discounts on special occasions such as your wedding anniversary or your birthday. ❻The most appealing benefit of surprise marketing is that it possesses the potential to instantly build a bond with prospects and customers.

解説レクチャー

1

❶～❹:マーケティングの最終的な目的は、商品を売ることだと述べられています。

❺:マーケティング戦略の1つに、サプライズマーケティングというものがあるとのことです。

❻～❾:誕生日などの特別な日ではない日にもらうプレゼントの方が、誕生日などにもらうプレゼントよりも嬉しく感じるようです。

❿～⓫:科学的にも、予想外のことが喜びをもたらすと説明しています。「驚き」という側面が、人の体験に影響するということですね。

2

❶～❷:消費者は非常に多くの広告にさらされているので、他の広告より目立つものを作るのが難しいと言っています。

❸:よって、「驚き」をマーケティング構想に組み込む会社が増えつつあるそうです。

❹～❻:教授が学生にサプライズマーケティングの概要を掴んだかどうかを問うていますね。

3
学生がサプライズマーケティングがどんなものか当たりを付けています。

4
❶～❷:学生が述べたクーポンや割引がサプライズマーケティングの具体例だとコメントしています。
❸～❺:サプライズマーケティングの定義が出ています。予想外の利益や経験を人々に与えることにより、顧客の関心を引く手法ですね。
❻:サプライズマーケティングの最大の魅力は、顧客と瞬時につながりを作ることができるということだと述べています。

聞き取りメモ例

marketing
sell < product / service
memorable
surprise marketing
happy ↗ unexpected

hard to stand out
↓
incorporate surprise
coupon
discount
draw attention
loyal customer
special event

L02_Q2

2. What can be inferred about the marketing industry today?

(A) Devising a campaign that can draw consumers' attention is becoming difficult.
(B) The marketing industry looks to neuroscientific journals for new ideas.
(C) Surprise marketing is the tactic most widely used in the industry today.
(D) Marketing companies have entirely changed the goal of marketing.

今日のマーケティング業界について何が推測できますか。

(A) 顧客の注意を引くキャンペーンを立案することが難しくなっている。
(B) マーケティング業界は新しいアイデアを得ようと、神経科学の雑誌を当てにする。
(C) surprise marketingは今日業界内で最も広く使われている戦略である。
(D) マーケティング会社はマーケティングの目的を完全に変えた。

教授の2❶と2❷によると、「現代は広告であふれており、他のものよりも目立つのが難しい」ということがわかります。これはつまり、消費者の目を引くのが難しいということなので、(A)が正解です。(B)は言及がありません。(C)についてですが、「最も幅広く用いられている(most widely used)」という発言はありません。(D)はマーケティングの目的はいつも同じだと1❷～1❸にあります。

□ devise X: Xを立案する　□ look to X for Y: YのためにXに頼る

5～6 | 問3～4 解説レクチャー

L02_Script05-06

5 P: ❶As people's lifestyles change, the forms of marketing also change. ❷So . . . let's take a quick look at one or two examples. ❸Well . . . many companies are making good use of electronic vouchers. ❹They send you special offers and messages that you can read from your computer or a mobile phone. ❺Many people today have a computer and mobile phone, making them an effective medium for marketing. ❻Recent technologies are really great. ❼For example . . . you're walking down the street. ❽You suddenly get a notification to your mobile phone. ❾It's a notification from a certain fast-food restaurant saying it has an offer of a free drink available for you. ❿And you go "A free drink!?" ⓫You didn't have a plan to go and eat in the restaurant, but hearing the free drink offer, which was totally unexpected, you might choose to stop by and grab something there. ⓬This is an example of surprise marketing involving a surprise reward.

6 P: ❶But really, that surprise doesn't have to be a free coupon or a discount. ❷Here's another example of surprise marketing which doesn't involve any rewards. ❸Some time ago, British Rail was looking for an advertising company with innovative marketing schemes to promote their railway services. ❹Some representatives of British Rail visited one advertising agency to have a meeting. ❺They were waiting in a meeting room of the advertising company. ❻Ten minutes past the appointment, nobody turned up. ❼Twenty minutes . . . still no one. ❽Thirty minutes past the appointment, still . . . nobody turned up. ❾After being kept waiting for about an hour, the representatives of British Rail got angry and decided to leave the room. ❿Just as they left the room, the people

from the advertising company barged in and said, "You've just experienced what British Rail customers experience every day." ⓫The creative imagination of the advertising company paid off, and they got the contract with British Rail. ⓬The firm succeeded in making a huge impact on the officials of British Rail, and this impact, or surprise, is what got them the contract. ⓭It's amazing that the advertising company played such a risky game, given what was at stake.

解説レクチャー

5

❶:人々の生活スタイルが変わるにつれて、マーケティングの手法も変わっていくとのことです。

❷~❺:携帯やパソコンにメールでクーポンなどを送る例を挙げています。こういった機器はほとんどの人が持っているので、有効な手段だと述べています。

❻~⓬:また、携帯に突然「無料ドリンク」のお知らせが届く場合も挙げられています。それが理由で、行く予定のなかった店に行くこともあるかもしれません。

6

❶~❷:クーポンなどのご褒美以外のサプライズマーケティングの例もあると述べています。

❸~❾:ある鉄道会社は顧客を増やすために広告会社を探していたとのことです。会社の代表団がある広告会社を訪れたとき、そこで1時間ほど待たされたそうです。当然、彼らは怒ったとあります。

❿:彼らが帰ろうとしたとき、広告会社の人が入ってきて「これこそが御社の利用客が毎日経験していることです」と伝えたそうです。要するに、「その鉄道会社の利用客は長時間待たされることが多い」ということを身をもって体験させたのです。

⓫~⓭:このサプライズにより、広告会社は大口の仕事を受注することができたと言っています。

聞き取りメモ例

• electric voucher
phone → [restaurant
free drink]
unexpected
eat sth there

somethingのことです

• railway
10 min nobody turned
20
30
1 hour leave
||
[what customers experienced every day]

win a contract

L02_Q3

3. Why can a free drink from a fast-food restaurant be effective?

(A) Because customers are often thirsty
(B) Because menu items are usually not free
(C) Because a free drink offer is very rare
(D) Because people do not have to choose their drinks

なぜファストフードレストランの無料ドリンクは効果的となり得ますか。

(A) 顧客はのどが渇いていることが多いから
(B) メニューにある商品は普通無料ではないから
(C) 無料ドリンクの提供はとても珍しいから
(D) 人々は飲み物を選ぶ必要がないから

❺❼からファストフードレストランの無料の飲み物についての話が展開されます。この場合のsurprise rewardとは、通常は代金のかかるものが無料で提供されるため、そのことが驚きを生むということだとわかります。よって、(B)が正解です。(A)は言及がありません。(C)も講義で言及がありません。また具体例として挙げられている以上、比較的一般的な手法であることが予測されます。(D)ですが、「選ぶ必要がない」といった話は講義中には出てきません。

L02_Q4

4. Why does the professor talk about the example of British Rail?

(A) To show how powerful monetary incentives can be in marketing
(B) To demonstrate rewards are not always necessary to attract customers
(C) To remind students of the importance of being on time for meetings
(D) To examine how surprise marketing helped British Rail win a contract

教授はなぜBritish Railの事例について話していますか。

(A) マーケティングにおいて金銭的インセンティブがどれほど強力になり得るかを示すため
(B) 顧客を引き付けるためには対価がいつも必要というわけではないということを示すため
(C) 会議に時間通りに行くことの重要性を学生に再認識させるため
(D) surprise marketingがどのようにBritish Railが契約を勝ち取る一助になったかを分析するため

❻❷以降で「ご褒美を与えるわけではない」サプライズマーケティングの手法について述べられています。この具体例がBritish Railなので、(B)が正解です。これと同じ理由で(A)は誤りだとわかりますね。(C)のような内容が講義からは読み取れません。(D)についてですが、契約を勝ち取ったのはBritish Railではなく広告会社なので誤りです。

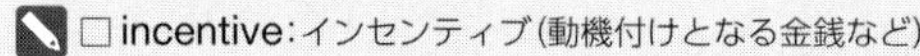

□ incentive：インセンティブ（動機付けとなる金銭など）

7～10 | 問5 解説レクチャー

L02_Script07-10

7 P: ❶We briefly talked about how "surprise" matters for marketing with a couple of examples. ❷Let's now take a closer look at why elements of surprise have such potential in marketing. ❸One reason is that surprise amplifies emotions. ❹Fear, anger, sadness, happiness . . . we have a variety of emotions. ❺What's unique about surprise is that it strengthens the intensity of our emotions. ❻For instance, if you are surprised and angry, you are furious because surprise boosts your anger. ❼In contrast, a pleasant surprise, a combination of happiness and surprise, can make you not just happy, but very happy. ❽This explains why a surprise gift is particularly effective. ❾A surprise gift surprises the person who receives it. ❿At the same time, that person feels glad or happy. ⓫You know, usually, no one gets angry when he or she receives a gift. ⓬The feeling of happiness is intensified by "surprise." ⓭Have any of you experienced something like this? ⓮Anyone? ⓯Why are you smiling Josh?

8 S: ❶Me? ❷Well . . . I, I don't know, but speaking of a surprise gift, I gave a ring to my fiancée in a sudden manner. ❸She looked surprised, but you know . . . it worked!

9 P: ❶Ha ha. ❷That's a good example. ❸The technique you used is surprise marketing. ❹Well, you didn't sell anything, but in effect, you marketed yourself. ❺So as we learned today, involving "surprise" in your marketing is a very effective way to sell things or convince people.

10 P: ❶Finally, even though surprise marketing is an extremely powerful marketing tactic, it is only so when it's carefully thought out and properly implemented. ❷In some cases, it can go wrong, and in fact, very wrong. ❸The reason should be clear if you remember what I said about how emotions can be powerful when combined with surprise.

解説レクチャー

7

❶～❷:なぜ驚きがマーケティングにおいて効果的なのか、その理由について踏み込んでいくとのことです。

❸～❺:驚きは種々の感情を増幅すると説明しています。

❻～❼:例えば、怒りと同時に驚きを覚えれば怒りが強くなり、驚きと喜びを組み合わせれば喜びが強くなるとのことです。

❽～⓯:サプライズプレゼントが喜びを増幅させるのも、この理由によるということですね。

8

❶～❸:この学生は、サプライズで婚約者に指輪を渡し、プロポーズに成功したと述べています。自らの体験を具体例として語ったわけですね。

9

❶～❺:教授も、学生の手法がサプライズマーケティングの手法と同じだと同意しています。

10

❶:サプライズマーケティングは入念な準備、適切な運用が行われなければ、失敗すると述べています。

❷～❸:驚きは感情を増幅させるので、マイナスの方向に向かうと悪影響というわけです。

聞き取りメモ例

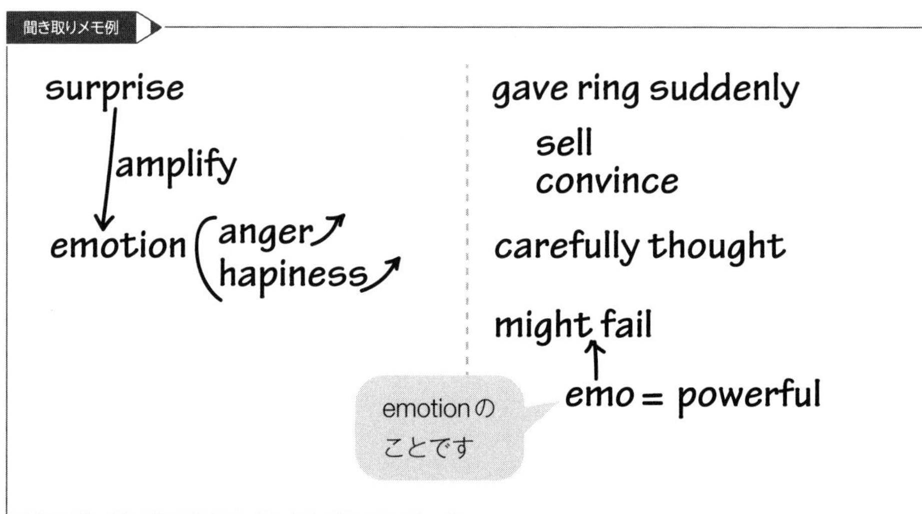

L02_Q5

5. What can be inferred about a poorly laid out surprise marketing campaign?

(A) It can nonetheless be a powerful marketing campaign.
(B) It can lead to amplifying negative emotions of customers.
(C) It still remains to be seen whether bad campaign could lead to a disaster.
(D) It should be studied thoroughly for future reference.

計画が貧弱なsurprise marketingのキャンペーンについて何が推測できますか。

(A) それでも強力なマーケティングキャンペーンになりうる。
(B) それは顧客の負の感情を増幅することにつながりうる。
(C) 悪いキャンペーンが大失敗を招くか否かはまだわからない。
(D) それは今後のために徹底的に研究されるべきである。

⑩❷で「サプライズマーケティングが悪い方向に向かうこともある」と述べられています。その後、「驚きは感情が強くなることもある」とあります。そこから貧弱なサプライズマーケティングは顧客が抱く負の感情を増幅させる可能性があると推測できるので、(B)が正解です。(A)のnonethelessは「貧弱な計画であるにもかかわらず」という意味です。逆接なので、powerfulが「良い意味で強力」ということになるため、⑩の内容に矛盾します。(C)は「まだわからない」とぼやかしていますが、講義では驚きが感情を増幅するので、貧弱な計画は悪い方向に向かうとあります。講義の内容に矛盾するので、誤りです。(D)にあるような今後の研究については、講義では言及されていません。

□ nonetheless：それにもかかわらず　□ amplify X：Xを増幅する　□ remain to be Vpp：まだ～されていない　□ thoroughly：完全に

問 6 解説レクチャー

L02_Q6

6. Listen again to part of the lecture and then answer the question.

Professor:
The firm succeeded in making a huge impact on the officials of British Rail, and this impact, or surprise, is what got them the contract. It's amazing that the advertising company played such a risky game, given what was at stake.

What does the professor mean when he says this?

"It's amazing that the advertising company played such a risky game, given what was at stake."

(A) Winning a contract is like a game that involves some risk.
(B) The tactics of the advertising company could have failed completely.
(C) The risky nature of the contract will cost the advertising company a lot of money.
(D) The advertising company could have won a contract using conventional tactics.

講義の一部をもう一度聞いて、設問に答えてください。

教授：
その会社はBritish Railの社員にとても大きなインパクトを与えることに成功し、このインパクト、つまり驚きが彼らに契約をもたらしたのです。何がかかっていたかを考えれば、広告会社がそのような危険な賭けに出たことは驚きです。

「何がかかっていたかを考えれば、その広告会社がそのような危険な賭けに出たことは驚きです」と言うとき、教授は何を意図していますか。

(A) 契約を勝ち取るということは、リスクを伴うゲームのようなものである。
(B) その広告会社の戦略は完全な失敗に終わったかもしれなかった。
(C) その契約が持つリスクはその広告会社にとって高くつくことになる。
(D) その広告会社は、従来の戦略を使っても契約を取れていただろう。

先方が怒り、広告会社が鉄道会社との大口契約を結ぶ機会を失っていたかもしれません。このことをriskyと表現しています。言い換えれば、大失敗になる恐れもあったわけです。よって(B)が正解です。(A)は契約を取ることにはリスクが伴うということを一般化しているため誤りです。講義中での具体例は驚きを利用したため、リスクを伴ったにすぎません。また、講義では契約自体がリスクを含んでいることへの言及はないので、(C)は誤りです。(D)は常識的に考えれば間違いではないかもしれませんが、講義の内容から読み取ることはできません。

□ win a contract：契約を取る　□ conventional：従来の

1

P: Professor S: Student

Listen to part of a lecture in a business marketing class.

1 P: ❶Marketing tactics have evolved significantly over the years as customers desire a more personalized experience.
❷However, the ultimate aim of marketing remains the same . . . sell your products.
❸Sell your services.
❹Basically, you wanna make your products or services memorable and unforgettable so that people keep buying what you offer.
❺One strategy for accomplishing this is "surprise marketing."
❻I'm sure you've received birthday presents on your birthday from your friends or parents.
❼It's nice to know there's somebody who celebrates your special day, isn't it?
❽But, you know what?
❾You're likely to feel happier if you get a present on a non-special day.
❿There's some neuroscientific research data indicating that the part of the human brain associated with pleasure showed increased activity when the event was unexpected.
⓫So, how people perceive a certain event differs depending on whether it's expected or unexpected.

ビジネスマーケティングの授業での講義の一部を聞きなさい。

1 P: ❶消費者が一人一人により特化した経験を求めるにつれて、マーケティング戦略は長きにわたり、著しく進化してきました。
❷しかしながら、マーケティングの最終的な目標は同じままです…商品を売るということです。
❸サービスを売るということです。
❹基本的に、あなたの提供するものを人々が買い続けるようにするために商品やサービスを覚えやすく、そして記憶に残るようにしたいと思うはずです。
❺これを成し遂げる１つの戦略が、'surprise marketing' です。
❻皆さんはきっと友達や両親から誕生日にプレゼントを受け取ったことがあると思います。
❼皆さんの特別な日を祝ってくれる誰かがいるということはとても素敵なことでしょう。
❽しかし、いいですか。
❾特別でない日にプレゼントをもらったほうがより嬉しく感じやすいのです。
❿神経科学の研究データは、快楽に関連する人間の脳の一部分は、ある特定の出来事が予期されていないものであったときに、活動が活発化したことを示しています。
⓫ですから、ある特定の出来事をどのようにとらえるかは、それが予期されていたか、されていなかったかによって変化するのです。

1
- ☐ tactic：戦略
- ☐ neuroscientific：神経科学の
- ☐ depending on X：Xによって

1 as customers (S) desire (V)
asは接続詞、「～するにつれて」

remain (V) the same (C)「同じままである」
the sameは文法的には補語。

[so that] people (S) keep (V) buying ...「…を買い続けるようにするために」
so thatは「目的」を意味する接続詞。

the part of the human brain (S) (associated with pleasure) showed (V) (increased) (M) activity (O)
the partが主語、showedが述語動詞、increased activityが目的語。

how people perceive a certain event (S) differs (V)
how people perceive a certain eventという名詞節が主語、differsが述語動詞。

2-4

2 P: ❶Today's consumers are exposed to a vast array of advertisements and digitalized experiences.
❷Therefore, it's extremely hard to come up with a campaign that stands out among many others out there.
❸Consequently, with increasing awareness of the power of surprise in the context of marketing, more and more marketing companies today are trying to incorporate elements of surprise into their marketing schemes.
❹So, what is this much-talked-about surprise marketing?
❺Any guesses?
❻Well, you guys should have a pretty good idea of it given what I have talked about so far.

3 S: Is it like giving out coupons or offering discounts?

4 P: ❶Yes, exactly, so that's one form of surprise marketing.
❷Coupons and discounts are good examples.
❸Surprise marketing tries to draw customers' attention by offering them something unexpected.
❹It starts by targeting groups of people who will receive an unexpected reward or experience.
❺Surprise campaigns include offering special privileges to loyal customers . . . or discounts on special occasions such as your wedding anniversary or your birthday.
❻The most appealing benefit of surprise marketing is that it possesses the potential to instantly build a bond with prospects and customers.

2 P: ❶今日の消費者は、とてつもなく多くの広告や、デジタル化された体験にさらされています。
❷そのため、そこらじゅうにある多くの広告の中でも目立つものを考え出すのは、非常に難しいことなのです。
❸結果として、マーケティングという分野の中で「驚き」の力への意識が高まり、今日ではますます多くのマーケティング会社が「驚き」の要素をマーケティング構想の中に組み込もうとしているのです。
❹では、このよく語られる surprise marketing とは何なのでしょうか。
❺何だと思いますか。
❻ええ、これまで私が話してきたことを考えれば、とてもいい答えが思い浮かぶはずですよ。

3 S: それはクーポンを配ったり、割引をしたりするというようなことですか。

4 P: ❶ええ、その通りです、ですからそれが surprise marketing の一形態ですね。
❷クーポンや割引はとてもいい例です。
❸ surprise marketing は、消費者に予期していない何かを提供することによって、彼らの注意を引こうとするのです。
❹それは、予期しない報酬や体験を受け取る人のグループをターゲットにすることから始めます。
❺サプライズキャンペーンは、常連客に対して特別優待、または結婚記念日や誕生日などの特別な機会に割引をすることも含みます。
❻ surprise marketing の最大の魅力は、それが見込み客や現実の顧客と即座につながりをつくる潜在力を有しているということです。

2
- ☐ be exposed to X：X にさらされる
- ☐ stand out：目立つ
- ☐ among others out there：そこらじゅうにある（others は other campaigns の意味）
- ☐ consequently：結果として
- ☐ incorporate X into Y：X を Y に組み込む
- ☐ scheme：構想
- ☐ much-talked-about：よく語られる、よく話題に上る

4
- ☐ draw one's attention：～の関心を引く
- ☐ reward：報酬
- ☐ privilege：特権
- ☐ loyal customer：常連客

2 given (what I have talked about so far) → given［名詞 /that SV］
「～ということを考えると」（given ≒ considering）

3 Is it like giving out ...「…を配るようなことですか」
like は前置詞

5

5 P: ❶As people's lifestyles change, the forms of marketing also change.
❷So . . . let's take a quick look at one or two examples.
❸Well . . . many companies are making good use of electronic vouchers.
❹They send you special offers and messages that you can read from your computer or a mobile phone.
❺Many people today have a computer and mobile phone, making them an effective medium for marketing.
❻Recent technologies are really great.
❼For example . . . you're walking down the street.
❽You suddenly get a notification to your mobile phone.
❾It's a notification from a certain fast-food restaurant saying it has an offer of a free drink available for you.
❿And you go "A free drink!?"
⓫You didn't have a plan to go and eat in the restaurant, but hearing the free drink offer, which was totally unexpected, you might choose to stop by and grab something there.
⓬This is an example of surprise marketing involving a surprise reward.

5 P: ❶人々の生活スタイルが変わるにつれて、マーケティングの手法も変化します。
❷では…例を一つ二つ簡単に見てみましょう。
❸多くの会社が電子クーポンを活用しています。
❹彼らは、コンピューターや携帯から閲覧できる、特別なオファーやメッセージを送ります。
❺今日の多くの人々がコンピューターや携帯電話を持っていますが、そのことがそれら（コンピューターや携帯）をマーケティングにおいて効果的な媒体にするのです。
❻近年の技術は本当に素晴らしいです。
❼例えば、あなたが道を歩いているとします。
❽突然、あなたの携帯電話にお知らせが届きます。
❾それは、無料ドリンクをお楽しみいただけます、と書かれた、あるファストフードレストランからのお知らせです。
❿するとあなたは、「無料ドリンク!?」と言います。
⓫あなたはそのレストランに行って食事をする予定はありませんでしたが、全く予期していなかった無料ドリンクのプレゼントがあると聞き、そこに立ち寄り何かを買う選択をするかもしれません。
⓬これは予想しないご褒美を使ったsurprise marketingの一例です。

5
- □ voucher：クーポン
- □ stop by：立ち寄る（byは副詞）
- □ grab X：Xをさっと買って食べる

5 Many people today have a computer and mobile phone, <u>making</u> them an effective medium for marketing

making以下は、Many people today ... phoneまでを意味上の主語とする分詞構文。Many people today have a computer and mobile phone, which makes them (=a computer and mobile phone) an effective medium for marketingと読み替えてもよい。

6

6 P: ❶But really, that surprise doesn't have to be a free coupon or a discount.
❷Here's another example of surprise marketing which doesn't involve any rewards.
❸Some time ago, British Rail was looking for an advertising company with innovative marketing schemes to promote their railway services.
❹Some representatives of British Rail visited one advertising agency to have a meeting.
❺They were waiting in a meeting room of the advertising company.
❻Ten minutes past the appointment, nobody turned up.
❼Twenty minutes . . . still no one.
❽Thirty minutes past the appointment, still . . . nobody turned up.
❾After being kept waiting for about an hour, the representatives of British Rail got angry and decided to leave the room.
❿Just as they left the room, the people from the advertising company barged in and said, "You've just experienced what British Rail customers experience every day."
⓫The creative imagination of the advertising company paid off, and they got the contract with British Rail.
⓬The firm succeeded in making a huge impact on the officials of British Rail, and this impact, or surprise, is what got them the contract.
⓭It's amazing that the advertising company played such a risky game, given what was at stake.

6 P: ❶しかし実際は、そのサプライズは無料クーポンや割引でなくてもいいのです。

❷どのようなご褒美も使わない surprise marketing のもう1つの例を今から紹介します。

❸かつて、British Rail は、鉄道サービスの販売促進をする革新的なマーケティング構想を持った広告会社を探していました。

❹ British Rail の何人かの代表者が商談をしにある広告代理店を訪れました。

❺彼らはその広告代理店の会議室で待機していました。

❻約束の時間を 10 分過ぎても、誰も姿を見せません。

❼ 20 分…まだ誰も来ません。

❽ 30 分を過ぎても、まだ誰も来ませんでした。

❾約 1 時間待たされた後、British Rail の担当者は怒り、部屋を出ることにしました。

❿彼らが部屋を出ようとしたちょうどその時、広告会社の担当者が入ってきて言いました、「これこそが御社の利用客が毎日経験していることなのです」と。

⓫広告会社の独創的な発想が功を奏し、British Rail の仕事を受注したのです。

⓬その会社は British Rail の社員にとても大きなインパクトを与えることに成功し、このインパクト、つまり驚きが彼らに契約をもたらしたのです。

⓭何がかかっていたかを考えれば、広告会社がそのような危険な賭けに出たことは驚きです。

6
- □ innovative：革新的な
- □ representative：代表者
- □ turn up：現れる
- □ barge in：押し入る
- □ pay off：功を奏する
- □ given X：Xを考えれば
- □ at stake：賭けの対象となっている

6 Ten minutes (past the appointment)「約束の時間から 10 分が過ぎて」
(past the appointment = M)

pastは前置詞。

what got them the contract
(what = S, got = V, them = O_1, the contract = O_2)

O_1にO_2を与える。このgetはgiveのような意味。

7-8

7 P: ❶We briefly talked about how "surprise" matters for marketing with a couple of examples.
❷Let's now take a closer look at why elements of surprise have such potential in marketing.
❸One reason is that surprise amplifies emotions.
❹Fear, anger, sadness, happiness . . . we have a variety of emotions.
❺What's unique about surprise is that it strengthens the intensity of our emotions.
❻For instance, if you are surprised and angry, you are furious because surprise boosts your anger.
❼In contrast, a pleasant surprise, a combination of happiness and surprise, can make you not just happy, but very happy.
❽This explains why a surprise gift is particularly effective.
❾A surprise gift surprises the person who receives it.
❿At the same time, that person feels glad or happy.
⓫You know, usually, no one gets angry when he or she receives a gift.
⓬The feeling of happiness is intensified by "surprise."
⓭Have any of you experienced something like this?
⓮Anyone?
⓯Why are you smiling Josh?

8 S: ❶Me?
❷Well . . . I, I don't know, but speaking of a surprise gift, I gave a ring to my fiancée in a sudden manner.
❸She looked surprised, but you know . . . it worked!

7

P: ❶私たちは、2、3の例とともに、マーケティングにとって、いかに「驚き」が大切かを簡単に話し合いました。
❷ではマーケティングにおいて、なぜ驚きの要素がそのような潜在力を持っているのか、より詳しく見てみましょう。
❸その1つの理由は、驚きが感情を増幅するからです。
❹恐怖、怒り、悲しみ、幸福…私たちは様々な感情を持っています。
❺驚きが他と違う点は、私たちの感情をさらに激しくするということです。
❻例えば、もしあなたが驚き怒っているのであれば、驚きが怒りを強めるため、あなたは激怒するでしょう。
❼対照的に、喜ばしい驚き、幸福と驚きの組み合わせは、あなたを単に幸せにするのではなく、とても幸せにするのです。
❽これによって、なぜサプライズギフトが特に効果的なのかがわかります。
❾サプライズギフトは、それを受け取る人を驚かせるのです。
❿同時に、その人は嬉しい、もしくは幸せだと感じます。
⓫ふつう、ギフトをもらって怒る人はいませんよね。
⓬その幸福の感情が、驚きによって強められるのです。
⓭誰かこのようなことを経験したことはありますか。
⓮誰か。
⓯Josh、なぜにこにこしているのですか。

8

S: ❶僕ですか。
❷さあ…なぜでしょう。でも、サプライズギフトと言えば、私は予告なしにフィアンセに指輪を贈りました。
❸彼女は驚いたように見えましたが、ええ、うまく行きました！

7

- ☐ amplify X：Xを増幅させる
- ☐ a variety of X：様々なX
- ☐ strengthen X：Xを強める
- ☐ intensity：激しさ
- ☐ furious：激怒した
- ☐ intensify X：Xを強める

8

- ☐ speaking of X：Xに関して言えば
- ☐ in a X manner：Xな方法で

9-10

9 P: ❶Ha ha.
❷That's a good example.
❸The technique you used is surprise marketing.
❹Well, you didn't sell anything, but in effect, you marketed yourself.
❺So as we learned today, involving "surprise" in your marketing is a very effective way to sell things or convince people.

10 P: ❶Finally, even though surprise marketing is an extremely powerful marketing tactic, it is only so when it's carefully thought out and properly implemented.
❷In some cases, it can go wrong, and in fact, very wrong.
❸The reason should be clear if you remember what I said about how emotions can be powerful when combined with surprise.

9 P: ❶はは。
❷それはいい例ですね。
❸あなたが使ったテクニックが surprise marketing なのです。
❹まあ、あなたは何も売りませんでしたが、実質的にあなた自身をマーケティングしたのです。
❺ですから、今日私たちが学習した通り、「驚き」をマーケティングに組み込むことは、物を売ったり人を説得したりするのにとても効果的な方法なのです。

10 P: ❶最後に、surprise marketing は極めて強力なマーケティング戦略ですが、それは入念に準備され、適切に運用されたときに限られるのです。
❷ある場合には間違った方向に、それも、とても間違った方向に行ってしまう可能性があるのです。
❸感情が驚きと組み合わされたときにどのように強力になるかについて、私が言ったことを覚えていれば、その理由は明らかなはずです。

9
- [ ] in effect：実質的に

10
- [ ] go wrong：失敗する

10 even though surprise marketing is an extremely powerful marketing tactic,
it(S) is(V) [only] so(C) (when it's carefully thought out and properly implemented)

soは補語を代用する語、so=an extremely powerful marketing tactic。またonlyはwhen以下を修飾。
it is an extremely powerful marketing tactic only when it's carefully thought out ...と解釈する。

リスニング問題 3 会話

CAMPUS CONVERSATION

問題演習の流れ

- □ 音声が流れている間は、問題は読めません。会話が終わり、最初の問題音声が流れ始めたらページをめくって、5分以内に解答しましょう。
- □ 1問の解答時間は20秒を目安にしています。問題を読み上げた後に解答時間として20秒のポーズ（音声なし）が入っていますので、その間に解答をマークしてください。
- □ メモは自由に取ってください。
- □ 3回解けるように、3回分のマークシートを問題ページに用意しています。解く日付を記入してからマークしてください。

Web解答方法

- □ 本試験では各選択肢の左に表示されるマークをクリックして解答します。本試験と同様の方法で取り組みたい場合は、Webで解答できます。
- □ インターネットのつながるパソコン・スマートフォンで、以下のサイトにアクセスしてWeb上で解答してください。

extester.com

- □ 操作方法は、p.13 ～ 14の「USA Club Web学習の使い方」をご参照ください。

学習の記録

学習開始日	年　　月　　日	学習終了日	年　　月　　日
学習開始日	年　　月　　日	学習終了日	年　　月　　日
学習開始日	年　　月　　日	学習終了日	年　　月　　日

リスニング問題 3 会話　音声

 L03

聞き取りメモ

L03_Q1

1. What was the main purpose of the student's visit to the professor?

(A) To register for a biochemistry class
(B) To ask about the difference of viruses and bacteria
(C) To clarify things he didn't understand in the class
(D) To decide the topic of a report

L03_Q2

2. According to the professor, what is the fundamental difference between viruses and bacteria?

(A) Bacteria can grow and reproduce by themselves but viruses cannot.
(B) The structure of bacteria is much simpler than viruses'.
(C) Bacteria are single-celled while viruses are multi-celled.
(D) Only bacteria can infect a host to obtain protein needed for reproduction.

L03_Q3

3. According to the professor, why are antibiotics not effective on viruses?

(A) Each virus has unique shapes, making drug design impossible.
(B) Many viruses have acquired resistance to antibiotics.
(C) Viruses do not have any structures or functions that antibiotics can perceive as targets.
(D) The cell wall of viruses is too thick to penetrate.

L03_Q4

4. What is the professor's attitude toward the student's idea about the topic for the report?

(A) She is enthusiastic about it.
(B) She could not fully comprehend what the student proposes.
(C) She believes the student must pick a completely different topic.
(D) She thinks it may be inappropriate.

L03_Q5

5. Listen again to part of the conversation and then answer the question.
Why did the professor say this?

(A) To stress that this topic is controversial
(B) To confirm that the student is correct
(C) To confess that she does not agree with the student
(D) To make sure whether viruses are dead or alive

 1. **(C)** 2. **(A)** 3. **(C)** 4. **(D)** 5. **(B)**

1~6 | 問 1~2 解説レクチャー

L03_Script01-06 S: Student P: Professor

1
S: Hi Professor Brown.
P: ❶Ah, hello! ❷It's always nice to see students during office hours.

2
S: This is my first time to take a biochemistry class, and everything is new.
P: ❶So you are learning. ❷And do you have any questions?

3
S: ❶Yes. ❷I was surprised by something in your lecture. ❸I always thought antibiotics were used to kill viruses. ❹But, after your lecture, I realized I might've been wrong.
P: ❶That's a common misconception. ❷Antibiotics are designed to kill bacteria, NOT viruses. ❸The name itself, "antibiotics", suggests that. ❹"Anti" means against and "biotic" refers to life. ❺So basically, these agents are not effective against viruses.

4
S: ❶But then, aren't viruses and bacteria similar? ❷They are both tiny, and . . .
P: ❶Well, they're fundamentally different. ❷Bacteria are single-celled living organisms with their own cellular structures, with which they can grow and reproduce. ❸In other words, they are living. ❹On the other hand, viruses aren't truly "alive", at least in a traditional sense.

5
S: ❶Not alive? ❷I've always pictured viruses as tiny living organisms.
P: ❶In short, viruses lack the structures or parts to function independently. ❷They don't have cell membranes, mitochondria, and many important proteins. ❸Viruses' structure is much simpler, and they can't grow or reproduce by themselves. ❹So, viruses need to infect a host cell and use the host's cellular materials to reproduce, which means . . .

6
S: They are not considered living organisms.
P: That's dead on!

解説レクチャー

※1S:1の学生の発言　1P:1の教授の発言

1S〜3S:導入部です。生化学の学生から教授に質問があると分かりますね。

3P〜6P:抗生物質の定義を教授が説明しています。さらに、そこからウイルスとバクテリアの違いについて細かく説明していますね。

聞き取りメモ例

biochemistry

まず何の授業についての質問をしにきているのかメモをします。biochemistryの授業についてのものなのでここをメモします

antibio kill ×virus ○bacteria

その後antibioticsがvirusではなくbacteriaを殺すというメモをします

vはvirus
bはbacteriaを表しています

v　simple　　grow/reproduce

b　single cell

その後2つの違いについて説明するので特徴をメモします

L03_Q1

1. What was the main purpose of the student's visit to the professor?

(A) To register for a biochemistry class
(B) To ask about the difference of viruses and bacteria
(C) To clarify things he didn't understand in the class
(D) To decide the topic of a report

学生が教授を訪ねた一番の目的は何でしたか。

(A) 生化学のクラスに登録するため
(B) ウイルスとバクテリアの違いについて尋ねるため
(C) 授業でわからなかったことをはっきりさせるため
(D) レポートのテーマを決めるため

2P ～ 3S のやりとりから、学生が質問するために来たことが分かります。よって、Cが正解です。Aは、すでに生化学の授業を取っているため不適切。Bは、教授とのやり取りによって生じた話題です。学生が教授の元に来た当初の目的ではありません。Dは会話の最後で突発的に生じた話題なので誤りです。

□ clarify:～を解明する

L03_Q2

2. According to the professor, what is the fundamental difference between viruses and bacteria?

(A) Bacteria can grow and reproduce by themselves but viruses cannot.
(B) The structure of bacteria is much simpler than viruses'.
(C) Bacteria are single-celled while viruses are multi-celled.
(D) Only bacteria can infect a host to obtain protein needed for reproduction.

教授によると、ウイルスとバクテリアの根本的な違いは何ですか。

(A) バクテリアは自分で成長し増殖できるが、ウイルスはできない。
(B) バクテリアの構造はウイルスの構造よりもずっと単純である。
(C) バクテリアは単細胞であるが、ウイルスは多細胞である。
(D) 宿主に感染して生殖に必要なタンパク質を得ることができるのは、バクテリアだけである。

4P ~ 5P で、教授がウイルスとバクテリアの違いを説明しています。4P ❷において、「バクテリアは単細胞の生物で…成長し増殖することができる」と述べられているため、Aが正解です。本文のgrow and reproduceという表現が、そのまま選択肢で用いられています。Bは、5P ❸で「ウイルスの構造は（バクテリアの構造より）もっと単純」とあるため誤り。Cは「ウイルスは多細胞である」という記述が本文にないため誤り。そもそもウイルスのほうが単純な構造なので多細胞はありえません。Dは、5P ❹で「ウイルスは宿主細胞に感染する」とあるため誤りです。

□ multi-celled:多細胞の

7～9 | 問3～4 解説レクチャー

L03_Script07-09　S: Student　P: Professor

7
S: ❶Ha ha. ❷It's getting interesting. ❸Well, so, my next question would be, why antibiotics kill bacteria but not viruses?
P: ❶Good question. ❷Antibiotics are designed to target structures or functions unique to bacteria, such as their cell walls or some enzymes. ❸Viruses don't have these elements. ❹Thus, antibiotics aren't effective against viruses.

8
S: ❶Wow, this sheds light on so much. ❷Well, I just came up with an idea. ❸Can I use this topic in my report?
P: ❶Well, it can be an interesting topic, but remember what we discussed today was covered in one section of Chapter 1. ❷To make it acceptable, consider exploring how antibiotics inhibit bacterial reproduction from a biochemical perspective. ❸Include biochemical reactions that were covered in other chapters as well. ❹Chemical reactions involved in protein synthesis can be a good example. ❺That way, you can make it more comprehensive and appropriate for the material to be graded.

9
S: ❶That sounds challenging but interesting. ❷Thank you, Professor. ❸I'll consider your advice.

解説レクチャー

※7S：7の学生の発言　7P：7の教授の発言

7S～7P：生徒がさらに別の質問をしています。

8S～9S：生徒がレポートのトピックについて相談しています。教授はそれに対してアドバイスをしていますね。

聞き取りメモ例

L03_Q3

3. According to the professor, why are antibiotics not effective on viruses?

(A) Each virus has unique shapes, making drug design impossible.
(B) Many viruses have acquired resistance to antibiotics.
(C) Viruses do not have any structures or functions that antibiotics can perceive as targets.
(D) The cell wall of viruses is too thick to penetrate.

教授によると、抗生物質がウイルスに効かないのはなぜですか。

(A) ウイルスはそれぞれが特有の形をしているため、薬剤開発が不可能だから。
(B) 多くのウイルスが抗生物質に対する耐性を獲得しているから。
(C) ウイルスには、抗生物質が標的と認識できるような構造や機能はないから。
(D) ウイルスの細胞壁が厚すぎて浸透しないから。

7P ❷❸で「抗生物質はバクテリアに特有な構造や機能を標的にする。ウイルスにはこれらの要素がない」とあります。つまり、ウイルスは抗生物質が標的とする構造や機能を持たないということなのでCが正解です。なお、残りの選択肢は本文に記述がないため誤りです。

□ **resistance to:** ～に対する耐性・抵抗力 □ **perceive A as B:** AをBと認識する・みなす
□ **penetrate:** ～に浸透する

L03_Q4

4. What is the professor's attitude toward the student's idea about the topic for the report?

(A) She is enthusiastic about it.
(B) She could not fully comprehend what the student proposes.
(C) She believes the student must pick a completely different topic.
(D) She thinks it may be inappropriate.

学生が考えたレポートのテーマについて、教授はどのような態度を取っていますか。

(A) 非常に興味を引かれている。
(B) 学生の案を十分に理解できなかった。
(C) 学生が完全に別のトピックを選ぶ必要があると考えている。
(D) 不適切かもしれないと考えている。

8P ❶に、「面白いトピックかもしれませんが、今日話したことは第1章のセクションの一つで扱っていることを忘れないでください」とあるため、学生が扱おうとしているトピックをそのままレポートの題材にするのは、避けるべきだと教授が考えているようです。よってDが正解となります。Aは、教授が積極的にそのトピックを推していることになるため誤り。Bは、教授が学生の発言を完全には理解していないことになるので誤り。教授は完全に異なるトピックを選ぶよう指示しているわけではないのでCも誤りです。

□ be enthusiastic about:～に熱中している　□ comprehend:～を理解する

問5 解説レクチャー

L03_Q5

5. Listen again to part of the conversation and then answer the question.

Professor:
So, viruses need to infect a host cell and use the host's cellular materials to reproduce, which means . . .

Student:
They are not considered living organisms.

Professor:
That's dead on!

Why did the professor say this?

"That's dead on!"

(A) To stress that this topic is controversial
(B) To confirm that the student is correct
(C) To confess that she does not agree with the student
(D) To make sure whether viruses are dead or alive

会話の一部をもう一度聞いて、設問に答えてください。

教授：

ですから、ウイルスは宿主細胞に感染し、宿主の細胞物質を利用して増殖する必要があります。つまり・・・

学生：

生物とはみなされない。

教授：

その通り！

なぜ教授は「その通り！」と言いましたか。

(A) このトピックが論争の的になっていることを強調するため
(B) 学生は正しいと明言するため
(C) 実は学生の意見に賛成できないのだと言うため
(D) ウイルスが死んでいるか生きているかを確かめるため

教授の発言に対して学生が正しい内容を返答しているため、Bが正解です。That's dead onという表現を知らなくても、文脈と発言のテンションから正解を導き出してください。残りの選択肢は全て「正しい」ことを示す表現とはなりません。

□ stress that節:〜だと強調する　□ controversial:論争の的になる　□ confess that節:〜だと認める

S: Student　P: Professor

Listen to part of a conversation between a student and his biochemistry professor.

1 S: Hi Professor Brown.
P: ❶Ah, hello!
❷It's always nice to see students during office hours.

2 S: This is my first time to take a biochemistry class, and everything is new.
P: ❶So you are learning.
❷And do you have any questions?

3 S: ❶Yes.
❷I was surprised by something in your lecture.
❸I always thought antibiotics were used to kill viruses.
❹But, after your lecture, I realized I might've been wrong.
P: ❶That's a common misconception.
❷Antibiotics are designed to kill bacteria, NOT viruses.
❸The name itself, "antibiotics", suggests that.
❹"Anti" means against and "biotic" refers to life.
❺So basically, these agents are not effective against viruses.

4 S: ❶But then, aren't viruses and bacteria similar?
❷They are both tiny, and . . .
P: ❶Well, they're fundamentally different.
❷Bacteria are single-celled living organisms with their own cellular structures, with which they can grow and reproduce.
❸In other words, they are living.
❹On the other hand, viruses aren't truly "alive", at least in a traditional sense.

学生と生化学の教授との会話の一部を聞きなさい。

1
S: こんにちは、ブラウン先生。
P: ❶ああ、こんにちは！
❷面談時間に学生と会うのはいつもいいものですよ。

2
S: 生化学の授業は初めてで、何もかもが新鮮です。
P: ❶そうですか、勉強中というわけですね。
❷何か質問はありますか。

3
S: ❶はい。
❷先生の講義で驚いたことがあります。
❸抗生物質はウイルスを死滅させるために使うものだとずっと思っていました。
❹でも、先生の講義を受けて、私は間違っていたかもしれないと気づきました。
P: ❶それはよくある誤解なんです。
❷抗生物質は殺菌するためのもので、ウイルスを死滅させるためのものではありません。
❸「抗生物質」という名前自体がそれを示しています。
❹「アンチ（anti）」は「対抗して（against）」という意味で、「バイオティック（biotic）」は「生命（life）」を表します。
❺ですから、基本的にこれらの物質はウイルスには効きません。

4
S: ❶でも、ウイルスとバクテリアは似ていませんでしょうか。
❷どちらも小さいし・・・
P: ❶いや、根本的に違います。
❷バクテリアは単細胞の生物で、独自の細胞構造を持ち、成長し増殖することができます。
❸つまり、生きているのです。
❹一方、ウイルスは、少なくとも従来の意味では、本当に「生きている」わけではありません。

- □ biochemistry：生化学

1
- □ office hours：面談時間、勤務時間、オフィスアワー

3
- □ antibiotics：抗生物質
- □ virus：ウイルス
- □ might've been=might have been：～だったかもしれない
- □ misconception：思い違い、誤解
- □ bacteria：バクテリア、細菌
- □ against：～に対抗して・反対して
- □ refer to：～に当てはまる
- □ agent：物質
- □ effective：効果のある

4
- □ tiny：とても小さい
- □ fundamentally：根本的に
- □ single-celled：単細胞の
- □ living organism：生物、有機体
- □ cellular structure：細胞構造
- □ reproduce：繁殖する、増殖する

3 I ... thought antibiotics were used 〈to kill viruses〉.
抗生物質は〈ウイルスを殺すために〉使われると思っていた。

be used to do ～するために使われる
used to do かつて～した
be used to doing ～するのに慣れている
を混同しないように注意

5-7

5 S: ❶Not alive?
❷I've always pictured viruses as tiny living organisms.
P: ❶In short, viruses lack the structures or parts to function independently.
❷They don't have cell membranes, mitochondria, and many important proteins.
❸Viruses' structure is much simpler, and they can't grow or reproduce by themselves.
❹So, viruses need to infect a host cell and use the host's cellular materials to reproduce, which means . . .

6 S: They are not considered living organisms.
P: That's dead on!

7 S: ❶Ha ha.
❷It's getting interesting.
❸Well, so, my next question would be, why antibiotics kill bacteria but not viruses?
P: ❶Good question.
❷Antibiotics are designed to target structures or functions unique to bacteria, such as their cell walls or some enzymes.
❸Viruses don't have these elements.
❹Thus, antibiotics aren't effective against viruses.

5

S: ❶生きていないのですか？
❷ウイルスは小さな生命体だとずっと思っていましたが。

P: ❶要するに、ウイルスには独立して機能するための組織や器官がないのです。
❷細胞膜も、ミトコンドリアも、多くの重要なタンパク質も持っていません。
❸ウイルスの構造はもっと単純で、単独では成長も増殖もできません。
❹ですから、ウイルスは宿主細胞に感染し、宿主の細胞物質を利用して増殖する必要があります。つまり・・・

6

S: 生物とはみなされない。

P: その通り！

7

S: ❶ははは。
❷興味が湧いてきました。
❸それでは、次の質問なのですが、なぜ抗生物質は殺菌はするのにウイルスは死滅させられないのですか。

P: ❶いい質問です。
❷抗生物質はバクテリアに特有の構造や機能、例えば細胞壁や一部の酵素などを標的にするように設計されています。
❸ウイルスはそのような要素を持っていません。
❹ですから、抗生物質はウイルスには効かないのです。

5

- ☐ picture：～を心に描く・想像する
- ☐ in short：要するに
- ☐ lack：～を欠く
- ☐ structure：組織、構造
- ☐ function：機能を果たす
- ☐ membrane：膜組織
- ☐ mitochondria：ミトコンドリア
- ☐ protein：タンパク質
- ☐ infect：～に感染する
- ☐ host cell：宿主細胞（ウイルスなどが寄生している細胞）
- ☐ cellular material：細胞物質

6

- ☐ consider A B：AをBとみなす
- ☐ be dead on：まったく正しい

7

- ☐ target：～を標的とする
- ☐ be unique to：～に特有だ
- ☐ cell wall：細胞壁
- ☐ enzyme：酵素
- ☐ element：要素、成分
- ☐ be effective against：～に対して効果がある

6 They (S) are not considered (V) living organisms (C).

consider O C「OをCだとみなす」の受動態

8-9

8 S: ❶Wow, this sheds light on so much.
❷Well, I just came up with an idea.
❸Can I use this topic in my report?

P: ❶Well, it can be an interesting topic, but remember what we discussed today was covered in one section of Chapter 1.
❷To make it acceptable, consider exploring how antibiotics inhibit bacterial reproduction from a biochemical perspective.
❸Include biochemical reactions that were covered in other chapters as well.
❹Chemical reactions involved in protein synthesis can be a good example.
❺That way, you can make it more comprehensive and appropriate for the material to be graded.

9 S: ❶That sounds challenging but interesting.
❷Thank you, Professor.
❸I'll consider your advice.

8 S: ❶へえ、これによって多くのことが解明できますね。
❷ええと、今思いついたんですが。
❸レポートでこのテーマを扱ってもいいでしょうか。
P: ❶そうですね、面白いトピックかもしれませんが、今日話したことは第１章のセクションの一つで扱っていることを忘れないでください。
❷レポートの条件に合うように、抗生物質がバクテリアの繁殖をどのように阻害するのか、生化学的な観点から探ることを検討してみてください。
❸他の章で取り上げた生化学反応も含めてください。
❹タンパク質の合成に関わる化学反応がいい例になります。
❺そうすれば、より包括的となり、評価する題材としてふさわしい内容にすることができます。

9 S: ❶それは大変そうですが、面白そうです。
❷先生、ありがとうございます。
❸先生のアドバイスを念頭において検討します。

8
- [ ] shed light on : ～に解明の光を当てる（～の説明となる）
- [ ] come up with :（解決策など）を思いつく
- [ ] acceptable : 受け入れられる
- [ ] explore :（問題など）を探求する
- [ ] inhibit : ～を抑制する
- [ ] reproduction : 繁殖
- [ ] from a ... perspective : ～の観点から
- [ ] (be) involved in : ～に関係している
- [ ] synthesis : 合成
- [ ] comprehensive : 包括的な

9
- [ ] challenging : やりがいのある

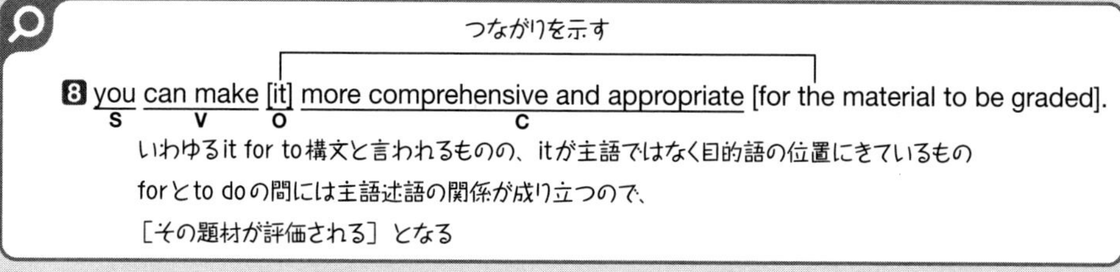

つながりを示す

8 you (S) can make (V) [it] (O) more comprehensive and appropriate (C) [for the material to be graded].

いわゆるit for to構文と言われるものの、itが主語ではなく目的語の位置にきているもの
forとto doの間には主語述語の関係が成り立つので、
［その題材が評価される］となる

リスニング問題 4 講義

ASTRONOMY

問題演習の流れ

- □ 音声が流れている間は、問題は読めません。講義が終わり、最初の問題音声が流れ始めたらページをめくって、5分以内に解答しましょう。
- □ 1問の解答時間は20秒を目安にしています。問題を読み上げた後に解答時間として20秒のポーズ（音声なし）が入っていますので、その間に解答をマークしてください。
- □ メモは自由に取ってください。
- □ 3回解けるように、3回分のマークシートを問題ページに用意しています。解く日付を記入してからマークしてください。

Web解答方法

- □ 本試験では各選択肢の左に表示されるマークをクリックして解答します。本試験と同様の方法で取り組みたい場合は、Webで解答できます。
- □ インターネットのつながるパソコン・スマートフォンで、以下のサイトにアクセスしてWeb上で解答してください。

extester.com

- □ 操作方法は、p.13 ～ 14の「USA Club Web学習の使い方」をご参照ください。

学習の記録

学習開始日	年　月　日	学習終了日	年　月　日
学習開始日	年　月　日	学習終了日	年　月　日
学習開始日	年　月　日	学習終了日	年　月　日

リスニング問題 4 講義　音声

 L04

Astronomy

聞き取りメモ

L04_Q1

1. What is the lecture mainly about?

(A) The process by which gold can be produced
(B) The difference between the Sun and other stars
(C) A detailed description of chemical reactions
(D) How large stars in the universe end their life cycle

L04_Q2

2. Why did the professor talk about the ring on his finger?

(A) To show how rare the materials used for the ring are
(B) To pull the audience into the topic of the lecture
(C) To deflect people's attention from technical details
(D) To explain the mechanism of supernova explosions

L04_Q3

3. What is the supposed reason why a star explodes when it dies?

(A) Iron is originally a highly explosive element.
(B) The conversion of hydrogen to helium provides the energy for an explosion.
(C) There are too many elements packed into a limited space.
(D) The star has no internal energy to sustain its own structure.

L04_Q4

4. What is the professor's opinion about computer simulations used for the research of supernova explosions?

(A) They can be used effectively only by specialized researchers.
(B) They have not generated conclusive data yet.
(C) They are currently in wide use.
(D) They are too expensive to keep developing.

L04_Q5

5. Which of the following are necessary to predict when there will be a star explosion? *Choose two answers.*

(A) How big it is
(B) What color it is
(C) How dense it is
(D) How bright it is

L04_Q6

6. What does the professor say about a stellar wind?

(A) It is the major force that converts helium into carbon and silicon.
(B) It contributes to the formation of heavy elements such as gold.
(C) It breaks heavy elements such as gold and silver down into smaller elements.
(D) It is a continuous stream of wind blowing between stars.

1. **(D)** 2. **(B)** 3. **(D)** 4. **(B)** 5. **(A) (B)** 6. **(B)**

問 1 解説レクチャー

L04_Q1

1. What is the lecture mainly about?

(A) The process by which gold can be produced
(B) The difference between the Sun and other stars
(C) A detailed description of chemical reactions
(D) How large stars in the universe end their life cycle

この講義の主題は何ですか。

(A) 金が生成される過程
(B) 太陽と他の星の違い
(C) 化学反応の詳細な説明
(D) 宇宙の大きい星がどのようにそのライフサイクルを終えるか

講義のはじめに星の誕生に軽く触れ、その後は主に超新星爆発の話をしています。よって(D)が正解です。(A)と(C)は講義で出てきますが、断片的な情報ですので主旨とは言えません。(B)は講義で触れられていません。

□ chemical reaction:化学反応

1~3 | 問 2 解説レクチャー

L04_Script01-03

1 **Professor:**
❶Let's start today's class. ❷I want everyone to look at my ring finger. ❸I'm married, so I wear a ring on my left ring finger. ❹What is it made of? ❺The color of this ring looks gold, but actually, it's a composite of gold, silver, and copper. ❻Have you ever thought about how gold, silver, copper, and other precious metals were formed? ❼Mystery, isn't it? ❽That's today's topic.

2 ❶When you look up at the night sky, I'm sure that you wonder about the stars. ❷Twinkling . . . beautiful . . . far away . . . if you keep looking at them, you realize that they differ in color and brightness. ❸Like humans, each star is unique and different. ❹Like humans or any other creature, stars also have a life cycle. ❺They are born, grow, get old, and die. ❻Stars aren't living creatures, but they do have a life cycle. ❼They are born in the heart of galaxies from what is called a nebula, which is a big mixture of gas and rocks in the galaxy. ❽Once formed, stars spend most of their lifetime as a burning and shining mass. ❾You know, those are the stars that we look at in the night sky. ❿The stars are mainly composed of hydrogen and helium gas, and they're like nuclear reactors turning hydrogen, the lightest element, into helium, the second lightest element. ⓫The same applies to the Sun. ⓬It is made up of mostly hydrogen and helium, and what the Sun is doing is converting hydrogen into helium.

3 ❶All stars shining in the sky are basically the same. ❷Simply put, they are shining by converting hydrogen into helium and getting energy from the conversion. ❸But the amount of hydrogen in the star is finite. ❹Stars keep burning hydrogen, and when they run out of hydrogen, they die. ❺Particularly, big stars—those that are eight times larger than the Sun—end their life with an astronomical event called a "supernova explosion." ❻A supernova explosion is a big explosion of a dying star. ❼The star explodes and ends its life.

解説レクチャー

1

❶～❺:教授が指にはめている指輪の素材を学生に問うています。

❻～❽:指輪の素材である金属がどのように生まれたのかが講義のテーマのようです。指輪という身近な具体例から、アカデミックなテーマに誘導しています。

2

❶～❸:星のことについて話しています。それぞれの星は色や輝きが違うと述べています。

❹～❻:星にもライフサイクルがあるそうです。

❼:星は、ガスと岩で構成される星雲（nebula）から生まれると述べています。

❽～❾:生まれた星は、燃えて輝き続けるそうです。夜空に見えるのはこのような星だとのことです。

❿:星は水素をヘリウムに変換するので、原子炉のように作用するそうです。

⓫～⓬:太陽も同じように、水素をヘリウムに変換するとのことです。

3

❶〜❷:あらゆる星は、水素をヘリウムに変換してエネルギーを得ていると説明しています。
❸〜❹:しかし水素は有限なので、水素が尽きると星は死ぬと述べています。
❺〜❼:大きな星が死ぬとき、「超新星」と呼ばれる大爆発が起こるそうです。

聞き取りメモ例

astronomy
ring gold→silver•copper
color bright
each diff
life cycle
nebula gas & rock

Hydrogen Helium
Sun [Hy→He]
get energy
light
No Hy= die
supernova explosion

L04_Q2

2. Why did the professor talk about the ring on his finger?

(A) To show how rare the materials used for the ring are
(B) To pull the audience into the topic of the lecture
(C) To deflect people's attention from technical details
(D) To explain the mechanism of supernova explosions

教授はなぜ指にはめている指輪について話しましたか。

(A) 指輪に使われている物質がどれほど稀少なものかを示すため
(B) 聴衆を、その講義のトピックへと誘導するため
(C) 専門的で細かい話から人々の注意をそらすため
(D) 超新星爆発のメカニズムを説明するため

❶❷で教授は自分がはめている指輪を学生に見せています。その後、❶❻～❽で講義のトピックの導入をしているので(B)が正解だとわかります。教授は別に指輪を見せびらかしているわけではないので(A)は誤りです。(C)はこの具体例の後にやや専門的な説明が始まるため、誤りです。(D)については指輪の話はあくまでテーマの導入であって、超新星爆発を説明するためのものではありません。

□ deflect X: Xをそらす

4 | 問 3 解説レクチャー

L04_Script04

4 ❶So why does a supernova explosion happen? ❷Why do those big stars explode when they die? ❸Here's the more detailed mechanism. ❹As a very big star goes along, it turns hydrogen into helium and that's how energy is generated in a star. ❺Right? ❻As I mentioned earlier? ❼OK. ❽The star will begin to turn helium into carbon. ❾Carbon is important for life, as you may all know. ❿That's how carbon is born. ⓫Basically, light elements collide with each other and form heavier elements. ⓬Hydrogen to helium, helium to carbon, to neon, to oxygen, and to silicon. ⓭This fusion process continues until the core of the star turns into iron. ⓮Iron is the last stage of this series of conversions. ⓯Iron cannot readily combine to form a heavier element. ⓰The reaction in the core of the star was the source of energy that sustained the life of the star, but if iron can't react to become another element, there's no more reaction in the core. ⓱The star cannot generate energy to sustain its structure, and finally, the star explodes.

解説レクチャー

4

❶～❼：超新星の仕組みを説明するに当たって、星が水素をヘリウムに変換することでエネルギーを得ることをおさらいしています。

❽～❿：星は次にヘリウムを炭素に変換するとのことです。

⓫～⓮：軽い元素は互いに衝突し、より重い元素を作り出すと説明しています。最終的に星の核が鉄になると述べています。

⓯～⓱：鉄は容易に他の元素と結びつくことはないとのことです。化学反応が起こりにくいのでエネルギーが生み出されず、構造を維持できずに爆発してしまうと述べています。

聞き取りメモ例

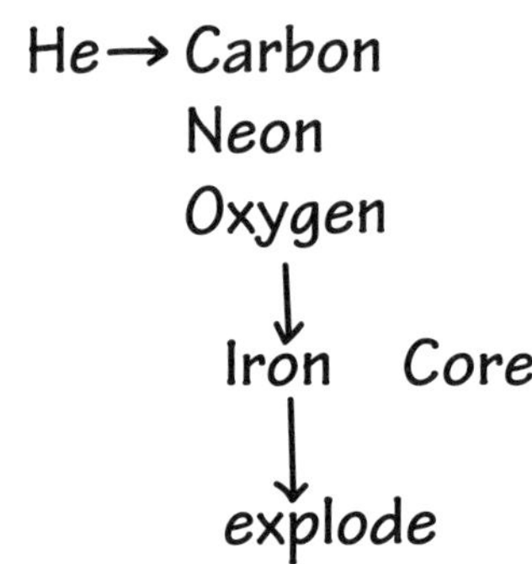

comp simulation
get larger
↓
explode

L04_Q3

3. What is the supposed reason why a star explodes when it dies?

(A) Iron is originally a highly explosive element.
(B) The conversion of hydrogen to helium provides the energy for an explosion.
(C) There are too many elements packed into a limited space.
(D) The star has no internal energy to sustain its own structure.

星が死ぬときに爆発する理由は何だと考えられていますか。

(A) 鉄はもともととても爆発しやすい元素だ。
(B) 水素からヘリウムへの変換は、爆発のためのエネルギーを供給する。
(C) 限られた空間の中にあまりに多くの元素が閉じ込められている。
(D) 星はそれ自身の構造を維持するための内部エネルギーを持たない。

4⑯以降に「構造を維持するエネルギーが不足するので爆発する」とあります。よって(D)が正解です。(A)と(C)のような発言は講義の中で出てきません。水素をヘリウムに変換するのは核融合のプロセスなので、(B)は誤りです。

□explosive：爆発しやすい　□element：要素、元素　□conversion：変換　□pack X into Y：XをYに閉じ込める

5~7 | 問 4~5 解説レクチャー

L04_Script05-07

5 ❶Our understanding of the exact mechanism isn't satisfactory yet because current computer models cannot account for the full amount of energy transferred and material ejected. ❷You know, we can do a series of simulations using computers, but we really can't cut open stars like onions. ❸So there are many things that remain unknown or unproven. ❹However, what we know is that a star gets larger and larger before the supernova explosion. ❺And a star gets redder and redder over time. ❻Therefore, we can tell which star is about to die and experience a supernova explosion. ❼Using a telescope, we can observe stars out there. ❽The fine differences in color can be analyzed, often with the aid of computer programs. ❾We can also estimate the size of the star as well as whether the star is expanding over time, and if so, at what pace. ❿Considering all these, we can predict the timing of the astronomical explosion.

6 ❶A supernova explosion is very rare and only a few have been observed in history. ❷The first in recent times was recorded in 185 AD by the Chinese. ❸Since then, people have observed and sometimes recorded these events. ❹It is said that, on average, a recognizable supernova explosion happens every 50 years. ❺If you are lucky, you may get to see the event once or maybe twice in your life.

7 ❶Although a big supernova explosion can be detected with the naked eye, it's best if you have a telescope because there are some interstellar dust clouds and particles within the Earth's atmosphere that can make this fantastic astronomical event invisible to us. ❷In fact, thanks to the invention of telescopes that allow the observation of distant galaxies, the number of known supernova explosions has dramatically increased.

解説レクチャー

5

❶~❸:現在のコンピューターモデルで、超新星の爆発を完全に理解できるわけではないとのことです。まだまだわからないことがたくさんあると述べています。

❹~❻:超新星爆発の前に星は大きくなり、かつ赤みがかると説明しています。よって、どの星が爆発するかを予測できるとのことです。

❼~❽:望遠鏡とコンピュータープログラムで、星の色における微妙な違いがわかるそうです。

❾~❿:さらに、星の大きさやその星が膨張しているのか、もしそうならどれくらいのスピードで膨張しているのかもわかるとのことです。

6

❶〜❸:超新星爆発は非常に珍しいものだと述べています。

❹〜❺:超新星爆発は50年に1度ほど起こるそうです。

7

❶:超新星爆発は肉眼でも観察できますが、望遠鏡を使うのがベストだとのことです。

❷:望遠鏡のおかげで、発見される超新星爆発の数が劇的に増えたと述べています。

聞き取りメモ例

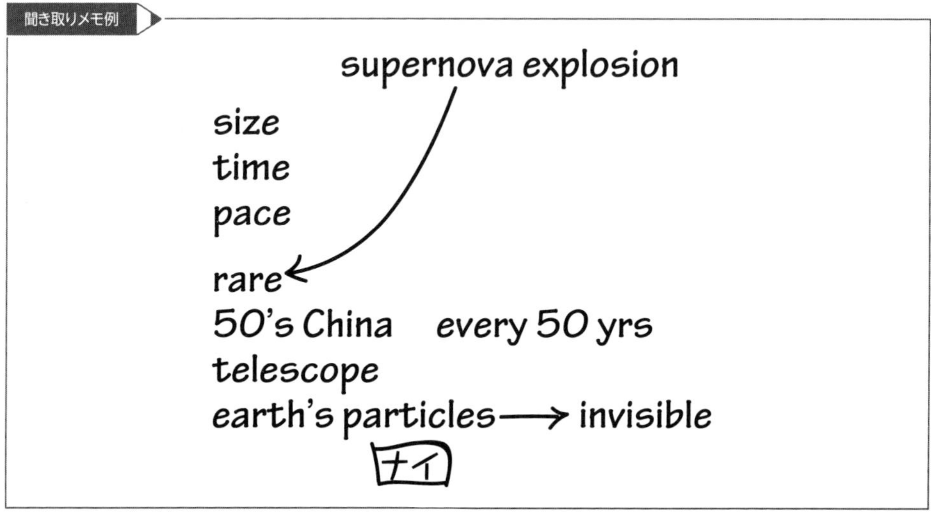

L04_Q4

4. What is the professor's opinion about computer simulations used for the research of supernova explosions?

(A) They can be used effectively only by specialized researchers.
(B) They have not generated conclusive data yet.
(C) They are currently in wide use.
(D) They are too expensive to keep developing.

超新星爆発の研究に使われるコンピューターのシミュレーションについて、教授はどう考えていますか。

(A) それらは専門的な研究者によってのみ効果的に使われる。
(B) それらは決定的なデータを未だ作り出せていない。
(C) それらは今では広く利用されている。
(D) それらを開発し続けるのは高くつきすぎる。

5❶や5❷で「コンピューターモデルが完全に超新星爆発の仕組みを説明できるわけではない」とあるので、(B)が正解です。(A)は講義の中で言及がありません。(C)の「広く利用されている」というのは教授の発言からは読み取れません。(D)ですが、コストについての話は講義では出てきません。

□ conclusive：決定的な

L04_Q5

5. Which of the following are necessary to predict when there will be a star explosion? *Choose two answers.*

(A) How big it is
(B) What color it is
(C) How dense it is
(D) How bright it is

星の爆発がいつ起こるかを予測するには、以下の内どれが必要ですか。2つ選んでください。

(A) どれだけそれが大きいか
(B) それがどんな色か
(C) それがどのくらい高密度か
(D) それがどれほど明るいか

5❾で「大きさ」に触れているので(A)は正解です。また、5❺で「ますます赤くなる」とあるので(B)も正解です。

□ dense：密度が高い、濃い

8~9 | 問6 解説レクチャー

L04_Script08-09

8 ❶So what happens after a supernova explosion? ❷A supernova explosion is the finale of the life cycle of a star, but I haven't talked about the aftermath. ❸Let's connect the dots. ❹Right before the explosion, the star contains not only light elements, but also heavier elements such as silicon, argon, oxygen, carbon, etc. ❺But the star does NOT really contain elements heavier than iron. ❻Gold, silver, copper . . . these are heavier than iron, so they are not present in the star before the explosion. ❼It is AFTER the explosion that these heavier elements are formed. ❽The impact of a supernova explosion is so big that it generates a powerful shockwave called a "stellar wind." ❾This stellar wind is enormously powerful. ❿Due to the powerful wind, elements around the place hit each other and heavier elements such as gold are created. ⓫By the way, you can't make artificial gold. ⓬You don't have the power of a stellar wind.

9 ❶A supernova explosion is the last, final moment of a star, I said. ❷But the word "supernova" literally means "super new star." ❸Interesting, isn't it? ❹The end of one star leads to the creation of many other new things. ❺That includes this ring on my finger.

解説レクチャー

8

❶~❸:超新星爆発の後に何が起こるかを説明するようです。

❹~❼:爆発の前は、鉄より重い元素は星の中に含まれていないとのことです。ところが爆発の後、鉄よりも重い金や銀などの元素が形成されるとあります。

❽~❿:爆発により、恒星風と呼ばれる強力な衝撃波が生じるとのことです。それにより、元素同士が衝突しより重い元素が生成されると説明しています。

⓫~⓬:恒星風のように強力な衝撃を人為的に生み出せないため、金を人工的に作ることは不可能だということです。

9

❶~❺:supernovaは文字通りに取ると「超新しい星」という意味だと述べています。ある星が一生を終えることにより、新しいものが生み出されるからだそうです。

聞き取りメモ例

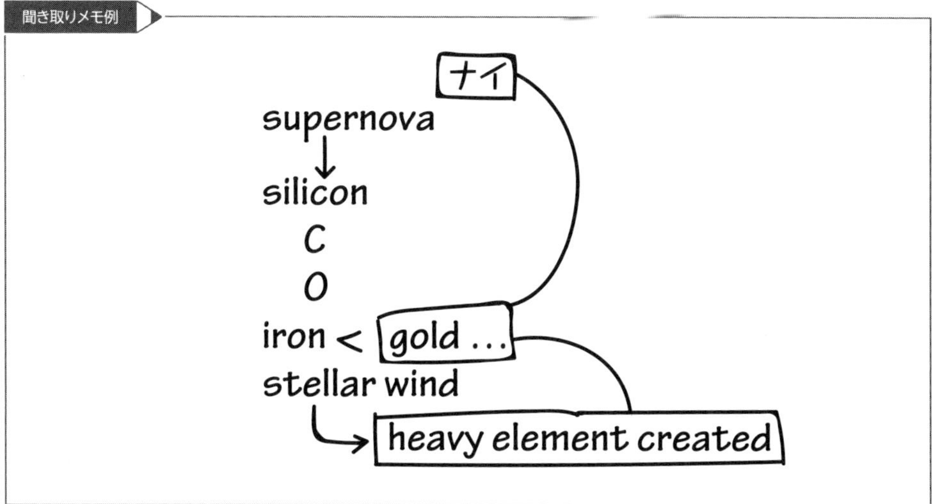

L04_Q6

6. What does the professor say about a stellar wind?

(A) It is the major force that converts helium into carbon and silicon.
(B) It contributes to the formation of heavy elements such as gold.
(C) It breaks heavy elements such as gold and silver down into smaller elements.
(D) It is a continuous stream of wind blowing between stars.

恒星風について、教授は何を述べていますか。

(A) それはヘリウムを炭素とケイ素に変換する主要な力だ。
(B) それは金のような重い元素の形成をもたらす。
(C) それは金や銀のような重い元素を破壊して、より小さな元素にする。
(D) それは星間に吹き続ける風の流れだ。

8 8～10で、恒星風の衝撃により、金などの元素が生み出されると説明されているので、(B)が正解です。(A)ですが、炭素やケイ素は8 4から、爆発の前に星に存在することがわかります。(C)は講義の内容とは真逆です。恒星風によって元素が衝突し、より重い元素が生成されるという説明が8 10にありました。(D)は講義では言及がありません。

1-2

Listen to part of a lecture in an astronomy class.

1 **Professor:**
❶Let's start today's class.
❷I want everyone to look at my ring finger.
❸I'm married, so I wear a ring on my left ring finger.
❹What is it made of?
❺The color of this ring looks gold, but actually, it's a composite of gold, silver, and copper.
❻Have you ever thought about how gold, silver, copper, and other precious metals were formed?
❼Mystery, isn't it?
❽That's today's topic.

2 ❶When you look up at the night sky, I'm sure that you wonder about the stars.
❷Twinkling . . . beautiful . . . far away . . . if you keep looking at them, you realize that they differ in color and brightness.
❸Like humans, each star is unique and different.
❹Like humans or any other creature, stars also have a life cycle.
❺They are born, grow, get old, and die.
❻Stars aren't living creatures, but they do have a life cycle.
❼They are born in the heart of galaxies from what is called a nebula, which is a big mixture of gas and rocks in the galaxy.
❽Once formed, stars spend most of their lifetime as a burning and shining mass.
❾You know, those are the stars that we look at in the night sky.
❿The stars are mainly composed of hydrogen and helium gas, and they're like nuclear reactors turning hydrogen, the lightest element, into helium, the second lightest element.
⓫The same applies to the Sun.
⓬It is made up of mostly hydrogen and helium, and what the Sun is doing is converting hydrogen into helium.

天文学の授業での講義の一部を聞きなさい。

1

❶今日の授業を始めましょう。
❷皆さんに私の薬指を見ていただきたいです。
❸私は結婚しているので、左手の薬指に指輪をしています。
❹これは何でできているのでしょうか。
❺この指輪の色は金色に見えますが、実際は金、銀、銅の合成物です。
❻皆さんは今までに金、銀、銅、その他の貴金属がどのようにしてできたか考えたことがありますか。
❼謎ですよね。
❽これが今日のテーマです。

2

❶夜空を見上げると、皆さんはきっと星のことを考えると思います。
❷きらめいていて、美しくて、遠くにある…それらを見続けると、色や輝きがそれぞれ違うということがわかります。
❸人間と同様に、それぞれの星は唯一無二であり、他の星とは異なります。
❹人間や他のあらゆる生き物と同様に、星にもライフサイクルがあります。
❺生まれ、成長し、年老い、死ぬのです。
❻星は生き物ではありませんが、ライフサイクルを持っているのです。
❼それら（星）は、銀河の中のガスと岩の巨大な混合物である星雲と言われているものをもとに、銀河の中心で形成されます。
❽一度形成されると、星は燃えて光る塊としてその一生を送ります。
❾ええ、こうしたものが、夜空に見えている星なのです。
❿星は主に水素とヘリウムのガスでできていて、一番軽い元素である水素を、二番目に軽い元素であるヘリウムに変える原子炉のようなものなのです。
⓫同じことが太陽にも当てはまります。
⓬それ（太陽）は主に水素とヘリウムでできており、太陽の中では水素がヘリウムに変換されているのです。

1

- ☐ ring finger：薬指
- ☐ be made of X：Xからできている
- ☐ composite：合成物
- ☐ copper：銅

2

- ☐ wonder about X：Xに好奇心を持つ、Xについてあれこれ考える
- ☐ differ in X：Xにおいて異なっている
- ☐ galaxy：銀河
- ☐ what is called a nebula：いわゆる星雲と呼ばれているもの
- ☐ be composed of X：Xで構成されている
- ☐ turn X into Y：XをYに変える
- ☐ element：元素
- ☐ apply to X：Xに当てはまる
- ☐ convert X into Y：XをYに変換する

2 they do have a life cycle

doは動詞を強調する語。

Once formed → Once (they are) formed

「いったん星ができれば」

3-4

3

❶All stars shining in the sky are basically the same.
❷Simply put, they are shining by converting hydrogen into helium and getting energy from the conversion.
❸But the amount of hydrogen in the star is finite.
❹Stars keep burning hydrogen, and when they run out of hydrogen, they die.
❺Particularly, big stars—those that are eight times larger than the Sun—end their life with an astronomical event called a "supernova explosion."
❻A supernova explosion is a big explosion of a dying star.
❼The star explodes and ends its life.

4

❶So why does a supernova explosion happen?
❷Why do those big stars explode when they die?
❸Here's the more detailed mechanism.
❹As a very big star goes along, it turns hydrogen into helium and that's how energy is generated in a star.
❺Right?
❻As I mentioned earlier?
❼OK.
❽The star will begin to turn helium into carbon.
❾Carbon is important for life, as you may all know.
❿That's how carbon is born.
⓫Basically, light elements collide with each other and form heavier elements.
⓬Hydrogen to helium, helium to carbon, to neon, to oxygen, and to silicon.
⓭This fusion process continues until the core of the star turns into iron.
⓮Iron is the last stage of this series of conversions.
⓯Iron cannot readily combine to form a heavier element.
⓰The reaction in the core of the star was the source of energy that sustained the life of the star, but if iron can't react to become another element, there's no more reaction in the core.
⓱The star cannot generate energy to sustain its structure, and finally, the star explodes.

3

❶空で輝いている全ての星は、基本的には同じです。
❷端的に言えば、それらは水素をヘリウムに変換して、その変換からエネルギーを得ることによって光っているのです。
❸しかし星にある水素の量は有限です。
❹星は水素を燃やし続け、そして水素が尽きると死ぬのです。
❺特に、大きい星―太陽の8倍大きいもの―は、「超新星爆発」と呼ばれる天文現象とともにその生涯を終えます。
❻超新星爆発は死にゆく星の大爆発なのです。
❼星は爆発し、一生を終えます。

4

❶では、なぜ超新星爆発が起こるのでしょうか。
❷なぜ大きな星は、死ぬときに爆発するのでしょうか。
❸より詳細なメカニズムをこれから説明します。
❹巨大な星は歳月を経るにしたがって、水素をヘリウムに変え、そうして星の中でエネルギーが生成されます。
❺そうですよね。
❻私が先ほど説明した通りですね。
❼はい。
❽星は、ヘリウムを炭素に変換し始めます。
❾炭素は、皆さん全員が知っている通り、星の生涯にとって重要です。
❿こうして炭素が生まれます。
⓫基本的に、軽い元素はお互いに衝突し、より重い元素を形成します。
⓬水素がヘリウムに、ヘリウムが炭素に、そしてネオン、酸素、ケイ素に。
⓭この融合過程は、星の核が鉄に変化するまで進行していきます。
⓮鉄は一連の変換の最終段階なのです。
⓯鉄がさらに重い元素を形成するために結合することは、容易ではありません。
⓰星の核内の化学反応はその星の寿命を持続させるエネルギー源でしたが、もし鉄が反応によって他の元素になれなければ、核の中ではそれ以上の化学反応は起こりません。
⓱星はその構造を維持するためのエネルギーを生み出せなくなると、しまいには爆発するのです。

3

- ☐ **simply put**：簡潔に言うと（to put it simplyとも言う）
- ☐ **conversion**：変換
- ☐ **finite**：有限の
- ☐ **run out of X**：Xがなくなる
- ☐ **astronomical**：天文の
- ☐ **a dying star**：死にかけている星（dyingは「死んでいる」ではなく「死にかけている」）

4

- ☐ **go along**：〈事〉が進展する（この文脈では、「星が存在し続ける」という意味）
- ☐ **as I mentioned**：私が述べたように
- ☐ **as you may all know**：おそらく皆さんもご存じでしょうが
- ☐ **collide with X**：Xと衝突する
- ☐ **readily**：容易に
- ☐ **sustain X**：Xを持続させる

5-6

5 ❶Our understanding of the exact mechanism isn't satisfactory yet because current computer models cannot account for the full amount of energy transferred and material ejected.
❷You know, we can do a series of simulations using computers, but we really can't cut open stars like onions.
❸So there are many things that remain unknown or unproven.
❹However, what we know is that a star gets larger and larger before the supernova explosion.
❺And a star gets redder and redder over time.
❻Therefore, we can tell which star is about to die and experience a supernova explosion.
❼Using a telescope, we can observe stars out there.
❽The fine differences in color can be analyzed, often with the aid of computer programs.
❾We can also estimate the size of the star as well as whether the star is expanding over time, and if so, at what pace.
❿Considering all these, we can predict the timing of the astronomical explosion.

6 ❶A supernova explosion is very rare and only a few have been observed in history.
❷The first in recent times was recorded in 185 AD by the Chinese.
❸Since then, people have observed and sometimes recorded these events.
❹It is said that, on average, a recognizable supernova explosion happens every 50 years.
❺If you are lucky, you may get to see the event once or maybe twice in your life.

5

❶現在のコンピューターモデルでは、伝達されるエネルギーと放出される物質の総量が説明できないため、正確なメカニズムに対する私たちの理解は、まだ満足のいくものではありません。
❷ご存じの通り、コンピューターを使って一連のシミュレーションをすることはできますが、実際にタマネギのように星を輪切りにして開くことはできません。
❸そのため、まだ知られていない事象や証明されていない事象が多数存在します。
❹しかしながら、私たちが知っているのは超新星爆発の前に星はどんどん巨大化するということです。
❺そして時間を経る毎に星はどんどん赤みがかっていくのです。
❻そのため、私たちはどの星が死にそうで、超新星爆発を起こしそうなのかがわかるのです。
❼望遠鏡を使うと、宇宙の星を観察できます。
❽コンピュータープログラムの助けが必要なことが多いですが、些細な色の違いを分析できます。
❾私たちはまた、その星が時間とともに膨張しているのかどうか、もしそうだとするとどれくらいのスピードで膨張しているのかどうか、またその星の大きさを推測することも可能なのです。
❿これらのことを考慮すると、天体の爆発の時期を予測できるのです。

6

❶超新星爆発はとても稀で、歴史上でもほんの数回しか観察されていません。
❷近いところで初めてのものは中国人によって西暦185年に記録されています。
❸それ以来、人々はこうした現象を観察し、時々記録してきました。
❹人間が確認できる超新星爆発は、平均50年に1度起こると言われています。
❺もし幸運なら、人生の中で1度、もしかすると2度その現象を見ることができるかもしれません。

5

- □ account for X：Xを説明する
- □ remain unknown or unproven：未知のままか、証明されていないままである
- □ redder and redder→比較級を重ねると「変化」の意味になる
- □ be about to V：～しそうになる
- □ X as well as Y：YだけでなくXも
- □ considering X：Xを考慮すると

6

- □ only a few：ほとんどない
- □ on average：平均的に
- □ get to V：～する機会を得る

5 the full amount of energy (transferred) [and] material (ejected)

transferredとejectedはそれぞれenergyとmaterialを後置修飾する過去分詞。

we can do a series of simulations (using computers)

using computersは分詞構文、「コンピューターを使って～」

cut (V) open (C) stars (O) (like onions) (M)

cut X openで「Xを切って開く」という意味。like onionsは「タマネギのように」という意味。

7-9

7 ❶Although a big supernova explosion can be detected with the naked eye, it's best if you have a telescope because there are some interstellar dust clouds and particles within the Earth's atmosphere that can make this fantastic astronomical event invisible to us.
❷In fact, thanks to the invention of telescopes that allow the observation of distant galaxies, the number of known supernova explosions has dramatically increased.

8 ❶So what happens after a supernova explosion?
❷A supernova explosion is the finale of the life cycle of a star, but I haven't talked about the aftermath.
❸Let's connect the dots.
❹Right before the explosion, the star contains not only light elements, but also heavier elements such as silicon, argon, oxygen, carbon, etc.
❺But the star does NOT really contain elements heavier than iron.
❻Gold, silver, copper . . . these are heavier than iron, so they are not present in the star before the explosion.
❼It is AFTER the explosion that these heavier elements are formed.
❽The impact of a supernova explosion is so big that it generates a powerful shockwave called a "stellar wind."
❾This stellar wind is enormously powerful.
❿Due to the powerful wind, elements around the place hit each other and heavier elements such as gold are created.
⓫By the way, you can't make artificial gold.
⓬You don't have the power of a stellar wind.

9 ❶A supernova explosion is the last, final moment of a star, I said.
❷But the word "supernova" literally means "super new star."
❸Interesting, isn't it?
❹The end of one star leads to the creation of many other new things.
❺That includes this ring on my finger.

7 ❶大きな超新星爆発は肉眼でも観察できますが、この素晴らしい天文現象を見えなくしてしまう星間ガスの雲や地球の大気中の粒子の存在により、もし望遠鏡を持っていればベストでしょう。
❷実際、望遠鏡の発明のおかげで遠くの銀河の観察が可能になったので、発見される超新星爆発の数も劇的に増えました。

8 ❶では、超新星爆発の後では何が起こるのでしょうか。
❷超新星爆発で星の一生は終わりますが、その後どうなるのかについてはまだ話していません。
❸では点をつないで全体像を見ましょう。
❹爆発の直前、星は軽い元素だけでなく、ケイ素、アルゴン、酸素、炭素などの比較的重い元素も含んでいます。
❺しかし星は鉄よりも重い元素は実際含んでいません。
❻金、銀、銅…これらは鉄よりも重いので、爆発前の星には存在しないのです。
❼これら比較的重い元素が形成されるのは爆発の後なのです。
❽超新星爆発の衝撃はとても大きく、恒星風と呼ばれる強力な衝撃波を生み出します。
❾この恒星風はとてつもなく強いのです。
❿その強い風によって、その周りの元素同士が衝突し、金のような比較的重い元素も生成されるのです。
⓫ところで、人工の金というものはつくることができません。
⓬恒星風の強さを生み出せませんからね。

9 ❶私は、超新星は星の最期の決定的な瞬間だと言いました。
❷しかし、'supernova' という単語は文字通りにとれば、「超新しい星」という意味なのです。
❸面白いでしょう。
❹ある星の死は、多くの他の新しい物の誕生につながります。
❺その中に、私の指のこの指輪が含まれているのです。

7
- ☐ naked eye：肉眼
- ☐ interstellar：星と星の間の
- ☐ invisible：目に見えない

8
- ☐ finale：終局
- ☐ aftermath：余波
- ☐ shockwave：衝撃波
- ☐ due to X：Xが原因で

9
- ☐ lead to X：Xをもたらす

8 right before X「Xの直前に」

rightは副詞

It is AFTER the explosion that these heavier elements are formed

強調構文。after the explosionが強調されている。

リスニング問題5 講義

FILM

問題演習の流れ

□ 音声が流れている間は、問題は読めません。講義が終わり、最初の問題音声が流れ始めたらページをめくって、5分以内に解答しましょう。

□ 1問の解答時間は20秒を目安にしています。問題を読み上げた後に解答時間として20秒のポーズ（音声なし）が入っていますので、その間に解答をマークしてください。

□ メモは自由に取ってください。

□ 3回解けるように、3回分のマークシートを問題ページに用意しています。解く日付を記入してからマークしてください。

Web解答方法

□ 本試験では各選択肢の左に表示されるマークをクリックして解答します。本試験と同様の方法で取り組みたい場合は、Webで解答できます。

□ インターネットのつながるパソコン・スマートフォンで、以下のサイトにアクセスしてWeb上で解答してください。

extester.com

□ 操作方法は、p.13 ～ 14の「USA Club Web学習の使い方」をご参照ください。

学習の記録

学習開始日	年　月　日	学習終了日	年　月　日
学習開始日	年　月　日	学習終了日	年　月　日
学習開始日	年　月　日	学習終了日	年　月　日

リスニング問題 5 講義 音声

 L05

Silent Film

聞き取りメモ

L05_Q1

1. What is the lecture mainly about?

(A) Principal components of silent films
(B) Charlie Chaplin's great talent
(C) Why silent films became obsolete
(D) Social impacts of silent films

L05_Q2

2. How is the lecture organized?

(A) By listing all characteristics of silent films one by one
(B) By explaining the events of the Silent Film Era chronologically
(C) By describing key aspects of silent films along with a famous figure's biography
(D) By providing short biographies of some major figures in the era

L05_Q3

3. Why did the professor explain City Lights in which Chaplin acted?

(A) To name one of the most popular films that Chaplin produced
(B) To clarify the fact that silent films often contained serious and dark themes
(C) To emphasize the importance of sticking to details to be a successful actor
(D) To reveal the fact that involved actors were not satisfied with how the movie was created

L05_Q4

4. How did Chaplin portray the gold rush in his film?

(A) He focused on the dark side of the theme.
(B) He actually mined gold and shot the scene.
(C) He took a neutral approach to a controversial issue.
(D) He included enjoyment even for sad accidents.

L05_Q5

5. What is the professor's opinion of silent films?

(A) They are too primitive and barely watchable.
(B) They are great and deserve more admiration.
(C) She thinks silent films are extremely underestimated today.
(D) She believes modern films with sound are more attractive.

L05_Q6

6. Listen again to part of the lecture and then answer the question.
What does the professor imply when she says this?

(A) Some students might not know who Charlie Chaplin is.
(B) Almost everyone knows who Charlie Chaplin is.
(C) Most people have seen more than one movie starring Charlie Chaplin.
(D) Students must pay more attention to his name.

1. **(A)**　2. **(C)**　3. **(C)**　4. **(D)**　5. **(B)**　6. **(B)**

問1 解説レクチャー

L05_Q1

1. What is the lecture mainly about?

(A) Principal components of silent films
(B) Charlie Chaplin's great talent
(C) Why silent films became obsolete
(D) Social impacts of silent films

講義の主題は何ですか。

(A) 無声映画の主な構成要素
(B) Charlie Chaplinの素晴らしい才能
(C) 無声映画が廃れた理由
(D) 無声映画の社会的影響

講義の前半では、無声映画の理解を促すために「音楽」や「演技」が重要だったと述べられています。後半では、無声映画のテーマが、社会現象などの人々に関連したものであったと説明されています。これらは、無声映画を構成する主な要素について述べていることになるので、(A)が正解です。(B)のChaplinはあくまで無声映画を説明する上での具体例です。(C)に関しては❼❶以降で無声映画が廃れた理由が説明されていますが、局所的に言及されているため主旨ではありません。(D)は❻❶以降で無声映画が社会と人をつなぐとあるため、内容は誤りとは言えないでしょう。しかし、断片的な情報ですので、主旨とは言えません。

□principal:主要な

❶～❸｜問2 解説レクチャー

L05_Script01-03

❶ **Professor:**
❶Let's move on to a new chapter, which is about silent films. ❷Anyone familiar with silent films? ❸Silent films are films with no spoken dialogue. ❹That means that there is no conversation that you can hear. ❺It may sound a little bit odd, but at that time, all films were silent, and the silent films had a huge impact on society, business, and people's everyday lives. ❻They were originally developed in the UK around 1880, and they became popular with Americans very quickly. ❼Actually, silent films were so influential that they even overcame the language barrier and people all across the world enjoyed them.

2 ❶Well, the word "silent" usually means no sound. ❷However, silent films are not completely sound-less or quiet. ❸Actually, they're accompanied by music . . . often live music. ❹Everybody here knows Thomas Edison right? ❺He invented a photographic apparatus that enabled people to create short films, and set the standard that all silent films should be accompanied by an orchestra, when he attended the first motion picture exhibition in the United States in 1895. ❻I used the term "motion pictures" just now. ❼Films were literally motion pictures, or a series of pictures shown at a time very quickly.

3 ❶Today, we use a VIDEO camera to shoot a movie. ❷Right? ❸The "movie" is a combination of images and sound. ❹On the other hand, people back then did NOT have a video camera. ❺What they had was just a simple camera . . . a camera that can take pictures ONLY. ❻So, you know what I'm getting at. ❼There was no technology to attach voice to the moving pictures. ❽By the way, the word "movies" that we often use today is a short form of "Moving Pictures." ❾Neat, huh?

解説レクチャー

1

❶～❹:今回のテーマは無声映画だと述べています。会話の音声がない映画のことですね。

❺:どの映画にも音声がなく、当時はこれが当たり前だったそうです。

❼:無声映画は言葉の壁を超えるので、世界中で鑑賞されていたとのことです。

2

❶～❸:無声映画は全く音がないというわけではなく、生演奏の音楽が伴っていたとあります。

❹～❺:Edisonが短編映画を作る装置を発明し、無声映画にオーケストラをつけることを標準化したと述べています。

❻～❼:motion pictureは「1枚1枚の連続した写真が素早く映されるもの」ということだと説明しています。

3

❶～❼:昔はビデオカメラがなく、写真しか撮れなかったと述べています。音声を画像と組み合わせる技術がなかったのです。

❽～❾:moviesはMoving Picturesの短縮形だと述べています。

聞き取りメモ例

silent film
impact soci business ppl
1880 UK
↓
US
lg barrier
overcome
+ music

languageのことです

Edison
+ オーケストラ
motion pic
camera　pic only
no tech　voice

L05_Q2

2. How is the lecture organized?

(A) By listing all characteristics of silent films one by one
(B) By explaining the events of the Silent Film Era chronologically
(C) By describing key aspects of silent films along with a famous figure's biography
(D) By providing short biographies of some major figures in the era

講義はどのように構成されていますか。

(A) 無声映画の全ての特徴を一つ一つ列挙することによって
(B) 年代順に無声映画時代の出来事を説明することによって
(C) 有名人の伝記とともに無声映画の主要な特徴を説明することによって
(D) その時代の何人かの主要人物の短い伝記を提示することによって

無声映画の主要な特徴を述べつつ、❹以降でChaplinを具体例にした説明が行われているので(C)が正解です。(A)では「全ての特徴(all characteristics)」が誤りです。講義で説明された内容が全てであるとする根拠はありません。(B)は「時系列に(chronologically)」が誤りです。講義は音楽や演技という特徴の説明から始まっています。(D)ですが、主にChaplinについては述べられていますが、他の人物の伝記といったものは出てきません。

□ chronologically：時系列に　□ biography：伝記

4～5 | 問3解説レクチャー

L05_Script04-05

4 ❶OK. ❷Since there was no speech in the films, the live music that played with the films was important for the audience to fully appreciate the stories. ❸Of course, besides live music, the actors' acting techniques were extremely important. ❹It was essential that actors emphasized body language and facial expressions. ❺Such emphasis on body language and facial expressions enabled the audience to better understand what was being portrayed in the scene and how actors were feeling. ❻Charlie Chaplin was one of many actors who dedicated himself to paying close attention to such detailed acting techniques. ❼Who hasn't heard his name? ❽OK . . . he is an actor who paid very close, meticulous attention to every movement in his films. ❾He moved to numerous companies in different locations, including London, California, and New York, but no matter where he acted, he stuck to his professionalism of fine-adjusting his body language and facial expressions. ❿In fact, Charlie was known as a perfectionist, the king of the re-take. ⓫Let me give you an example. ⓬In 1931, he was working on producing a film titled City Lights. ⓭In shooting the scenes, he was so concerned about subtle details of a certain scene that he demanded to reshoot the scene 342 times. ⓮342 times of retakes just for one scene! ⓯Such careful attention to even the slightest details led him to become one of the most well-known figures in film history. ⓰Like him, other actors needed to pay close attention to fine acting techniques, and this was one of the biggest things that differentiated good actors from not-so-good ones.

5 ❶During the Silent Film Era, some actors began to create their own films. ❷Because actors in this era really had to be particular about fine acting techniques, they themselves often became filmmakers by using their own knowledge about acting skills from their experience. ❸Let's refer again to Charlie Chaplin. ❹After he finished his contract with the Mutual Film Corporation in 1917, he decided to make his own private studio to try directing. ❺In total, he created um, over 70 films.

解説レクチャー

4

❶～❷:生演奏の音楽は、観客がストーリーを理解するために必要だったそうです。

❸～❺:音楽に加え、俳優のボディーランゲージや表情も、観客がストーリーを理解する上で重要だと言っています。

❻～❽:演技に細心の注意を払った人で有名なのがChaplinですね。

❾～❿:Chaplinは演技に関して完璧主義者だったようです。何度も撮り直したそうです。

⓫～⓯:具体例として、City Lightsという映画で1つのシーンを342回も撮り直したことが挙げられています。彼が世界的に有名になった一因は、ここにあるようです。

⑯:演じる技術の差が、優秀な俳優か否かを決定づけたとのことです。

5

❶~❷:演技にこだわりをもっていた俳優は、自身が監督となって映画を撮ることもあったそうです。

❸~❺:Chaplinの例がまた挙げられています。彼は自分のスタジオを作り、70本以上の映画を撮ったと説明があります。

聞き取りメモ例

film + live music
actors — [body lg / facial expressions]

Chaplin
attention
companies
1931 City lights
342 reshoot - 1 scene
good actor

own film　actor → film maker
C: 1917 own studio
70 films

L05_Q3

3. Why did the professor explain City Lights in which Chaplin acted?

(A) To name one of the most popular films that Chaplin produced
(B) To clarify the fact that silent films often contained serious and dark themes
(C) To emphasize the importance of sticking to details to be a successful actor
(D) To reveal the fact that involved actors were not satisfied with how the movie was created

なぜ教授はChaplinが出演したCity Lightsの説明をしましたか。

(A) Chaplinが制作した中で最も人気がある映画の1つを挙げるため
(B) 無声映画が深刻で陰惨なテーマをよく扱ったという事実を明確にするため
(C) 俳優として成功を収めるためには、細部にこだわることが重要であることを強調するため
(D) 出演した俳優が、その映画の作り方に満足していなかったという事実を明らかにするため

City Lightsという固有名詞を聞き取れたでしょうか。この問題は講義で具体例に言及した意図を問うています。4❻以降で、Chaplinが細かい点に注意を払っていた俳優だとわかります。4⓬以降、作品例としてCity Lightsが登場します。また4⓯から、演技にこだわったからこそ成功したとわかります。よって、(C)が正解です。(A)については、Chaplinが作った映画であることは正しいです。ただし、Chaplinのこだわりを例証するためにCity Lightsが言及されているので、(A)は誤りです。(B)ですが、これはThe Gold Rushという映画に関する説明なので誤りです。(D)は講義で言及がありません。

6～7｜問 4～5 解説レクチャー

L05_Script06-07

6 ❶Now, silent films were entertainment that really reflected filmmakers' own personal lives and what was occurring around them. ❷In other words, a number of films made in the era were based on real events and stories occurring at the time. ❸Charlie's films, The Kid . . . and . . . what was that . . . oh . . . The Gold Rush . . . these are good examples. ❹The Kid, which deals with issues of poverty and parent-child separation, is thought to have been influenced by Charlie's own experience of losing his own child with his second wife, Lita Grey, after divorce. ❺Similarly, The Gold Rush is grounded in the actual social phenomenon. ❻The 19th century observed a great deal of discoveries of gold in America, Canada, and other countries. ❼Many people looked for gold, but many people died due to accidents when they went mining to seek their fortune. ❽Charlie succeeded in expressing such a serious and dark social phenomenon in a comical way. ❾So, themes depicted in silent films were often associated with real events . . . ❿Silent films were media that connected society and the audience.

7 ❶Unfortunately, although many people and movie stars contributed to the prosperity of silent films, they became obsolete in the 1930s. ❷Well, technology finally developed enough to let people enjoy films with sound and voices. ❸Once the early films with voice were produced in 1927, the production of silent films stopped within a decade. ❹Although there's a widely held misconception that silent films are primitive and barely watchable by modern standards, this misconception only comes from the poor preservation conditions of those films. ❺In fact, as mentioned earlier, there are many great films from the Silent Film Era. ❻And I must say this . . . silent films are still alive. ❼There are a certain number of filmmakers and people who are producing silent films even now! ❽I really recommend that you watch a film titled "The Artist" produced in 2011 in France. ❾This is a silent film produced in modern day. ❿This movie, "The Artist," was nominated for ten Academy Awards. ⓫And, it won five in the year 2012.

解説レクチャー

6

❶～❷:無声映画は、監督の生活や身の周りで生じた出来事を描いていたとのことです。
❸:The Kid やThe Gold Rushという映画が具体例として挙げられています。
❹:The Kidは、Chaplinが離婚で2番目の妻との子と離れ離れになったことに影響されたそうです。
❺～❽:The Gold Rushも、実際のゴールドラッシュという出来事に基づいているとのことです。社会の暗い側面をコミカルに描くことにChaplinは成功したと述べています。
❾～❿:無声映画のテーマと社会の出来事の関係をまとめています。

7

❶～❸:20世紀初頭に音声付きの映画が誕生すると、まもなく無声映画は廃れてしまったそうです。
❹～❺:無声映画が現代人にとって見るに堪えないという考えは誤りだと述べています。単に、保存状態がよくないだけだそうです。実際、素晴らしい無声映画はたくさん存在するとのことです。
❻～❼:さらに、今でも無声映画を作っている人々がいると続けています。
❽～⓫:教授のおすすめはThe Artistだそうです。「アカデミー賞の候補になった」と述べることで、The Artistが素晴らしい映画であることを保証しています。

聞き取りメモ例

Gold Rush poverty
↑
based own experience
lose child
look for gold
die
dark phenom
comical way
connect society
audience

1930's すたれる
1927 voice
SF not worth watching
↕
No
the artist 2011
Academy award

L05_Q4

4. How did Chaplin portray the gold rush in his film?

(A) He focused on the dark side of the theme.
(B) He actually mined gold and shot the scene.
(C) He took a neutral approach to a controversial issue.
(D) He included enjoyment even for sad accidents.

Chaplinは映画の中でゴールドラッシュをどのように描きましたか。

(A) 彼はそのテーマの暗い側面に焦点を当てた。
(B) 彼は実際に金を採掘してそのシーンを撮影した。
(C) 彼は議論を呼ぶ問題に対して中立的なアプローチをした。
(D) 彼は悲しい事故にさえも愉快さを加えた。

❻❸から映画The Gold Rushの話が始まります。❻❼は「人々が事故で亡くなったこと」、❻❽は「コミカルな方法で、深刻な社会現象を描いた」と説明しています。よって、(D)が正解です。a serious and dark social phenomenonがsad accidents、in a comical wayがenjoymentで言い換えられています。(A)は「暗い側面(dark side)」は正しいのですが、❻❽の「コミカルな方法で(in a comical)」という発言がないので誤りです。(B)の「Chaplinが実際に金を採掘して」というような内容は講義では言及がありません。(C)ですが、中立的であるという発言はありません。

□ controversial：議論を呼ぶような、物議をかもす

L05_Q5

5. What is the professor's opinion of silent films?

(A) They are too primitive and barely watchable.
(B) They are great and deserve more admiration.
(C) She thinks silent films are extremely underestimated today.
(D) She believes modern films with sound are more attractive.

無声映画に対する教授の意見はどうですか。

(A) 原始的過ぎて、見るに堪えない。
(B) 素晴らしく、もっと称賛されてしかるべきだ。
(C) 無声映画は今日極めて過小評価されていると考えている。
(D) 音声付きの現代の映画の方が魅力的だと思っている。

❼❶で無声映画が廃れてしまったことを残念だと嘆いています。その後、無声映画の素晴らしさを、アカデミー賞を受賞した作品にも言及しつつ述べているので、(B)が正解です。❼❹で、「無声映画が原始的で見るに堪えないという考えは誤解だ」と述べているので、(A)は誤りです。(C)についてですが、アカデミー賞を受賞したことにも触れているので、「極めて過小評価されている(extremely underestimated)」というのは教授の意見とは合いません。(D)は、教授は無声映画の素晴らしさについて述べているため、誤りです。

□ deserve X: Xに値する　□ admiration: 称賛　□ underestimate X: Xを過小評価する

問6 解説レクチャー

L05_Q6

6. Listen again to part of the lecture and then answer the question.

Professor:
Charlie Chaplin was one of many actors who dedicated himself to paying close attention to such detailed acting techniques. Who hasn't heard his name?

What does the professor imply when she says this?

"Who hasn't heard his name?"

(A) Some students might not know who Charlie Chaplin is.
(B) Almost everyone knows who Charlie Chaplin is.
(C) Most people have seen more than one movie starring Charlie Chaplin.
(D) Students must pay more attention to his name.

講義の一部分をもう一度聞いて、設問に答えてください。

教授：
Charlie Chaplinは、細かい演技の技術に細心の注意を払うことを追求した多くの俳優の一人でした。彼の名前を聞いたことがない人がいるでしょうか。

「彼の名前を聞いたことがない人がいるでしょうか」と言うとき、教授は何を示唆していますか。

(A) 何人かの学生はCharlie Chaplinが誰なのか知らないかもしれない。
(B) ほとんど全員がCharlie Chaplinが誰なのかを知っている。
(C) ほとんどの人がCharlie Chaplin主演の映画を複数観たことがある。
(D) 学生たちは彼の名前にもっと注意を払うべきだ。

Who hasn't heard his name?は「誰が彼の名前を聞いたことがないだろうか」という意味ですが、いわゆる反語で「聞いたことがない人などいないだろう」という意味だと解釈できます。よって(B)が正解です。教授は字義通り「聞いたことがない人はいますか」と質問をしているわけではないので、(A)は誤りです。(C)の「複数」というのは言いすぎです。教授の発言からは読み取れません。(D)も教授の発言からは読み取れません。

□ star X: Xを主演させる

1-2

Listen to part of a lecture in a film class.

1 **Professor:**
❶Let's move on to a new chapter, which is about silent films.
❷Anyone familiar with silent films?
❸Silent films are films with no spoken dialogue.
❹That means that there is no conversation that you can hear.
❺It may sound a little bit odd, but at that time, all films were silent, and the silent films had a huge impact on society, business, and people's everyday lives.
❻They were originally developed in the UK around 1880, and they became popular with Americans very quickly.
❼Actually, silent films were so influential that they even overcame the language barrier and people all across the world enjoyed them.

2 ❶Well, the word "silent" usually means no sound.
❷However, silent films are not completely sound-less or quiet.
❸Actually, they're accompanied by music . . . often live music.
❹Everybody here knows Thomas Edison right?
❺He invented a photographic apparatus that enabled people to create short films, and set the standard that all silent films should be accompanied by an orchestra, when he attended the first motion picture exhibition in the United States in 1895.
❻I used the term "motion pictures" just now.
❼Films were literally motion pictures, or a series of pictures shown at a time very quickly.

映画の授業での講義の一部を聞きなさい。

1

❶次の章に進みましょう。無声映画です。
❷誰か無声映画について詳しい人はいますか。
❸無声映画とは、会話の音声がない映画のことです。
❹つまり、その映画の中では何の会話も聞こえないということです。
❺少し変に思えるかもしれませんが、当時全ての映画が無音であり、無声映画は社会、ビジネス、人々の日常生活に多大な影響を及ぼしたのです。
❻もともと無声映画は 1880 年頃イギリスで発展し、その後急速にアメリカ人に人気が出ました。
❼実際、無声映画の影響力はとても大きかったので、それらは言葉の障壁を超えるに至り、世界中の人々が楽しんだのです。

2

❶さて、'silent' という単語は通常「無声」を意味します。
❷しかし、無声映画は完全に無音ないし静かというわけではありません。
❸実際のところ、それらには音楽、しばしば生演奏の音楽が伴っています。
❹ここにいる皆さんは Thomas Edison のことを知っていますよね。
❺彼は、人々が短編映画を製作することを可能にする写真撮影装置を発明し、1895 年アメリカで初めての motion pictures 上映会に出席したとき、全ての無声映画にオーケストラをつけることを一般化しました。
❻私はたった今、'motion pictures' という用語を使いました。
❼映画は文字通り 'motion pictures'、すなわち一度に素早く表示される一連の写真でした。

1

- ☐ odd：変な
- ☐ influential：影響力のある
- ☐ language barrier：言葉の壁

2

- ☐ be accompanied by X：X を伴う
- ☐ live music：生演奏の音楽
- ☐ apparatus：装置
- ☐ set the standard：標準化する
- ☐ exhibition：会
- ☐ literally：文字通り
- ☐ a series of X：一連の X
- ☐ at a time：一度に

1 Anyone familiar with silent films? → (Is) anyone familiar with X?
「Xに詳しい人はいますか」

3 ❶Today, we use a VIDEO camera to shoot a movie.
❷Right?
❸The "movie" is a combination of images and sound.
❹On the other hand, people back then did NOT have a video camera.
❺What they had was just a simple camera . . . a camera that can take pictures ONLY.
❻So, you know what I'm getting at.
❼There was no technology to attach voice to the moving pictures.
❽By the way, the word "movies" that we often use today is a short form of "Moving Pictures."
❾Neat, huh?

3

❶今日私たちは映画を撮影するためにビデオカメラを使います。
❷そうですよね。
❸「映画」とは、複数の画像と音声の組み合わせです。
❹一方、人々は当時ビデオカメラを持っていませんでした。
❺彼らが持っていたのはただの簡素なカメラ…写真しか撮ることのできないカメラでした。
❻そういうわけで、私が言いたいことはわかりますよね。
❼動画に音声を加える技術はなかったのです。
❽ところで、私たちが今日よく使う'movies'という単語は、'Moving Pictures'の短縮形なのです。
❾(ネーミングが)なかなかいいでしょう。

3

- ☐ get at X：Xを暗示する
- ☐ attach X to Y：XをYに付ける
- ☐ neat：巧みな、適切な

4

4 ❶OK.
❷Since there was no speech in the films, the live music that played with the films was important for the audience to fully appreciate the stories.
❸Of course, besides live music, the actors' acting techniques were extremely important.
❹It was essential that actors emphasized body language and facial expressions.
❺Such emphasis on body language and facial expressions enabled the audience to better understand what was being portrayed in the scene and how actors were feeling.
❻Charlie Chaplin was one of many actors who dedicated himself to paying close attention to such detailed acting techniques.
❼Who hasn't heard his name?
❽OK . . . he is an actor who paid very close, meticulous attention to every movement in his films.
❾He moved to numerous companies in different locations, including London, California, and New York, but no matter where he acted, he stuck to his professionalism of fine-adjusting his body language and facial expressions.
❿In fact, Charlie was known as a perfectionist, the king of the re-take.
⓫Let me give you an example.
⓬In 1931, he was working on producing a film titled City Lights.
⓭In shooting the scenes, he was so concerned about subtle details of a certain scene that he demanded to reshoot the scene 342 times.
⓮342 times of retakes just for one scene!
⓯Such careful attention to even the slightest details led him to become one of the most well-known figures in film history.
⓰Like him, other actors needed to pay close attention to fine acting techniques, and this was one of the biggest things that differentiated good actors from not-so-good ones.

4

❶はい。
❷映画の中にセリフがなかったので、映画とともに生演奏された音楽は、観客が筋書きを完全に理解するために重要でした。
❸もちろん、生演奏の音楽の他にも、俳優たちの演技の技術が極めて重要でした。
❹俳優たちがボディーランゲージや表情を強調することは必要不可欠だったのです。
❺そのようなボディーランゲージや表情の強調によって、観客は、そのシーンで何が描写されているのか、また俳優がどう感じているのかをよりよく理解できるようになりました。
❻Charlie Chaplinは、細かい演技の技術に細心の注意を払うことを追求した多くの俳優の一人でした。
❼彼の名前を聞いたことのない人がいるでしょうか。
❽はい…彼は、映画の中の全ての動きに対して、かなり細かいところまで行き届いた注意を払った俳優です。
❾彼はロンドン、カリフォルニア、そしてニューヨークを含む様々な場所の数々の会社を渡り歩きましたが、どこで演技をしようとも、ボディーランゲージと表情を微調整する専門技術にこだわりました。
❿実際、Charlieは完璧主義者、撮り直しの王として知られていました。
⓫例を挙げます。
⓬1931年に、彼はCity Lightsというタイトルの映画製作に取り組んでいました。
⓭シーンを撮影するとき、彼はあるシーンの些細な部分がどうしても気になり、そのシーンの撮り直しを342回要求したのです。
⓮たった1つのシーンに対して342回の撮り直しですよ！
⓯そのようなかなり小さな部分にまで行き届く慎重さが、彼を映画史における最もよく知られた人物の1人にしたのです。
⓰他の俳優も彼のように細かな演技の技術に細心の注意を払う必要があり、これがいい俳優とそれほどでもない俳優を分けた最も大きな要因の1つでした。

4

- □ appreciate X：Xを理解する、Xの価値を認める
- □ portray X：Xを描写する
- □ dedicate oneself to X：Xに専心する
- □ pay close attention to X：Xに細心の注意を払う
- □ detailed：細かい
- □ who hasn't heard his name?：誰が彼の名前を聞いたことがないだろうか。いや誰でもある（いわゆる反語）
- □ meticulous：細かいことによく気を配る
- □ numerous：数々の
- □ no matter where SV：どこで～しようとも
- □ stick to X：Xにこだわる、Xにつき従う
- □ lead X to V：Xが～することにつながる
- □ figure：（有名な）人物
- □ fine acting techniques：細かな演技の技術
- □ differentiate X from Y：XをYと区別する

4 to (better) understand「よりよく理解するために」
betterはunderstandを修飾する副詞

5-6

5 ❶During the Silent Film Era, some actors began to create their own films.
❷Because actors in this era really had to be particular about fine acting techniques, they themselves often became filmmakers by using their own knowledge about acting skills from their experience.
❸Let's refer again to Charlie Chaplin.
❹After he finished his contract with the Mutual Film Corporation in 1917, he decided to make his own private studio to try directing.
❺In total, he created um, over 70 films.

6 ❶Now, silent films were entertainment that really reflected filmmakers' own personal lives and what was occurring around them.
❷In other words, a number of films made in the era were based on real events and stories occurring at the time.
❸Charlie's films, The Kid . . . and . . . what was that . . . oh . . . The Gold Rush . . . these are good examples.
❹The Kid, which deals with issues of poverty and parent-child separation, is thought to have been influenced by Charlie's own experience of losing his own child with his second wife, Lita Grey, after divorce.
❺Similarly, The Gold Rush is grounded in the actual social phenomenon.
❻The 19th century observed a great deal of discoveries of gold in America, Canada, and other countries.
❼Many people looked for gold, but many people died due to accidents when they went mining to seek their fortune.
❽Charlie succeeded in expressing such a serious and dark social phenomenon in a comical way.
❾So, themes depicted in silent films were often associated with real events . . .
❿Silent films were media that connected society and the audience.

5 ❶無声映画時代、何人かの俳優は、自分の映画を製作し始めました。
❷この時代の俳優は、細かい演技の技術について本当にこだわらなければならなかったため、自らの経験から得た演技技術の知識を生かして、自分自身で映画製作者となったのです。
❸ Charlie Chaplin に話を戻しましょう。
❹彼が 1917 年 Mutual Film Corporation との契約を終了した後、監督に挑戦するため、自身のプライベートスタジオを作ることを決めました。
❺合計で、彼は、えーっと、70 本以上の映画を製作しました。

6 ❶さて、無声映画は、映画製作者自身の私生活や、彼らの周りで起こっていたことを反映した娯楽作品でした。
❷言い換えると、その時代に製作された多くの映画は、当時実際にあった出来事や話に基づいていたのです。
❸ Charlie の映画、The Kid と、あれは何でしたっけ、ああ、The Gold Rush、これらはいい例です。
❹貧困、親子の別離という問題を扱った The Kid は、離婚の後で 2 番目の妻、Lita Grey との子供と離れ離れになったという、チャーリー自身の経験に影響を受けたと考えられています。
❺同様に、The Gold Rush は実際の社会現象に基づいています。
❻ 19 世紀にはアメリカ、カナダ、そして他の国々で金が何度も発見されました。
❼多くの人々が金を探し求めましたが、成功を求めて採鉱に行った先で、多くの人々が事故で亡くなりました。
❽チャーリーはそのような深刻で陰惨な社会現象を、コミカルな方法で表現することに成功しました。
❾つまり、無声映画で描かれるテーマはしばしば実際の出来事と結びついていたのです。
❿無声映画は社会と観客をつなぐメディアだったのです。

5
- ☐ be particular about X：X にこだわる
- ☐ refer to X：X について言及する
- ☐ in total：合計で

6
- ☐ in other words：言い換えると
- ☐ deal with X：X を扱う
- ☐ be grounded in X：X に基づく
- ☐ mine：採鉱する
- ☐ depict X：X を描く

6 The 19th century observed ...
「19 世紀が…を目撃した」 → 「19 世紀に…が生じた」

7

7 ❶Unfortunately, although many people and movie stars contributed to the prosperity of silent films, they became obsolete in the 1930s.
❷Well, technology finally developed enough to let people enjoy films with sound and voices.
❸Once the early films with voice were produced in 1927, the production of silent films stopped within a decade.
❹Although there's a widely held misconception that silent films are primitive and barely watchable by modern standards, this misconception only comes from the poor preservation conditions of those films.
❺In fact, as mentioned earlier, there are many great films from the Silent Film Era.
❻And I must say this . . . silent films are still alive.
❼There are a certain number of filmmakers and people who are producing silent films even now!
❽I really recommend that you watch a film titled "The Artist" produced in 2011 in France.
❾This is a silent film produced in modern day.
❿This movie, "The Artist," was nominated for ten Academy Awards.
⓫And, it won five in the year 2012.

7

❶多くの人々や映画スターが無声映画の繁栄に貢献しましたが、残念なことに、1930年代に無声映画は廃れてしまいました。
❷ええ、ついに、観客が音と声が聞ける映画を楽しめるまでに技術が発達したのです。
❸1927年に初期の音声付き映画が製作されると、無声映画の製作は10年もしないうちに終わってしまいました。
❹無声映画は原始的で、現代の標準からすると見るに堪えないという誤解がよくありますが、この誤解は（無声）映画の悪い保存状態に起因するだけのものなのです。
❺実際、先ほども言及した通り、無声映画時代に作られたものには素晴らしい映画が多くあります。
❻そして、これは言わないといけませんね…無声映画はまだ生きているのです。
❼今でも無声映画を製作している一定数の映画製作者や人々が存在します。
❽フランスで2011年に製作された'The Artist'という映画を観ることを強くお勧めします。
❾これは現代に製作された無声映画です。
❿この映画、'The Artist'は10部門でアカデミー賞にノミネートされました。
⓫そして、2012年には5部門で賞を取ったのです。

7

- □ contribute to X：Xに貢献する
- □ prosperity：繁栄
- □ obsolete：廃れた
- □ a widely held misconception：広く信じられている誤解
- □ primitive：原始的な
- □ barely：ほとんど～ではない（≒hardly）
- □ misconception：誤解

7 as mentioned earlier → as (is) mentioned earlier
「先ほど述べられたように」

リスニング問題6 会話

CAMPUS CONVERSATION

問題演習の流れ

- □ 音声が流れている間は、問題は読めません。会話が終わり、最初の問題音声が流れ始めたらページをめくって、5分以内に解答しましょう。
- □ 1問の解答時間は20秒を目安にしています。問題を読み上げた後に解答時間として20秒のポーズ（音声なし）が入っていますので、その間に解答をマークしてください。
- □ メモは自由に取ってください。
- □ 3回解けるように、3回分のマークシートを問題ページに用意しています。解く日付を記入してからマークしてください。

Web解答方法

- □ 本試験では各選択肢の左に表示されるマークをクリックして解答します。本試験と同様の方法で取り組みたい場合は、Webで解答できます。
- □ インターネットのつながるパソコン・スマートフォンで、以下のサイトにアクセスしてWeb上で解答してください。

extester.com

- □ 操作方法は、p.13 ～ 14の「USA Club Web学習の使い方」をご参照ください。

学習の記録

学習開始日	年　月　日	学習終了日	年　月　日
学習開始日	年　月　日	学習終了日	年　月　日
学習開始日	年　月　日	学習終了日	年　月　日

リスニング問題 6 会話 音声

 L06

聞き取りメモ

L06_Q1

1. Why does the student go to see his professor?

(A) To talk about a certain mathematical model
(B) To seek advice on a topic for the upcoming task
(C) To brief the professor on how other students are doing
(D) To ask the professor if he can work alone

L06_Q2

2. Why is the student concerned about his preparation for the presentation?

(A) He was assigned a position to talk in the class as the first speaker.
(B) He must make all the presentation slides without anyone's help.
(C) He may not have enough time to wrap up his materials.
(D) He has not found necessary information sources for his speech.

L06_Q3

3. What is indicated about the search theory? *Choose two answers.*

(A) It has far-reaching implications for people's economic activities.
(B) It deals with people's purchasing behavior.
(C) It is difficult to mathematically prove the validity of the theory.
(D) It helps to analyze issues regarding labor and employment.

L06_Q4

4. What does the professor suggest that the student do in his presentation? *Choose two answers.*

(A) To illustrate how the theory can be used in real life
(B) To spare some time for discussion
(C) To include advanced materials not covered in the class
(D) To present precise details of a theory

L06_Q5

5. Listen again to part of the conversation and then answer the question.
Why did the professor say this?

(A) To indicate that the student may have missed the chance to talk with him
(B) To warn the student of a possibility of failing a course
(C) To suggest that the student make another appointment
(D) To complain that he had to cancel his meeting

 1. **(B)** 2. **(C)** 3. **(B) (D)** 4. **(A) (B)** 5. **(A)**

1~7 | 問 1~2 解説レクチャー

L06_Script01-07 S: Student P: Professor

1
S: ❶Hello, Professor Osborne. ❷I have an appointment with you at 2:00.
P: ❶Hi, Oliver. ❷Well, it's already ten past two. ❸You really should try to be on time from next time. ❹It's fortunate that I don't have any meetings after your appointment. ❺If I did, you would be the one who would have to suffer the consequences.

2
S: ❶I'm awfully sorry. ❷I'll never let this sort of thing happen again.
P: ❶It's OK, as long as you're more careful next time. ❷So, how's everything?

3
S: Well, I'm getting quite busy now that the final exam period is just around the corner, but other than that, I'm doing okay.
P: ❶We're in the same boat then! ❷But at least, you'll have a long summer vacation after the exam. ❸I'll be spending most of my summer grading your exams and preparing course materials for the next semester. ❹And I'll also be doing some investigations for my research. ❺Man, I wish I was a student and had a longer break. ❻Well . . . anyway . . . what do you wanna talk about today?

4
S: Well, I'd like your opinion about my topic for the in-class presentation.
P: ❶Oh right! ❷We're having the oral presentation next week in the class. ❸I almost forgot . . . actually, you're the first presenter. ❹Right?

5
S: ❶Yes. ❷I'll be the first speaker, but that's not really an issue. ❸I need to hurry up and get the preparation done. ❹I'm running out of time.
P: ❶Then, why don't you work in a team?

6
S: ❶Some of them are working in groups. ❷But, I don't really like group work, so I'm trying to do it by myself. ❸Anyway, they seem to be doing okay, too.
P: Well, it's up to you, but feel free to talk to me when you are stuck.

7
S: Well, we're supposed to choose one of the economics theories from the textbook, and discuss it beyond what we've learned in class, right?
P: Right.

解説レクチャー

1S～**2P**：学生が教授と会う時間に遅刻したことがわかります。If I did, you would be the one ... は、If I had a meeting after your appointment, you would be the one ...「もし会議があったら、困るのは学生だっただろう」ということです。幸い、教授にはこの後用事がないようです。

2P～**3S**：学生の近況を聞いています。期末試験に向けた勉強で忙しいとのことです。

3P：We're in the same boatは「同じ船」つまり「同じ状況にある」という意味です。夏休みの間、教授は試験を採点したり、次の学期に向けて授業準備をしたり、研究のために調査をしたりする必要があるそうです。

4S：学生がクラスで発表するプレゼンテーションについて聞きに来たとわかります。

4P～**5S**：学生が最初の発表者です。準備の時間が少ないことが気がかりなようですね。

5P～**6S**：学生はグループではなく、一人で準備を行いたいようです。

6P～**7P**：学生は経済理論の1つを選び、授業で学んだ以上のことをプレゼンで話す必要があるとのことです。

聞き取りメモ例

late
busy final
summer vac
busy [scoring
　　 ______
class presentation
first presenter
hurry

work in a team
↕
don't like
economic theory
beyond

L06_Q1

1. Why does the student go to see his professor?

(A) To talk about a certain mathematical model
(B) To seek advice on a topic for the upcoming task
(C) To brief the professor on how other students are doing
(D) To ask the professor if he can work alone

なぜ学生は教授に会いに行っていますか。

(A) ある数理モデルについて話すため
(B) 今度の課題のトピックについて助言を求めるため
(C) 他の学生がどうしているか教授に手短に説明するため
(D) 彼が一人で作業してもいいか教授に尋ねるため

3Pから**4P**までの発言により、プレゼンテーションのアドバイスをもらいに来たことがわかるので、(B)が正解です。presentationをtaskと、next weekをupcomingと言い換えていますね。(A)は数学理論に関する話は登場しますが、それが教授に会いに行く目的ではありません。(C)ですが、他の学生の様子に関する発言はありますが、これも教授に会いに行く目的ではありません。(D)はすでに一人で活動しているため、誤りです。

□ upcoming：今度の、これから生じる予定の

L06_Q2

2. Why is the student concerned about his preparation for the presentation?

(A) He was assigned a position to talk in the class as the first speaker.
(B) He must make all the presentation slides without anyone's help.
(C) He may not have enough time to wrap up his materials.
(D) He has not found necessary information sources for his speech.

学生はなぜプレゼンの準備に関して心配していますか。

(A) 彼が最初のスピーカーとして授業で話す役割を与えられた。
(B) 彼は誰の助けも借りずに全てのプレゼンのスライドを作らなければならない。
(C) 資料を完成させるのに十分な時間がないかもしれない。
(D) スピーチに必要な情報源を見つけられていない。

5S ❸〜❹で「急いで準備を終えなければいけない。時間が足りなくなりそうだ」と述べているので、(C)が正解です。running out of timeをnot have enough timeで言い換えています。(A)は5S ❷で「最初の発表者だが、それは問題ではない」と述べているので誤りです。(B)に関しては、一人で活動することを選んでいる以上、義務ではありません。(D)は会話中での言及がありません。

□ wrap up X: Xを完成させる

8〜14 | 問3〜4 解説レクチャー

L06_Script08-14

8 S: ❶So I found this really interesting theory called "search theory" when I was skimming through the textbook. ❷I learned that search theory deals with how consumers make a decision about whether they buy a certain product or not. ❸Besides, it seems the theory has an application in labor economics. ❹But . . . the thing is that I'm not really sure if I should discuss it from a theoretical perspective or practical perspective.

P: So you're thinking about two approaches . . . theoretical and practical.

9 S: Yes, exactly.

P: ❶Hmm. ❷We've been treating many theories without really exploring their real-world applications or having discussions about their practical use. ❸So, I suggest that you introduce applications of the theory, you know, real-world examples that we didn't have chance to touch on. ❹For example, using this model, we can tackle things like unemployment or job hunting and their effects in a highly systematic and sophisticated way. ❺This is an advanced course open only to seniors, so they'll be able to follow some complicated or advanced topics.

10 S: ❶Right. ❷That's what I thought first. ❸But I've actually found the mathematical model behind the theory quite interesting. ❹Search theory is based on a mathematical model called the General Equilibrium Model. ❺I'm not really interested in all the fancy tricks used in the proof or the complicated math with its cryptic symbols and stuff. ❻What I'm really fascinated about is the fact that a seemingly pure mathematical theorem has a place in economics and how economists have incorporated it into economic theories. ❼Do you think I could probably talk about that? ❽You know, since this mathematical viewpoint is also something we didn't go too much into detail about.

P: ❶We only looked at it briefly, so I'm a bit worried about whether everybody will be able to follow your presentation. ❷I totally agree that math is one of the most important subjects to understand economics. ❸But the math used in search theory is quite advanced, most of which is beyond the scope of the typical undergraduate student.

11 S: ❶Yes, I'm aware of that. ❷My intention is to emphasize the basic idea of the mathematical model. ❸I won't go into the technical details. ❹I will make sure that even somebody without an advanced knowledge of mathematics can understand.

P: ❶I see. ❷If that's the case, it might work. ❸Well, since you're so passionate about this theory, why don't you give it a try?

12 S: Yes, I will!

P: ❶And, be sure to have some time for discussion and questions at several points in your presentation. ❷Maybe talk for 10 minutes, then stop and make sure everybody is with you. ❸Then continue again, like that.

13 S: ❶That's a good idea. ❷I'll definitely do that!

P: ❶Shall I go over your presentation outline once it's ready? ❷I'd be happy to comment on whether the level of your presentation is right for the audience.

14 S: ❶That would be a tremendous help. ❷Thank you, professor. ❸I will let you know as soon as I'm finished with the first draft.

解説レクチャー

8S: 学生は探索理論（search theory）に興味があるようです。これは消費者が購買の決定を下す方法に関する理論だそうです。問題は、理論的側面と実用的側面のどちらに焦点を当てるべきかで学生が迷っているということです。

8P ~ 9P：教授は、探索理論の実社会での応用について話すよう勧めています。例えば、この理論を用いて、失業や就職活動とそれがもたらす影響に取り組むことができると述べています。4年生向けの授業なので、込み入った内容のプレゼンでも問題ないとのことですね。
10S：学生が興味を持っているのは、理論の背景にある数学的モデルです。とくに、複雑な数式ではなく、純粋な数学の定理が経済学において役割を持ち、また経済学者がそれを経済理論に応用しているということに興味を持っていますね。
10P：教授は、他の学生がプレゼンについてこられるかどうかを気にしています。学生が興味を持っている数学の理論は、学部生レベルを超えているものが多いからだそうです。
11S ~ 12S：学生は、理論の基本的概念を強調することに留めると述べています。数学の応用知識がなくても、ついていけるようにするとのことです。それを聞いて、教授も許可を出しています。
12P ~ 13S：プレゼンの途中で質疑応答の時間を設けるよう助言しています。
13P ~ 14S：教授がプレゼンの概要をチェックすると申し出ています。それに対して学生は、原案が完成したら教授に見せると述べています。

聞き取りメモ例

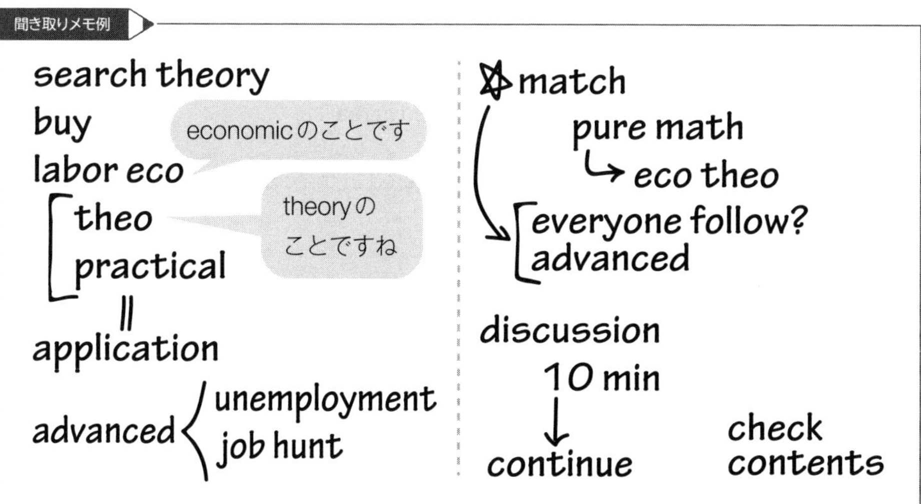

L06_Q3

3. What is indicated about the search theory? *Choose two answers.*

(A) It has far-reaching implications for people's economic activities.
(B) It deals with people's purchasing behavior.
(C) It is difficult to mathematically prove the validity of the theory.
(D) It helps to analyze issues regarding labor and employment.

探索理論について何が示されていますか。2つ選んでください。

(A) 人々の経済活動に広範な影響を与えている。
(B) それは人々の購買行動を対象としている。
(C) その理論の有効性を数学的に証明することは難しい。
(D) それは労働と雇用に関する問題を分析するのに役立つ。

8Sによると探索理論は「消費者が購買の決定を下す方法」に関する理論なので(B)が正解です。また9P❹で、この理論を用いて、「失業や就職活動、またそれらがもたらす影響」を扱うことができるとあります。これは(D)に一致しますね。よって、(B)と(D)が正解です。なお、探索理論そのものが人々の経済活動に影響を及ぼすわけではないので、(A)は誤りですね。(C)は会話中に言及がありません。

□implication:影響(通常複数形)　□regarding X: Xに関する

L06_Q4

4. What does the professor suggest that the student do in his presentation? *Choose two answers.*

(A) To illustrate how the theory can be used in real life
(B) To spare some time for discussion
(C) To include advanced materials not covered in the class
(D) To present precise details of a theory

教授は、学生にプレゼンの中で何をするよう提案していますか。2つ選んでください。

(A) どのようにその理論が現実の生活で使われるかを解説すること
(B) 議論の時間を取ること
(C) 授業でカバーされていない高度なレベルの資料を含めること
(D) 理論の正確な詳細を示すこと

教授は9P❸で「理論の応用」、つまり「実生活での応用の具体例」について述べることを提案しています。よって1つ目の正解は(A)です。9P❸のapplicationをcan be usedと、real-worldをreal lifeと、examplesをillustrateという動詞でそれぞれ言い換えています。さらに、12P❶で「質疑応答の時間を取ること」を提案しているので(B)も正解です。(C)については10P❶で「全ての学生がプレゼンを理解できるかどうか不安だ」と教授が述べています。高度な内容を入れることを提案するはずがありません。(D)は会話中に言及がありません。

□cover X: X(授業内容など)を扱う(カバーする)

問5解説レクチャー

L06_Q5

5. Listen again to part of the conversation and then answer the question.

Professor:
Hi, Oliver. Well, it's already ten past two. You really should try to be on time from next time. It's fortunate that I don't have any meetings after your appointment. If I did, you would be the one who would have to suffer the consequences.

Why did the professor say this?

"If I did, you would be the one who would have to suffer the consequences."

(A) To indicate that the student may have missed the chance to talk with him
(B) To warn the student of a possibility of failing a course
(C) To suggest that the student make another appointment
(D) To complain that he had to cancel his meeting

会話の一部をもう一度聞いて、設問に答えてください。

教授：
Oliverさん、こんにちは。ええと、もう2時10分ですね。次から時間通りに来るようにした方がいいですよ。Oliverさんとの約束の後に会議がなくて、よかったです。もしあれば、割を食うのはOliverさんでしょうから。

なぜ教授は「もしあれば、割を食うのはOliverさんでしょうから」と言いましたか。

(A) 学生が自分と話す機会を逃してしまったかもしれないということを示すため
(B) 授業の単位を落としてしまう可能性を学生に警告するため
(C) 学生にまた予約をするよう提案するため
(D) 会議を中止しなければならなかったと苦情を言うため

If I didはIf I had a meeting after your appointment、つまり「Oliverさんとの約束の後に会議があったなら」という意味です。you would be the one who would have to suffer the consequencesの部分は「相談ができないという形で割りを食うのはOliverさんでしょう」という意味です。よって、「教授と話す機会を逃していたかもしれない」という意味の(A)が正解です。(B)と(D)は会話から読み取ることができません。(C)は「学生にまた予約をするよう提案する」という意味です。つまり、教授と学生の話が次回に持ち越されるということなので誤りです。

1-4 S: Student P: Professor

Listen to a conversation between a student and his economics professor.

1
S: ❶Hello, Professor Osborne.
❷I have an appointment with you at 2:00.
P: ❶Hi, Oliver.
❷Well, it's already ten past two.
❸You really should try to be on time from next time.
❹It's fortunate that I don't have any meetings after your appointment.
❺If I did, you would be the one who would have to suffer the consequences.

2
S: ❶I'm awfully sorry.
❷I'll never let this sort of thing happen again.
P: ❶It's OK, as long as you're more careful next time.
❷So, how's everything?

3
S: Well, I'm getting quite busy now that the final exam period is just around the corner, but other than that, I'm doing okay.
P: ❶We're in the same boat then!
❷But at least, you'll have a long summer vacation after the exam.
❸I'll be spending most of my summer grading your exams and preparing course materials for the next semester.
❹And I'll also be doing some investigations for my research.
❺Man, I wish I was a student and had a longer break.
❻Well . . . anyway . . . what do you wanna talk about today?

4
S: Well, I'd like your opinion about my topic for the in-class presentation.
P: ❶Oh right!
❷We're having the oral presentation next week in the class.
❸I almost forgot . . . actually, you're the first presenter.
❹Right?

学生と経済学の教授の会話を聞きなさい。

1
S: ❶ Osborne 先生、こんにちは。
❷ 2 時に予約をしていたんですが。
P: ❶ Oliver さん、こんにちは。
❷ええと、もう 2 時 10 分ですね。
❸次から時間通りに来るようにした方がいいですよ。
❹ Oliver さんとの約束の後に会議がなくて、よかったです。
❺もしあれば、割を食うのは Oliver さんでしょうから。

2
S: ❶本当にすみません。
❷こんなことはもう二度としません。
P: ❶次からもっと気を付けるようにすれば、大丈夫ですよ。
❷ところで、最近はどうですか。

3
S: そうですね、もうすぐ期末試験があるので忙しいですが、それ以外はうまくやっています。
P: ❶では私と同じ状況ですね！
❷だけど少なくとも、Oliver さんは試験の後には、長い夏休みがあるじゃないですか。
❸私は皆さんの試験を採点し、次の学期に向けて授業の資料を用意することに夏の大半を費やす予定です。
❹あと、研究のための調査もする予定です。
❺学生になって、もっと長い休みが取れたらいいんですけど。
❻ところで、今日は何について話したいのですか。

4
S: ええと、クラスで発表するプレゼンのトピックについて、ご意見を伺いたいんです。
P: ❶ああそうでした！
❷来週授業で口頭でのプレゼンテーションをするんでしたね。
❸忘れかけていました…そう言えば、Oliver さんが最初のプレゼンターです。
❹合ってましたか。

1
- ☐ on time：時間通りに
- ☐ consequence：（悪い）結果

2
- ☐ this sort of X：この種のX
- ☐ as long as SV：～する限り

3
- ☐ now that SV：今や～なので
- ☐ around the corner：まもなくやってくる
- ☐ other than X：Xを除けば
- ☐ be in the same boat：同じような悪い状況にいる
- ☐ grade X：Xを採点する

1 ten past two「2 時 10 分」
pastは「～を過ぎて」という意味の前置詞なので「2時を過ぎて10分経った状態」ということ。

5-8

5 S: ❶Yes.
❷I'll be the first speaker, but that's not really an issue.
❸I need to hurry up and get the preparation done.
❹I'm running out of time.
P: Then, why don't you work in a team?

6 S: ❶Some of them are working in groups.
❷But, I don't really like group work, so I'm trying to do it by myself.
❸Anyway, they seem to be doing okay, too.
P: Well, it's up to you, but feel free to talk to me when you are stuck.

7 S: Well, we're supposed to choose one of the economics theories from the textbook, and discuss it beyond what we've learned in class, right?
P: Right.

8 S: ❶So I found this really interesting theory called "search theory" when I was skimming through the textbook.
❷I learned that search theory deals with how consumers make a decision about whether they buy a certain product or not.
❸Besides, it seems the theory has an application in labor economics.
❹But . . . the thing is that I'm not really sure if I should discuss it from a theoretical perspective or practical perspective.
P: So you're thinking about two approaches . . . theoretical and practical.

5

S: ❶はい。
❷私が最初に発表するんですが、特にそれは問題ではありません。
❸急いで準備を終わらせなければいけないんです。
❹時間が足りなくなってきました。
P: それなら、チームで作業してはどうですか。

6

S: ❶中にはグループで作業を進めている人もいます。
❷でも、グループワークがあまり好きではないので、一人でしようと思っています。
❸とにかく、グループでやっている人もうまくやっているようですし。
P: ええ、それは Oliver さん次第ですが、行き詰まったときには私に遠慮なく言ってください。

7

S: ええと、教科書から経済理論を1つ選んで、授業で習った以上のことを論じないといけないんですよね。
P: そうです。

8

S: ❶あの、教科書を流し読みしていたら、「探索理論」と呼ばれるとても面白い理論を見つけたんです。
❷探索理論は、ある商品を買うか否かに関する決定を、どのように消費者が下すかに焦点を当てているということを学びました。
❸それに、その理論は労働経済学へも応用できるようなんです。
❹ただ…実は、それを理論的な観点から議論すべきか、実用的な観点から議論すべきかで迷っているんです。
P: つまり、理論的アプローチと実用的アプローチの2つを考えているのですね。

5
- □ get X done：Xを終わらせる
- □ run out of X：Xが足りなくなる

6
- □ be up to X：X次第である
- □ be stuck：行き詰まる

7
- □ beyond X：Xを超えて

8
- □ skim through X：Xをざっくりと読む
- □ application：応用性

8 the thing is that ... 「問題は…ということだ」
説明や理由を述べるときに使う表現

9-10

9
S: Yes, exactly.
P: ❶Hmm.
❷We've been treating many theories without really exploring their real-world applications or having discussions about their practical use.
❸So, I suggest that you introduce applications of the theory, you know, real-world examples that we didn't have chance to touch on.
❹For example, using this model, we can tackle things like unemployment or job hunting and their effects in a highly systematic and sophisticated way.
❺This is an advanced course open only to seniors, so they'll be able to follow some complicated or advanced topics.

10
S: ❶Right.
❷That's what I thought first.
❸But I've actually found the mathematical model behind the theory quite interesting.
❹Search theory is based on a mathematical model called the General Equilibrium Model.
❺I'm not really interested in all the fancy tricks used in the proof or the complicated math with its cryptic symbols and stuff.
❻What I'm really fascinated about is the fact that a seemingly pure mathematical theorem has a place in economics and how economists have incorporated it into economic theories.
❼Do you think I could probably talk about that?
❽You know, since this mathematical viewpoint is also something we didn't go too much into detail about.
P: ❶We only looked at it briefly, so I'm a bit worried about whether everybody will be able to follow your presentation.
❷I totally agree that math is one of the most important subjects to understand economics.
❸But the math used in search theory is quite advanced, most of which is beyond the scope of the typical undergraduate student.

9 S: はい、その通りです。

P: ❶うーん。

❷今まで実生活における応用を詳しく見たり、実用的な用途についての議論をあまりせずに、多くの理論を論じてきました。

❸ですから、その理論の応用、つまり私たちが触れる機会がなかった実生活での例を紹介することをお勧めします。

❹例えば、このモデルを使って、失業や就職活動のようなもの、そしてそれらがもたらす影響に、かなり体系的かつ高度なやり方で取り組むことができます。

❺4年生のみに開かれた上級のクラスですから、複雑で高度なテーマにもついていけるでしょう。

10 S: ❶そうですね。

❷それが一番始めに考えたことです。

❸ただ実は、その理論の裏にある数理モデルがとても面白いと思ったんです。

❹探索理論は、一般均衡モデルと呼ばれる数理モデルに基づいています。

❺証明に使われる凝ったテクニックや、よくわからない記号を使った複雑な数学自体にはあまり興味がありません。

❻私がとても興味をそそられるのは、純粋な数学の定理に見えるものが経済学の中で役割を持っているということと、経済学者がそれを経済理論に応用しているということです。

❼そのことについて話してもいいと思いますか？

❽この数学的な観点は、あまり詳細に立ち入らなかったことでもありますし。

P: ❶私たちはそれを簡単に考察しただけなので、皆がOliverさんのプレゼンについていけるかどうか少し心配です。

❷数学は経済学を理解するための最も重要な科目の一つだということには、私も全く同感です。

❸ですが探索理論に用いられている数学はとても高度なもので、その大部分は普通の学部生レベルを超えているんです。

9

- □ touch on X：Xに触れる、言及する
- □ tackle X：Xに取り組む
- □ sophisticated：高度な
- □ senior：大学4年生

10

- □ fancy：複雑な
- □ cryptic：謎めいた
- □ fascinate X：Xを魅了する
- □ have a place：役割を持つ
- □ incorporate X into Y：XをYに組み入れる
- □ a bit：少し（≒ a little）
- □ scope：領域、範囲
- □ undergraduate student：学部生

10 found (V) the mathematical model (O) (behind the theory) (M) quite interesting (C)

「その理論の裏にある数理モデルがとても興味深いと思った」

11–14

11 S: ❶Yes, I'm aware of that.
❷My intention is to emphasize the basic idea of the mathematical model.
❸I won't go into the technical details.
❹I will make sure that even somebody without an advanced knowledge of mathematics can understand.
P: ❶I see.
❷If that's the case, it might work.
❸Well, since you're so passionate about this theory, why don't you give it a try?

12 S: Yes, I will!
P: ❶And, be sure to have some time for discussion and questions at several points in your presentation.
❷Maybe talk for 10 minutes, then stop and make sure everybody is with you.
❸Then continue again, like that.

13 S: ❶That's a good idea.
❷I'll definitely do that!
P: ❶Shall I go over your presentation outline once it's ready?
❷I'd be happy to comment on whether the level of your presentation is right for the audience.

14 S: ❶That would be a tremendous help.
❷Thank you, professor.
❸I will let you know as soon as I'm finished with the first draft.

11 S: ❶はい、それはわかっています。
❷私の意図は、その数理モデルの基本的概念を強調することにあるんです。
❸専門的な詳細については立ち入らないつもりです。
❹数学に関しての応用知識を持っていない人でも理解できるようにします。
P: ❶なるほど。
❷だとすれば、うまくいくかもしれませんね。
❸そうですね、Oliver さんがそれほどこの理論に夢中なのであれば、やってみてはいかがですか。

12 S: はい、やってみます！
P: ❶それと、プレゼンの途中に何度か、質疑応答の時間を取るようにしてください。
❷例えば 10 分話したら、中断して皆さんがついてこれているか確かめる。
❸それから再開する、というように。

13 S: ❶それはいい考えですね。
❷そうします！
P: ❶その準備ができ次第、私がプレゼンのアウトラインをチェックしましょうか。
❷ Oliver さんのプレゼンのレベルが聞く側にとってちょうどいいかどうかについて是非コメントしたいのですが。

14 S: ❶それはとても助かります。
❷ありがとうございます、先生。
❸原案が出来上がり次第すぐ連絡します。

11
- ☐ detail：詳細
- ☐ be the case：事実である
- ☐ give it a try：それを試してみる

12
- ☐ be with X：Xの話に付いて行く

13
- ☐ once SV：いったん～すれば

14
- ☐ tremendous：巨大な

リスニング問題 7 講義

GEOGRAPHY

問題演習の流れ

- ☐ 音声が流れている間は、問題は読めません。講義が終わり、最初の問題音声が流れ始めたらページをめくって、5分以内に解答しましょう。
- ☐ 1問の解答時間は20秒を目安にしています。問題を読み上げた後に解答時間として20秒のポーズ（音声なし）が入っていますので、その間に解答をマークしてください。
- ☐ メモは自由に取ってください。
- ☐ 3回解けるように、3回分のマークシートを問題ページに用意しています。解く日付を記入してからマークしてください。

Web解答方法

- ☐ 本試験では各選択肢の左に表示されるマークをクリックして解答します。本試験と同様の方法で取り組みたい場合は、Webで解答できます。
- ☐ インターネットのつながるパソコン・スマートフォンで、以下のサイトにアクセスしてWeb上で解答してください。

extester.com

- ☐ 操作方法は、p.13 ～ 14の「USA Club Web学習の使い方」をご参照ください。

学習の記録

学習開始日	年　　月　　日	学習終了日	年　　月　　日
学習開始日	年　　月　　日	学習終了日	年　　月　　日
学習開始日	年　　月　　日	学習終了日	年　　月　　日

リスニング問題7 講義 音声

 L07

Geography

Positive feedback loops

The albedo effect

聞き取りメモ

L07_Q1

1. What aspect of glaciers does the professor mainly discuss?

(A) How multiple factors determine the overall amount of glaciers
(B) How the melting of glaciers affects the environment
(C) How they are affected chiefly by human activities
(D) How they change shape from one period to another

L07_Q2

2. What does the professor say about the interglacial period?

(A) It is a period during which glaciers gain mass.
(B) It is marked by low temperatures.
(C) It is characterized by increased melting of glaciers.
(D) It is the phase in which there was hardly any ice in the Arctic.

L07_Q3

3. According to the professor, what does "albedo" represent?

(A) The brightness of light coming from the Sun
(B) The type of light absorbed in the surface of the Earth
(C) The amount of light sent back by the Earth's surface
(D) The color of the light reflected by the ocean

L07_Q4

4. What does the professor say about the red-colored algae growing on glaciers?

(A) They release greenhouse gases such as CO_2.
(B) Their cells change color once exposed to the Sun.
(C) They are capable of directing the Sun's heat back into space.
(D) They contribute to negative feedback loops.

L07_Q5

5. What are the two examples of man-made negative feedback the professor discusses? *Choose two answers.*

(A) Using too much electricity
(B) Cutting down trees
(C) Driving large-sized vehicles
(D) Burning natural resources

L07_Q6

6. Listen again to part of the lecture and then answer the question.
Why does the professor say this?

(A) To remind the student of the importance of repeating main points
(B) To indicate that what the student said is not completely correct
(C) To make sure that the students understand the concept
(D) To remind the student of the need to study harder

 1. **(A)** 2. **(C)** 3. **(C)** 4. **(D)** 5. **(B) (D)** 6. **(B)**

1～9 | 問1～3 解説レクチャー

L07_Script01-09 P: Professor S: Student

1 P: ❶Today we are talking about glaciers, in particular how they form and melt away. ❷A glacier is simply a gigantic body of ice moving under its own weight. ❸You might have heard on the news or read in newspapers that they're melting worldwide and people seem to make a big fuss about it. ❹How do melting glaciers affect us or any other living creatures on the Earth? ❺Well, the truth is that glaciers are like the Earth's air conditioner, helping to regulate the climate as we know it today. ❻However, there is clear evidence that the Earth is losing its ice. ❼I'm sure many of you are familiar with the consequences, but just in case you aren't, let me remind you. ❽The global glacier loss is a big contributing factor in rising sea water levels and global temperatures. ❾We tend to think humans are to blame for these changes, but the reality is . . . we don't know precisely to what degree human activities are contributing to this . . . because nature also plays its role. ❿The Earth has seen glaciers form and melt long before the development of human civilization. ⓫That is, there have been periods marked by more glaciers and periods marked by fewer glaciers. ⓬The periods of glacier advances are called glacial periods, and the periods of glacial losses are called interglacial periods. ⓭So a glacial period is a period of building ice, whereas an interglacial period is a period of melting ice. ⓮And the Earth has been going back and forth between these two periods since its birth.

2 P: ❶So the next question arises. ❷What causes the fluctuation of the Earth's climate? ❸Well . . . the climate of the Earth is subject to what we call "positive feedback loops" and "negative feedback loops." ❹Don't worry. ❺I'll go over each process with some examples later. ❻Once the idea clicks, the concept and the mechanism of these loops become much clearer.

3 P: ❶Let's first look at positive feedback loops. ❷Do any of you know what positive feedback loop means? ❸You can guess.

4 S: Well, if something happens in a loop, the same things are repeated over and over, so I guess in a positive feedback loop, at least in the context of the environment, something good for the environment happens again and again?

5 P: ❶Good guess. ❷You're right about certain things repeating themselves. ❸Let me give you a precise definition. ❹So . . . in the context of glaciers, a positive feedback loop is a series of repeating events that help the formation of glaciers. ❺For instance, suppose that the air temperature drops. ❻Then the amount of ice and snow covering the Earth grows. ❼Ice and snow reflect sunlight. ❽You know, so the sunlight hitting the surface of the Earth is bounced back to space, leading to a colder climate. ❾A colder climate means more ice and more snow. ❿See, this whole process repeats itself.

6 P: ❶The example I just gave has to do with "the albedo effect." ❷Albedo is a measure of how much light is reflected by a surface, and the albedo effect refers to how things like ice, snow, water, land, etc. reflect solar radiation. ❸High albedo means lots of reflection, and low albedo . . . little reflection. ❹The Earth's surface has many different colors, and each color has an effect on the Earth's temperature. ❺Ice and snow are white, or light colored, so they have a high albedo. ❻They send a lot of the Sun's energy back into space and prevent the surface from heating up. ❼Clouds prevent the sunlight from reaching the Earth's surface, so they cool the Earth too. ❽Dark-colored surfaces like the oceans, on the other hand, have a low albedo. ❾They absorb the Sun's heat, warming the Earth.

7 P: ❶Let's now look at negative feedback loops. ❷Now that you know what a positive feedback loop is, you should be able to guess what this is. ❸In the context of glaciers, a negative feedback loop is a cycle where a series of events leads to the melting of glaciers. ❹One example of a negative feedback is volcanic eruptions. ❺When a volcano erupts near a glacier, the resulting molten lava melts the surrounding ice. ❻This means less solar energy is reflected and hence more heat is absorbed. ❼The Earth gets warmer and more ice melts, leading to even more land being exposed to the Sun and even more melting of glaciers. ❽This is a negative feedback cycle. ❾Ice keeps melting.

8 P: ❶Another interesting player of negative feedback is algae. ❷There are several kinds of algae that grow on melting surfaces of glaciers.

9 S: So they have low albedo.

解説レクチャー

1

❶～❹:氷河の影響というテーマを導入しています。

❺:氷河をエアコンで例えています。

❻～❽:氷河がなくなることにより、海面上昇と気温上昇が生じると説明しています。

❾:一般的に地球環境の変化は人間の責任だと考える人が多いですが、人間だけでなく、自然の影響もあるとのことです。

❿～⓮:氷河が増える時期である氷河期 (glacial period) と、氷河が減る時期の間氷期 (interglacial period) を地球は繰り返してきたと述べています。

2

❶:the next question により、話が転換するとわかります。

❷～❻:positive feedback loopsとnegative feedback loopsという用語を出しています。

3

❶～❸:positive feedback loopsの意味がわかるか学生に聞いています。

4

学生が当たりを付けています。something good for the environment happens again and againという発言がわかりやすいですね。「環境にとって望ましいことが繰り返し生じる」という意味です。

5

❶～❹:学生の発言を受けてpositive feedback loopの説明を始めています。

❺～❿:具体例が挙げられています。「気温が下がる → 氷や雪が増える → 太陽光が反射されるため、さらに気温が下がる」というプロセスが、何度も繰り返されると説明しています。

6

❶～❷:アルベドの定義が述べられています。「地表で反射される光の量」を表す尺度だとのことです。その後、アルベド効果を説明しています。

❸～❻:氷や雪は白いのでアルベドが高いと述べています。その結果、地球が冷えるということです。

❼:さらに雲も太陽光を遮るので、地球の寒冷化に一役買うと続けています。

❽～❾:海などの表面の色が濃いものはアルベドが低いそうです。

7

❶～❸:negative feedback loopが氷河を解かすものだと説明しています。

❹～❾:火山の噴火がnegative feedback loopの具体例として挙げられています。「火山の噴火 → 溶岩が氷を解かす → 太陽光の反射が減る → さらに地球が温暖になる → さらに氷が解ける」というプロセスが説明されています。

8

❶～❷：藻類もnegative feedback loopの一因になると述べています。

9

❶：藻類がnegative feedback loopの一因になっている理由を、この学生は理解しているようです。

聞き取りメモ例

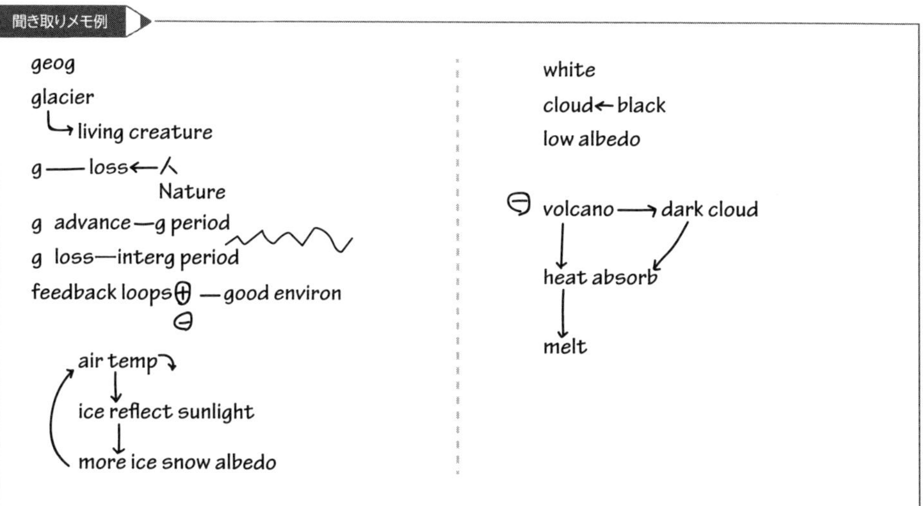

L07_Q1

1. What aspect of glaciers does the professor mainly discuss?

(A) How multiple factors determine the overall amount of glaciers
(B) How the melting of glaciers affects the environment
(C) How they are affected chiefly by human activities
(D) How they change shape from one period to another

教授は氷河の何について主に論じていますか。

(A) どのように多くの要因が氷河の総量を決定するのか
(B) どのように氷河の融解が環境に影響を与えるのか
(C) どのようにそれら（氷河）が主に人間の活動によって影響を受けるのか
(D) どのようにそれら（氷河）が時代の移り変わりとともに形を変えるのか

講義では主に氷河の形成と融解について取り扱っています。雲や雪、火山噴火、人間活動などが要因となり、氷河の増減をもたらすという内容なので、(A)が正解です。(B)については氷河の融解に関して言及はしていますが、これは断片的な情報です。(C)は「主に人間の活動によって」が誤りです。❶❾で「人間が与える影響の程度は不明」とありました。(D)は「形を変える」ことについて講義の中で言及がありません。

□ chiefly:主に

L07_Q2

2. What does the professor say about the interglacial period?

(A) It is a period during which glaciers gain mass.
(B) It is marked by low temperatures.
(C) It is characterized by increased melting of glaciers.
(D) It is the phase in which there was hardly any ice in the Arctic.

教授は間氷期について何と言っていますか。

(A) 氷河が大きくなる時期である。
(B) 低い気温が特徴的である。
(C) 氷河の融解の増加が特色である。
(D) 北極に氷河がほとんどなかった時期である。

❶⓬に「氷河が減る時期のことを間氷期（interglacial period）と呼ぶ」とあります。また❶⓭には「氷が解ける時期」ともあります。よって、「氷河の融解が増加する」と述べている(C)が正解です。(A)の内容は氷河期のことを指しているので誤りです。(B)については講義では言及がありません。(D)は「氷河がほとんどない(hardly any)」とは述べられていません。あくまで減るだけですね。

L07_Q3

3. According to the professor, what does “albedo” represent?

(A) The brightness of light coming from the Sun
(B) The type of light absorbed in the surface of the Earth
(C) The amount of light sent back by the Earth’s surface
(D) The color of the light reflected by the ocean

教授によると、アルベドは何を意味していますか。

(A) 太陽から届く光の明るさ
(B) 地表に吸収される光の種類
(C) 地表が跳ね返す光の量
(D) 海が反射する光の色

6❷で「アルベドは地表が反射した光の量を示す尺度」と述べられているので(C)が正解です。6❷のhow muchはthe amount of、reflectedはsent backとそれぞれ言い換えられています。

10～12 | 問4～5 解説レクチャー

L07_Script10-12

10 P: ❶Right. ❷These algae reflect less solar radiation and hence absorb more heat. ❸As the glaciers with these algae absorb more sunlight, the pace of melting accelerates even further and more algae grow on the melting glaciers. ❹Sometimes, scientists refer to this phenomenon as blood snow, for the cells of the algae are reddish and hence the affected ice becomes red. ❺As we have seen, many components are involved in these loops.

11 P: ❶And, you also need to know this: the positive feedback loop and the negative feedback loop are competing with each other. ❷They are not in equilibrium. ❸There's a period during which the positive loop wins and the Earth gets colder and colder and there's lots of ice. ❹There's also a period during which the negative loop wins and the Earth gets warmer and warmer. ❺There's relatively less ice during this period . . . ❻Which loop wins is determined by many different factors as we've just discussed.

12 P: ❶So far, we've focused on positive and negative feedback loops occurring naturally. ❷But—unsurprisingly—human activities also act to trigger these loops. ❸Although we don't know exactly to what extent human activities are affecting the balance of the two loops, what is apparent is that humans are contributing more to the negative loop than to the positive loop.❹One activity is deforestation, which leads to an increase in greenhouse gases such as CO_2 because fewer trees means that less greenhouse gases are absorbed. ❺Another one, and probably the most notable one . . . is the burning of fossil fuels. ❻As we burn fossil fuels to, say, generate electricity, we produce greenhouse gases. ❼These gases trap the Sun's heat in the atmosphere, which raises the air temperature and melts large portions of glaciers. ❽This then lowers the Earth's albedo, as discussed earlier, and triggers even more melting of glaciers.

解説レクチャー

10

❶～❸:「藻類が太陽光を吸収 → 氷が解ける → さらに藻類が繁殖する」というプロセスが説明されています。

❹:blood snowの定義を確認しています。藻類の細胞が赤みがかっているため、氷が赤く見えるということだそうです。

❺:positive feedback loopとnegative feedback loopに影響をもたらす要因は多くあるとこれまでの話をまとめています。

11

❶～❷:positive feedback loop と negative feedback loop は、同時ではなく相互に競い合っていると説明しています。

❸～❻:positive feedback loopが優勢なときは地球が寒くなり、negative feedback loopが優勢なときは暖かくなるとあります。また、この時期は氷が少ないとも述べられています。

12

❶～❸:人間はpositive feedback loopよりもnegative feedback loopに対してより多くの影響を与えているとのことです。ただし、影響の程度は不明だそうです。

❹:一例として森林破壊が挙げられています。CO_2の増加による温暖化ですね。

❺～❽:別の例として挙げられているのが化石燃料の使用です。温室効果ガスが増えることにより、地球の温度が上がります。その結果、氷河が解けると説明しています。

聞き取りメモ例

algae　absorb　sunlight
heat

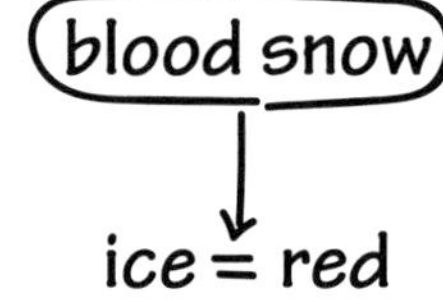

⊕ vs ⊖ ← human

deforestation
↓
CO2

burning fossil fuel
↓
greenhouse gas

L07_Q4

4. What does the professor say about the red-colored algae growing on glaciers?

(A) They release greenhouse gases such as CO_2.
(B) Their cells change color once exposed to the Sun.
(C) They are capable of directing the Sun's heat back into space.
(D) They contribute to negative feedback loops.

教授は氷河の表面に繁殖する赤い色の藻類について何と言っていますか。

(A) CO_2などの温室効果ガスを放出する。
(B) 太陽にさらされると細胞の色が変わる。
(C) 太陽の熱を宇宙に向けて跳ね返す能力がある。
(D) negative feedback loopの原因となる。

まず❽で「藻類がnegative feedbackの一因となる」とあります。さらに、❿❹で「その藻類の細胞が赤い」とあります。よって、赤い藻類がnegative feedback loopの原因となると言えるので、(D)が正解です。(A)と(B)は講義で言及されていません。(C)についてですが、これらの藻類は太陽の熱を吸収するので誤りです。

L07_Q5

5. What are the two examples of man-made negative feedback the professor discusses? *Choose two answers.*

(A) Using too much electricity
(B) Cutting down trees
(C) Driving large-sized vehicles
(D) Burning natural resources

教授が論じている人為的なnegative feedbackの2つの例はどれですか。2つ選んでください。

(A) 過剰な電力の使用
(B) 木々の伐採
(C) 大型車両の運転
(D) 自然資源の燃焼

⑫❷から人間がnegative feedback loopに影響を及ぼす事例が述べられています。⑫❹に「森林破壊」とあるため、「木を切り倒す」という意味の(B)は正解です。⑫❺に「化石燃料を燃やすこと」とあるので(D)も正解です。⑫❺のfossil fuelsをnatural resourcesと言い換えています。(A)と(C)については言及がありません。

□vehicle:車両、乗り物

問6 解説レクチャー

L07_Q6

6. Listen again to part of the lecture and then answer the question.

Student:
Well, if something happens in a loop, the same things are repeated over and over, so I guess in a positive feedback loop, at least in the context of the environment, something good for the environment happens again and again?

Professor:
Good guess. You're right about certain things repeating themselves.

Why does the professor say this?

"Good guess. You're right about certain things repeating themselves."

(A) To remind the student of the importance of repeating main points
(B) To indicate that what the student said is not completely correct
(C) To make sure that the students understand the concept
(D) To remind the student of the need to study harder

もう一度講義の一部を聞いて、設問に答えてください。

学生：
えっと、もし循環の中で何かが起こったら同じことが何度も繰り返されるので、positive feedback loopでは、少なくとも環境という面においては、環境にとって望ましいことが何度も繰り返し生じる、ということでしょうか。

教授：
いい推測ですね。あることが繰り返されるという点は正しいです。

教授はなぜ「いい推測ですね。あることが繰り返されるという点は正しいです」と言っていますか。

(A) 要点を繰り返すことの重要性を学生に気付かせるため
(B) 学生の発言が完全に正しいわけではないことを示すため
(C) 学生が概念を理解していることを確認するため
(D) 勉強をもっと頑張る必要があると学生に気付かせるため

❸で教授にpositive feedback loopsの意味がわかるかと聞かれて、学生がその意味を❹では推測して答えています。教授は学生の答えを受けて、❺❷で「あることが繰り返されるという点は正しいです」と限定して学生の発言は正しいと認めています。しかし、裏を返せば別の部分は正しくないということです。よって(B)が正解です。

1 P: Professor S: Student

Listen to part of a lecture in a geography class.

1 P: ❶Today we are talking about glaciers, in particular how they form and melt away. ❷A glacier is simply a gigantic body of ice moving under its own weight. ❸You might have heard on the news or read in newspapers that they're melting worldwide and people seem to make a big fuss about it. ❹How do melting glaciers affect us or any other living creatures on the Earth? ❺Well, the truth is that glaciers are like the Earth's air conditioner, helping to regulate the climate as we know it today. ❻However, there is clear evidence that the Earth is losing its ice. ❼I'm sure many of you are familiar with the consequences, but just in case you aren't, let me remind you. ❽The global glacier loss is a big contributing factor in rising sea water levels and global temperatures. ❾We tend to think humans are to blame for these changes, but the reality is . . . we don't know precisely to what degree human activities are contributing to this . . . because nature also plays its role. ❿The Earth has seen glaciers form and melt long before the development of human civilization. ⓫That is, there have been periods marked by more glaciers and periods marked by fewer glaciers. ⓬The periods of glacier advances are called glacial periods, and the periods of glacial losses are called interglacial periods. ⓭So a glacial period is a period of building ice, whereas an interglacial period is a period of melting ice. ⓮And the Earth has been going back and forth between these two periods since its birth.

地理学の授業での講義の一部を聞きなさい。

1 P: ❶今日は氷河について、とりわけそれらがどのように形成され、解けてなくなるのかについてお話しします。
❷簡単に言うと、氷河はそれ自体の重さによって動く巨大な氷の塊です。
❸皆さんもそれら（氷河）が世界中で解けていて、人々がそれについて大騒ぎをしている、というニュースを聞いたり新聞で読んだりしたことがあるかもしれませんね。
❹氷河の融解は私たちや地球上の他の生き物にどのような影響を与えるのでしょうか。
❺そうですね、実際のところ氷河は、今日知られている気候の調節に役立つ地球のエアコンのようなものなのです。
❻とはいえ、地球から氷がなくなりつつあることの明らかな証拠があります。
❼それがどのような結果を招くのか皆さんもご存じと思いますが、念のため説明します。
❽世界規模の氷河の消失は、海面上昇と気温上昇の大きな要因となるということです。
❾これらの変化は人間に責任があると考えがちですが、現実には…どの程度人間の活動に起因するのかは正確にはわかっていません。なぜなら自然もまたその要因になっているからです。
❿地球では、人類の文明が発達するずっと以前から、氷河はできたり解けたりを繰り返してきました。
⓫つまり、氷河の増加が際立つ時期もあれば、氷河の減少が際立つ時期もあったのです。
⓬氷河が増大する時期は氷河期と呼ばれ、氷河が減少する時期は間氷期と呼ばれます。
⓭氷河期は氷がつくられる時期で、間氷期は氷が解ける時期です。
⓮そして、地球は誕生以来、この2つの時期を交互に繰り返してきたのです。

1
- ☐ glacier：氷河
- ☐ in particular：特に
- ☐ melt away：解けてなくなる
- ☐ gigantic：巨大な
- ☐ make a fuss：大騒ぎする
- ☐ regulate X：Xを調節する
- ☐ be familiar with X：Xをよく知っている
- ☐ in case：～の場合に備えて
- ☐ be to blame：責任がある
- ☐ precisely：正確に
- ☐ to what degree SV：どの程度～するのか
- ☐ civilization：文明
- ☐ mark X：Xを特徴付ける
- ☐ whereas：一方で
- ☐ go back and forth：前後に行ったり来たりする

1 You might have heard (V) ... or read (V) ... (that they're melting ...) (O)

have heardとhave readの目的語はthat節。

the climate (as we know it)「我々が知っているような気候」

名詞＋as we know itで「我々が知っているような名詞」という意味。

2-5

2 P: ❶So the next question arises.
❷What causes the fluctuation of the Earth's climate?
❸Well . . . the climate of the Earth is subject to what we call "positive feedback loops" and "negative feedback loops."
❹Don't worry.
❺I'll go over each process with some examples later.
❻Once the idea clicks, the concept and the mechanism of these loops become much clearer.

3 P: ❶Let's first look at positive feedback loops.
❷Do any of you know what positive feedback loop means?
❸You can guess.

4 S: Well, if something happens in a loop, the same things are repeated over and over, so I guess in a positive feedback loop, at least in the context of the environment, something good for the environment happens again and again?

5 P: ❶Good guess.
❷You're right about certain things repeating themselves.
❸Let me give you a precise definition.
❹So . . . in the context of glaciers, a positive feedback loop is a series of repeating events that help the formation of glaciers.
❺For instance, suppose that the air temperature drops.
❻Then the amount of ice and snow covering the Earth grows.
❼Ice and snow reflect sunlight.
❽You know, so the sunlight hitting the surface of the Earth is bounced back to space, leading to a colder climate.
❾A colder climate means more ice and more snow.
❿See, this whole process repeats itself.

2

P: ❶すると、次の疑問が湧いてきます。
❷地球の気候変動は、何によって引き起こされるのかということです。
❸そうですね…地球の気候は positive feedback loop と negative feedback loop と呼ばれるものに左右されます。
❹心配しないでください。
❺後ほどそれぞれのプロセスを具体例を挙げて説明します。
❻その考え方がわかれば、これらの循環の概念や仕組みが明確になります。

3

P: ❶まず始めに、positive feedback loop を見てみましょう。
❷誰か positive feedback loop の意味がわかる人はいますか。
❸推測でも構いません。

4

S: えっと、もし循環の中で何かが起こったら同じことが何度も繰り返されるので、positive feedback loop では、少なくとも環境という面においては、環境にとって望ましいことが何度も繰り返し生じる、ということでしょうか？

5

P: ❶いい推測ですね。
❷あることが繰り返されるという点は正しいです。
❸もっと正確に定義してみましょう。
❹つまり…氷河において positive feedback loop とは、氷河の形成を促進する一連の事象が繰り返されることです。
❺例えば、気温が下がるとしましょう。
❻すると地球を覆う氷と雪の量が増えます。
❼氷と雪は太陽光を反射します。
❽ということは、地球の表面に当たる太陽光は宇宙に跳ね返り、より寒冷な気候になるというわけです。
❾寒冷な気候は氷と雪が増えることを意味します。
❿そう、このように全体のプロセスが繰り返されるのです。

2

- ☐ fluctuation：変動
- ☐ be subject to X：Xの影響を受ける
- ☐ go over X：Xについて説明する

5

- ☐ definition：定義
- ☐ bounce back：跳ね返す、反射する

5 You're right about (certain things [S′] repeating [V′] themselves [O′])

aboutの目的語はcertain things repeating themselves全体。 certain thingsはrepeatingという動名詞に対する意味上の主語。

6-8

6 P: ❶The example I just gave has to do with "the albedo effect."
❷Albedo is a measure of how much light is reflected by a surface, and the albedo effect refers to how things like ice, snow, water, land, etc. reflect solar radiation.
❸High albedo means lots of reflection, and low albedo . . . little reflection.
❹The Earth's surface has many different colors, and each color has an effect on the Earth's temperature.
❺Ice and snow are white, or light colored, so they have a high albedo.
❻They send a lot of the Sun's energy back into space and prevent the surface from heating up.
❼Clouds prevent the sunlight from reaching the Earth's surface, so they cool the Earth too.
❽Dark-colored surfaces like the oceans, on the other hand, have a low albedo.
❾They absorb the Sun's heat, warming the Earth.

7 P: ❶Let's now look at negative feedback loops.
❷Now that you know what a positive feedback loop is, you should be able to guess what this is.
❸In the context of glaciers, a negative feedback loop is a cycle where a series of events leads to the melting of glaciers.
❹One example of a negative feedback is volcanic eruptions.
❺When a volcano erupts near a glacier, the resulting molten lava melts the surrounding ice.
❻This means less solar energy is reflected and hence more heat is absorbed.
❼The Earth gets warmer and more ice melts, leading to even more land being exposed to the Sun and even more melting of glaciers.
❽This is a negative feedback cycle.
❾Ice keeps melting.

8 P: ❶Another interesting player of negative feedback is algae.
❷There are several kinds of algae that grow on melting surfaces of glaciers.

6

P: ❶今挙げた例は「アルベド効果」と関係があります。
❷アルベドは光がどのくらい地表で反射されるかを表す尺度であり、アルベド効果とは氷や雪や水や陸地などが太陽放射を反射することを指します。
❸高いアルベドは反射が大きいことを意味し、低いアルベドは…反射が小さい。
❹地球の表面には様々に異なる色があり、それぞれの色は地球の気温に影響を与えます。
❺氷と雪は白または薄い色なので、アルベドは高くなります。
❻それらは太陽エネルギーの多くを宇宙に送り返し、地表が熱くなるのを防ぎます。
❼雲は太陽光が地球表面に届くのを遮るため、それもまた地球を冷やすことになります。
❽一方、海などの濃い色の表面では、アルベドは低くなります。
❾それらは太陽の熱を吸収し、地球を暖めるのです。

7

P: ❶次に negative feedback loop を見てみましょう。
❷皆さんは positive feedback loop が何なのかがもうわかっているので、こちらが何なのかはもう推測できるでしょう。
❸氷河において negative feedback loop とは、氷河の融解にいたる一連の事象のサイクルのことです。
❹ Negative feedback の一例が火山の噴火です。
❺氷河の近くの火山が噴火すると、それに伴う溶岩が周りの氷を溶かします。
❻これは、太陽エネルギーの反射が少なくなり、したがって熱の吸収がより多くなることを意味します。
❼地球はより温暖になり、より多くの氷が解けることで、さらに多くの地面が太陽にさらされ、さらなる氷河の融解につながります。
❽これが negative feedback のサイクルです。
❾氷が解け続けるのです。

8

P: ❶ Negative feedback をもたらすもう 1 つの興味深い要因は藻類です。
❷融解する氷河の表面に繁殖する藻類には何種類かあります。

6
- □ X have to do with Y：XはYと関係がある
- □ radiation：放射

7
- □ now that：今や〜なので
- □ volcanic：火山の
- □ eruption：噴火
- □ molten lava：溶岩
- □ the surrounding ice：周りにある氷
- □ even more land：さらに多くの土地
- □ be exposed to X：Xにさらされる

8
- □ algae：藻類

9-11

9 S: So they have low albedo.

10 P: ❶Right.
❷These algae reflect less solar radiation and hence absorb more heat.
❸As the glaciers with these algae absorb more sunlight, the pace of melting accelerates even further and more algae grow on the melting glaciers.
❹Sometimes, scientists refer to this phenomenon as blood snow, for the cells of the algae are reddish and hence the affected ice becomes red.
❺As we have seen, many components are involved in these loops.

11 P: ❶And, you also need to know this: the positive feedback loop and the negative feedback loop are competing with each other.
❷They are not in equilibrium.
❸There's a period during which the positive loop wins and the Earth gets colder and colder and there's lots of ice.
❹There's also a period during which the negative loop wins and the Earth gets warmer and warmer.
❺There's relatively less ice during this period . . .
❻Which loop wins is determined by many different factors as we've just discussed.

9 S: つまり、アルベドが低いということですね。

10 P: ❶その通り。
❷これらの藻類は太陽放射の反射を減らし、したがって熱の吸収を増加させます。
❸このような藻類が付着した氷河が吸収する太陽光が増えるとともに融解がさらに加速し、より多くの藻類が繁殖することになります。
❹科学者たちは時折この現象を、藻類の細胞が赤みがかっていて、その影響で氷が赤く見えることから赤雪と呼びます。
❺これまで見てきたように、こうした循環には多くの構成要素があるのです。

11 P: ❶そして、これも知っておく必要がありますが、positive feedback loop と negative feedback loop は相互に競い合っています。
❷この 2 つは均衡していないのです。
❸ Positive loop が勝って、地球の寒冷化が進み、大量の氷が存在する時期があります。
❹また negative loop が勝り、地球の温暖化が進む時期もあります。
❺この時期は比較的氷が少ないのです…。
❻どちらの循環が勝るのかは、今話し合ったように多くの要因によって決まります。

10
- [ ] hence：ゆえに
- [ ] refer to X as Y：X を Y と呼ぶ

11
- [ ] in equilibrium：均衡して

10 the pace ... accelerates even further

further は far の比較級。「さらに加速する」という意味。

for the cells (S) ... are (V) reddish

for は「等位接続詞」で「理由」を表す。

⓬

⓬ P: ❶So far, we've focused on positive and negative feedback loops occurring naturally.
❷But—unsurprisingly—human activities also act to trigger these loops.
❸Although we don't know exactly to what extent human activities are affecting the balance of the two loops, what is apparent is that humans are contributing more to the negative loop than to the positive loop.
❹One activity is deforestation, which leads to an increase in greenhouse gases such as CO_2 because fewer trees means that less greenhouse gases are absorbed.
❺Another one, and probably the most notable one . . . is the burning of fossil fuels.
❻As we burn fossil fuels to, say, generate electricity, we produce greenhouse gases.
❼These gases trap the Sun's heat in the atmosphere, which raises the air temperature and melts large portions of glaciers.
❽This then lowers the Earth's albedo, as discussed earlier, and triggers even more melting of glaciers.

⓬ P: ❶ここまでは自然に起こるpositiveとnegativeのfeedback loopに焦点を当ててきました。
❷しかし、驚くには当たりませんが、人間活動もこれらの循環の引き金となります。
❸人間活動がこの2つの循環のバランスにどの程度影響しているかは正確にはわかりませんが、はっきりしていることは、人間はpositive loopよりもnegative loopにより多くの影響を与えているということです。
❹その活動の一つは森林破壊で、樹木の減少により温室効果ガスの吸収が減るため、CO_2などの温室効果ガスの増加につながります。
❺もう一つ、おそらく最も顕著な人間活動は…化石燃料の使用です。
❻私たちが、例えば発電のために化石燃料を燃やすと、温室効果ガスが排出されます。
❼これらのガスは大気圏に太陽の熱を閉じ込め、気温を上昇させ、氷河の大部分を解かします。
❽そうしてこれが、先程話したように、地球のアルベドを低下させ、さらなる氷河融解の引き金となるのです。

⓬
- ☐ notable：顕著な
- ☐ burn X：Xを燃やす
- ☐ portion：部分

リスニング問題8 会話

目標解答時間 5分

CAMPUS CONVERSATION

問題演習の流れ

- □ 音声が流れている間は、問題は読めません。会話が終わり、最初の問題音声が流れ始めたらページをめくって、5分以内に解答しましょう。
- □ 1問の解答時間は20秒を目安にしています。問題を読み上げた後に解答時間として20秒のポーズ（音声なし）が入っていますので、その間に解答をマークしてください。
- □ メモは自由に取ってください。
- □ 3回解けるように、3回分のマークシートを問題ページに用意しています。解く日付を記入してからマークしてください。

Web解答方法

- □ 本試験では各選択肢の左に表示されるマークをクリックして解答します。本試験と同様の方法で取り組みたい場合は、Webで解答できます。
- □ インターネットのつながるパソコン・スマートフォンで、以下のサイトにアクセスしてWeb上で解答してください。

extester.com

- □ 操作方法は、p.13 ～ 14の「USA Club Web学習の使い方」をご参照ください。

学習の記録

学習開始日	年　　月　　日	学習終了日	年　　月　　日
学習開始日	年　　月　　日	学習終了日	年　　月　　日
学習開始日	年　　月　　日	学習終了日	年　　月　　日

リスニング問題 8 会話 音声

L08

聞き取りメモ

L08_Q1

1. Why does the student go to see the counselor?
   (A) To inquire about financial opportunities
   (B) To seek advice on choosing courses
   (C) To talk about a way to improve his grade in a math class
   (D) To confirm that he can earn money

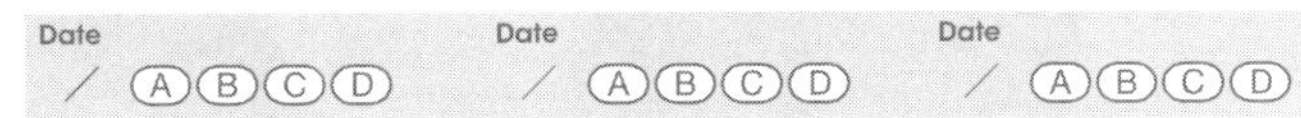

L08_Q2

2. Why did the student struggle in the mathematics course in his first semester?
   (A) Because he was not good at mathematics when he was in high school
   (B) Because he did not devote himself to preparing for the exam
   (C) Because the exams were more difficult than other subjects' exams
   (D) Because he took a class that was not designed for freshmen

L08_Q3

3. In what ways are need-based scholarships different from GPA-based ones? *Choose two answers.*
   (A) Academic performance is not a requirement.
   (B) Students can apply twice a year if they need additional support.
   (C) Students can receive a greater amount of money for their tuition.
   (D) Applicants need to provide information about earnings.

L08_Q4

4. What does the counselor offer to do for the student?

(A) Help him collect necessary documents
(B) Contact the person responsible for the issue
(C) Talk to the student's professor about his grades
(D) Review the student's scholarship application form

L08_Q5

5. Listen again to part of the conversation and then answer the question. What does the counselor mean when she says this?

(A) To confirm that the student finished paying the fee
(B) To admit that the math class is hard
(C) To show that she was surprised at the expensive tuition
(D) To acknowledge that the experience was meaningful

 1. **(A)**　2. **(B)**　3. **(A) (D)**　4. **(B)**　5. **(D)**

1～7 | 問 1～2 解説レクチャー　L08_Script01-07　C: Counselor　S: Student

1
C: ❶Hello, James. ❷How are you doing?
S: ❶I'm doing great. ❷You?

2
C: ❶Things are a bit hectic these days, but I'm getting by. ❷So, what brought you here?
S: ❶Well, I was looking for some ways to financially support myself, and I saw in the university bulletin that the school offers some scholarships. ❷I was wondering, you know, if there is anything I could apply to . . .

3
C: ❶Ah, I see. ❷That's a concern for almost all students. ❸Well, the university does indeed provide several scholarships with different requirements. ❹Let me see what we've got at the moment. ❺Mmm . . . one second . . . ❻We're accepting applications right now for scholarships offered on academic performance. ❼If I'm not mistaken, this is your third semester, right?
S: Yes, that's right.

4
C: ❶Okay, to be eligible for these scholarships, your grade point average or GPA must be above a certain threshold. ❷What is your GPA to date?
S: Well, off the top of my head, I would say it's 3.9ish out of 4.0.

5
C: ❶Wow, I must say I'm impressed. ❷That's quite an achievement.
S: ❶Thank you. ❷I've been trying to boost my GPA over the last two semesters. ❸The only class I really struggled in was college mathematics, which I took in the first semester. ❹I was always good at math, so I didn't spend enough time studying for the exams. ❺I really regret it.

6
C: ❶That's pretty common among freshmen actually. ❷They tend to perform rather poorly, sorry, I mean . . . not as well as they think they can, in the subjects they're actually good at.
S: ❶So I'm not the only one, it seems. ❷I'm ashamed to say this but I kinda assumed college courses were just an extension of high school studies. ❸Obviously, I was wrong. ❹I learned it the hard way.

7
C: You surely paid the price for it!
S: Yeah, I think I've come quite a long way since then.

聞き取りポイント

2S:学生が相談に来た理由は、奨学金のことについて聞くためだとわかります。

3C~**4C**:現在、利用可能な奨学金は成績要件があるものだそうです。GPAの最低ラインが定められていると述べています。

4S~**5C**:学生のGPAは3.9という大変素晴らしい成績のようです。

5S~**6C**:数学が得意という理由で試験勉強に十分な時間を割かなかったため、数学の授業で苦労したと学生が述べています。これは新入生によくあることだとカウンセラーも認めています。

6S:この学生は、大学は高校の延長線だと思っていたと明かしています。だから数学を真面目に勉強しなかったのですね。

7C:paid the price for itは「そのために対価を払った」という意味です。この文脈では「失敗し、そのかいもあって、大学は高校とは違うということを学んだ」という意味でしょう。

7S:I've come quite a long way since then は「そのとき以来、長距離を移動してきた」が直訳ですが、「失敗から学んで以来、非常に成長した」という意味です。

聞き取りメモ例

hectic

scholarships

look for financial help

• academic

3rd semester

3.9

bulletin

math

not study enough

← high school good

learned from 失敗

L08_Q1

1. Why does the student go to see the counselor?

(A) To inquire about financial opportunities
(B) To seek advice on choosing courses
(C) To talk about a way to improve his grade in a math class
(D) To confirm that he can earn money

学生はなぜカウンセラーのところへ行っていますか。

(A) 財政支援を受ける機会について尋ねるため
(B) 授業を選ぶ際にアドバイスを求めるため
(C) 数学の授業で成績を上げる方法について相談するため
(D) 自分がお金を稼げることを確認するため

2Sで、この学生が奨学金のことを尋ねに来たとわかります。よって(A)が正解です。2S❶のscholarshipsをfinancial opportunitiesと言い換えていますね。(B)と(C)ですが、この会話は授業のことではないため誤りです。また、この会話ではお金を「稼ぐこと」ではなく「奨学金」について尋ねているため、(D)は誤りです。

L08_Q2

2. Why did the student struggle in the mathematics course in his first semester?

(A) Because he was not good at mathematics when he was in high school
(B) Because he did not devote himself to preparing for the exam
(C) Because the exams were more difficult than other subjects' exams
(D) Because he took a class that was not designed for freshmen

学生はなぜ1学期目に数学の授業で苦労しましたか。

(A) 彼は高校のとき数学が苦手だったから
(B) 試験勉強に専念しなかったから
(C) その試験が他の科目の試験よりも難しかったため
(D) 1年生向けでない授業を履修したため

5S ❸で「大学で苦労した唯一のクラスが数学だった」と述べています。また、続く 5S ❹で「試験に向けて十分な時間を割かなかった」ともあります。よって、(B)が正解です。5S ❹の spend enough time を devote himself to と、studying for を preparing for とそれぞれ言い換えていますね。(A)は 5S ❹に「いつも数学は得意だった」とあるので、誤りです。(C)が紛らわしいです。確かに「難しかった」のですが、「他の科目よりも難しかった」ことを示唆する発言はありません。(D)の「1年生向けでない授業」というのは内容からはうかがえません。

□ devote oneself to Ving：～することに専念する

8～15｜問 3～4 解説レクチャー

L08_Script08-15

8 C: ❶You definitely have. ❷In fact, according to your transcript, it looks like you got the highest grade possible in all your other classes. ❸Magnificent! ❹So, since you have such an excellent GPA, you should definitely apply for some GPA-based scholarships. ❺To increase your chances of getting the scholarship, I suggest you include a statement in your application form showing your commitment to maintaining high academic performance. ❻In addition, maybe you should elaborate on how you could contribute to the university. ❼Many students make the mistake of emphasizing only their academic achievement. ❽But, you know, that part is obvious from their transcript.

S: ❶Thank you for sharing useful tips. ❷Do you also have information about how much I'd be able to receive from these scholarships?

9 C: ❶Let me see . . . ❷Give me a moment . . . ❸The numbers range from $1,000 to $10,000. ❹The exact amount will be only available on your offer letter. ❺On average though, it should be sufficient to cover ten credits, which are about half the credits most of the students take in a semester. ❻Please bear in mind though that you can only apply once a year. ❼And also note that you can't receive two scholarships at the same time.

S: ❶Got it. ❷Any other scholarships available?

10 C: The university also offers some need-based scholarships.

S: Need-based meaning . . . ?

11 C: ❶Need-based scholarships are financial aid provided based on the financial situations of students. ❷For this kind of financial support, what matters is your financial situation, and you would need to supply us with official documents to prove it. ❸There are some conditions regarding the household income. ❹They don't see your academic performance, though . . . ❺The need-based scholarships are only meant to support students experiencing financial hardships.
S: ❶I see. ❷Do you know how much those scholarships will cover?

12 C: ❶Well, I don't . . . seem . . . ❷Hmm. ❸Apparently, they operate on a slightly different schedule. ❹I'll let you know when the details become available.
S: ❶That would be great. ❷Thanks!

13 C: ❶However, since your GPA is very high, I think you should consider applying for one of those GPA-based scholarships. ❷Besides, unlike the need-based ones, you only need to submit an application form and your official transcript.
S: ❶Yeah, I guess you're right. ❷Where can I get the application form?

14 C: ❶It's available at the scholarship office, which is in the building across from this one. ❷They should be able to give you more details . . . ❸Actually, you should talk to Kelly there. ❹She's in charge of the applications. ❺Shall I give her a call and let her know you're coming now?
S: ❶Yes, please. ❷I'll be on my way. ❸Thanks for your help.

15 C: Any time.

解説レクチャー

8C：この学生は、数学以外の科目では最高の成績を取ったことがわかります。よって、奨学金に申し込むことができますね。さらに奨学金をもらう可能性を高めるために、学業に励むことを誓約するための書類（a statement）を同封することが勧められています。さらに、大学にどのように貢献できるかを考えるようにも言われています。

8S：奨学金の額に話題が移ります。

9C：具体的な金額は奨学金をもらう人しかわからないとのことです。平均すると、1学期の単位の半分を賄う額になることが多いようです。また、1年に1回しか申し込めず、同時に2つの奨学金を受けることもできないと説明しています。

11C：GPAによって決まる奨学金だけでなく、財政状況に応じて支給される奨学金もあるようです。世帯収入を証明する書類が必要ですね。この奨学金は成績を考慮しないと言っています。

11S ~ **12C** : 財政状況に応じて支給される奨学金の額に話題が移りますが、カウンセラーの人は知らないようです。they operate on a slightly different scheduleは「成績に応じて支給される奨学金と財政状況に応じて支給される奨学金が、異なるスケジュールで動いているため、まだ後者の具体的な情報が開示されていない」ということを示唆しています。
13C : 成績がいいのでGPAベースの奨学金を勧めています。さらに、財政状況に応じて支給される奨学金とは異なり、必要書類は申込書類と成績証明書だけだとの説明があります。
14C : 申込書は奨学課（the sholarship office）で入手可能だと述べています。
14C ~ **15C** : カウンセラーの人が奨学課の女性に電話して、この学生が向かうことを知らせてくれるようです。それに対して、学生が感謝を伝えています。

聞き取りメモ例

• academic transcript statement commitment contribute to Univ $1,000–10,000 10 credits only one	• need based financial situation doc prove income $? [A]—application /transcript get from office Kelly

L08_Q3

3. In what ways are need-based scholarships different from GPA-based ones?
Choose two answers.

(A) Academic performance is not a requirement.
(B) Students can apply twice a year if they need additional support.
(C) Students can receive a greater amount of money for their tuition.
(D) Applicants need to provide information about earnings.

必要に応じた奨学金は、GPAに応じた奨学金とどのように異なりますか。2つ選んでください。

(A) 学業成績は要件でない。
(B) 学生は、さらなる支援が必要であれば、年に2回申し込める。
(C) こちらの方が学生は授業料のためにより多くのお金を受け取ることができる。
(D) 応募者は収入に関する情報を提供しなければならない。

11C❹に「学業成績を考慮しない」とあります。よって(A)は正解です。さらに、11C❷に「財政状況を証明する公的な書類を提出する必要がある」とあります。よって(D)も正解です。11C❷のdocuments to prove itをinformation about earningsと言い換えています。(B)と(C)は会話の中で言及がありません。

□tuition:授業料 □applicant:申込者 □earnings:収入

L08_Q4

4. What does the counselor offer to do for the student?

(A) Help him collect necessary documents
(B) Contact the person responsible for the issue
(C) Talk to the student's professor about his grades
(D) Review the student's scholarship application form

カウンセラーは、学生のために何をすることを申し出ていますか。

(A) 必要書類を集める手助けをすること
(B) その件の責任者に連絡を取ること
(C) 彼の成績に関して彼の教授に話すこと
(D) 彼の奨学金申込書類をチェックすること

14C❺で、奨学金の申し込みを担当している人に電話することを申し出ています。よって、(B)が正解です。14C❹のgive ... a callをcontactと、in charge ofをresponsible forとそれぞれ言い換えていますね。(A)と(C)、(D)については会話の中で言及されていません。

問5 解説レクチャー

L08_Q5

5. Listen again to part of the conversation and then answer the question.

Student:
So I'm not the only one, it seems. I'm ashamed to say this but I kinda

assumed college courses were just an extension of high school studies. Obviously, I was wrong. I learned it the hard way.

Counselor:
You surely paid the price for it!

What does the counselor mean when she says this?

Counselor:
You surely paid the price for it!

(A) To confirm that the student finished paying the fee
(B) To admit that the math class is hard
(C) To show that she was surprised at the expensive tuition
(D) To acknowledge that the experience was meaningful

会話の一部分をもう一度聞いて、設問に答えてください。

学生：
では、私だけではないようですね。こんなことを言うのは恥ずかしいのですが、大学の授業はただの高校の延長だと思っていました。明らかに、それは間違っていました。私は苦い経験をしてそのことを学びました。

カウンセラー：
だけど、失敗のかいがありましたね。

「だけど、失敗のかいがありましたね」と言うとき、カウンセラーは何を意図していますか。

(A) 学生が授業料を払い終えたことを確認するため
(B) 数学の授業が難しいということを認めるため
(C) 高い授業料に驚いたことを示すため
(D) その経験が意味のあることだったと認めるため

pay the price for Aで「Aのつけを払う」という意味ですが、これがわからなくても文脈から意味を推測することができます。学生は「大学の授業はただの高校の延長だと思っていたが間違っていた」と述べ、「失敗してそれを学んだ」と続けています。つまり、カウンセラーの発言は「学生が失敗から学んだということ」を言い改めているものなので、(D)が正解ですね。(A)と(C)は発言とは無関係です。**7C**のpriceという語から、(A)や(C)を選ばないように気を付けましょう。

1–5 C: Counselor S: Student

Listen to a conversation between a counselor and a student.

1 C: ❶Hello, James.
❷How are you doing?
S: ❶I'm doing great.
❷You?

2 C: ❶Things are a bit hectic these days, but I'm getting by.
❷So, what brought you here?
S: ❶Well, I was looking for some ways to financially support myself, and I saw in the university bulletin that the school offers some scholarships.
❷I was wondering, you know, if there is anything I could apply to . . .

3 C: ❶Ah, I see.
❷That's a concern for almost all students.
❸Well, the university does indeed provide several scholarships with different requirements.
❹Let me see what we've got at the moment.
❺Mmm . . . one second . . .
❻We're accepting applications right now for scholarships offered on academic performance.
❼If I'm not mistaken, this is your third semester, right?
S: Yes, that's right.

4 C: ❶Okay, to be eligible for these scholarships, your grade point average or GPA must be above a certain threshold. ❷What is your GPA to date?
S: Well, off the top of my head, I would say it's 3.9ish out of 4.0.

5 C: ❶Wow, I must say I'm impressed.
❷That's quite an achievement.
S: ❶Thank you.
❷I've been trying to boost my GPA over the last two semesters.
❸The only class I really struggled in was college mathematics, which I took in the first semester.
❹I was always good at math, so I didn't spend enough time studying for the exams.
❺I really regret it.

カウンセラーと学生との会話を聞きなさい。

1
C: ❶こんにちは、James さん。
❷調子はどうですか。
S: ❶とてもいいですよ。
❷調子はいかがですか。

2
C: ❶最近少し忙しいですが、何とかやっています。
❷それで、今日はどうしたんですか。
S: ❶ええと、経済的に自活する方法を探していたら、大学の掲示板で大学が奨学金を提供していることを知ったんです。
❷何か、その、申し込めるものがあるかなと思ったのですが。

3
C: ❶ああ、なるほど。
❷それはほぼ全ての学生にとっての悩みですね。
❸ええと、大学は確かにいくつかの奨学金を様々な要件のもとに提供しています。
❹今何があるかちょっと見てみますね。
❺うーん、少し待ってくださいね。
❻現在学業成績に応じて提供されている奨学金の申し込みを受け付けていますね。
❼確か、今は 3 学期目ですよね。
S: ええ、そうです。

4
C: ❶わかりました。これらの奨学金を受ける資格を得るためには、あなたの評定の平均、GPA がある一定の基準より上である必要があります。
❷今までの GPA は何ですか。
S: ええと、今すぐに思せる限りでは、4 の内 3.9 くらいだと思います。

5
C: ❶あら、とてもいいですね。
❷素晴らしい成績です。
S: ❶ありがとうございます。
❷この 2 学期間 GPA を上げようとしてきたんです。
❸本当に苦労した授業は、1 学期目に履修した大学数学だけでした。
❹今までずっと数学が得意だったので、試験勉強に十分な時間を割かなかったんです。
❺それをとても後悔しています。

2
- □ hectic：忙しい
- □ get by：なんとかやり過ごす、切り抜ける
- □ bulletin：掲示板
- □ scholarship：奨学金

3
- □ requirement：要件
- □ have got：持っている（≒ have）
- □ at the moment：今は
- □ one second：ちょっと待ってください
- □ application：申し込み
- □ be mistaken：間違っている
- □ semester：学期

4
- □ be eligible for X：X を得る資格がある
- □ grade point average：評定平均
- □ threshold：基準、入口
- □ to date：今までの
- □ off the top of my head：すぐに思い出す限りでは
- □ -ish：〜くらい

5
- □ boost X：X を押し上げる
- □ [over/for] the [last/past] X：ここ X 間
- □ struggle：苦労する

6-8

6 C: ❶That's pretty common among freshmen actually.
❷They tend to perform rather poorly, sorry, I mean . . . not as well as they think they can, in the subjects they're actually good at.
S: ❶So I'm not the only one, it seems.
❷I'm ashamed to say this but I kinda assumed college courses were just an extension of high school studies.
❸Obviously, I was wrong.
❹I learned it the hard way.

7 C: You surely paid the price for it!
S: Yeah, I think I've come quite a long way since then.

8 C: ❶You definitely have.
❷In fact, according to your transcript, it looks like you got the highest grade possible in all your other classes.
❸Magnificent!
❹So, since you have such an excellent GPA, you should definitely apply for some GPA-based scholarships.
❺To increase your chances of getting the scholarship, I suggest you include a statement in your application form showing your commitment to maintaining high academic performance.
❻In addition, maybe you should elaborate on how you could contribute to the university.
❼Many students make the mistake of emphasizing only their academic achievement.
❽But, you know, that part is obvious from their transcript.
S: ❶Thank you for sharing useful tips.
❷Do you also have information about how much I'd be able to receive from these scholarships?

6
C: ❶それは1年生には実際、とてもよくあることですよ。
❷彼らの成績はあまりよくないという傾向があるのです、ごめんなさい、私が言いたいのは、彼らは実際に得意な科目で、思ったほどいい成績を取れないのです。
S: ❶では、私だけではないようですね。
❷こんなことを言うのは恥ずかしいのですが、大学の授業はただの高校の延長だと思っていました。
❸明らかに、それは間違っていました。
❹私は苦い経験をしてそのことを学びました。

7
C: だけど、失敗したかいがありましたね。
S: ええ、あれ以来、非常に成長したと思います。

8
C: ❶そのとおりですね。
❷実際、あなたの成績証明書によると、他の全ての授業では最高の成績を収めているように見受けられます。
❸素晴らしい！
❹そのような素晴らしいGPAを持っているので、GPAに応じたいくつかの奨学金に絶対に申し込んだほうがいいですよ。
❺奨学金を受けられる可能性を高めるために、高い学業成績を維持することを誓約する書類を申込書類に追加することをお勧めします。
❻そして、あなたがどんなことで大学に貢献できるかについて詳しく述べたほうがいいでしょう。
❼多くの学生が、彼らの学業成績のみを強調する間違いを犯します。
❽しかし、それは成績証明書を見れば明らかですよね。
S: ❶役に立つご助言を教えていただきありがとうございます。
❷これらの奨学金からどのくらい受け取れるかもおわかりですか。

6
- ☐ kinda→kind of：少し（副詞として用いる）
- ☐ extension：延長
- ☐ the hard way：苦労して

7
- ☐ pay the price：対価を払う

8
- ☐ transcript：成績証明書
- ☐ the highest grade possible：可能な限り最高の
- ☐ magnificent：素晴らしい
- ☐ commitment：専心
- ☐ elaborate on X：Xを詳述する
- ☐ emphasize X：Xを強調する
- ☐ tip：助言

9-12

9 C: ❶Let me see . . .
❷Give me a moment . . .
❸The numbers range from $1,000 to $10,000.
❹The exact amount will be only available on your offer letter.
❺On average though, it should be sufficient to cover ten credits, which are about half the credits most of the students take in a semester.
❻Please bear in mind though that you can only apply once a year.
❼And also note that you can't receive two scholarships at the same time.
S: ❶Got it.
❷Any other scholarships available?

10 C: The university also offers some need-based scholarships.
S: Need-based meaning . . . ?

11 C: ❶Need-based scholarships are financial aid provided based on the financial situations of students.
❷For this kind of financial support, what matters is your financial situation, and you would need to supply us with official documents to prove it.
❸There are some conditions regarding the household income.
❹They don't see your academic performance, though . . .
❺The need-based scholarships are only meant to support students experiencing financial hardships.
S: ❶I see.
❷Do you know how much those scholarships will cover?

12 C: ❶Well, I don't . . . seem . . .
❷Hmm.
❸Apparently, they operate on a slightly different schedule.
❹I'll let you know when the details become available.
S: ❶That would be great.
❷Thanks!

9 C: ❶そうですね。
❷ちょっと待ってくださいね。
❸額は 1000 ドルから 10000 ドルまで幅があります。
❹正確な額は、採用通知でしかわかりません。
❺しかし平均では、10 単位分、つまりほとんどの学生が 1 学期間に取得する単位の半分ぐらいを賄うには十分のはずです。
❻1 年に 1 回しか申し込めないということを覚えておいてください。
❼また、同時に 2 つの奨学金を受けられないということにも注意してくださいね。
S: ❶わかりました。
❷他に応募可能な奨学金は。

10 C: 大学は必要に応じた奨学金も提供していますね。
S: 必要に応じたというのは…。

11 C: ❶必要に応じた奨学金とは、学生の財政状況に基づいて提供される財政上の支援です。
❷この種の財政支援にとって重要なのはあなたの財政状況で、それを証明する公的書類を提出しなければならないでしょう。
❸世帯収入に関するいくつかの条件があります。
❹しかしこちらはあなたの学業成績は考慮されません…。
❺必要に応じた奨学金は、財政的に困っている学生を支援するためだけのものなのです。
S: ❶わかりました。
❷これらの奨学金はいくら負担してくれるかわかりますか。

12 C: ❶いいえ、わからないようで…。
❷うーん。
❸どうも他とは少し違ったスケジュールで動いているようです。
❹詳細がわかり次第お知らせします。
S: ❶それは助かります。
❷ありがとうございます。

9
- □ give me a moment：少々お待ちください
- □ range：ある範囲にわたる【動詞】
- □ from X to Y：XからYまで
- □ offer letter：採用通知書
- □ on average：平均して
- □ sufficient to V：～するのに十分な
- □ credit：履修単位
- □ bear in mind that SV：～ということを心に留めておく、覚えておく
- □ note that SV：～ということに注意する

11
- □ supply X with Y：XにYを与える
- □ regarding X：Xに関して【前置詞】
- □ household：世帯の
- □ be meant to V：～することを意図している

12
- □ apparently：見たところによると、どうやら

⑬-⑮

⑬ C: ❶However, since your GPA is very high, I think you should consider applying for one of those GPA-based scholarships.
❷Besides, unlike the need-based ones, you only need to submit an application form and your official transcript.
S: ❶Yeah, I guess you're right.
❷Where can I get the application form?

⑭ C: ❶It's available at the scholarship office, which is in the building across from this one.
❷They should be able to give you more details . . .
❸Actually, you should talk to Kelly there.
❹She's in charge of the applications.
❺Shall I give her a call and let her know you're coming now?
S: ❶Yes, please.
❷I'll be on my way.
❸Thanks for your help.

⑮ C: Any time.

13 C: ❶しかし、あなたのGPAはとても高いので、GPAに応じた奨学金の1つに申し込むことを考えたほうがいいと思います。
❷それに、必要に応じた奨学金とは違って、申込書類と公式の成績証明書を提出するだけでいいんですよ。
S: ❶ええ、確かにそうですね。
❷どこでその申込書類が手に入りますか。

14 C: ❶この建物の向かい側の建物にある奨学課で入手できます。
❷そこに行けばもっと詳しく教えてもらえるでしょう。
❸そうだ、そこにいるKellyさんに話すといいでしょう。
❹彼女は申し込みの担当です。
❺彼女に今からあなたが行くと電話しましょうか。
S: ❶ええ、お願いします。
❷今からそこに向かいます。
❸助かりました。ありがとうございました。

15 C: またいつでもどうぞ。

14
- ☐ across from X：Xの向かい側に
- ☐ be in charge of X：Xの担当だ
- ☐ be on one's way：～に行く途中だ

15
- ☐ any time：いつでも

リスニング問題9 講義

PHYSICS

問題演習の流れ

- □ 音声が流れている間は、問題は読めません。講義が終わり、最初の問題音声が流れ始めたらページをめくって、5分以内に解答しましょう。
- □ 1問の解答時間は20秒を目安にしています。問題を読み上げた後に解答時間として20秒のポーズ（音声なし）が入っていますので、その間に解答をマークしてください。
- □ メモは自由に取ってください。
- □ 3回解けるように、3回分のマークシートを問題ページに用意しています。解く日付を記入してからマークしてください。

Web解答方法

- □ 本試験では各選択肢の左に表示されるマークをクリックして解答します。本試験と同様の方法で取り組みたい場合は、Webで解答できます。
- □ インターネットのつながるパソコン・スマートフォンで、以下のサイトにアクセスしてWeb上で解答してください。

extester.com

- □ 操作方法は、p.13 ～ 14の「USA Club Web学習の使い方」をご参照ください。

学習の記録

学習開始日	年　　月　　日	学習終了日	年　　月　　日
学習開始日	年　　月　　日	学習終了日	年　　月　　日
学習開始日	年　　月　　日	学習終了日	年　　月　　日

リスニング問題 9 講義　音声

 L09

Physics

聞き取りメモ

L09_Q1

1. What is the lecture mainly about?

(A) Two physical phenomena and their applications
(B) New methods of electricity generation
(C) A promising theory about fusion and fission
(D) Particles making up an atom

L09_Q2

2. How does the professor introduce students to the main subject?

(A) By illustrating a technical concept using familiar examples
(B) By sharing relevant historical events
(C) By explaining an underlying theory
(D) By reminding students of its applications

L09_Q3

3. Why did the professor mention uranium and plutonium?

(A) To simplify the explanation about fission
(B) To give an example of large unstable atoms
(C) To name atoms that are more suitable for fusion
(D) To discuss the potential risks involved

L09_Q4

4. Why do people have high expectations of electricity generation by fusion rather than fission? *Choose two answers.*

(A) Because it produces a smaller amount of harmful waste
(B) Because it is less likely to result in lethal accidents
(C) Because it is capable of producing a greater amount of energy
(D) Because it requires little regular maintenance

L09_Q5

5. How does the professor feel about cold fusion?

(A) He is indifferent to the development of the new technology.
(B) He asserts that cold fusion casts extreme danger to human beings.
(C) He firmly believes that the technology has promising future.
(D) He is skeptical about whether it will be useful.

L09_Q6

6. In the lecture, the professor describes a number of characteristics of fusion and fission. Indicate whether each of the following is a characteristic of fusion or fission.

	Fusion	Fission
(1) It is the reaction taking place inside the Sun.	(A)	(B)
(2) A great deal of energy is needed to start a reaction.	(A)	(B)
(3) High-speed neutrons are used to generate energy.	(A)	(B)
(4) It occurs in an environment with high pressure.	(A)	(B)
(5) It is used in nuclear power generation.	(A)	(B)

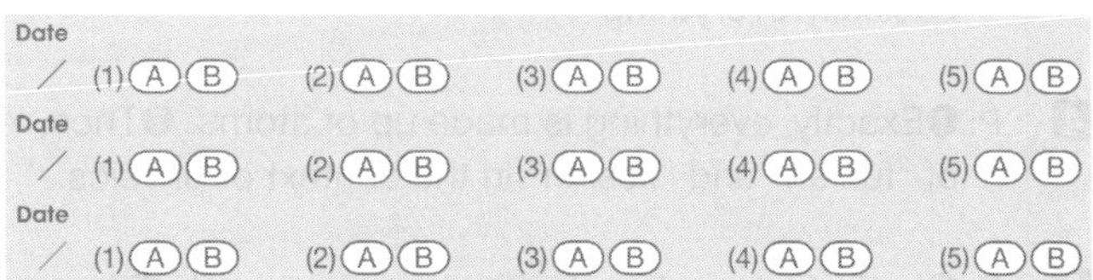

1. **(A)**　2. **(A)**　3. **(B)**　4. **(A) (C)**　5. **(D)**　6. (1) **(A)** (2) **(A)** (3) **(B)** (4) **(A)** (5) **(B)**

1〜6 | 問 1〜2 解説レクチャー

L09_Script01-06　P: Professor　S: Student

1 P: ❶Today, we're talking about something slightly technical: fission and fusion. ❷Fission . . . and fusion . . . ❸Imagine that you're enjoying a party. ❹Let's say you're a boy. ❺And at the party, you meet a certain girl. ❻The moment you see her, you find her really attractive. ❼You talk to her and it appears she's interested in you, too. ❽A few days later, you ask her to go out for a date and, fortunately, she says yes. ❾So now, you two are a couple. ❿So TWO people came closer and became ONE unit. ⓫That's fusion. ⓬Now, here comes the sad part. ⓭As you get to know her better, you discover that you two don't have much in common, and eventually both of you decide to break up. ⓮So, ONE unit or couple separates into TWO individuals. ⓯This is an everyday example of fission. ⓰Fission . . . and fusion . . . ⓱Well, now that we're vaguely acquainted with what fusion and fission are, at least in terms of interpersonal relationships, let's now dive in and see the bigger picture of what they are in the context of physics.

2 P: ❶Just to recap, an atom is a basic unit of matter. ❷You can think of it as a basic building block of objects around us. ❸Every solid, liquid, and gas is made up of atoms such as hydrogen, oxygen, carbon, gold, silver, uranium, mercury, and so on. ❹Does anyone have any questions so far? ❺Everybody fine with the concept of atoms?

3 S: So, atoms are the basic elements of things like water, air, rocks, our clothing, and basically everything.

4 P: ❶Exactly, everything is made up of atoms. ❷Then, let's make clear the concept of "fusion" and "fission" in the context of physics.

5 P: ❶Let's first explore fusion in more detail. ❷As you see it graphically on the first slide, "fusion" is two atoms colliding and combining together to form a single, heavier atom. ❸Two hydrogen atoms bump into each other and form one helium atom . . . this is an example of fusion, and this is what's happening in the center of the Sun. ❹I'll omit the details, but a fusion reaction produces a huge amount of energy. ❺Well, let me be a little more precise. ❻You first have to supply some energy to start a fusion reaction, and once the fusion reaction happens, it produces a far greater amount of energy. ❼So you end up getting a lot of energy from this reaction. ❽Fusion occurs under extremely high temperatures and pressures, like in the center of a star, or like the Sun as I just mentioned. ❾That's why the Sun is very hot.

6 S: Fusion provides the heat and energy.

解説レクチャー

1

❶:今回のテーマが分裂と融合だとわかります。

❸:例え話が始まりますね。

❹~⓫:融合とは「1つになること」だとわかります。

⓬~⓯:一方、分裂とは「バラバラになること」という意味だそうです。

2

❶~❺:原子を定義しています。メインテーマへの橋渡しです。

3

学生が教授の説明を理解していることを示しています。

5

❶:firstにより、まずは融合の説明が行われると考えられます。

❸:水素が衝突してヘリウムになるという例で融合を説明しています。これが太陽の中心部分で生じていることでもあると述べています。

❹:融合は莫大なエネルギーを生み出すようです。融合の定義から、特性へと話題が転換していますね。

❺:詳細な説明が続くことが示唆されています。

❻:supply energy → fusion → more energy というプロセスが説明されています。

❽:融合は、高温と高圧の環境で生じるとのことです。

6

融合が熱とエネルギーを生み出すと述べています。

聞き取りメモ例

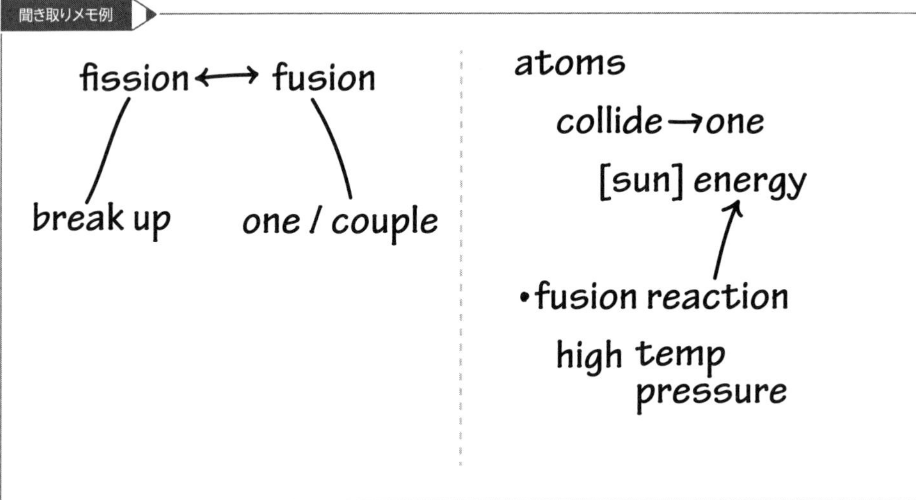

L09_Q1

1. What is the lecture mainly about?

(A) Two physical phenomena and their applications
(B) New methods of electricity generation
(C) A promising theory about fusion and fission
(D) Particles making up an atom

講義の主題は何ですか。

(A) 2つの物理現象とその応用
(B) 新たな発電の方法
(C) 融合と分裂に関する有望な学説
(D) 原子を構成する粒子

1❶で分裂と融合について話すと述べられています。その後、融合がどんな現象かを説明し、7❼では水素爆弾などの兵器に使われると述べています。8から分裂がどういった現象なのかを説明し10で原子力発電への応用について述べています。つまり2つの現象がどういったものなのかを説明し、それらの応用法について述べているので、(A)が正解です。(B)は、教授の11に新たな技術に関する発言がありますが、講義の主旨ではありません。(C)についてはpromising「有望な」が誤りです。講義ではすでに確立している理論を説明しています。(D)も講義の主旨ではありません。

□promising：有望な

L09_Q2

2. How does the professor introduce students to the main subject?

(A) By illustrating a technical concept using familiar examples
(B) By sharing relevant historical events
(C) By explaining an underlying theory
(D) By reminding students of its applications

教授はどのようにして学生たちに主題を導入していますか。

(A) 身近な例を用い、専門的な概念を説明することによって
(B) 関連する歴史上の出来事を共有することによって
(C) 基礎となる理論を説明することによって
(D) 学生たちにその応用の仕方を思い出させることによって

1で教授は、融合と分裂を男女の関係に例えています。惹かれあうのが融合、別れるのが分裂です。よって、専門的な概念を慣れ親しんだ例で示すとした(A)が正解です。例え話は構成や意図、目的を問う問題に関わりやすいので注意してください。(B)については歴史上の出来事に関する発言はありません。また、特定の理論に関する言及はないので(C)は誤りです。(D)ですが、応用に関する説明は講義の後半で登場します。導入には使われていません。

□ underlying：根底にある

7～11 | 問 3～5 解説レクチャー

L09_Script07-11

7 P: ❶Now you see how it works. ❷Great. ❸So, I said you first need to provide some energy to start a fusion reaction. ❹You need a greater amount of energy to trigger a fusion reaction than to trigger a fission reaction. ❺So it is more difficult to initiate a fusion reaction. ❻On the other hand, fusion produces three to four times the energy that fission does. ❼The amount of energy fusion produces is so great that it has been used to create a deadly weapon, the hydrogen bomb. ❽Well, some scientists are also trying to use the power of fusion peacefully by designing a fusion reactor to produce electricity. ❾However, it's difficult to control a fusion reaction, and the prospect of seeing fusion being used commercially, at least in the near future, is pretty slim. ❿Besides, the cost involved in creating the necessary conditions for a fusion reaction is high, and it is slowing the progress of the development.

8 P: ❶Next, let's look into fission, the splitting of one atom into two, in more detail. ❷Compared to the fusion, we need much less energy to trigger a fission reaction. ❸As the picture in the next slide shows . . . here . . . in fission, an atom disintegrates or breaks up. ❹You don't need high temperatures or pressure for this. ❺A fission reaction takes place when a large unstable atom collides with particles called neutrons moving at a high speed.

9 S: What exactly do you mean by an unstable atom?

10 P: ❶Well, things might get a bit technical, so I was hoping to discuss it in the latter half of the lecture, but we might as well talk about it now rather than later since you brought it up. ❷I'll try to simplify this. ❸OK, so unstable atoms are usually large-sized atoms. ❹The size of hydrogen atoms or helium atoms is rather small. ❺On the other hand, there are many large atoms such as uranium or plutonium atoms. ❻Usually, atoms get more unstable as the size increases. ❼Technically, I should talk about the structure of the nucleus and the balance of protons VS neutrons. ❽But, umm, I'll skip that part for now. ❾Okay, that was bit of a side note. ❿So, when an unstable atom is bombarded by high-speed neutrons, the target atom breaks up into two or more smaller atoms and neutrons. ⓫This process also produces a large amount of energy. ⓬By the way, the energy produced by a fission reaction is what heats water inside nuclear reactors and produces electricity in a nuclear power plant.

11 P: ❶So far, we've been able to take advantage of the commercial use of electricity generated by fission, but not by fusion. ❷The low energy requirement for starting a reaction has made the technological development of fission relatively easier. ❸But some scientists are endeavoring to utilize the energy produced by "fusion" as well to generate electricity. ❹Fusion produces three to four times as much energy as fission, and it creates less radioactive waste. ❺In this regard, there may be tremendous merits in fusion-based electricity generation. ❻However, there are some obstacles the researchers must overcome as I mentioned earlier. ❼In the past, a few researchers developed what they called cold fusion, a technology they claimed would allow us to generate electricity at a significantly lower cost. ❽However, it was eventually rejected, and even though research is still underway into this innovative technology, the majority of scientists today take it with a pinch of salt.

解説レクチャー

7

❶~❸:直前の内容を確認しています。

❹~❺:分裂よりも融合の方がエネルギーを要するので、融合を引き起こす方が難しいと述べられています。

❻:同時に、融合の方が分裂よりも多くのエネルギーを生み出すそうです。

❼:融合の生み出すエネルギーの大きさを示す具体例として水素爆弾が挙げられています。

❽~❾:融合を制御するのは難しいので、平和的利用の可能性は低いと教授は考えています。

❿:また、適当な条件下で融合の反応を引き起こすためのコストが高いことも問題として挙げられています。

8

❶:今度は分裂の説明です。

❷~❹:分裂は融合ほどエネルギーが必要ではないと言っています。分裂では原子が分解します。また高温や高圧の環境も不要だそうです。つまり、融合と対比関係にあるわけです。

❺:大きい不安定な原子が衝突したときに分裂が生じるとあります。

9

不安定な原子についての説明が次に来ると予測できます。

⓾

❶〜❻：不安定な原子は比較的大きいそうです。例えばウランやプルトニウムが当てはまります。一般的に、原子が大きくなればなるほど不安定になるとのことです。

❼〜❾：詳しい話は飛ばすと述べています。

❿〜⓫：不安定な原子が衝突すると、より小さな原子や中性子へと分裂するということです。この過程で大きなエネルギーが生じるそうです。

⓬：分裂が原子力発電において用いられていることを理解しておきましょう。

⓫

❶〜❷：融合ではなく分裂によって電力を得ていると述べられています。分裂の方が必要となるエネルギーが少ないからだと説明しています。

❸〜❺：ところが、融合による発電が可能となれば、より多くの電力を生み出すことができ、かつ放射性廃棄物も減るという利点があるとのことです。

❻：ですが、融合による発電には様々な困難が伴うそうです。

❼〜❽：cold fusion「常温核融合」と呼ばれる手法で発電しようとしたが、結局はうまくいかなかったと述べています。大半の科学者が、融合を用いた発電に懐疑的なようです。

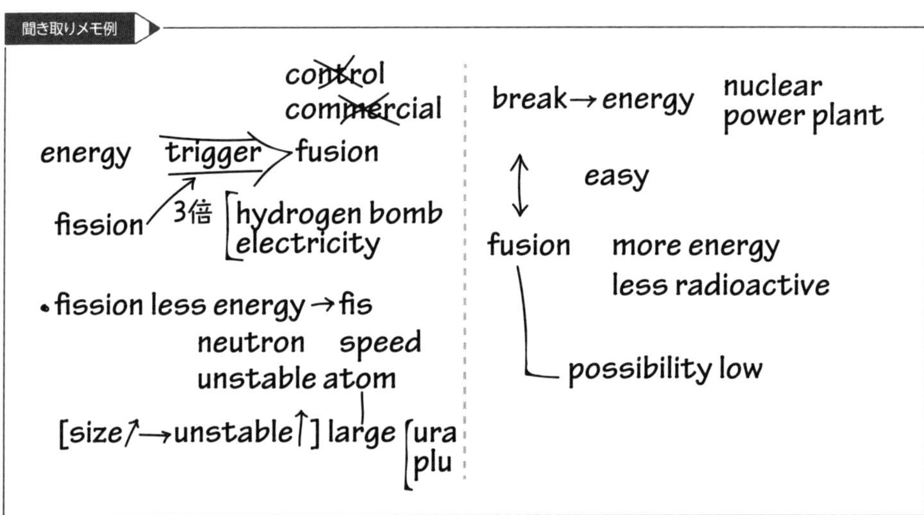

L09_Q3

3. Why did the professor mention uranium and plutonium?

(A) To simplify the explanation about fission
(B) To give an example of large unstable atoms
(C) To name atoms that are more suitable for fusion
(D) To discuss the potential risks involved

教授はなぜウランとプルトニウムに言及しましたか。

(A) 分裂の説明を簡素化するため
(B) 大きな不安定な原子の例を挙げるため
(C) より融合に適した原子の名前を挙げるため
(D) 潜在的リスクについて議論するため

⑩❺から、ウランとプルトニウム原子は大きいとわかります。さらに⑩❸に不安定なものは原子が大きいとあるので、この2つの部分から(B)が正解だとわかります。(A)については確かに、教授の⑩❷にsimplifyが登場します。しかしこの段階では、ウランやプルトニウムに関する発言がないので誤りです。(C)は、ウランとプルトニウムは融合ではなく分裂の文脈で登場するため、誤りです。(D)は講義の中でウランやプルトニウムに関するリスクについては言及されていません。常識に惑わされないようにしましょう。

L09_Q4

4. Why do people have high expectations of electricity generation by fusion rather than fission? *Choose two answers.*

(A) Because it produces a smaller amount of harmful waste
(B) Because it is less likely to result in lethal accidents
(C) Because it is capable of producing a greater amount of energy
(D) Because it requires little regular maintenance

人々が分裂ではなく融合による発電に高い期待を寄せるのはなぜですか。2つ選んでください。

(A) 生み出す有害廃棄物が少ないため
(B) 壊滅的な事故が起こる可能性が低いため
(C) 多くのエネルギーを発生させることができるため
(D) 定期点検をほとんど必要としないため

⓫❸に融合を発電に使おうとしている科学者がいることが述べられています。(A)は教授の⓫❹に「核融合の方が、放射性廃棄物が少ない」とあるため正解です。(C)は教授の⓫❹に「核分裂の3~4倍のエネルギーを生み出す」とあるため正解です。(B)と(D)は講義で言及がありません。よって(A)と(C)が正解です。

□ lethal：致命的な

L09_Q5

5. How does the professor feel about cold fusion?

(A) He is indifferent to the development of the new technology.
(B) He asserts that cold fusion casts extreme danger to human beings.
(C) He firmly believes that the technology has promising future.
(D) He is skeptical about whether it will be useful.

教授は常温核融合についてどう感じていますか。

(A) 新しい技術の開発に無関心である。
(B) 常温核融合は人間に大きな危機をもたらすと主張している。
(C) その技術は将来有望であると固く信じている。
(D) その技術が役立つかどうかに懐疑的である。

教授の発言⓫❼に「過去には、数名の科学者たちが、常温核融合と呼ばれる技術を開発し」とあります。しかし⓫❽で「今日の大多数の科学者は懐疑的な見方をしている」と述べているので(D)が正解です。take X with a pinch of saltは「Xをうのみにしない」という意味です。教授をthe majority of scientistsに含めるべきかどうかは難しいのですが、特に否定しているわけではないので、多数派の意見に賛成していると考えてよいでしょう。「考え」や「態度」に関わる箇所は出題される可能性が高いと思って聞きましょう。(A)は「無関心である」という発言はありません。(B)ですが「常温核融合が危険である」とは述べていません。(C)までの内容は講義からはうかがえません。

□ be indifferent to X：Xに無関心な　□ skeptical：懐疑的な

問 6 解説レクチャー

L09_Q6

6. In the lecture, the professor describes a number of characteristics of fusion and fission. Indicate whether each of the following is a characteristic of fusion or fission.

	Fusion	Fission
(1) It is the reaction taking place inside the Sun.	(A)	(B)
(2) A great deal of energy is needed to start a reaction.	(A)	(B)
(3) High-speed neutrons are used to generate energy.	(A)	(B)
(4) It occurs in an environment with high pressure.	(A)	(B)
(5) It is used in nuclear power generation.	(A)	(B)

教授は講義の中で、融合と分裂の多くの特徴を説明しています。下記の内、どれが融合でどれが分裂の特徴かを示してください。

	融合	分裂
(1) 太陽の中で起こっている反応だ。	(A)	(B)
(2) 反応を引き起こすためには、最初に大量のエネルギーを投入する必要がある。	(A)	(B)
(3) エネルギーを生み出すには、高速で移動する中性子が使われる。	(A)	(B)
(4) 高圧下で発生する。	(A)	(B)
(5) 原子力発電に使用されている。	(A)	(B)

5❸に「これが融合の一例であり、太陽の中心で起こっていること」とあるので、(1)は融合に関することだとわかります。7❹や8❷に融合や分裂反応を引き起こす際に必要になるエネルギー量の比較をした発言があります。そこから(2)が融合に関することだとわかります。8❺に「分裂現象は、大きくて不安定な原子が、高速で動いている中性子と呼ばれる粒子とぶつかることで引き起こされる」とあるので、(3)が分裂に関することだとわかります。5❽に「融合は高温高圧状態下で引き起こされる」とあるので、(4)は融合に関することだとわかります。10⓬に「この分裂反応によって生まれたエネルギーが、原子力発電所の原子炉の中の水を熱し、電力を生み出している」とあるので、(5)は分裂に関することだとわかります。

1-2 P: Professor S: Student

Listen to the following discussion in a physics class.

1 P: ❶Today, we're talking about something slightly technical: fission and fusion.
❷Fission . . . and fusion . . .
❸Imagine that you're enjoying a party.
❹Let's say you're a boy.
❺And at the party, you meet a certain girl.
❻The moment you see her, you find her really attractive.
❼You talk to her and it appears she's interested in you, too.
❽A few days later, you ask her to go out for a date and, fortunately, she says yes.
❾So now, you two are a couple.
❿So TWO people came closer and became ONE unit.
⓫That's fusion.
⓬Now, here comes the sad part.
⓭As you get to know her better, you discover that you two don't have much in common, and eventually both of you decide to break up.
⓮So, ONE unit or couple separates into TWO individuals.
⓯This is an everyday example of fission.
⓰Fission . . . and fusion . . .
⓱Well, now that we're vaguely acquainted with what fusion and fission are, at least in terms of interpersonal relationships, let's now dive in and see the bigger picture of what they are in the context of physics.

2 P: ❶Just to recap, an atom is a basic unit of matter.
❷You can think of it as a basic building block of objects around us.
❸Every solid, liquid, and gas is made up of atoms such as hydrogen, oxygen, carbon, gold, silver, uranium, mercury, and so on.
❹Does anyone have any questions so far?
❺Everybody fine with the concept of atoms?

物理学の授業での次の議論を聞きなさい。

1 P: ❶今日の授業は少しばかり専門的です。トピックは分裂と融合です。
❷分裂と融合…。
❸自分がパーティーを楽しんでいる様子を想像してみてください。
❹あなたは男の子だとしましょう。
❺そのパーティーであなたはある女の子と出会います。
❻あなたは彼女を見た瞬間、惚れてしまいます。
❼そしてあなたは彼女に声をかけます。すると、どうも彼女もあなたに関心を抱いているようです。
❽数日後、あなたは彼女をデートに誘うことにします。幸運にも彼女はあなたの誘いを快諾してくれます。
❾そしてあなたたち２人は付き合うことになりました。
❿２人の人間が近づき１つになった。
⓫これが融合です。
⓬さて、次は悲しい局面です。
⓭彼女をよく知るにつれて、あなたは彼女とあまり共通点がないことに気付き、そして結局２人は別れることを決意します。
⓮１つの集合体であるカップルが離れ、２人の別々の人間になる。
⓯これが日常生活で言う分裂の例です。
⓰分裂と融合…。
⓱さて、少なくとも人間関係における融合と分裂が、漠然とではありますが、何なのかわかったところで、次は物理学において融合と分裂が何なのかを大局的に見ていくことにしましょう。

2 P: ❶端的に言うと、原子は物質の基本単位でしたね。
❷私たちの周りにある物を構成する基本的要素であると考えてもらって差し支えありません。
❸全ての固体、液体、そして気体は、水素、酸素、炭素、金、銀、ウラン、水銀などの原子でできています。
❹今までのところで何か質問はありますか。
❺皆さん、原子の概念は理解できたということでいいですね。

1
- ☐ Let's say …：例えば…だと考えましょう
- ☐ the moment SV：～するとすぐに
- ☐ it appears (that) SV：～のようだ
- ☐ get to V：～するようになる
- ☐ be aquainted with X：Xを知る、Xと知り合いになる
- ☐ in terms of X：Xという観点で
- ☐ dive in：潜る、深く考察する

2
- ☐ to recap：要約すると（≒ in summary）
- ☐ think of X as Y：XをYとみなす

2 Everybody fine with the concept ...? → (Is) everybody fine with X?
「Xに関しては全員大丈夫ですか」be動詞の疑問文では、be動詞が省略されることがある。

3–6

3 S: So, atoms are the basic elements of things like water, air, rocks, our clothing, and basically everything.

4 P: ❶Exactly, everything is made up of atoms.
❷Then, let's make clear the concept of "fusion" and "fission" in the context of physics.

5 P: ❶Let's first explore fusion in more detail.
❷As you see it graphically on the first slide, "fusion" is two atoms colliding and combining together to form a single, heavier atom.
❸Two hydrogen atoms bump into each other and form one helium atom . . . this is an example of fusion, and this is what's happening in the center of the Sun.
❹I'll omit the details, but a fusion reaction produces a huge amount of energy.
❺Well, let me be a little more precise.
❻You first have to supply some energy to start a fusion reaction, and once the fusion reaction happens, it produces a far greater amount of energy.
❼So you end up getting a lot of energy from this reaction.
❽Fusion occurs under extremely high temperatures and pressures, like in the center of a star, or like the Sun as I just mentioned.
❾That's why the Sun is very hot.

6 S: Fusion provides the heat and energy.

3 S: つまり、原子は水、空気、岩、私たちの服など、つまり全てを構成する基本的要素ということですね。

4 P: ❶その通りです。全て原子から成っています。
❷それでは、物理学においての融合と分裂の概念を明らかにしましょう。

5 P: ❶まず最初に融合をもっと詳しく見ていくことにします。
❷最初のスライドの図からわかるように、融合は２つの原子が衝突し結合することにより、１つのより重い原子が生じることを指します。
❸２つの水素原子がぶつかり合い、そして１つのヘリウム原子となる…これが融合の一例であり、太陽の中心で起こっていることです。
❹詳細は割愛しますが、融合反応は莫大なエネルギーを生み出します。
❺いや、もう少し正確に説明しましょう。
❻融合反応を引き起こすには、まずエネルギーを供給しなければなりません。ひとたび融合反応が起こると、供給したエネルギーを遥かに超える量のエネルギーが発生します。
❼つまり、この反応から多くのエネルギーを得ることができるというわけです。
❽融合は、恒星の中心や、先ほど述べたように、太陽の中心のような高温高圧状態下で引き起こされるものです。
❾太陽が高温なのはこのためなんですね。

6 S: 融合は熱とエネルギーを発生させるということですね。

5
- ☐ explore X：Xを見ていく
- ☐ in detail：細かく
- ☐ bump into X：Xにぶつかる
- ☐ omit X：Xを割愛する
- ☐ precise：厳密な、正確な
- ☐ end up Ving：結局～する

4 make (V) clear (C) the concept (O) ... → make the concept ... clear
「その概念を明確にする」SVOCがSVCOという語順になっている。

5 "fusion" (S) is (V) (two atoms (S′) colliding and combining (V′) together) (C)
two atomsはcolliding and combiningという動名詞に対する意味上の主語。

7-9

7 P: ❶Now you see how it works.
❷Great.
❸So, I said you first need to provide some energy to start a fusion reaction.
❹You need a greater amount of energy to trigger a fusion reaction than to trigger a fission reaction.
❺So it is more difficult to initiate a fusion reaction.
❻On the other hand, fusion produces three to four times the energy that fission does.
❼The amount of energy fusion produces is so great that it has been used to create a deadly weapon, the hydrogen bomb.
❽Well, some scientists are also trying to use the power of fusion peacefully by designing a fusion reactor to produce electricity.
❾However, it's difficult to control a fusion reaction, and the prospect of seeing fusion being used commercially, at least in the near future, is pretty slim.
❿Besides, the cost involved in creating the necessary conditions for a fusion reaction is high, and it is slowing the progress of the development.

8 P: ❶Next, let's look into fission, the splitting of one atom into two, in more detail.
❷Compared to the fusion, we need much less energy to trigger a fission reaction.
❸As the picture in the next slide shows . . . here . . . in fission, an atom disintegrates or breaks up.
❹You don't need high temperatures or pressure for this.
❺A fission reaction takes place when a large unstable atom collides with particles called neutrons moving at a high speed.

9 S: What exactly do you mean by an unstable atom?

7 P: ❶もう融合が理解できたようですね。
❷その調子です。
❸私は融合反応を引き起こすためには、まず一定のエネルギーを供給する必要があると言いました。
❹実は、融合反応を引き起こすためには、分裂反応を引き起こすよりも大きなエネルギーが必要です。
❺つまり、融合反応を引き起こす方が難しいというわけなんです。
❻その一方、融合反応は分裂反応が生み出すエネルギーの3倍から4倍の量のエネルギーを発生させます。
❼融合反応が生み出すエネルギーは莫大なため、水素爆弾という兵器の開発に利用されました。
❽さて、その一方で、核融合炉を設計し、それを用いて電力を発生させようと、融合反応が生み出すエネルギーの平和的活用を試みる科学者もいます。
❾しかしながら、融合反応を制御することは困難で、少なくとも近い将来、核融合が商業的に利用される可能性は低いでしょう。
❿そのうえ、融合反応を発生させるために必要な環境をつくり出すためには多額の費用がかかり、それが開発の足かせとなっている側面があります。

8 P: ❶次に、分裂をより詳しく見ていきましょう。分裂は、1つの原子が2つの原子に分かれることでしたね。
❷分裂反応を引き起こすために必要なエネルギーは、融合反応を引き起こすために必要なそれに比べずっと小さいものです。
❸次のスライドの、ええっと、ここにあるように、分裂では原子が分解します、つまり別れるのです。
❹この現象を発生させるためには、高温も高圧も必要ありません。
❺分裂現象は、大きくて不安定な原子が、高速で動いている中性子と呼ばれる粒子とぶつかることで引き起こされるのです。

9 S: 不安定な原子とは具体的に何ですか。

7
- ☐ work：機能する
- ☐ trigger X：Xを引き起こす
- ☐ initiate X：Xを引き起こす
- ☐ reactor：炉
- ☐ slim：（見込みなどが）わずかな

8
- ☐ look into X：Xを詳しく見る
- ☐ disintegrate：分解する
- ☐ take place：生じる
- ☐ collide with X：Xにぶつかる
- ☐ particle：粒子
- ☐ neutron：中性子

7 fusion (S) produces (V) (three to four times) the energy (O) that fission does
three to four timesは「3～4倍の」という意味。doesはproduceを意味する代用表現。

⑩

⑩ P: ❶Well, things might get a bit technical, so I was hoping to discuss it in the latter half of the lecture, but we might as well talk about it now rather than later since you brought it up.
❷I'll try to simplify this.
❸OK, so unstable atoms are usually large-sized atoms.
❹The size of hydrogen atoms or helium atoms is rather small.
❺On the other hand, there are many large atoms such as uranium or plutonium atoms.
❻Usually, atoms get more unstable as the size increases.
❼Technically, I should talk about the structure of the nucleus and the balance of protons VS neutrons.
❽But, umm, I'll skip that part for now.
❾Okay, that was bit of a side note.
❿So, when an unstable atom is bombarded by high-speed neutrons, the target atom breaks up into two or more smaller atoms and neutrons.
⓫This process also produces a large amount of energy.
⓬By the way, the energy produced by a fission reaction is what heats water inside nuclear reactors and produces electricity in a nuclear power plant.

⑩ P: ❶うーん、少し専門的になるので講義の後半で話そうと思っていたのですが、質問してくれたので今話したほうがいいかもしれませんね。
❷わかりやすく説明しますね。
❸ええっと、不安定な原子というのは、通常大きな原子のことを指しています。
❹水素原子やヘリウム原子はサイズ的にかなり小さい部類に入ります。
❺一方で、ウランやプルトニウムといった大きな原子も数多くあるのです。
❻通常、原子は大きくなればなるほど不安定になります。
❼厳密には、原子核の構造や陽子と中性子のバランスを議論する必要があります。
❽でも、うーん、今はやめておきましょう。
❾話が少し逸れてしまいましたね。
❿つまり、不安定な原子が高速で移動する中性子と衝突すると、その原子が２つあるいはそれ以上の小さい原子と中性子に分裂するのです。
⓫この過程では大きなエネルギーも発生します。
⓬ところで、この分裂反応によって生まれたエネルギーが原子力発電所の原子炉の中の水を熱し、電力を生み出しているのです。

⑩
- □ technical：専門的な
- □ the latter half：後半部分
- □ might as well V：～しても同じだろう
- □ bring X up：X（話題）を持ち出す
- □ simplify X：Xを単純化する
- □ bit of X：ちょっとしたX（≒ just / only）
- □ bombard X：Xに衝突させる

⑩ what(S) heats(V) water(O)
heatsは動詞。

⓫

⓫ P: ❶So far, we've been able to take advantage of the commercial use of electricity generated by fission, but not by fusion.
❷The low energy requirement for starting a reaction has made the technological development of fission relatively easier.
❸But some scientists are endeavoring to utilize the energy produced by "fusion" as well to generate electricity.
❹Fusion produces three to four times as much energy as fission, and it creates less radioactive waste.
❺In this regard, there may be tremendous merits in fusion-based electricity generation.
❻However, there are some obstacles the researchers must overcome as I mentioned earlier.
❼In the past, a few researchers developed what they called cold fusion, a technology they claimed would allow us to generate electricity at a significantly lower cost.
❽However, it was eventually rejected, and even though research is still underway into this innovative technology, the majority of scientists today take it with a pinch of salt.

11 P: ❶現在に至るまで、私たちは核分裂により発生した電力の商業的利用の恩恵を受けてきましたが、核融合による発電はまだ実現していません。

❷分裂反応を引き起こすために必要なエネルギーが小さいことから、分裂の技術的開発は比較的容易なものでした。

❸しかしながら、融合によって生み出されるエネルギーを利用して、電力を発生させようと努力している科学者たちもいます。

❹融合は分裂の3倍から4倍のエネルギーを発生させる上、その過程で生み出される放射性廃棄物の量は分裂のそれより少ないのです。

❺この観点から、融合による発電は大きなメリットがあるかもしれません。

❻しかし、先ほど言ったように、科学者たちが乗り越えなければならない壁も存在します。

❼過去には、数名の科学者たちが、常温核融合と呼ばれる技術を開発し、彼らはこの技術のお陰で、発電のコストが大幅に下げられると主張しました。

❽しかし、結局この技術は受け入れられませんでした。現在でもこの革新的な技術の研究は続いているものの、今日の大多数の科学者は懐疑的な見方をしています。

11

- ☐ so far：現在に至るまで
- ☐ relatively：比較的
- ☐ endeavor to V：～する努力をする
- ☐ utilize X：Xを利用する
- ☐ X as well：Xも（≒too）
- ☐ radioactive：放射性の
- ☐ in this regard：この観点から
- ☐ electricity generation：発電
- ☐ obstacle：壁
- ☐ (be) underway：進行中である
- ☐ take X with a pinch of salt：Xを疑って聞く

11 a technology (they claimed would allow us to generate electricity)
→ a technology ([that] they claimed would allow us ...)
（[that] = S′, they = S″, claimed = V″, would allow = V′）
省略されている関係代名詞は、wouldに対する主格として機能する。いわゆる「連鎖関係詞」。

リスニング問題10 講義

ART HISTORY

問題演習の流れ

- □ 音声が流れている間は、問題は読めません。講義が終わり、最初の問題音声が流れ始めたらページをめくって、5分以内に解答しましょう。
- □ 1問の解答時間は20秒を目安にしています。問題を読み上げた後に解答時間として20秒のポーズ（音声なし）が入っていますので、その間に解答をマークしてください。
- □ メモは自由に取ってください。
- □ 3回解けるように、3回分のマークシートを問題ページに用意しています。解く日付を記入してからマークしてください。

Web解答方法

- □ 本試験では各選択肢の左に表示されるマークをクリックして解答します。本試験と同様の方法で取り組みたい場合は、Webで解答できます。
- □ インターネットのつながるパソコン・スマートフォンで、以下のサイトにアクセスしてWeb上で解答してください。

extester.com

- □ 操作方法は、p.13 ～ 14の「USA Club Web学習の使い方」をご参照ください。

学習の記録

学習開始日	年　　月　　日	学習終了日	年　　月　　日
学習開始日	年　　月　　日	学習終了日	年　　月　　日
学習開始日	年　　月　　日	学習終了日	年　　月　　日

リスニング問題 10 講義 音声

L10

Art history

聞き取りメモ

L10_Q1

1. What is the lecture mainly about?

(A) A comparison of outdoor art and indoor art
(B) Difficulties involved in oil painting
(C) Effects of light on the color of painting
(D) A new art style made popular by a certain group of artists

L10_Q2

2. What can be inferred about the color preparation used for painting before the 19th century?

(A) Not too many people had the skill to create the right colors.
(B) It took longer to prepare colors from pigments than it does now.
(C) The color mixing could be done only inside a room.
(D) It was as simple and straightforward as it is today.

L10_Q3

3. According to the professor, what are the inventions that caused plein-air painting to flourish? *Choose two answers.*

(A) Paint stored in a tube
(B) A canvas that can withstand rain
(C) A portable wooden framework
(D) Easy-to-carry smaller brushes

L10_Q4

4. Why did the professor mention a grasshopper in reference to the work of Van Gogh?

(A) To emphasize that nature sometimes presented difficulties for plein-air artists

(B) To give an example of what Van Gogh often depicted

(C) To explain that a grasshopper was a common subject for Impressionists

(D) To name a subject that was difficult to draw due to its fast movement

Date / (A)(B)(C)(D) Date / (A)(B)(C)(D) Date / (A)(B)(C)(D)

L10_Q5

5. How did plein-air painters draw people who did not stop and pose in a street?

(A) By memorizing the scene outdoors and completing the work indoors

(B) By depicting subjects' movements making rough and quick sketches

(C) By taking some pictures and referring to them later

(D) By working as a group and referring to each other's work

L10_Q6

6. What is an "artists' colony"?

(A) People passing by in the street depicted by painters

(B) Experts with highly specialized techniques in painting

(C) An assembly of people who are painting the same thing

(D) A group of artists who are trying to expand their territory

1. **(D)** 2. **(B)** 3. **(A) (C)** 4. **(A)** 5. **(B)** 6. **(C)**

1 | 問1 解説レクチャー

L10_Script01

1 **Professor:**
❶OK today, we're going to talk about plein-air painting. ❷Plein-air painting is nothing really rare or special today, but let me go ahead and explain what it is, how it began, and some other interesting points about the new art style. ❸Now, in the 19th century in France, there was an art movement called "Impressionism." ❹Briefly, Impressionists analyzed colors and the reflection of light found in nature more precisely than before. ❺In a sense, they tried to depict nature using more precise colors and light. ❻It is these people, Impressionists, who popularized plein-air painting. ❼So, what is plein-air painting? ❽What does it mean? ❾Well, it's not really possible to translate the term "plein-air painting" directly, but simply put—it means "outdoors painting." ❿OK, so what I'm saying is that plein-air painters paint outdoors, in nature. ⓫The Impressionists, like Claude Monet and his contemporaries, loved trying to capture the light while they were painting outside. ⓬Painting outdoors is nothing new or special for us today, you might say. ⓭But back then, this was a completely new way of painting, and we can say that it was revolutionized by new inventions.

解説レクチャー

❶~❷:今回のテーマは、plein-air painting (以下PAP) の定義と起源、そしてその興味深い側面だと述べています。講義の内容が予測できます。

❸~❺:印象派の画家は、自然界の色や光をより正確に描こうとしたとのことです。ちなみに、印象派はTOEFL頻出です。

❻:印象派がPAPを有名にしたと言っています。

❼~❿:PAPの簡単な定義は「野外での絵画制作」だそうです。

⓫:印象派の具体例として「クロード・モネ」が挙げられています。

⓬~⓭:当時、新たな発明品によってPAPに革命が生じたそうです。

聞き取りメモ例

Plein air painting
nature color light
impressionist Monet
outdoor in nature
new way
↓
invention

L10_Q1

1. What is the lecture mainly about?

(A) A comparison of outdoor art and indoor art
(B) Difficulties involved in oil painting
(C) Effects of light on the color of painting
(D) A new art style made popular by a certain group of artists

この講義は主に何についてのものですか。

(A) 屋外と屋内の美術の比較
(B) 油彩画に伴う困難
(C) 絵画の色に対する光の効果
(D) ある特定の画家のグループによって人気になった新しい芸術スタイル

教授の説明❶において、PAPがテーマだとわかります。さらに❶❸～❶❻において、印象派の画家がPAPを有名にしたともあります。❶❻のpopularizedをmade popularに、Impressionistsをa certain group of artistsでそれぞれ言い換えている(D)が正解です。他の選択肢は全て講義の主旨と無関係です。

□ effect of X on Y: XのYに対する影響

2～3｜問 2～3 解説レクチャー

L10_Script02-03

2 ❶So, what do I mean by new inventions? ❷Well . . . plein-air painting became popular in the early 19th century. ❸And, before that time, paints were manually made in the artists' studio, inside a room. ❹The artist would have to buy dry pigments and then grind those pigments with oils in order to create a certain color. ❺Just imagine the process compared to what we do now. ❻And . . . you can also imagine how hard it would be to take all the heavy equipment outside to work in nature. ❼But, in the early 1800s, something innovative was starting to get manufactured. ❽And this really, I mean really, changed the way artists would work. ❾That invention was paints in tubes. ❿They could buy premade paints in small tubes, so they would save an enormous amount of time. ⓫Another thing was the easel, you know . . . the wooden frame that supports the canvas. ⓬I bet when I say easel, you imagine those huge, wooden frames, or easels, in artists' studios. ⓭Yes, and now imagine having to carry those around with you, walking somewhere outside, trying to find a nice spot to paint. ⓮Well, so someone clever thought, "OK, there must be a way to make these easels smaller, less heavy, and still have them serve their purpose." ⓯And, so the French easel, called the pochade, was invented. ⓰The French easel looks very much like a suitcase which can be expanded, and . . . and so this was very convenient for the Impressionists. ⓱It is still used nowadays by contemporary plein-air painters. ⓲Now, I am not saying that plein-air, or painting outdoors, was invented at this time. ⓳No, not at all. ⓴Artists had long painted outdoors, but with the introduction of paints in tubes and portable easels, the popularity of plein-air painting increased widely . . . OK?

3 ❶OK, now that we know what plein-air painting is, let's talk about the most common subject or thing that artists would paint. ❷Well, what would you say was painted the most? ❸Think about it. ❹The artists were outside, most likely somewhere in nature, and so as you can guess, a logical subject would be landscapes. ❺You see, the artists had a lot of freedom by choosing to paint outdoors. ❻They could literally pick any spot they found worth painting, and transfer the image onto their canvas. ❼But, when working outdoors, there were a few challenges the artists would face. ❽The light changes quickly, and morning, afternoon, and evening light are all different, so the artists would have to paint quickly in order to capture that certain time of day. ❾If they couldn't finish on that day, they would either come back some other day at the same time to continue painting, or they finished the paintings back in the studio according to their rough sketches and also from their memory.

解説レクチャー

2

❶:新しい発明品についての説明を始めています。
❷~❹:PAPが有名になるまでは、顔料を買って色を作る必要があったと言っています。
❺~❻:❹の作業が大変なものであることがわかります。続く❻でも、you can also imagine how hard ... とあります。また外で絵を描くには、重い道具を持ち出す必要もあったと説明があります。自ら顔料を買わなければならず、また重い道具を持ち出す必要もあったのですね。
❼~❿:チューブ入りの絵の具が登場します。これが時間の節約になったとのことです。
⓫~⓱:さらに、より軽くて持ち運びしやすいイーゼル(画架)も登場しました。折り畳み式で、現代でも用いられていると言っていますね。
⓲~⓴:これらの発明によりPAPの人気が上がったとのことです。

3

❶~❻:PAPにおいて、画家が題材にするものは風景だそうです。
❼~❽:問題点は、野外だと光が変化するので素早く描く必要があるということだと説明しています。
❾:描き終わらない場合は、また翌日の同じ時間に再開するか、スタジオに持ち帰って記憶を頼りに描く必要があると述べています。

聞き取りメモ例

19C ← manually inside
dry pigment+oil
heavy equipment
• [paint in tubes
• easel
↓
smaller less heavy
French easel]
↓
popular

subject
landscape
light changes
→ quickly paint
come back
or
do it in studio

L10_Q2

2. What can be inferred about the color preparation used for painting before the 19th century?

(A) Not too many people had the skill to create the right colors.
(B) It took longer to prepare colors from pigments than it does now.
(C) The color mixing could be done only inside a room.
(D) It was as simple and straightforward as it is today.

19世紀以前に絵画に使われた絵の具を準備することについて何が推測できますか。

(A) 正しい色を作る技術を持っていた人はそれほど多くなかった。
(B) 顔料から絵の具を作るのに今より長い時間がかかった。
(C) 色を混ぜ合わせることは屋内でのみできた。
(D) それは今日と同じくらい単純で容易だった。

2❸から19世紀初頭以前の絵の具に関する話が始まります。2❹で、絵の具を準備することがいかに大変だったのかが述べられています。2❿では、「チューブ入りになったことにより、非常に多くの時間が節約できた」と述べられています。裏を返せば、19世紀初頭以前は絵の具の準備に、より多くの時間がかかっていたということなので、(B)が正解です。(C)ですが、onlyなどの断定的な語はダミーの選択肢になることが多いです。

□straightforward:容易な、容易に理解できる

L10_Q3

3. According to the professor, what are the inventions that caused plein-air painting to flourish? *Choose two answers.*

(A) Paint stored in a tube
(B) A canvas that can withstand rain
(C) A portable wooden framework
(D) Easy-to-carry smaller brushes

教授によれば、plein-air paintingをはやらせる要因となった発明品は何ですか。2つ選んでください。

(A) チューブに入った絵の具
(B) 雨に耐えられるキャンバス
(C) 持ち運びが可能な木の枠組み
(D) 持ち運びが簡単な小さめの筆

❷❼～❷❿では「チューブに入った絵の具」、❷⓫～❷⓰では「イーゼル」が言及されています。そして❷⓴で、「この2つがPAPの人気を高めた」とあるので、(A)と(C)が正解です。easelは難語ですが、❷⓬でwooden frames, or easelsと言い換えています。(D)ですが、持ち運びやすくなったのは筆ではなくイーゼルです。

□ withstand X: Xに耐える

4～6 | 問 4～6 解説レクチャー

L10_Script04-06

4 ❶There were other hurdles. ❷Let's call them obstacles—insects, sand, strong winds and so on. ❸You see, nature isn't ideal all the time. ❹It could start raining any moment, and the artist wouldn't be able to finish his painting. ❺If the rain was too harsh, it could undermine the painting. ❻So it's easier said than done. ❼How many of you have heard of Van Gogh? ❽Well, he was one of the artists who loved painting outdoors. ❾And a fun fact—it is not uncommon to find little parts of sand in his paintings. ❿Actually, not so long ago, researchers found a grasshopper in one of his paintings! ⓫Can you imagine that, an actual grasshopper on a Van Gogh painting? ⓬This is very interesting, because it tells us what conditions he was working in. ⓭It helps us imagine Van Gogh standing somewhere in the grass, trying to paint a landscape, and uh, well, grasshoppers hopping around, making it harder for him to keep his canvas clean!

5 ❶OK. ❷Well, besides landscapes, artists would also paint buildings, streets, and people. ❸So, they tried to portray everyday life. ❹Well, people wouldn't pose as a usual model would, but they would move around, doing whatever they were doing. ❺And, the artists would usually capture these movements with bold and quick brushstrokes, so they could actually just create an impression of the person in front of them.

6 ❶I don't know if some of you had the opportunity to spot some plein-air painters somewhere on the street, but you know, nowadays plein-air courses are quite popular. ❷The good part is that, you don't really have to be a professional artist to join, and they make courses for beginners, so everyone can experience what it's like to paint outside. ❸Also, to this day, "artists' colonies" are popular. ❹An artists' colony is a group of artists that agrees on a place, and meets up there to paint together. ❺Each can work in his or her favorite technique. ❻So, after they're done, they can compare each other's works, and it's quite interesting to see different depictions of the same subject. ❼So, plein-air is a quite interesting way of painting and being in nature at the same time.

解説レクチャー

4

❶～❻:他の問題点としては、虫や強風などの自然からの影響があると言っています。具体例として雨が強調されています。

❼～⓭:ゴッホの絵には砂や本物のバッタが入り込んでいるそうです。

5

❶～❸:風景に加えて、建物や人物なども描かれているとのことです。

❹～❺:人物は動き回るため、動きのイメージを大胆に描くことが求められるそうです。

6

❶～❷:最近は、PAPの授業が人気だそうです。素人でも参加することができるというのが利点ですね。

❸～❻:artists' colonyは、ともに同じ場所で絵を描く集団のことだと定義されています。参加者は好みの技術を用いることができるとのことです。同じ集団だからと言って、同じ技術である必要はないとのことです。描き終わったら、お互いの絵を比較すると述べています。

❼:教授はPAPを、絵画と自然体験を融合した興味深い活動だと評しています。

聞き取りメモ例

rain hard
Van Gogh
grasshopper

• building
• street
• ppl move

capture
impression

• not pro
• artists colony paint together same subject

L10_Q4

4. Why did the professor mention a grasshopper in reference to the work of Van Gogh?

(A) To emphasize that nature sometimes presented difficulties for plein-air artists
(B) To give an example of what Van Gogh often depicted
(C) To explain that a grasshopper was a common subject for Impressionists
(D) To name a subject that was difficult to draw due to its fast movement

教授はなぜVan Goghの絵画に関連してバッタに言及しましたか。

(A) 自然が時折plein-air paintersに困難をもたらしたことを強調するため
(B) Van Goghがよく描いたものの例を提示するため
(C) 印象派にとってバッタが普通の題材だったことを説明するため
(D) 素早い動きによって、描くことが難しかった題材を挙げるため

4❶～4❻は「自然の影響がPAPにもたらした困難」について述べています。さらに4❿以降で、ゴッホの絵にバッタが入っていることを述べていました。これは自然の影響の具体例ですね。よって、(A)が正解です。(B)はexampleという語にひっかからないよう気を付けましょう。ゴッホがバッタを描いたわけではありません。(C)は講義の中で言及されていません。(D)についても言及がありません。difficultという語に惑わされないようにしましょう。

L10_Q5

5. How did plein-air painters draw people who did not stop and pose in a street?

(A) By memorizing the scene outdoors and completing the work indoors
(B) By depicting subjects' movements making rough and quick sketches
(C) By taking some pictures and referring to them later
(D) By working as a group and referring to each other's work

路上で立ち止まってポーズを取ることをしなかった人々を、plein-air paintersはどのように描きましたか。

(A) 戸外でのシーンを記憶し、部屋の中で作品を仕上げることによって
(B) 大まかで素早いスケッチをし、題材の動きを描くことによって
(C) 写真を何枚か撮り、後にそれらを参照することによって
(D) 集団で取り組み、お互いの作品を参照することによって

❺❹～❺❺によると、「大胆かつ素早い筆さばきで、動く人々を描く」とあります。❺❺のbold and quick brushstrokesをrough and quick sketchesと言い換えている(B)が正解です。(A)についてですが、❸❾に選択肢と同様の内容がありますが、人の描き方に関するものではないため、誤りです。(C)は講義の中で言及がありません。(D)に関しては❻❻に「お互いの作品を比べる」という発言がありますが、絵の描き方ではないので誤りです。

L10_Q6

6. What is an "artists' colony"?

(A) People passing by in the street depicted by painters
(B) Experts with highly specialized techniques in painting
(C) An assembly of people who are painting the same thing
(D) A group of artists who are trying to expand their territory

artists' colonyとは何ですか。

(A) 画家たちによって描かれた、道を通り過ぎる人々
(B) 絵画における、高度に専門化した技術を持つ専門家
(C) 同じものを描く人々の集まり
(D) 守備範囲を広げようとする画家のグループ

artists' colonyについては❻❸以降に説明がありました。同じ場所に集まって、同じ題材を描く集団のことです。よって(C)が正解です。❻❹groupがassemblyに、❻❻のthe same subjectがthe same thingでそれぞれ言い換えられていますね。(A)は風景の他にPAPで描かれたものの1つです。(B)は専門家であることとartists' colonyの関係は特に読み取れないので誤りです。(D)については「自分の守備範囲を広げる」という発言はありません。

□assembly:人々の集まり

1

Listen to part of a lecture in an art history class.

1 **Professor:**
❶OK today, we're going to talk about plein-air painting.
❷Plein-air painting is nothing really rare or special today, but let me go ahead and explain what it is, how it began, and some other interesting points about the new art style.
❸Now, in the 19th century in France, there was an art movement called "Impressionism."
❹Briefly, Impressionists analyzed colors and the reflection of light found in nature more precisely than before.
❺In a sense, they tried to depict nature using more precise colors and light.
❻It is these people, Impressionists, who popularized plein-air painting.
❼So, what is plein-air painting?
❽What does it mean?
❾Well, it's not really possible to translate the term "plein-air painting" directly, but simply put—it means "outdoors painting."
❿OK, so what I'm saying is that plein-air painters paint outdoors, in nature.
⓫The Impressionists, like Claude Monet and his contemporaries, loved trying to capture the light while they were painting outside.
⓬Painting outdoors is nothing new or special for us today, you might say.
⓭But back then, this was a completely new way of painting, and we can say that it was revolutionized by new inventions.

美術史の授業での講義の一部を聞きなさい。

1 ❶では今日は plein-air painting についてお話しします。
❷plein-air painting は今日においては、珍しいものでも特別なものでもありませんが、それが何なのか、どのように始まったのか、またその新しい芸術スタイルのその他の興味深い側面をいくつか説明させてください。
❸さて、19 世紀のフランスでは、「印象主義」と呼ばれる芸術運動がありました。
❹端的に言えば、印象派の画家たちは、自然に見られる色や光の反射を以前よりも正確に分析しました。
❺ある意味、彼らはより正確な色や光を用いて自然を描写しようとしたのです。
❻plein-air painting を有名にしたのは、これらの人々、印象派の画家だったのです。
❼では、plein-air painting とは何なのでしょうか。
❽それは何を意味するのでしょうか。
❾ええ、'plein-air painting' という用語を直接翻訳するのは実際のところ不可能ですが、端的に言えば「野外での絵画制作」を意味します。
❿ですから私が言っているのは、plein-air painters は、戸外の自然の中で絵を描くということです。
⓫Claude Monet や彼と同時代の画家たちに見られる印象派の画家は、戸外で絵を描く際に光を捉えようとする試みを好みました。
⓬今日私たちにとっては、戸外で絵を描くことは何も新しい、特別なことではないと、皆さんは言うかもしれません。
⓭しかし当時、これは全く新しい絵画の描き方で、新しい発明品による革命的な描き方に変わったと言えるかもしれないのです。

1
- ☐ go ahead : 話を進める
- ☐ depict X : Xを描く
- ☐ simply put : 端的に言えば
- ☐ contemporary : 同時代の人
- ☐ revolutionize X : Xに革命的変化を起こす

1 It is these people, Impressionists, who popularized plein-air painting
いわゆる強調構文でthese people, Impressionistsが強調されている。

2

2 ❶So, what do I mean by new inventions?
❷Well . . . plein-air painting became popular in the early 19th century.
❸And, before that time, paints were manually made in the artists' studio, inside a room.
❹The artist would have to buy dry pigments and then grind those pigments with oils in order to create a certain color.
❺Just imagine the process compared to what we do now.
❻And . . . you can also imagine how hard it would be to take all the heavy equipment outside to work in nature.
❼But, in the early 1800s, something innovative was starting to get manufactured.
❽And this really, I mean really, changed the way artists would work.
❾That invention was paints in tubes.
❿They could buy premade paints in small tubes, so they would save an enormous amount of time.
⓫Another thing was the easel, you know . . . the wooden frame that supports the canvas.
⓬I bet when I say easel, you imagine those huge, wooden frames, or easels, in artists' studios.
⓭Yes, and now imagine having to carry those around with you, walking somewhere outside, trying to find a nice spot to paint.
⓮Well, so someone clever thought, "OK, there must be a way to make these easels smaller, less heavy, and still have them serve their purpose."
⓯And, so the French easel, called the pochade, was invented.
⓰The French easel looks very much like a suitcase which can be expanded, and . . . and so this was very convenient for the Impressionists.
⓱It is still used nowadays by contemporary plein-air painters.
⓲Now, I am not saying that plein-air, or painting outdoors, was invented at this time.
⓳No, not at all.
⓴Artists had long painted outdoors, but with the introduction of paints in tubes and portable easels, the popularity of plein-air painting increased widely . . . OK?

2

❶では、新しい発明品とは何を意味するのでしょうか。
❷ええ…plein-air painting は 19 世紀の初頭に流行しました。
❸それ以前は、絵の具は、画家のスタジオ内、部屋の中で手作業によって作られていました。
❹画家は乾燥顔料を買い、特定の色を作り出すために、それらの顔料を油といっしょにすりつぶさなければなりませんでした。
❺今日私たちがすることと比較してそのプロセスを想像してみてください。
❻そうすれば、自然の中で制作するために重い道具を戸外に持ち出すことがどれ程大変なことかも想像がつくでしょう。
❼しかし 1800 年代初頭、革新的なあるものが作られ始めていたのです。
❽そしてこれが本当に、誇張ではなく本当に、画家たちが絵を描く方法を変えたのです。
❾その発明品とはチューブに入った絵の具です。
❿小さなチューブに入った、あらかじめ作られた絵の具を買うことができたため、実に多くの時間を節約することができたのです。
⓫もう一つはイーゼルでした、あの、キャンバスを支える木のフレームのことです。
⓬私がイーゼルと言うと、画家のスタジオにあるとても大きい木のフレーム、すなわちイーゼルを思い浮かべるでしょう。
⓭そうです、では絵画を描くのにいい場所を見つけようとして、戸外を歩きながら、それらを持ち運ばなければならないことを想像してみてください。
⓮そして、賢い誰かが「そうだ、これらのイーゼルをより小さく、より軽くして、それでもなおそれらが目的を果たせるようにする方法があるはずだ」と考えたのです。
⓯そして、ポシャドと呼ばれるフランスのイーゼルが発明されたのです。
⓰そのフランスのイーゼルは、サイズを大きくできるスーツケースによく似ていたため、印象派の画家たちにとってとても便利だったのです。
⓱それは現代の plein air painters によって現在も使われています。
⓲ところで、私は plein-air、つまり野外での絵画制作がこの時に始まったとは言っていません。
⓳全く違います。
⓴画家たちは長い間戸外で制作をしていたのですが、チューブ入り絵の具と持ち運び可能なイーゼルの登場によって、plein-air painting の人気がとても高まったのです…わかりましたか。

2

- ☐ manually : 手で、自力で
- ☐ dry pigment : 乾燥顔料
- ☐ grind X : X を挽く
- ☐ enormous : 巨大な
- ☐ easel : 画架
- ☐ serve one's purpose : 役目を果たす

3 ❶OK, now that we know what plein-air painting is, let's talk about the most common subject or thing that artists would paint.
❷Well, what would you say was painted the most?
❸Think about it.
❹The artists were outside, most likely somewhere in nature, and so as you can guess, a logical subject would be landscapes.
❺You see, the artists had a lot of freedom by choosing to paint outdoors.
❻They could literally pick any spot they found worth painting, and transfer the image onto their canvas.
❼But, when working outdoors, there were a few challenges the artists would face.
❽The light changes quickly, and morning, afternoon, and evening light are all different, so the artists would have to paint quickly in order to capture that certain time of day.
❾If they couldn't finish on that day, they would either come back some other day at the same time to continue painting, or they finished the paintings back in the studio according to their rough sketches and also from their memory.

3

❶いいですね、では plein-air painting が何かはもうわかったので、画家たちが描いた最も一般的な題材やものについて話しましょう。
❷さて、一番描かれたものは何だと思いますか。
❸考えてみてください。
❹画家たちは戸外、おそらく自然のどこかにいました。皆さんが推測できるように、題材は必然的に風景になるでしょう。
❺ご存じでしょうが、画家たちは野外での絵画制作を選択することによって、多くの自由を手に入れたのです。
❻彼らは、描くに値すると考えた場所は、まさにどこでも選ぶことができ、そのイメージをキャンバス上に模写することができたのです。
❼しかし、野外で絵画制作をする際、画家が直面するいくつかの困難がありました。
❽光は素早く変化し、午前から午後、夜と、光は全て異なるため、画家は一日のうちの特定の時間を（絵の中に）捉えるため、素早く描く必要がありました。
❾もしその日に仕上げることができなければ、彼らは制作を続けるために別の日の同じ時間に戻って来るか、もしくはスタジオに持って帰っておおまかなスケッチや記憶を頼りに仕上げていたのです。

3

- [ ] subject：対象、題材
- [ ] as you can guess：ご想像のとおり
- [ ] a logical subject：合理的に考えて適切な題材
- [ ] landscape：風景
- [ ] literally：文字通り
- [ ] worth Ving：～する価値がある
- [ ] according to X：Xに従って

4-5

4 ❶There were other hurdles.
❷Let's call them obstacles—insects, sand, strong winds and so on.
❸You see, nature isn't ideal all the time.
❹It could start raining any moment, and the artist wouldn't be able to finish his painting.
❺If the rain was too harsh, it could undermine the painting.
❻So it's easier said than done.
❼How many of you have heard of Van Gogh?
❽Well, he was one of the artists who loved painting outdoors.
❾And a fun fact—it is not uncommon to find little parts of sand in his paintings.
❿Actually, not so long ago, researchers found a grasshopper in one of his paintings!
⓫Can you imagine that, an actual grasshopper on a Van Gogh painting?
⓬This is very interesting, because it tells us what conditions he was working in.
⓭It helps us imagine Van Gogh standing somewhere in the grass, trying to paint a landscape, and uh, well, grasshoppers hopping around, making it harder for him to keep his canvas clean!

5 ❶OK.
❷Well, besides landscapes, artists would also paint buildings, streets, and people.
❸So, they tried to portray everyday life.
❹Well, people wouldn't pose as a usual model would, but they would move around, doing whatever they were doing.
❺And, the artists would usually capture these movements with bold and quick brushstrokes, so they could actually just create an impression of the person in front of them.

4

❶困難は他にもありました。
❷それらを「障壁」と呼びましょう。昆虫、砂、強風などです。
❸ご存じのように自然は常に理想的なわけではありません。
❹いつ何時雨が降り出すかわかりませんし、画家が絵画を仕上げられないかもしれません。
❺もし雨がとても強ければ、絵画を台無しにしてしまうかもしれません。
❻だから「言うは易く行うは難し」なのです。
❼皆さんのうち何人が Van Gogh のことを話に聞いたことがありますか。
❽彼は戸外で絵を描くのが好きな画家の一人でした。
❾そして面白いことに、彼の絵画の中に砂粒が見つかるのは稀なことではありません。
❿なんと、少し前に研究者たちが、彼の絵画の中にバッタを発見したのです。
⓫想像できますか、Van Gogh の絵の中に本物のバッタがいたんですよ。
⓬それは、彼がどんな環境で制作に励んでいたのかを物語るとても興味深いものです。
⓭それは、Van Gogh が草原のどこかに立ち、風景を描こうとしていると、そうですね、バッタが周りを跳びまわって、Gogh がキャンバスをきれいな状態に保つのが難しくなっているところを想像すればわかるでしょう。

5

❶はい。
❷風景の他に、画家は建物、道路、そして人々も描いていました。
❸そう、彼らは日常生活を描写しようとしたのです。
❹人々は普通のモデルがするようにポーズをとらず、何をする場合でも、それをそのまま続けて動き回っていました。
❺そして、画家はたいていこれらの動きを大胆な、素早い筆さばきでとらえたので、実際に彼らの目の前の人の印象をまさに作り出すことができたのです。

4

- ☐ hurdle：困難
- ☐ obstacle：障壁
- ☐ harsh：強い
- ☐ undermine X：Xを台無しにする
- ☐ easier said than done：言うは易く行うは難し
- ☐ grasshopper：バッタ
- ☐ help X V：Xが～する助けとなる
- ☐ imagine X Ving：Xが～しているところを想像する

5

- ☐ as a usual model would：普通のモデルがするように
- ☐ capture X：Xを捉える
- ☐ brushstroke：筆さばき

4 nature isn't ideal all the time

not ... allは部分否定なので「常に…というわけではない」という意味。

6

6 ❶I don't know if some of you had the opportunity to spot some plein-air painters somewhere on the street, but you know, nowadays plein-air courses are quite popular.
❷The good part is that, you don't really have to be a professional artist to join, and they make courses for beginners, so everyone can experience what it's like to paint outside.
❸Also, to this day, "artists' colonies" are popular.
❹An artists' colony is a group of artists that agrees on a place, and meets up there to paint together.
❺Each can work in his or her favorite technique.
❻So, after they're done, they can compare each other's works, and it's quite interesting to see different depictions of the same subject.
❼So, plein-air is a quite interesting way of painting and being in nature at the same time.

6 ❶皆さんの中に、路上のどこかで plein-air painter を見る機会のあった人がいるかどうかわかりませんが、最近 plein-air の授業はとても人気ですよね。
❷うれしいことに、受講するにはプロの画家である必要は全くありませんし、初心者向けの授業も用意されているので、誰もが戸外で絵を描くことがどのようなものかを経験できます。
❸また、今日に至るまで「画家のコロニー」は人気です。
❹画家のコロニーとは、場所を決め、絵を描くためにそこに集まる画家の集団です。
❺各人が、自分の好みの技術を用いて絵が描けます。
❻ですから、描き終わったら、お互いの作品を比較できます。同じ題材の違った描写を見るのはとても面白いものです。
❼ plein-air は、絵を描くと同時に自然の中にいるということが実感できるとても興味深い方法なのです。

6 what it is like to paint「～絵を描くことがどのようなものなのか」

itはto paintを指す仮主語。なお、likeは前置詞。

著者：

森田 鉄也（もりた てつや）

武田塾 English Director、武田塾豊洲校・高田馬場校・国立校・鷺沼校オーナー。株式会社メタフォー代表取締役。慶應義塾大学文学部英米文学専攻卒。東京大学大学院言語学修士課程修了。TOEFL iBT 115 点、TOEFL ITP 660 点、TOEIC L&R 990 点（90 回以上）、TOEIC S&W 400 点、国連英検特 A 級、英検 1 級、ケンブリッジ英検 CPE、英単語検定 1 級、通訳案内士（英語）、英語発音検定満点、TEAP 満点、GTEC CBT 満点、IELTS 8.0、日本語教育能力検定試験合格。英語教授法 TEFL・CELTA 取得。
『TOEIC L&R TEST 単語特急 新形式対策』（朝日新聞出版）、『ミニ模試トリプル 10 TOEIC L&R テスト』（スリーエーネットワーク）など著書多数。
YouTube チャンネル：Morite2 English Channel、ユーテラ授業チャンネル

日永田 伸一郎（ひえいだ しんいちろう）

英語講師。大学受験予備校やオンライン予備校で中学生と高校生を相手に英語を教えている。早稲田大学国際教養学部卒。トロント大学に 1 年間留学。趣味で TOEFL iBT 満点と IELTS バンド 9.0 を目指している。現在は TOEFL iBT 117 点、IELTS 8.0 を保持。好きなことはピアノ、将棋、サッカー、本を買いあさること。

山内 勇樹（やまうち ゆうき）

UCLA（カリフォルニア大学ロサンゼルス校）卒。脳神経科学専攻。留学サポート・語学学習を提供する株式会社 Sapiens Sapiens の代表講師兼最高責任講師。TOEFL iBT 120 点、TOEIC L&R 990 点、TOEIC S&W 400 点、英検 1 級（成績優秀者表彰）、ケンブリッジ英検 CPE（C2）、通訳翻訳士資格などさまざまな資格・スコアを保有。アメリカ、イギリス、カナダなど世界中の名門大学、大学院、ビジネススクール、法学校に合格者を出し続けている留学のスペシャリスト。企業の英語指導としての顧問、指導実績も多数。高校での客員講師としても授業を行っている。書籍、雑誌、新聞、講演、ワークショップ、動画配信などを通じ、TOEFL 指導や留学サポートの教育を幅広く提供している。趣味はバスケットボール、登山、神社巡り、流れ星の観測、バーベキュー、マリオカートなど。

装幀・本文デザイン　斉藤 啓（ブッダプロダクションズ）
DTP　有限会社ギルド
イラスト　トミタミドリ
音源制作　TMTレコーディングスタジオ
ナレーター　Howard Colefield／Iain Gibb／Nadia McKechnie／Rachel Walzer
写真提供　PIXTA（ピクスタ）: ©bst2012（P.337）
Shutterstock.com: ©Dmytro Zinkevych（P.273）、©Nejron Photo（P.291、P.383）、©LightField Studios（P.319）、©Matej Kastelic（P.359、P.403）、©amenic181（P.427）、©BearFotos（P.447、P.471）

極めろ！ TOEFL iBT® テスト リーディング・リスニング解答力　第2版

2019 年 8 月 8 日　初　版第 1 刷発行
2024 年 4 月 30 日　第 2 版第 1 刷発行

著　者　森田 鉄也　日永田 伸一郎　山内 勇樹
発行者　藤嵜 政子
発行所　株式会社　スリーエーネットワーク
〒 102-0083　東京都千代田区麹町 3 丁目 4 番
トラスティ麹町ビル 2 F
電話：03-5275-2722［営業］03-5275-2726［編集］
https://www.3anet.co.jp/
印刷・製本　萩原印刷株式会社

ISBN978-4-88319-943-3　C0082